Buddhist Thought and Culture

Buddhist Thought and Culture

Indo-Japan Seminar on Buddhist Philosophy

With Special Reference to the Thoughts and Works of Professor Hajime Nakamura

Edited by
S.R. Bhatt

Originals

(an imprint of Low Price Publications)
Delhi-110052

Distributed by
D.K. Publishers Distributors (P) Ltd.
4834/24, Ansari Road, Darya Ganj,
New Delhi-110002
Phones: 51562573, 51562575, 51562577
e-mail: dkpd@del3.vsnl.net.in
visit us at: www.dkpd.com

First Published 2005
Rs. 475

ISBN 81-88629-30-8

Published by
Originals
(an imprint of Low Price Publications)
A-6, Nimri Commercial Centre,
Near Ashok Vihar Phase-IV,
Delhi-110052
Phones: 27401672, 27452453
e-mail: lpp@nde.vsnl.net.in
visit us at: www.lppindia.com

Printed at
D K Fine Art Press P Ltd.
Delhi-110052

PRINTED IN INDIA

Foreword

India and Japan have very old cultural contacts. Many travelers and scholars have contributed immensely to this living tradition between the two countries. Among these names Professor Hajime Nakamura and Kaviguru Rabindranath Tagore in contemporary times come to the forefront. Nakamura was an outstanding thinker and interpreter of Indian culture. He was a scholar of international repute and a recipient of many prestigious awards in Japan and India apart from several other countries of the world. He was a great friend of India and an ardent admirer of Indian culture. He was closely associated with Dr. S. Radhakrishnan, the late President of our Republic, who had profuse admitation for him.

In the words of Dr. K. R. Narayanan, another former President of the republic of India, "Nakamura was well known in India as one of the outstanding and eminent scholars, and true friend of our country".

The central axis of Nakamura's scholarship was Indian which he studied and expounded with remarkable depth and compression, and with admirable width and breadth of philosophical perspectives. He was proud of his association with Indian culture and he declared this in unequivocal terms. His perceptive understanding of Indian culture and his exposition of all the systems of Indian philosophical thought were excellent. The sweep of his scholarship was exceedingly vast and encompassing. In every field of his research he was original, novel, pioneering and authoritative.

The quality and quantity of Nakamura's published works are astonishing, far exceeding than the works of any single individual in our times.

He has published more than 1000 books and research papers in Japanese and other European languages, mostly in Japanese. It would indeed be a pity and regrettable if his seminal contributions to world culture remain unknown or inaccessible to non-Japanese scholars due to language barrier.

The present Volume is an outcome of Indo-Japan International Seminar in the form of a befitting tribute and discharge of "*Guru ṛṇa*" to the late Nakamura. The papers included here reflect his astounding scholarship in all systems of philosophical thoughts of classical and modern India. It is hoped that this Volume would significantly contribute to better understanding not only of Indian philosophical systems but also of the rise and spread of Buddhism in Japan.

D. P. Chattopadhyaya

Chairman
Centre for Studies in Civilizations
Kolkata and New Delhi
September14, 2004

Preface

The history of human kind has witnessed rise of many cultures and civilizations on the surface of the earth. Though human thoughts and value pursuits know no geographical boundaries or barriers, there is something unique and distinctive in each individual culture and civilization that gets shared, or perhaps may remain unshared as well, at trans-geographical spheres. These unique and distinctive elements have developed some times in isolation but quite often they have interacted and interfaced between and among themselves. In this process of sharing there have been encounters and confluences, assimilations and absorptions, fortifications or admixtures of identities, submerging or over powering of identities etc. In these enterprises and adventures one thing emerges out prominently and that is the fact that the values posited, pursued and realized in each individual culture and civilization are global and universalizable and yet the ways they are posited, pursued and realized are uniquely local. Therefore there is striking similarity and also bewildering diversity. The commonalities and contrasts are vivid and glaring, wonderous and baffling but they are academically quite stimulating and interesting. In the absence of tangible historical records, or extinction of some such records, many facets of these human achievements are eclipsed to our awareness and may remain so for ever. Some of the archeological findings, deeper explorations and newer researches are providing us glimpses of scattered and concealed evidences which need to be worked on though it may not be easy.

A systematic comparative study of cultures and civilizations of the world in their interactions and mutual relations will certainly be helpful not only in self-awareness but also in forging universal solidarity and in bringing about world peace. Though this enterprise is primarily theoretical it will surely have practical orientations and pragmatic outputs. In keeping these considerations a series of intercultural and intercivilizational dialogues and colloquia were organized by Indian Council of Philosophical Research, New Delhi. The present Volume incorporates the papers presented in Indo-Japan international Seminar which was funded by Japan Foundation (Asia Center) and in which the Eastern Institute, Tokyo, collaborated academically. In this seminar scholars from India, Japan, South Korea, China and Vietnam participated. The seminar was planned around the works and thoughts of Professor Hajime Nakamura, an outstanding thinker of international repute who contributed immensely and significantly towards intercultural and intercivilizational studies and understanding.

The basic foundation of Professor Nakamura's scholarship was no doubt Indian thought which he investigated and expounded with unprecedented greatness and comprehension, and with remarkable width and breadth of philosophical perspectives, but his field of research has been exceedingly vast encompassing both Eastern and Western thoughts, ancient and modern. In every field of his research he has been original, fresh, pioneering and authentic. For example, his book "The Structure of Logic" is a unique and marvelous synthesis of Eastern and Western Logics. His another book, "A Comparative History of Ideas" is global in scope and covers features and problems of thought which are common to East and West. But his perspective is Asian with an Indian emphasis. It is a very well documented work.

Professor Nakamura's publications are astonishingly large and of varied subject matter. As per the information provided by Professor Sengaku Mayeda, Professor

Nakamura has published more than 1000 books and research papers in Japanese and European languages, but mostly in Japanese. It is indeed a matter of great loss to non-Japanese scholars that his seminal contributions to world culture have remained either unknown or inaccessible to them due to language barrier, as has been pointed out by many scholars.

This seminar was a modest attempt to bring to the fore his remarkable and insightful contributions. Through this publication of the proceedings of the seminar it shall be possible for the English knowing world to be acquainted with and to evaluate and appreciate the tremendous work Professor Nakamura has accomplished. This Volume contains papers on Indian Buddhism, Japanese Buddhism and Korean Buddhism. Professor Nakamura was a Buddhist by faith and conviction but he was a great Vedāntin by training. In him we find a desirable symbiosis of Buddhism and Vedānta. He had close acquitance with and deep insight into all other systems and traditions of philosophical thought of classical and contemporary India. The papers of eminent scholars included here provide glimpses of some facets of his magnificient scholarship. In the publication of this Volume it is hoped that it will stimulate renewal of cross-cultural interactions which will help and contribute in mutual understanding and mutual enrichment. It may also consolidate and revitalize humanity's common spiritual resources for universal well-being.

I would like to take this opportunity to thank the Japan Foundation, the Eastern Institute and the Indian Council of Philosophical Research for organizing the Seminar and making it a grand success. I also thank Shri Pradeep Mittal of Originals (an imprint of Low Price Publications) for bringing out the Proceedings of the Seminar in a book form so elegantly within a short period of two months.

I further thank the eminent scholars who have contributed learned papers. The members of the Staff of Indian Council of Philosophical Research deserve sincere thanks for providing infra-structural facilities without which it would not have been possible to organize this Seminar. I particularly thank Shri S. Sreekumaran and Shri Mohinder Chopra for their help.

S.R. Bhatt

MP-23, Maurya Enclave,
Pitampura
Delhi-110088
September 22, 2004

Contents

1

Buddhism in India and in Japan

S R Bhatt

"Caratha bhikkave cārikam bahujanahitāya bahujanasukhāya
Lokānukampāya atthāya hitāya sukhāya devamanussānām"

O Monks! Move around for the well-being of every one,
For the happiness of every one,
Showering compassion on the entire world,
For the good, for the welfare, for the happiness
Of divine and human.

(Vinaya Piṭaka I.23)

I

The advent of Śākyamuni, the Buddha, initially the light of Asia and now of the entire world, has been a significant event in the history of world culture and civilization. Born in a royal family and brought up in all material prosperity and physical comforts, he was restless with pain and suffering, finitude and evanescence of the mundane life. After intense study and interactions with scholars of his time, and undertaking profound reflections and deep maditation he gained inslight into the nature of Reality and the phenomenal world. He could find out the root cause of the malady and the way to get rid of it. Having attained enlightenment, he did not remain self-centered, benevolent and merciful heart as he had. He was not contented with his own emancipation and longed and strived for the emancipation of all suffering beings. He showed to the humanity the sure path of *Nirvāṇa,* a way to eradicate suffering and to escape from the labyrinth of the cycle of birth and death (*bhava cakra*). It consisted of a symbiosis of wisdom (*prajñā*) and conduct *(śīla*), ethics (*caryā*) and meditative practice (*dhyāna*). These are the four pillars of the enlightened way of life, he pointed out. He realized the 'Four Noble Truths', practiced them in the form of the 'Noble Eight-fold Path' in his own life and subsequently exhorted people about them after having been convinced about their efficacy. The Path shown by him was so beneficial that it redeemed the sorrows and sufferings of humankind and provided them succor and solace. That is why he was regarded as a Great Healer (*Bhaiṣajya Guru*) and a liberator (*Tāyin*).

II

The Buddha has been the finest product of Indian culture. In the words of Mrs. Rhys Davids, "He was the greatest and wisest, and best of that long line of reformers who have tried to infuse new strength into the religious life of India".[1] He was an inheritor of an old tradition as well as creator of a new outlook. In his own words, "Even so have I, O Monks!, seen an ancient way, an ancient road, traversed by the supremely enlightened ones of the olden times."[2] The Buddha was a well-read and well-versed person with a critical bent of mind and subtle logical acumen. He was well steeped in the Vedic lore and drew his ideas and inspirations from it. He was fully exposed to the rich and varied cultural milieu of his time. In order to arrive at the true knowledge of life and Reality he interacted with many erudite scholars of his day. He was not born in an intellectual void and his ideas did not grow up in a cultural vaccum. His reflections were not undertaken in isolation without any moorings in the ancient wisdom of his land. He had an open and assimilative mind and accommodated all those noble and sublime ideas available in the intellectual and meditational environment of his time that were agreeable to his experiences. There are many references to this effect in the Pali canons. The basic teachings of the Buddha have their Vedic ancestry. In fact his ideas sprang up as resurgent thoughts protesting against the distortions in the

Vedic wisdom that crept in later on in the vast temporal canvas of Indian history. He was born like a lotus of *saddharma* in the muddy water of cultural pollution. It should be noted that he did not condemn the Vedas but only those aberrations that were in violation of the Vedic spirit and about which even the Upaniṣads and the Gītā raised their voice. Of course, the Buddha was more vocal and emphatic. The way he reformulated them was both innovative and attractive. He imbibed all that was profound and sublime in the Vedic wisdom. In this sense he was the savior and purifier of the Vedic lore. He purified it and restated it with a new vigor. It was not for nothing that long before Vārāha, Agni and other Purāṇas accepted the Buddha as an *Avatāra* of Viṣṇu, one of the most revered Buddhist texts, the Laṇkāvatāra Sūtra, identified the Buddha with Viṣṇu and Rāma. He was worshipped along with Viṣṇu and Śiva or as Viṣṇu/Śiva, a tradition the remnants of which are there in Bodh Gaya, Puri etc. and this tradition is still alive in Indonesian, Nepalese and many other Hindu families.

III

The Buddha was a wise and practical person fully knowledgeable of human psychology, human needs and aspirations. He not only discerned the inner cravings of human heart and intellect, he knew the logic and language in which he was to communicate with the masses. So he gave discourse in the language and in the form with which people were conversant. During his life time itself he was recognized as 'Great Savior', an enlightened seer who visualized and realized the *summum bonum* of life. He founded a new monastic order, known as *samgha,* and gave a novel turn to the institution of *samnyāsa* directing it for universal well-being and happiness. The origin and spread of Buddhism has been a landmark in the history of India. A distinction can be drawn between monastic Buddhism and the Buddhism of the populace. Both the modes received great impetus during Buddha's lifetime. Even his royal parents and family members became his disciples. His popularity spread far and wide and his teachings provided solace and succor to the distressed people. He wondered from one place to another along with his disciples conversing with people in the language and idiom familiar to them. He mastered the art of discussion and debate and spread the radiance of his enlightened wisdom and righteous conduct without taking any rest out of mercy and compassion for the suffering humanity. Though he did not write anything his teachings were preserved and subsequently codified by his disciples who very intelligently and diligently collated and compiled them with mutual consultation. His teachings were prolific and stretched over a long span of time but all these were retained in memory and recollected by his immediate disciples who always accompanied him during his travels from one place to another. This apart his teachings were not theoretical and were exemplified in his conduct and in that of his disciples. Because of their practical nature it was easy to remember them. Almost the entire *Tripiṭaka* literature is a collection of the sayings, utterances, narratives, rules of the order and other teachings known as *Buddha vacana.*

Buddhism acquired popular recognition during the lifetime of the Buddha but soon after his *Mahāparinirvāṇa* it grew by leaps and bounds in India and outside. It is a lopsided view that there was a decline of Buddhism in India. Buddhism constitutes the very core of Indian mind and as a mode of thinking and a way of living it has a deep and unmitigated impact on Indian psyche and culture. It has great potential in ennobling Indian culture provided it remains free from polluting influence of the vested interests.

IV

We do not know the exact date of the introduction of Buddhism outside India and there are no definite historical records available to this effect. But there are positive evidences of Indian settlements in many parts of Asia practicing Vedic mode of living and this must have paved the way for the spread of Buddhism in those places. The prevalence of Vedic Dharma before the rise of Buddhism provided the fertile ground in Asian countries in particular for the acceptance and spread of Buddhism both through land and sea routes. There are sufficient clues available in this regard which need to be examined closely with a positive mind. However, historically it is well-known that it was Samrāṭ Aśoka who made phenomenal contribution to the preservation, propagation and spread of Buddhism in India and abroad. During his time Buddhism became quite vibrant and predominant not only in Greater India but also outside. Perhaps he was the first royal patron, a strong and ardent follower and a zealous propagator of Buddhism who sent missionaries, including his own children, to spread *saddharma* to near and far off places in Asia, Africa and Europe.

From the point of view of the cultural history of humankind it is indeed significant that originated in India Buddhism soon penetrated the whole of Asia, enamored the hearts of the masses, influenced the intellect of the elites and won over the spirits of the powerful rulers. Its intermingling with the local cultures and morass, and its deep and pervasive impact on the minds of the native people have been so intense and immense that it not only molded and reformulated the original thoughts, ideas and ideals, beliefs and practices of the countries of its *locale* but also brought about profound changes in their social, cultural and religious life. The people of these countries felt that Buddhism has something ennobling, enlightening and emancipating to offer. This apart, Buddhism also acted as a catalytic force in transforming the social conditions, in forging national unity and in bringing about political solidarity in those countries. In this grand cultural interface there are a few points that deserve serious attention of the world scholarship.

The transmission to and acceptance, assimilation, modification and trans-creation of Buddhism outside India, its birthplace and homeland, have been interesting and astonishing, which need meaningful and gainful intercultural studies to find out a ground for world brotherhood. For the Indians it is really significant to know as to how and why Buddhism could get such a fascination and strong foothold outside India with notable and unmitigated impact on thought and culture of these countries. For the people of these countries it is instructive to be aware of the Indian roots of their Buddhist view and way of life.

The Asian contribution in the preservation, propagation and furtherance of the Buddhist thought and culture cannot be underestimated. Once receptive of Buddhism these countries themselves became its exporters, so to say. The Indian seed yielded rich harvest on the Asian soil. This apart it can be said with great satisfaction that some of the valuable Buddhist literature lost in India has been found preserved elsewhere either in original or in translation etc. It is the needed task for the Indian scholars to restore it back in Indian languages. It is well known that Japan, Korea, China, Tibet, Thailand etc. have the proud privilege of preserving the largest and richest Buddhist cultural heritage. India with other countries like Germany, United States, U.K. and France can join hands with them in sharing, preserving and enriching the same. Some of these have great literary, artistic, cultural, philosophical and religious value and they can be regarded as classics of world literature, culture and civilization. In the past there have been attempts in India and elsewhere to collate and compile Buddhist literature. Since then a lot of new literature has come up and it is need of the time to have another compilation on a grand scale in a systematic, chronological and geographical order. It is a huge and stupendous task to be undertaken by a team of scholars to be sponsored by an international body like UNESCO. The spread and influence of Buddhism in almost whole of Asia in the course of several centuries evinces a common Asian mindset, shared modes of thinking and ways of living. Had there been no commonality of thought, belief systems and value patterns such a reception and absorption and intermingling would not have been possible. It is therefore not an exaggeration to say that there is something called Asian mind. However pluralistic and diversified it might be one can discern an underlying commonality that has made cross movement of ideas possible. Furthermore, the way, the ease and the swiftness with which this cultural appropriation and assimilation took place in local cultures, and atmospheres and environments, are suggestive of the metabolic dynamism of the Asian psyche.

It is really unfortunate that in modern times India and other Asian countries instead of directly interfacing each other and in a common way, view each other through a *tertim quid*. It is high time that we have now direct cultural understanding throwing off glasses of Western indologists and orientalists. In the hoary past we had direct linkages and cultural exchanges along with trade in material goods through sea and land routes. Trading in material goods has an ephemeral and transient value but exchange in thought and culture has a lasting impact. However, this should not be misunderstood as promotion of regionalism. Regional understanding is only a base for universal solidarity. Buddhism has been a universal religion and ecumenical character has been essential to it. It has displayed these features in its long history. It has tremendous potentiality to pave the way for universal interdependence, interconnectedness and interrelationship. Perhaps at no other time in human history this message of the Buddha is more needed than at present to redeem the distracted humanity. In this venture the Western ways of thinking and Western knowledge of science and technology could be tempered and seasoned with Buddhist spirituality and meditational intuitions following the noble middle path.

V

Japan is an important and presently very influential country that professes and practices Buddhism particularly of Mahāyāna variety. Buddhism has exerted an immeasurable influence on the thought and culture of Japan. Since its inception it has evolved into a form unique to Japan as it adopted itself to local culture and ethos so as to best suit the needs and the psyche of the people. It made adjustments with local modes of Nature worship and Shintoism. It was fortunate in receiving royal patronage and public support.

There were many rulers and scholarly religious leaders who contributed to the preservation, propagation and enrichment of Buddhism in Japan. Though coming from India people of Japan accepted it as their own religion and accorded highest regard for it. It is believed that Buddhism was officially introduced to Japan from Korea in the year 552 A.D. by a delegation sent by the king of Paekche, but in the words of Dr. Amarnath Thakur, "Nonetheless, this formal introduction of Buddhism did not represent the first contact of the Japanese people with the new faith. The traders and merchants or some of the immigrants from the Asiatic continent, who had settled prior to the 'Paekche delegation', also had brought the Buddhist teachings with them and very soon their religion made quite progress among the Japanese. Among the large number of immigrants' colonies there were some priests also and it is recorded that a monk of Chinese ancestry, Shiba-Tachito, had constructed a temple.[3] In fact the same has been the situation in respect of Korea as well where Buddhism entered directly from India much before the known historical record of its reaching there from China. There is therefore a need to have a fresh look to be undertaken by the scholars at the old historical records and to supplement them with other literary and traditional cultural evidences. The pre-historic evidences in the form of local traditions, folk tales etc. may be of some help in this regard.

As per the present information, according to the Chronicles of Japan, *Nihonshoki,* the semi-historical literature documenting the early history of Japan, Buddhism arrived in Japan in October 552 A.D. through a Korean delegation sent by a king of Paekche. Korea was then divided into four major and several smallar states. The state of Paekche was under the combined attack of the Silla and Koguryo states. In desperation the king sent an envoy with a delegation to the emperor of Japan for military assistance. As a mark of respect and consideration the delegation presented a statue of Śākyamuni Buddha and several Buddhist artifacts including the *Sūtras*. The message of the king of Paekche was as under :–

"The religion (Ho, Skt. Dharma) is the most excellent of all teaching, though difficult to master and hard to comprehend, even the sages of China would not have found it easy to grasp. It brings endless and immeasurable blessings and fruits even the attainment of supreme enlightenment. Just as the Cintamani jewel is said to fulfill every need according to desire, so the treasures of this glorious religion will never cease to respond in full to those who seek for it. Moreover, this religion has come to Korea from India and the people of the two countries are now ardent followers of its teachings and none are outside its pale."[4]

Japan then was far less developed than Korea. The Japanese emperor was very much impressed by the sublimity of the message, beauty of the Buddha image and the technology involved in its making which was unknown to the Japanese. The Buddhist gifts from Korea were received with mixed reaction in Yamato's royal court. The Shinto believers, particularly people of Mononobe clan, opposed it using as an excuse then prevalent epidemic as arising out of the wrath of the native gods. So they compelled the emperor to burn Buddha's statue. At that time a fire also took place burning down a big part of the palace and it was argued by the supporters of Buddhism, belonging to the Soga clan, that this was due to showing disrespect to the image of the Buddha. However, the government administrators recognized the need and worth of the new civilization to keep pace with the neighbouring countries and let Buddhism in. With acceptance by nobilities and capturing the hearts of people it acquired the status of a state religion. With royal patronage Buddhist temples were built which served as centers of religious ceremonies as well as social service. The monks functioned as teachers, doctors, nurses, cultivators etc. apart from serving as priests. They catered to the spititual and mundane needs of the people. Thus they were leaders in society and naturally the rulers supported and encouraged them.

Shotoku Taishi

The introduction and advancement of Buddhism in Japan was certainly due to the irresistible force of the new civilization but it received great impetus from Prince-Regent Shotoku Taishi, a strong personality who guided and consolidated Buddhist movement by his wisdom and insight. Shotoku is a title given to him that means holy and virtuous. He was the son of the Emperor Yomei. His mother was a Buddhist. He also had two Paekche monks as his tutors. He studied Buddhist texts thoroughly. Because of this background he became devout Buddhist. Though he was a regent to Empress Suiko, he wielded actual power and ruled Japan for thirty years. His rule is considered to be the golden period in Japanese history as it was marked by the phenomenal growth of Buddhist culture and national solidarity. There are many achievements to his credit. He established an efficient bureaucracy in the royal court, composed a moral and political code, proclaimed Buddhism as a state religion, contributed to the development of Buddhist art and architecture and undertook several charitable works. He wrote learned commentaries on three Buddhist scriptures, namely, Saddharmapuṇḍarīkasūtra, Vimalakīrtinirdeśa and Śrīmalādevīsimhanāda. These reflect a deep and scholarly understanding of Buddhism. During his reign the whole country was literary transformed. His contribution to the spread of Buddhism was immense as he provided full royal patronage to it. He was an ardent follower and zealous propagator of Buddhism. With indefatigable spirit he promoted Buddhism. Following the Saddharmapuṇḍarīka he appreciated the Buddhist conception of universal benevolence and distinguished it from the Confucian concept of propriety. He advocated the Buddhist ideals of eradication of egocentricity and cultivation of existential openness based on the principle of interconnectedness of all phenomena (*pratītyasamutpāda*). He emphasized the importance of realizing the Buddhist truths within a concrete human nexus by establishing unity between the mundane and the ultimate. It was world–affirming Buddhism, down to earth, and practical. He is still remembered with great respect and reverence in Japan as the father of Japanese Buddhism. Some people regard him to be the reincarnation of the Bodhisattva Avalokiteśvara. *It would be a befitting recognition of his highly significant contributions if a seminar could be organized by the Japan Foundation, or J.S.P.S., highlighting his exposition of Buddhism.* Such an outstanding and extraordinary person should be better known and emulated all over the world. His ideas are of great relevance to contemporary times in bringing about universal peace, prosperity and well-being.

Saicho

In the Nara period the Buddhist ideal of universal spiritual communion centered in Mahāvairocana Buddha got prominence following *Saddharmapuṇḍarīkasūtra* and *Avatamsakasūtra* that heavily influenced the Japanese mind. During this period an Indian Hīnayānist monk and a Chinese monk by the name Ganjin went to Japan to teach the importance of the practice of Buddhist precepts. During this time two great saint-scholars Saicho and Kukai came on the scene and gave a uniquely Japanese form to Buddhism. At the age of 19 Saicho was ordained as a monk. At 20 he wrote 'Genbun' in which he thus expressed his anguish and wish, "The three worlds are in suffering and peace is nowhere to be found. The sun of Śākyamuni and the moon of Maitreya no longer shine. Disasters will soon befall us." He expressed his sense of urgency of the need to revive Buddhism. He followed the Tien-tie or Tendai sect based on the *Saddharmapuṇḍarīkasūtra*. He gave lectures on this text at Mt. Hiei. He went to China and met a very eminent Chinese monk Chigi who had synthesized all Buddhist scriptures in a unique blend based on the *Saddharmapuṇḍarīkasūtra*. He had also undertaken a re-systematization of *samathavipasyanā* meditation. After one year Saicho returned to Japan. He advocated universality of liberation based on the *Ekāyana* theory. He emphatically stated that the Buddhist practice is not divorced from every day life. That is why he insisted on the realization of ultimate unity of the whole universe in terms of *'Tathatā'* in this very life. His teachings can be best summed up in the following last words to his disciples before he died, "Do not make Buddhist images for me and do not copy *sūtras* for me. Transmit what I have taught you to every one. Buddhist practice is not divorced from our every day lives, but if we are drawn only to the most trivial aspect of our lives, we will not be able to practice. Let us live properly between the world of practice and our every day world. Let us study the three teachings of *prajñā, samādhi* and śīla given by the Buddha and spread them with single-minded devotion and proper understanding. If you think it proper as I do, adhere to the teachings and practice and then at the appropriate time spread them so that they will be useful to all."

Kukai

A contemporary of Saicho, Kukai founded the Shingon sect, a Tāntric school centered round Mahāvairocana Buddha, in which individual mystical vitalities were coordinated with cosmic vitalities contained in Mahāvairocana Buddha. This form of Buddhism is technically known as Tantrayāna or Vajrayāna according to which one can attain Buddhahood in one's lifetime through the regulative practices of body (*mudrā*), speech (*mantra*) and mind (*maṇḍala*). With the help of two *maṇḍalas, Vajra* and *Garbha,* Shingon Buddhism explains and correlates empirical (*samsāra, saṃvṛti)* and trans-empirical (*nirvāṇa, paramārtha*). Kukai believed that *Dharmakāya* is personified as Mahāvairocana Buddha. *Dharmakāya* is the universal principal permeating the entire cosmos. All are manifestations of this principal and every one participates and partakes in the same *Buddhabhāva.* Kukai was very much impressed by these noble Buddhist ideas and on that basis argued in his work *Sankyo Shiki* for the superiority of Buddhism over Confucianism and Taoism. He was not satisfied with life as scholar and instead went off roaming the country as a wandering ascetic. He was as famous as Shotoku and made considerable contribution to preservation and propagation of Buddhism in Japan. He was a gifted artist, poet and sculptor. He also influenced Japanese art, culture and education. He was known for welfare activities.

Genshin, Honen and Shinran

In Hein and Kamakura periods Genshin, Honen and Shinran popularized *Sukhāvatī vyūhasūtra* and *Amitāyurdhyānasūtra.* Meditation on and worship of Amitābha Buddha gained prominence. It was believed that he resides in the paradise *Sukhāvatī* or *Tuṣita* and he can cure all illness. He is the Healing Buddha (*Bhaiṣajya Guru*). During this time a new sect by the name Jodo (Pure Land) came into existence. Genshin advocated chanting of the name of Amitāyus, known as *nembutsu,* as a means to be born in *Sukhāvatī* or *Tuṣita* heaven and attain enlightenment.

After Genshin Honen and his disciple Shinran popularized *nembutsu*. Honen maintained that the *nembutsu* is the way preferred by Amidā Buddha in his vow to save all beings and it is an easy way that every one can practice. Shinran joined Honen to propagate *nembutsu*. The followers of the traditional Tendai and other schools opposed both. They, however, made a formal declaration that their purpose was not to undermine the traditional schools. Although Shinran had very deep respect for Honen and insisted that he taught only what he learnt from Honen, it is quite clear that his ideas are innovative. One of the most important differences between the two is with regard to *nembutsu* as to whether it is innate or acquired. Honen maintained that it depends upon ones call for the mercy of Amidā and his resulting grace while Shinran argued that the Buddha-nature is inherent in all of us and therefore only through self-effort this is achieved. All of us have Amidā Buddha indwelling in us. This is how Shinran reconciled the 'Pure Land' teaching with the traditional Buddhist doctrines. Like Nāgārjuna he insisted that there is no dualism between *samsāra* and *nirvāṇa*. Therefore he asserted that it is possible to dwell upon Amidā Buddha's enlightenment while fully participating in the worldly activities. In *nembutsu* there is no difference between *samsāra* and *nirvāṇa*. He further maintained that one who practices *nembutsu* could do only good and no evil. Some teachers of Pure Land school were maintaining that after saying *nembutsu* one is already saved or emancipated and therefore can do good or evil. Shinran protested against such a false view. He insisted that one who practices *nembutsu* sincerely could do only good and no evil. D.T. Suzzuki, the Renzai Zen Master who popularized Zen Buddhism in the West, rated Shinran's sect, known as Shin, as an outstanding Japanese contribution to the world culture. Shinran had several able disciples who helped in making Zen flourish through out Japan.

Eisai and Hakuin

In the Kamakura period two sects of Zen, viz., Rinzai and Soto, came into existence. Eisai after his visit to China introduced Rinzai sect that was based on the practice of *Chān*

(Skt. *Dhyāna*). Hakuin popularized this sect later on. He was bold, witted and sometime enigmatic. There are many famous episodes about him. Once a samurai asked him "Monk, is there really such thing as heaven and hell?" Hakuin replied, "What is your profession?" "I am a samurai." he responded. Hakuin broke out in laughter, "A samurai? What does a fool like you know?" The samurai got very angry, pulled out his sword and said, "I will kill you." Hakuin stopped laughing and shouted back, "There! Hell." The samurai realized what had happened and withdrew his sword. Hakuin said, "There the doors of heaven are opened." The Renzai Zen technique of *Koan* is quite fascinating. In this the students are given an apparently illogical question to think over. Then the teacher constantly presses them for an answer. This is followed by 'Sesshin' that are intense sessions in which the teacher presses students even harder. The purpose is not to seek any logical or rational answer and there may be none. The real aim is to get the ego of the students destroyed or to make them realize that there is no logical answer to issues of life, or to point out incorrectness of any particular answer. The same *koan* can serve different purposes depending upon the situation, the disposition of the student and the intention of the teacher.

Dogen

Dogen, another prominent thinker, introduced the other variety of Zen, known as Soto Zen. He was a child genius. He pondered over the vexed issue that if every one is endowed with the Buddha-nature then why is there a need to train for and to attain enlightenment. He discussed this with Eisai and Myozen but was not satisfied. He went to China to study with Chinese monks. Later on the answer he found out was that though the Buddha-nature is amply present in every person, unless one practices it is not manifested; unless there is realization it is not attained. He opined, "To think practice and realization are not one is the heretical view. In the Buddha dharma practice and realization are identical. Because one's present practice is practice in realization, one's initial negotiation of the way in itself is the whole of original realization. Thus, even while one is directed to practice, he is told not to anticipate realization apart from practice because practice points directly to original realization. As it is already realization in practice, realization is endless; as it is practice in realization, practice is beginning-less." Thus there is no difference between practice and enlightenment. Enlightenment is not a goal to be attained at the end of practice for there is no end to practice. So if one is mindful in what one is doing then there is no distinction between practice and enlightenment. Take for example an accomplished artist. He does not cease to practice after becoming accomplished. Rather he displays greater and greater skill in producing newer masterpieces. In him enlightenment and practice go hand in hand.

Dogen further clarified that instead of saying, "All sentient beings have Buddha-nature", it should be said, "The whole of being is Buddha-nature." Similarly he pointed out that redemption from *samsāra* is not to be confined to the sentient world only but it is to be extended to all existence. Thus he widened the scope of *nirvāṇa* from human to cosmic and made it trans-anthropocentric. He gave a very illuminating understanding of *nirvāṇa*. It is not mere transcendence of impermanence but realization of impermanence as impermanence. Mere transcendence of impermanence and reaching the state of permanence is not Buddhistic. Genuine *nirvāṇa* consists in realization of impermanence and working for enlightenment of suffering-affected *samsāra*-bound beings. This is the flow of *Mahākaruṇā* in which *samsāra* and *nirvāṇa* become one as Nāgārjuna and Śāntideva have taught. This is what is meant by saying, "Do not abide in *samsāra* or *nirvāṇa*." This 'no-abiding' is the true *Buddhatva*. It is not turning away from *samsāra* but realizing *nirvāṇa* in *samsāra*, a symbiosis of *Mahābodhi* and *Mahākaruṇā*.

Dogen advocated "Deep mountain, quite valley" approach to life. Rinzai monks, on the other hand, dwelled mainly in towns and cities. The essence of Soto Zen teaching is, "Look into the mind and you will find *Buddhahood*." Dogen has emphasized this practice of meditation and contemplation in day to day living. The sum and substance of his teahing in his own words expressed in his masterpiece 'Shobo-genzo' is , "To study the way is to study the self. To study the self is to forget the self. To forget the self is to be enlightened by all things. To be enlightened by all things is to remove the barries between one's self and others."

In practice Dogen favors *Zazen* (sitting meditation) rather than *koan* that is favored by Hakuin. But emphasis on meditation and practice is common to both of them. Both belived that every being is possessed of *bodhicitta* or the seed of *Buddhahood*. Everyone is a sleeping Buddha and by meditation can realize enlightenment and gain a direct insight into the nature of reality.

Nichiren

Another notable thinker after Dogen is Nichiren. He was critical of Pure Land sect and propagated faith in the Lotus sūtra. He wanted its promulgation all over the world. He declared himself to be an incarnation of Bodhisattva of Supreme Action. He favored social activism. He believed that politics and society couldn't be detached from religion. Religion should form the basis of a prosperous and virtuous society. He believed that the ideal country is one that is governed by the Buddha dharma. He envisioned Japan as the land in which the true teaching of the Buddha was to be revived and from which it was to spread throughout the world. He firmly held that Japan is the only country whose destiny is linked to the Lotus teaching and its promulgation. He emphasized two important characteristics of the Lotus sūtra, viz., *Ekayāna* doctrine that advocated universal liberation and the doctrine of the eternally enlightened Buddha who is ever present. He insisted that only the latter half of the Lotus sūtra contains the final and supreme teaching. He further emphasized practical side of the religious conduct rather than mere theoretical study. He was firmly convinced that his teachings would liberate Japan from moral degeneration. Because of his strong views he suffered severe persecution but his convictions grew stronger and stronger. He was sentenced to death but escaped narrowly. His followers branched off into several sub-sects the most prominent among them was Soka Gakkai.

Tokugawa Period

In the Tokugawa period we find a number of Buddhist leaders who revived, restated or reformed their Buddhist traditions. Tenkei emphasized attainment of one's own enlightenment by oneself without seeking guidance of any teacher. In the same vein Suzuki Shosan rejected the authority of the previous masters and dissuaded people from forsaking their vocations in the world. He emphasied this-worldliness and social action. He advocated faithful pursuance of one's vocation. He maintained that realization of Buddhist truth in mundane activities entails appreciation of Buddhist practices within the concrete human social nexus. But he wanted that care had to be taken so that it does not degenerate into sheer profit seeking utilitarianism. All our afflictions come from attachment to body and material things. To be delivered from this attachment is the way to become the Buddha. Faithful performance of one's own duties is real Buddhist practice. His message could be expressed as, "Work is worship". He emphasized vocational ethics seasoned with distributive justice, a principle of mutual caring and sharing. He said, "Renounce desires and pursue gains single mindedly. But you should never enjoy the fruits of your labour by yourself. You should, instead, work for the good of all." Takuan, another Zen thinker, taught that the Law of the Buddha is the same as the Law of mundane existence. Hakuin also rejected formalistic and intellectual Zen and emphasized spirituality and ethical conduct. He recognized the traditional *koan* system. Tominaga Nakamoto advocated situational ethics. Jiun Sonja laid stress on the practice of 'Ten Virtues' as the essence of Buddhism. All these thinkers rejected monastic asceticism and advocated egalitarianism. Their teachings created a climate for Japan's rapid progress.

Buddhism in Modern Japan

In modern times even though Buddhism has lost its vantage position, the enlightened Buddhist leaders have tried to revitalize it. Among them Nishida Kitaro, D.T. Suzuki, Nanjo Bunyu, J. Takakusu and Hajime Nakamura are noteworthy. In contemporary times S. Mayeda, Masao Abe, Masaharu Anesaki, J Takasaki, Y. Matsunami, M. Tokunaga, H. Marui and many others have made significant contributions towards proper understanding of Buddhism. Nishida Kitaro and D.T. Suzuki were deeply involved in Zen practices. Both of them emphasized the Eastern ways of thinking as distinct from the Western ones. Nishida's emphasis on 'pure experience' and his advocacy of 'absolute Nothingness' have Buddhist tinge. Suzuki is well known as an exponent of Zen but he has been an authoritative interpreter of the Mahāyāna tradition. He expounded Zen as 'non-dualistic awakening'. He pointed out that the logic of *prajñā*-intuition is beyond the dualistic logic of the West though it includes the latter. Nishida also shared the same view. Hajime Nakamura emphasized this point as well. *All these thinkers and scholars have influenced and shaped the contemporary Japanese philosophy and the richness of their thoughts is yet to be adequately evaluated and fully appreciated outside Japan.* A host of scholars associated with *Bukkyo Dendo Kyokai* and with *The Eastern Institute* and two academic organizations, viz., *The Japanese Association of Indian and Buddhist Studies* and *The Japanese Association for South Asian Studies* have been doing phenomenal work in Buddhist studies. Buddhism is being seriously studied at many governmental and private universities.

In contemporary times Japan has made substantial contribution in the spread of Buddhism in Europe, United States of America, Canada, Australia etc. Thus after Korea and China Japan also has been an exporter of Buddhism. Once receptive of Buddhist thought Japan has been its zealous promoter and protector.

The contribution of Buddhism to Japanese national life, to its culture and civilization has been immense and valuable. It gave a new impetus to the development of arts, sciences, philosophy and literature. It was not just a religion but also an instrument of social service. Buddhist temples were seats of learning and social service. Society and temples were interrelated and they worked hand in hand for the amelioration of the suffering of the people. The Buddhist monks provided community leadership. There was also perfect matching of Buddhism and state machinery. Shotoku's rule can be cited as an example. Under the influence of Buddhism the entire country was literary transformed. Buddhism helped in broadening the mental vista of Japanese people, elevated their spiritual level, refined their aesthetic sense and accelerated material progress. It is hoped that Buddhism will continue to thrive in Japan and with missionary zeal she may spread Buddhist universal values of peace, cosmic unity, mutual caring and sharing, and general well being. Buddhism has taught Japan that there is a Deity who looks after the welfare of the whole universe and works for the redemption of all without any discrimination irrespective of any particular tribe, clan or nation. Let Japan disseminate this wisdom all over the globe once again. The ideals of *Buddhabhāva, Buddhakṣetra* etc. stand for this. In the past India gave the lead and now it is for Japan to take over the onerous task of leading the world in the field of spirituality apart from the fields of science and technology getting reinforcement from India. The present day Japan is facing the danger of extinction of its native culture nourished by Buddhism. The impact of Western consumerism and materialism has been devastating. India and Japan and in fact the whole of Asia are engulfed in a crisis. A renewal of cross cultural interactions will not only help and contribute to mutual understanding and mutual enrichment but it will also consolidate and vitalize common spititual roots and resources. If we look back to our long past the wisdom of those times will help us to understand each other more intimately for our mutual benefit and enhancement.

References

1 Buddhism p. 83.

2 (i) Samyutta Nikāya II, p. 106.

(ii) For Buddhism in India please refer "2500 Years of Buddhism (Ed.) P.V. Bapat, Publications Division, Govt. of India.

3 Buddhism in the Land of Rising Sun, Published in *Buddhism and Humanism*, International Buddhist Conference, Bodhgaya, 1995, p. 123.

4 Quoted from "History of Japanese Religion" p. 53 by Masaharu Anesaki.

5 The following account is based on Encyclopaedia of Asian Philosophies, Routledge, London.

2

Sharing the Aisles of the Future

Lokesh Chandra

Buddhism is wisdom and compassion, life and legend, beauty and bliss, as alive as a river that runs, or as a mountain upon which a glimmer of eternity descends. It takes me to the cosmic image of a solitary being, said a Japanese monk Kenjiu Kasawara who had gone to Oxford to study Sanskrit under Max Müller. He wrote of him: "I never found any guile in him, and I doubt whether, during the last four years, Oxford possessed a purer and nobler soul among her students than this poor Buddhist priest." It was a century and a quarter ago. He fell sick, returned home and passed away in 1883. Max Müller recalled: "I well remember how last year we watched together a glorious sunset from the Malvern Hills, and how, when the Western sky was, like a golden curtain, covering we knew not what, he said to me, 'that is what we call the Eastern gate of our Sukhāvatī, the Land of Bliss'. He looked forward to it, and he trusted he should meet there all who had loved him, and whom he had loved and that he should gaze on the Buddha Amitābha". Kasawara and Nanjio had been sent to England by the liberal-minded Shinshū sect founded by Shinran in the 13th century. Max Müller inspired both his students to trace Sanskrit texts in Japan. He also requested the Government of Great Britain to urge their Ambassador to the Imperial Court of Japan to locate Sanskrit manuscripts in their country. Emperor Meiji and his government were suppressing Buddhism and disowning their cultural heritage. They suddenly realized the international importance of the Buddhist legacy. Japan admired and wanted to emulate the insular empire of Great Britain. Hence the request of Max Müller through the British Ambassador was taken up enthusiastically and Buddhism found new heartbeats. The oldest Sanskrit manuscript on palm-leaves had been preserved at the Horyuji monastery since the year AD 609. It was a sensational discovery as such as ancient palm-leaf codex was not known till then, from India or anywhere else. Indian scholars were thrilled and through these Sanskrit manuscripts began India's modern interface with Japan in imperceptible bonds of the fragrance of a dream.

Kasawara gazing at the flaming Sun on the pensive calm of an eve at Oxford was pondering over his Home beyond the western mountains. In the Sanskrit phrase *astam eti* for 'the sun sets', the word *asta* means 'home'. The Sun goes home beyond the auspicious golden mountain: *astaṁ gacchati yatrārko girau hema-prabhe śubhe* (Rāmāyaṇa 4.37.22). What a point of reference for the imagining consciousness, an imagery of expanding consciousness. When the Sun goes home, he enters the womb of Fire to find a new existence (*atha yad astam eti tad agnāv eva yonau garbho bhūtvā praviśati*). As we assemble here in an India-Japan seminar we too are in quest of the Fire to raise the human state. We seek the ultra-living Fire that lives in our heart, in the sky, in the warmth of love. The first words of India in the Ṛgveda were: "*agnim īḍe purohitam*" "I pay homage to the Fire", the Fire that is in the joy of creation. Man is a creation of this Fire of joy, not a creation of need. As we assemble to ponder over the future of the Sanātana destiny of Indo-Japanese eternity, the last fifteen centuries of Buddhism invoke the intensity of Emperor Aśoka, Shotoku Taishi, the repose of Shinran, the dialectic of the light of Amidā in Sukhāvatī who asks of us:

> In the bright crystal of your eyes
>
> Show the havoc of fire, show its inspired works.

In the early morning light, the Sun (Savitā) stands out fiery red in all his majesty. This immense dazzling light exalts man, links him the small to the great, magnifies human destiny, and in such moments of exaltation the Indic man has sung for millennia, in the muted voice of his heart, the Gāyatrī:

"*oṁ tat savitur vareṇyaṁ bhargo devasya dhīmahi*" to invoke the glory and grandeur of Sun the Deity to implore him to import depths of substance.

The Taima *maṇḍala* of Japan, based on the Amitāyur-dhyāna-sūtra, begins with contemplation on the Sun about to set and looks like a drum suspended in space. This is the first of the sixteen contemplations to calm the mind and visualise Sukhāvatī. The sixteen contemplations in the outer court are the *ādhāra* and the inner sanctum is the *ādheya* of this Pure Land. The sixteen contemplations are on the (1) setting sun i.e. the eastern gate of Sukhāvatī, (2) water (lakes) of Sukhāvatī, (3) earth i.e. land of Sukhāvatī, (4) trees of Sukhāvatī, (5) ponds of Sukhāvatī, (6) mansions of Sukhāvatī, (7) lotus throne of Amidā, (8) Amidā trinity, (9) Amidā in his 'great body', (10) Avalokiteśvara, (11) Mahāsthāma-prāpta, (12) oneself in Sukhāvatī, (13) Amidā in his 'small body' (*sūkṣma-kāya*), (14) superior, (15) average, (16) inferior levels of karmas leading to nine degrees of birth.

The first six contemplations are related to the surrounds of Sukhāvatī (1-6), the next seven to Buddha Amitābha of this Paradise in his gross and subtle bodies alongwith his two main acolytes Avalokiteśvara and Mahāsthāmaprāpta (7-13), and the final three to the nine degrees of rebirths that a sādhaka can undergo dependent on his karmas (14-16). The Jodo tradition takes the setting Sun to symbolise Sukhāvatī in the west transcending the phenomenal world, and contemplations on the still crystalline waters of the Pure Land as a reality as it is mirrored in the pure mind. The 'land beyond' (*higan* 'other shore'), and the 'universe within' are reflection and serenity. The Sun in the Heavens, and the Lotus in the waters have been conjoined in some other sutras as well.

In the centre of the Taima *Maṇḍala* are the five meditations on the elements of *Tejas* represented by the Sun, *Āpaḥ* 'waters', *Pṛthivī* 'earth', the unspecified *Ākāśa* 'ether' represented by the *anāhata* or unstruck resonance of the musical instruments flying all over the heavens. These represent the *dhāraṇā* of the eight-fold/*aṣṭāṅga* Yoga. The East Asian tradition did not realise that these meditations are on the five elements, even though four great meditations (*shi-dai-kan*) had been detailed in the Chinese translation of a lost Sanskrit work 'The Secret Essential Methods of Meditation' done by Kumārajīva during the years AD 402-412 (T613, Nj779, K798). The flying musical instruments in the *maṇḍala* could not lead to the concept of contemplation on *Ākāśa* or other. They are part of *nāda-laya* detailed in the fourth chapter of the Haṭha-yoga-pradīpikā 4. 79-89 on *samādhi*. The sounds in nāda have three stages:

(1) Very loud sounds in the initial stage: like the surging ocean, thunder, kettle drums (*bherī*), and cymbals (*jharjhara*).

(2) Loud sounds in the intermediate stage: like the *mardala,* conch (*śaṅkha*), bell (*ghaṇṭā*), and *kāhala*.

(3) Subtle sounds in the final stage: like that of trinklets (*kiṅkiṇī*) flute (*vaṁśā*), *vīṇā* and bees (*bhramara*).

The mind absorbed in nāda becomes calm and collected in *anāhata*. The five meditations (*pañca-dhāraṇā*) on the five elements (*bhūta*) in Yoga are focussed on their symbols or their deities. The Tri-śikhi-brāhmaṇa-upaniṣad (2. 133 f.) points out that they can be visualised as symbols, while the Gheraṇḍa-saṁhitā names them:

earth element	as a yellow square	pārthivī dhāraṇā
water element	as a silvery crescent	āmbhasī dhāraṇā
fire element	as a red flame	āgneyī dhāraṇā
air element	as a smoke-coloured altar	vāyavī dhāraṇā
ether element	as lustrous deep black space	ākāśī dhāraṇā

They destroy all evil, affliction and sorrow (Gheraṇḍa-saṁhitā 3.72 f.). Thus we see a deep nexus between the Sukhāvatī contemplations and the yoga practices.

Shinran says in *The True Teaching, Practice and Realization of the Pure Land Way* that the Buddhist Dharma and secular ruler work together for the good of the people. The ruler is responsible for peace and benevolent rule, while Buddhist temples ensure divine protection for the state. This is the coming together of the 'two truths': the 'supramundane truth' (Jap. *shintai,* Skt. *paramārtha-satya*) and the 'mundane or secular truth' (Jap. *zokutai,* Skt. *saṁvṛti-satya*). In the Shinshu, the two truths signify the 'Buddha-dharma' (*buppō*) and 'the *rājadharma* or the sovereign's law' (*ōbō*). This conceptual frame-work preempts arbitrary governance and also promotes values.

The Longer Sukhāvatī-vyūha was translated by Lokakṣema the Yueh-chin, besides the Ajātaśatru-kaukṛtya-vinodana which is the basis of its promulgation. It had been translated earlier by An Shih-kao, the crown prince of Parthia, who gave the kingdom to his uncle, became a monk, and came to China in AD 148 and worked till AD 170. These two translations were done by speakers of Iranian languages. They brought together Sanskrit, Iranic and Chinese languages under the umbrella of Sukhāvatī a transcendent universe to ferry living beings to yonder shore of awakening. The trans-subjective reality of the Pure Land replaced the radically restrictive vision of the sinocentric world-view. The Sukhāvatī weltanschauung introduced the idealised reality of multiple universes, wherein any reality is as valid as any other. The barbarian or devil of the Classical Chinese formulations now became the Other. After all, the Chinese cavalries got their horses from the Yueh-chih and the Parthians. The Parthian shot was well-known as the custom for firing in retreat at the enemy. The intervention of Iranian and Iranised peoples in the translation of Sanskrit Sūtras into Chinese marks the beginning of one of the most impressive achievements of East Asian culture. Several objects of Iranian origin have been found in the Shosoin Repository like the lacquered ewer with a bird-headed spout, a gigaku mask of a drunken Persian king (*suiko-ō-men*) made of paulownia wood, or the biwa with the camel. The musical instruments, enlivened with *hu-yueh* 'Iranian music', achieved wide acclaim and they can be seen floating in the Sukhāvatī *maṇḍalas*.

The intercultural exchanges across the Silk Route, or better the Sūtra Route, had been initiated by Emperor Aśoka. He worked assiduously to spread the values of Dharma among the Yonas, Kambojas, and other peoples in the northwest of India and beyond. The four accounts in Chinese and Tibetan associate the foundation of Khotan in Central Asia to the son and ministers of Emperor Aśoka. Yotkan, the ancient capital of Khotan, has yielded a collection of coins from the first century AD bearing Chinese legends on one side and Indian Prakrit legends on the other. Buddhism in the northwestern and Central Asian regions gave rise to the great cultural values of East Asia. From central Asia Buddhism passed on to China, Korea and Japan. The Yueh-chih, Parthians, Sogdians, Kucheans and others translated the masterpieces of Buddhist Sūtras into Chinese. China was enriched by the new ideas flowing in from the 'Western Region' (*hsi-yu*). The concept of barbarians and Sinocentrism underwent changes. The multiple paradises of Buddhism, the sophistication and abstraction of Buddhist philosophy, the social and moral values harmonising all sectors of society, the opening up of monastic learning to high and low, the ideal beauty of sculptures and paintings in their soft diaphanous colours, and scores of other new syndromes of ideas and living gave a new world-view to East Asia. Emperor Aśoka initiated a movement whose dynamics can also rejuvenate the renewed image of the future. Aśoka's message was not only a religion, but the noblest form of creativity imbued with spirituality and social values that could endure over time. He gave a humane direction to the Inner Universe in the nobility of its meaning for life to be lived in harmony on the family level, in the harmony of sects, and the affinity of the human spirit with the other transcendent reality. He was the beloved of the gods (*Devānāṁpriyaḥ*), that is blessed by them, as well as one who saw to the fulfilment of public welfare (*Priyadarśī*). The noble and the real converged in the here-and-now. Emperor Aśoka gave rise to humanism in the Buddhist vision that transcended itself. Herein the ethical imperatives and social practices converged. His message became humanity in man, by rising above the self. We need to renew the images of Emperor Aśoka by invoking values as the highway of human existence.

Emperor Aśoka sent his emissaries to Srilanka, and according to local traditions to other parts of Southeast Asia known as Suvarṇabhūmi. The tribal ways of these areas were transformed into images of perfection, giving rise to sculptures, temple complexes, governmental institutions, writing, literature, philosophy, and so on. A rich development of religion, culture and civilization followed. Buddhism became the birth place of philosophical ideas, and all the influences in art and poetry which determined for two millennia, and still determine, the intellectual and spiritual life of millions. It became a tremendous civilizing influence.

Buddhism seeks for the coming century a human home in light, beauty and happiness of the horizons of the mind. From the invisible grounds of Emperor Aśoka flow the springs at which saps and juices come to enrich humanity after thousands of years. The mind has to be enjewelled in the interior spark of Enlightenment (*Bodhi*).

Lord Buddha spent the last rainy season at the Veṇuvana on the outskirts of Vaiśālī. Resting under a tree, the Buddha remarked: "this world is beautiful—it is a joy to live in it". The beauty of life is mirrored in the dancing belles on the element earth in the Taima *maṇḍala*. Life and humans are central in the message of Śākyamuni. For the first time in the religious history of man, Lord Buddha made human beings central to the totality of life, as well as to their transcendence, that is, life and the beyond were their own doing. It is a strong point of Buddhism and one of the important factors that conditioned its spread over Asia. Men of different cultures and different languages could find their being in the eternal message of Lord Śākyamuni.

The Buddha propounded the stability of societies in the Dīgha-nikāya 2.73: "...So long, Ānanda, as the Vajjians assemble in harmony and disperse in harmony; so long as they do their business in harmony; so long as..., just so long as they do these things, Ānanda, may the prosperity of the Vajjians be looked for and not their decay."

Lord Buddha represents the culmination of thought and social action. His is a dialogue not with a Supreme Brahman, but inspiring lessons for human beings. He was a lover of mankind. He urged each one to become what he/she really is down in the deepest, what one discovers himself to be in moments of loftiest meditation. Men had to get rid of hatred and malice, indulgence in lower desires, all lying and evil thoughts.

It has been rightly pointed out in the biography of Lord Buddha entitled *Lalitavistara,* that he studied 64 scripts at school. The Chinese script is among them. It means that there is no single divine language, but all languages are divine. In every language you can have a divine message. Other religions are wedded to the sanctity of one language. Buddhism accepted all the languages of the world. It means that all humans, wherever they reside are potential Buddhas, *Buddhāṅkura* in Sanskrit, that is Sprouting Buddhas, or Enlightened Beings in the making. This centrality of human beings is evident in Buddhism from very early times. Humans need not look up to an external Divine, but to the Divinity within themselves. The within is the beyond.

The Japanese syllabary of Fifty Sounds, to *goju-on,* was based on the Sanskrit sound system. It was to spread education to the common man. The new syllabary was a revolutionary step in Japan's civilisation: what was hitherto the prerogative of the pre-destined few became the potential privilege of all. The entire alphabet was woven into a poem wherein every syllable occurs once. This poem is called *Iroha.* It is based on the Mahāparinirvāṇa-sūtra. It runs in translation as follows:

Colours, gleam as they may,
How they blow away!
Who in this world of ours
Lasts for aye?
The deep mountains of ephemeral life
We've crossed this day.
No more shallow dreams we see.
Nor shall we inebriate be.

It is a free transcreation of the Sanskrit poem:

sarve saṁskārāḥ anityāḥ utpāda-vyaya-dharmiṇaḥ/
teṣāṁ vyupaśamaḥ sukham avadad mahāśramaṇaḥ//

The Chinese had constructed the Great Wall against the barbarians. The Yueh-chih were selling horses to China, and alongwith they brought Buddhist Sūtras to China. The horses were for the cavalry and hence power, and the Sūtras were virtue. This gave rise to the Chinese idea of Power and Virtue. In modern Japan it has become wealth and virtue (*fukoku yutoku*). The Yueh-chih impressed the Chinese with sophisticated Sūtras. They were not barbarians, but highly cultured. Dharmarakṣa the Yueh-chih translated for the first time several Buddhist sūtras into Chinese. Ninety five of them are found in the Taisho edition of the Chinese *Tripiṭaka.* Thus Buddhism was 'Power and Virtue', steeds and sūtras, providing security and the sublime. Confucianism was predominantly Palace Culture, while Buddhism was Peoples' Culture. Anyone could join the *Saṅgha* and rise irrespective of his status of birth. The beauty of the paintings and sculptures with their celebration of life contrasted sharply with the stiff contours of the funerary bas reliefs of the Han tombs.

At Hase, Kamakura stands the great image of Amidā, renowned as the Daibutsu, which is deservedly the symbol of Japan today. In the thirteenth century it was constructed by contributions of devotees of the Sukhāvatī sect. Five centuries ago, a tidal wave swept away its hall and since it has sat under the open sky. Despite its immensity, the statue has an aesthetic fluency. The statue gazes downward with an aura of divine compassion (*karuṇā*) while the devotees chant adoration to Amitābha 'Infinite Illumination', *nama Amida butsu,* so that there shines the light of illumination regained.

From the swordsmanship hall (*dōjō*) to the garden. No gardens in the world are more abstract and symbolic than those inspired by Zen. A Zen garden is a starting point for meditation, a possible gate to *satori,* to delivery from the bondage of illusion and the chain of reincarnation. It is the mystery of autonomy and spontaneity. Every stone has its innuendo, every blade of grass touches off a vortex of reflections. The Ryoanji garden with its naked expanse of white sand acting as a setting for stones takes us back to the sea, to the ocean of existence (*bhava-sāgara*). This supremely abstract monument, the *kare sansui,* the "dry landscape" garden, was designed in the late fifteenth century. The rocks, tiny mounts Fuji, simply mean *fuji,* not two, that is, peerless, the abolition of all distinctions, the *advaya*. There are both literal levels and symbolic tangents thereof, crossing the sea of illusion towards the shore of *satori* "illumination", to cross over the dry sandy ripples of the ocean of existence, the *bhava-sāgara*.

Zen is a product of the Chinese and Japanese soil from the Buddhist seed of Enlightenment, India's hut and Japanese bamboos, India's sophisticated thought and Japan's bizarre koans: all leading to self-reliance (*jiyū*) and self-being (*jizai*).

The world of imagery still flows into the stream of life in Japan. The roundish Daruma doll is a must for success in life. You buy it, its eyes are blank, you paint one pupil before embarking on a project (can well be an Election !), and if all ends well, the second pupil is added so that Daruma is rewarded by full sight. The Daruma doll is the Indian *ācārya* Bodhidharma, the founder of Zen Buddhism. He spent eight years in un-interrupted meditation. At last when he tried to stand up, he found that his legs had atrophied. Thus the ancient frontiers of the collective mind live on.

Along a road stands an egglike rock on a flat roundish base of another rock, with the Saṇskrit monogram RO : Sanskrit letters implying deeper levels. A modern Japanese girl in mini, her hair dyed blonde and perhaps with styrene injection for a rounded feminine form, stops by, graciously puts a tangerine on a piece of paper as an offering to the planets (*nava-graha*): RO is the symbolic syllable or bījākṣ ara for *nava-graha-pūjā*. Such are the frozen levels of culture ever echoing at different strata of existence and consciousness.

Japan of today is the manifestation (*suijaku*) of the universal essences (*honji*) of her Collective Conscious that not only survives but has been turned into a precious asset. The echoes of her consciousness are repeated at different levels of her life. Classical and contemporary are living symbols of vitality: steel and glass skyscrapers besides shops selling samurai swords. Japan fascinates the mind and ravishes the eyes. The electronics of today of frozen of culture pulsate in the warm reality of life in Japan.

The Meiji Restoration is a watershed in Japanese history. The dictum *wakon yosai* "Japanese spirit and Western techonology" has worked miracles. This is the ideal Asia needs today to rise from the ashes of inaction and hence dependence on the West. The language of Japan was always clear, goals precise, and hard work has been the ideal. In the 19th century a Japanese scholar visited the Louvre. A painting showed a sinner condemned to hard labour in hell. The astonished Japanese exclaimed: "Is hard work a punishment?" A Buddhist monk was known in India as *bhikṣu* 'one who begs alms' and as *śramaṇa* 'one who works hard'. The Sino-Japanese took the latter as *shamon* as the prime expression. Glory to labour or *karmaṇyevādhikāraste* in the words of the Gītā. Work alone can liberate us.

The Japanese Okakura Tenshin stayed at the home of poet Rabindranath Tagore in 1902. It led to the cultural renaissance of India. Out of his talks with the Indian poet, Tenshin crystallised his essay on *The Ideals of the East,* his first publication in English. Tenshin "The Heart of Heaven" launched the idea "Asia is one". Havell, Tagore, Coomaraswamy responded. The pioneers of modern Indian painting, Abanindranath Tagore, Nandlal Bose, and others, used Japanese brushes and colours and reflected the diaphanous aura of Japanese paintings in their new creativity. It was echoed in the researches of Coomaraswamy who found parallels for Vedic texts in Japanese art in his *Elements of Buddhist Iconography* published by the Harvard University in 1935. This cultural encounter left a deep impression on our national ethos. India linked freedom with Japan. Some of our revolutionaries sought refuge in Japan. The heroic struggle of Tenshin prevented the wholesale destruction of the cultural heritage of Japan in the orgy of foreignism sweeping the country. Yet, he spoke of the cup of humanity. The East and the West are not so apart, or in the words of Okakura: "humanity has met in a tea-cup".

Through Japanese life run the threads of an outward explosion and an inward implosion. The inner life moves in peace, serenity and meditation. The outer manifestation is stress and action. The Bodhisattvas take on two aspects: the one calm, serene, and benevolent and the other dynamic, passionate and terrifying. The ritual rhythms and symbolic behaviour converge, and become movement, action, miracle of achievement in a frenzy of merciless precision. The intangible perfume and the indefinable hue of the Japanese spirit create a modernisation that resists Westernisation. Japan is more modernised than Westernised, while the Philippines is more Westernised than modernised. Does a Westerner feel his eyes assuming an almond shape and his thoughts becoming Zen simply because he drinks tea? The adoption, diffusion and development of inventions have become the unequivocal 'we' of Japan. There is no veering of the Japanese mind toward the West, but a slight movement towards a neutral territory. 'Me' is the miracle. The Sanskrit word for miracle is *camatkāra* which originates from *ca mat* 'and mine, and mine'. It is the coming together of me and creativity. The word *camatkāra* refers to the remarkable *camaka* hymn of the Yajurveda. It is an affirmation of life, the substantiality of existence, which is to be attained by every me.

Buddhism with its many gods and goddesses represents pluralism, which is going to be the new sensibility. It is the openness to multiple forms of reality. They are the many structures of meaning and being in which we constantly live. No universal proposal for human meaning can come up: the depths can be lived out of the rag bag of the many. Pluralism gives depth, a resonance of the transcendant function.

Buddhism announces and owns expanding consciousness, a new humility in the diversity of our modern existence. Contemporary life can have no fixed horizons, fences, or boundaries. The emerging pluralistic universe seeks relevance in polytheism to purify, perfect and ennoble our existence. In polytheism man's free thinking and many-sided thinking has the power to create for himself new and individual eyes, always newer and more individualized.

The French writer André Malraux had said that Europe was seeking the Holy Grail. The Holy Grail is believed to be the chalice in which Saint Grael collected the blood of Christ after crucifixion . It was brought to Britain and was preserved and venerated for generations. When its keepers became impure, it vanished. Numerous knights went in search but could not find it. This search could succeed only if one who was perfectly chaste in thoughts, words and deeds (Jap. *sanmitsu*) undertook it. This Grail was the Alms-bowl of the Buddha, that went across Parthia to West Asia. Parthia was a Buddhist area. An Shih-kao the princes of Parthia was the second great translator of Buddhist *sūtras* into Chinese. The Bowl inherited such ethereal power that it was owned by Christianity as the Holy Grail. It has been a famous object of quest for the knights of Arthurian romance. Its quest is linked with gradual realization of spiritual meaning. It influenced poetic speculations and works, such as T.S. Eliot's *The Waste Land* (1922). Now the quest of the Western man is the White Man's burden and his rights of dominance under the euphemism of human rights. Today the Hindu-Buddhist culture of India and Japan is under the serious threat of globalization

The Threat of Globalization to Buddhism

The cultural foundations of the Hindu-Buddhist Commonwealth (HBC) are being threatened on the levels of economy through globalization, on the grounds of social behaviour patterns by electronic media, and in the case of defence through superior technology and interference. Japanese intellectuals have been reacting to the globalization tendencies with growing vehemence. Saeki Keishi of the Kyoto University, Kaneko Masaru and other Japanese intellectuals have pointed out the unfairness of globalization. Masaru has written a book entitled 'Antiglobalism' (Jap. *Han gurobarizumu*). The Japanese have been honestly outspoken. They say "Globalization is just another word for Americanization", "Is this greedy, survival-of- the-fittest capitalism really what we want", "We must not forget issues like Japanese tradition and cultural identity". Pierre Bourdieu divides resources into three types: economic capital, cultural capital and social capital. All the three fundamental bases of civilized life have run aground in the HBC. We seem to have lost sight of our strengths and are being led astray by the verbal bubble of the West. We need to read Keishi's "The End of Americanism" (*Amerikanizumu no shūen*). The fall of communism was a victory for human rights, and now the demise of globalism will be a victory of values. Globalization provides confrontation and hereby new opportunities to assess our traditions, and in the words of Emmanuel Todd of Paris, traditions are the heart of a culture. Family system stubbornly resists globalization and thus helps cultures preserve their individuality. Yamazaki Masakazu of the University of East Asia's Graduate School has pointed out that values common to all humanity are an illusion.

The constant stream of directives by the Allied Occupation against Shinto-Buddhist culture of Japan was the first experience of the Japanese people of a bulldozer-like pressure of an antagonistic and more powerful civilization. Civilization had swept the nation after the Meiji Restoration of 1868 with the slogan "Civilization and Enlightenment". In the post-war years, 'civilization' was replaced by 'culture', and the phrase "culture nation" (*bunka kokka*) emerged as a national slogan. The "Huntington shock" has led to the realization that cultures/civilizations wield power. The HBC cultures are objects of aesthetic contemplation, an appreciation of beauty and charm, nobility and fervour. The concept of culture/ civilization as power has made the Japanese reflect on self-awareness, and to nurture the "search for our roots." At the same time, the Japanese have commenced the scrutinisation of American civilization "as a kind of bastard or freak offspring of modern Europe" in the words of Saeki Shōichi.

The fundamental perception now is "we should accept what we are, namely, a distinctly minor civilization that operates best on a scale commensurate with its own physical size". The deconstruction of the *idée fixe* of the Yasukuni shrine as an emblem of militarism has been replaced by the shrine as a symbol of modernization. The Yasukuni is redolent of the ephemeral cherry blossom: a modern image of the Buddhist concept of *anityatā.* As silence gives new voices to historic symbols, the Japanese have noted the importance of 'linguistic sovereignty'. Takashina Shūji, Director General of the National Museum of Western Art, writes: "Preserving it is absolutely essential not only to safeguard the Japanese language but also to contribute to the world through the Japanese language and Japanese culture". The famed novelist Natsume Sōseki taught his students that the correct Japanese translation for "I love you" is *Tsuki ga tottemo aoi naa* "the moon is so blue tonight". This emotional expression has to work within in Japanese cultural framework. Kawakatsu Heita of the Waseda University says: "Culture emerged from our involvement with the land. The word *culture* comes from a word meaning 'to till the soil', which was eventually applied to cultivation of the spirit....We are suffering from...a cultural crisis, .. We have to return to the land again". The Japanese are becoming alive to the idea of civilization as power. A new self-awareness is emerging. All the varied civilizations cannot be measured by a single yardstick. "Heavyweight" civilizations have to acknowledge the existence of "lightweight" civilizations that posses a mysterious charm, refinement and unique flavour of belonging. It is difference between a "house" and a "home", an expression of inner identity, alive within, the cultural flowering of a dwelling. The West seeks to submerge our identities into an industrial civilization, that exaggerates the value of human rationality, and repudiates the transcendental which alone can give life meaning. As humans are not completely comfortable with modern industrial consumerism, the clash becomes internalized and spiritual. It is easy to be nihilistic and pronounce tradition and religion, symbols and significance, history and national identity as dead. To deny them is to deny ourselves. Human society is a system of symbols. Symbolic meaning holds sway in the realm of life. It preserves continuity and unity. Mass culture is being projected as a counterpoint to break up the fundamental dignity of sacred symbols and their vitality of spontaneous development. Artistic genres, traditional rituals and conventions, that is Form, are suffering from ignorance and contempt. Form is the very foundation and main stay of culture. The external Form of cultural manifestation is being undermined by the Christian concept of separation of religion and government, which was to annihilate the pagan Roman state. Now it has become a sacred cow. Today there is a 'crisis of Form', whereby contemporary society demonstrates spiritual and cultural shallowness. This Western framework does not apply to the U.K. where the Archbishop of Canterbury officiates at the coronation of the British Monarch, or to the USA where the President takes oath of office on a Bible. Secularization and cultural denigration (modernization) undermines the institutions of non-Western nations. The stronger this drive becomes, the greater is peoples' identification with their own culture. Kawakatsu speaks of "an encounter between a Japan of beauty and a West of strength...Beauty is not always something that wilts before might." To him the "way of the samurai" meant "the polishing of spirit and virtue so as to avoid war." The Meiji government let this spirit and virtue fall by the wayside in its headlong dash to build a wealthy state and strong army, with disastrous results. In his policy speech on 7 August 1998 Prime Minister Obuchi Keizo spoke of *fukoku yūtoku* 'a country of wealth and virtue'. The two Sino-Japanese characters of *Fuji* mean "rich" and "civilized." Heita says that "by turning itself into a country to both wealth and virtue, Japan can make itself as splendid as its Mount Fuji". Nakanishi Terumasa elaborates the Japanese sense of values and accomplishing economic vitality under three national goals "freedom and vitality, revival of history and tradition, and independence." Ishihara Shintarō, a member of the Japanese Parliament wrote "Learning to say no to America" as early as April 1990, wherein he minced no words: "there is no need to...get our ideals spoon-fed to us by the Americans." Nishibe Susumu has been forthright in his comments: "the spread of 'globalism' is nothing more or less than the 'Americanization of the world'...let us make the twentyfirst century the century of de-Americanization." Another commentator Etō Jun says: "the only way to make sense of it is to conclude that the object is to mass-produce self-hating Japanese." Kawachi Takashi of the Mainichi Shimbun warns: "those who feel victimized by post-cold-war trends regard economic globalization as a campaign to impose Western values, under which a country's development strategy and reform efforts are judged by how close they approach the Anglo-American model". He is positive in pointing out the core Asian values: "restraint of individual desires and ambitions, harmony with nature, and concert between the group and individual". Freedom and fairness have to go together. Lee O-young, once a Minister of Culture and Sports of the Republic of Korea, presents a new cultural paradigm:

(i) From a focus on politics and economics to an emphasis on civilization and culture.

(ii) The ability to unite the people culturally will be as important as political, military and economic might.

(iii) The wave of modernization is being replaced in Japan by a new but opposite wave of *datsu-Ō nyū-A* "get away from Europe and unite with Asia".

(iv) A new paradigm of *glocalism,* to bring together globalism and localism.

(v) A definition of the distinguishing features of Asian culture which is not fixed and absolute. In the domestic architecture of Japan and Korea, the interior and exterior are separated by a single thin sheet of paper. The *shōji* or paper homes are to welcome the sounds and breezes, the lovely chirping of birds and insects. It is an open culture as contradistinguished from Europe's culture of walls. It encourages openness.

(vi) Confucianism teaches that we are not born human but *become* human.

(vii) People are part of nature, not its rulers. In former times farmers used to plant three beans in one hole: one to be eaten by the insects in the ground, another by birds in the sky, and the last sprouts to be eaten by the people.

(viii) The environmental problems can be solved only by an alternative to the Judo-Christian tradition. The latter tradition views humankind apart from nature and ruling over it according to God's design.

(ix) The vocabulary of post-structuralism, with words prefixed by inter (internet, interactive, intertextuality) is a paradigm shift to relationality. It is the Chinese ideogram *ren* which combines the elements for 'person' and 'two'. It focuses on the individual and his surrounds acting in unison.

(x) Lee concludes: "At length we will hear, wafting in from the once-forgotten Asian steppe, a song that transcends the spiritual, emotional discord."

The European perceptions of eurocentrism and the general theory of civilizations are both structurings of a mind that has seen phenomenal advances during the last millennium. The Western mind is seeking room to move meaningfully in a pluralistic universe, while it is rooted in the meaning and being of its own thinking and understanding. It does not seek either a re-valuation or a trans-valuation of its *bodhicitta* (*bodaishin*) in the rich structures of consciousness of Buddhism, Hinduism, Taoism, Confucianism or Shintoism. To the westerner a "higher religion" will generate its own antagonisms and may become its own obituary. A uni-dimensional norm of humanity is against the deep reality of existence. We have to discover freedom to acknowledge variousness. All the centuries, climates, lands, languages can not be articulated according to a single symbol system. The 'new science' is bringing in indeterminism, plural logical systems, quarks without substance, irrational numbers, and so on. They compel us to a polycentric world, to a new sensibility of polytheistic consciousness. The new paradigms will have to be many-spendored, with a liveliness of sharing. It will not be a desire to control and manipulate societies through money or mind, sex or spirituality, power and privilege. No 'fundamental values' exist in a vacuum. They have a history of centuries, exegeses of hundreds of minds, the faith of millions, and now the dreadful power of techonology. So concepts like 'cultural commonality' and 'universalism' are counterproductive rather than creative. Buddhism has accepted and respected differences, the beauty of many forms, the eternality of various values. It has meshed the many in the harmony of divergence rather than of convergence.

Respect for the cultures, civilizations and religions of each other, and no interference or conversions by a subtle psychological agenda, should be the values of humankind in our century.

'True universality' will be rich diversity, with no single meaning. The various lines, the many realities will be lived in every one's deepest feelings. Religions in the plural, will be global in the sense that they will be rooted in human consciousness as the vision and faith of fellow beings, whatsoever their demographic numbers. Universality of civilization, rather than a universal civilization, will seek civil behaviour in the affirmation of diversity. Such a civilizaiton will be multiple and the centre will be everywhere.

3

India and Japan: Discovering Each Other

Sushila Narsimhan

We, Indians, can take pride in the fact that Gautama Buddha, one of the finest product of Indian culture, not only gained widespread acceptance and admiration outside India, but his teachings have also played a major role in enriching Asian culture and bringing a fusion of Asian civilizations. From India, Buddhism spread rapidly to several Asian countries like Tibet, Ceylon, Burma, China, Korea, and Japan. This smooth spread of Buddhism in Asian countries may be attributed partly to its ecumenical character and partly to the common Asian mindset, shared modes of thinking, commonality of belief systems and value patterns. Buddhism became a popular religion in China, despite the fact that the philosophy of Confucius, a contemporary of Buddha, was already well entrenched there. The same was in the case of Japan. The Japanese already had a native religion called *'Kami no michi'* (Way of God), and yet Buddhism found a prestigious place among the Japanese rulers and elites. In fact, it was only after coming into contact with Buddhism that the Japanese became conscious of their native religion, which they termed as *'Shintō'* to distinguish it from *'Butsudō'* (Way of Buddha).[1]

Japanese Discovery of India

Two principal elements of pre-modern Japanese culture were alien in origin. One, Buddhism derived from India, and the other, Confucianism derived from China. But, despite their foreign origins, both Buddhism and Confucianism were accepted, modified and assimilated by the Japanese as part of their indigenous cultural tradition along with Shinto.[2] A major reason for the ready acceptance of these foreign philosophies may be attributed to the character of the Japanese people who appreciate synthesis rather than analysis, harmony more than logical consistency. The Japanese were attracted to both Buddhism and Confucianism. While Confucianism spurred the Japanese to learn Chinese, Buddhism drew them towards the study of Sanskrit. In that age when overseas travels were difficult, the neighbouring China served as a source of information and learning. China also became the meeting point for the visiting Indian and Japanese monks and scholars. The two Japanese scholars, Kibi-no-Makibi (693-775) and Kōbō Daishi (Kūkai, 744-836), who are credited for evolving the *kana* syllabary, *katakana* and *hiragana,* had studied Sanskrit from the Indian scholars in China.[3] No wonder, one can find a close resemblance between Japan's fifty sound syllabary pattern of *a, i, u, e, o,* and the order of India's *devanāgari* letters. The sentence in Japanese language too is arranged in the same order as in Sanskrit–subject (*kartā*), object (*karma*), and verb (*kriyā*). The evolution of simple and phonetic *kana* was found very convenient because it enabled the Japanese to pen their thoughts in a living tongue that they had been speaking since antiquity. It is quite possible that, had India's *devanāgari* script penetrated into Japan before the Japanese came into contact with the Chinese character (*kanji*), the Japanese would have adopted the Indian script rather than the complicated *kanji,* and today there would have been no language barrier India and Japan!

The introduction of Buddhism and Confucianism not only contributed to the enrichment of Japanese culture and writing tradition, but also shaped the early Japanese world-view. The ancient Japanese people used to think that the world comprised of three components: *Tenjikū* (India), *Shintan* (China) and *Honchō* (Japan). Amongst these, very often *Tenjiku* was considered as the real world and a "paradise" or "utopia" since it was the birthplace of Buddha. From time to time, several zealous devotees of Buddha, like: Takaoka Shinnō (third son of Emperor Heijō, r. 806-810),[4] Myōe Shōnin Kōben (1173-1232) of Takao-zan (Yamashiro), and Minamoto-no-Sanetomo (1192-1219) of Kamakura, had made strenuous efforts to reach *Tenjiku* but their dream remained unrealized. Until the pre-modern era, *Tenjiku* was really the Heavenly Kingdom!

As a contrast, many Indian monks had managed to reach Korea,[5] and also Japan. Most of these had followed the Central Asian Silk route or the land route via northeastern India (known in China as the 'Southern Silk route') to reach Korea and China. As per historical records, the first Indian to enter Japan was Bodhisena, a *Brāhmaṇa* ascetic from South India. Bodhisena came to Japan via China along with his ten disciples, including Fo-che, a Vietnamese monk settled in Champa (present day Bhagalpur in Bihar), during the reign of Emperor Shomu (r. 724-748). He reached Nara, Japan's ancient capital, in 736 AD and stayed there until death in 760 AD. Delighted to hear the news of the arrival of a learned saint from the land of Buddha, the emperor with the help of a famous Buddhist monk Gyōki (670-749),[6] a Korean by birth, organized a get-together of about 10,000 people to felicitate him. The news of Gyōki's devotion to Buddhism had reached Bodhisena. Meeting Gyōki in person, Bodhisena exclaimed with sheer joy: "Oh! So you are the Japanese Mañjusrī (Bodhisattva)"[7] As per *Daianji Bodai deraiki* [Succession records of Tōdaiji temple], Bodhisena presented to Emperor Shomu several Indian items, incense-burners, 100 *tālapatra* (palmyra leaf) manuscripts in Brahmi writing, and 2000 grains of Buddha's body-relics. Bodhisena spent rest of his life in Nara and in 751 AD, after the demise of Gyōki, was made the *Dai Sōjō* (Chief priest). Thus, in 752, when the world's biggest gilded statue of Buddha (Buddhalocana) was installed in the Tōdaiji temple and the *kigen* rite (the ceremony of the opening of the Buddha's eyes) was performed, Bodhisena was the chief priest.[8] During the tenure of Bodhisena, Nara became a great centre of art and learning. Apart from teaching Sanskrit to his disciples, Bodhisena also wrote many books contributing to the richness of Japanese literature. Bodhisena also initiated the Japanese in religious music and dance based on Indian mythological themes thereby introducing several aspects of Indian Brāhmaṇical culture. Thus along with Buddhism, several aspects of Hindu culture also entered Japan. The Buddhist temples in Japan, besides having the idols of Buddha and Bodhisattava, also have many Hindu gods and goddesses, such as Brahmā (*Bon-ten*), Indra (*Taishaku-ten*), Varuṇa (*Suiten*), Ganeśa (*Shōten*), Kubera (*Bishamon*), Śiva (*Daikoku*), Catur-lokapāla (*Shi-tennō*), Sarasvati (*Benzai-ten*), and Śrī Lakṣmi (*Kichijō-ten*).

However, despite Japanese acquaintance with various aspects of Indian culture, their basic interest was from the very beginning conditioned by their curiosity to understand Buddhism and not to know India or investigate things Indian. As pointed out by Tokunaga Muneo of Kyoto University: "India attracted our attention chiefly as the birth place of Buddhism, particularly as the motherland of Mahāyāna Buddhism and the Indian philosophical schools closely related to it rather than to the Indian culture and civilization *per se*."[9] This lack of interest was partly due to the geographical barriers which made India an inaccessibly remote country, and partly because of language handicaps. Since Japan did not have a writing tradition as late as 8th century AD, it was difficult for the Japanese to understand any written text, be it in Sanskrit or in Chinese. Until then, the Japanese had to depend on Korean or Chinese interpreters. Moreover, whatever information or knowledge the Japanese had gathered about India and Buddhism came by way of China and Korea, relayed through Chinese interpretations and translations. And, since China's world-view was deeply coloured by the assumption of Chinese superiority, there was a natural tendency among the Chinese to look down upon all other countries as 'barbarians.' In this Sino-centric world, Japan was the 'eastern barbarian' and the Chinese interest in India was restricted primarily to the study of Buddhist *sūtra*.

By the 13th century, although Buddhism had disappeared from the country of its birth, it gained unprecedented popularity in Japan. The 14th century saw the blossoming of

Zen Buddhism, which because of its simplicity and close touch with reality and pragmatism, not only worked as a religious guide but also influenced the general life and culture of the Japanese people. This was the 'Golden Age' of Buddhism in Japan. However, after maintaining its predominant sway for almost 1000 years, Buddhism suffered a set back when the Tokugawa warrior regime came to power in early 17th century. The Tokugawa rule was preceded by a century of warfare. Determined to provide peace and stability to the country, the Tokugawa looked for a political philosophy which would consolidate their hold and ensure harmonious relationship among the people. The pragmatic warrior class interpreted monasticism and deserting one's parents, wife and children as 'escape' from worldly duties, hence unethical and inhumane.[10] The Confucians interpreted Buddha's teachings not only negatively but found its stress on asceticism and detachment from worldly life irrelevant to the prevailing social and political needs. So they turned to *Shushigaku* or the philosophy of Chu Hsi (1130-1200), a follower of Confucius. The Chu Hsi's brand of Confucianism with its stress on the precise moral evaluation of political acts, human behaviour and relationships answered the needs of the Tokugawa rulers who not only propagated it as a state ideology but also encouraged its study. Although Buddhism was not wiped out because every Japanese was required to register at a Buddhist temple on account of the *'terauke'* (temple registration) law, its popularity as a religious sect and spiritual philosophy had waned. Thus, so long Buddhism occupied the centre-stage of Japan's spiritual and cultural thought, India was cherished and venerated from afar as *Tenjiku* or the Heavenly Kingdom, but after the rise of Confucianism, both Buddhism and the country of its birth were pushed in the rear.

Since Buddhism and Confucianism had played such a deep and intrinsic role in Japan's cultural development, it was not possible for Japan to remain unaffected by the developments taking place in India and China, both of which had become victims of alien rule. For the warrior rulers of Japan, preservation of one's country's honour and independent polity or *kokutai* was the supreme-most duty (*taigi*). The ineptitude of the people of China and India to defend their country against foreign incursions did not go down well with the Japanese, particularly the scholars of *Kokugaku* (National Learning). The *Kokugaku* movement had developed in late-17th century in a setting of conscious opposition to the China-centred scholarship. Although it began as a movement for affirming the superiority of Japan and encouraging antiquarian literary study, it gradually became a medium for carrying powerful political message as well. A towering figure of *Kokugaku* movement, Motōri Norinaga (1730-1801) labeled India as "an old country" and China as "a middle-aged country". He urged his countrymen to shun both Buddhism and Confucianism, because in his opinion these external philosophies had polluted Japan's pristine spirit and turned the Japanese minds away from Japan's rich heritage and Shintoism.[11]

This kind of negative appraisal took the form of open attack in the mid-19th century when India became a full-fledged colony of Great Britain and China was reduced to a semi-colonial status, completely at the mercy of European powers. The thought that Japan might succumb to a similar fate as that of India and China generated a paranoid vision of the world among the Japanese. Fukuzawa Yukichi (1835-1901), a leading intellectual of 19th century, saw the countries of Asia as 'mirrors' that could reflect the situation of Japan. What perturbed him was that even the countries with long histories such as Turkey, India, and China were not spared. Excoriating their weaknesses, he said that Turkey—a great country of warrior "is an independent country only in name."[12] Alluding to India, he wrote in 1875, "The great spiritual land of India has become England's 'kitchen' and the descendants of Brahmā Prajāpati have become the slaves of the British,[13] whose sole business was to grow opium and sell it in China with great profits.[14] He foreboded a similar fate for China. From that time onwards, India and China, the erstwhile *Tenjiku* and *Shintan,* came to be perceived as "negative examples" or the "carts that had overturned."

Nevertheless, these overturned carts had left their tracks for all to see. The Japanese, known for their pragmatism, lost no time to take lessons from India's and China's disasters and resolved not to repeat those experiences in Japan. After Japan's forcible opening in 1854, the Japanese interest in the developments taking place in India increased. As India was already a colony of Great Britain, thc Japanese took India as a case study to understand the nature of British imperialism. The study of India gave a sense of urgency to the Japanese to plan for unification and consolidation of their nation. Thus, despite being ostracized as negative examples, India and China served as media of knowing not just the power of the West but also the prevailing international trends of the 'struggle for existence' and 'survival of the fittest'. To survive in this amoral and harsh world, the Japanese deemed it necessary to make their country rich and strong like the West.

Once the 'West' rose in the scale of values, 'Asia' inevitably fell. Japan's ability to safeguard its independence and resist the Western threat instilled a sense of superiority over other Asian countries. Thereafter, Asia came to be scorned not only by the Westerners but by the Asians themselves. This was most evident among the Europe-returned Japanese and the proponents of Westernization who perceived Asia as a primitive (*yaban*) continent. During their trips to Europe, the modernized Japanese felt greatly irked when the Westerners referred to Japan as "Asian."[15] In a setting, in which the Western world loomed so large, the Japanese began looking at Asia through Western intellectual glasses and found it as a backward continent. In a handbook of world geography written in 1869 for the children, Fukuzawa Yukichi clubbed India, China, and Korea together with Annam (present Vietnam), Burma, and Tibet, and described all of them as backward, illiterate, spiritless, and despised by the West. Not just that, he warned his countrymen that if Japan continued to associate with the backward Asian countries, traditions and values, the Westerners would dump Japan in the same category as rest of Asia and would remain apathetic to Japan's goal of attaining parity with the civilized nations of the West. To wean the Japanese from their cultural and emotional dependence on Asia, Fukuzawa advocated "*Datsu-A nyū*-Ō" (Leave Asia, enter Europe). Since geographically it was not possible to separate Japan from Asia, he wanted the Japanese to shed their Asian-ness, join the West and do what the Westerners were doing in Asia.

There were, however, some Japanese such as Arao Sei (1858-1896) and Sugita Teiichi (1851-1928), who expressed their solidarity with Asia and in 1880 formed a Society for Asian Revival (*Kō-A Kai*). Wary of seeing Japan drifting along Western ways, they argued that even though Japan had modernized itself on the model of the West, it should remain an Asian power, as Asia was where Japan lay geographically and historically. The society even envisaged a federation consisting of Annam, Burma, India, Korea, and Siam—the Asian countries either subjugated or threatened by Britain, France, and Russia. The news about Indian people forming a national organization (the Indian National Congress) and launching struggle against the British lent support to their pro-Asian activities. Hailing the news, a fortnightly magazine *Nihonjin* , started in 1888 by Miyake Setsurei (1860-1945) and Shiga Shigetaga (1863-1927), carried an article visualizing the possibility of India becoming "a new big independent country of Asia." The article rates the Indian people's struggle for freedom very highly and draws a sharp contrast with the earlier effort of 1857, referred to as an 'uprising' caused by religious fanaticism.[16] Miyake and Shiga not only disapproved their government's policy of appeasing the West but also the adulation of Western culture by the Japanese. The Japanese, Miyake stated, must promote the study of Asia as it would benefit not only Japan but the whole world. To wean the Japanese from their preference for Western over Asian values, Miyake wrote a treatise in 1891, *Shin-zen-bi Nihonjin,* in which he argued that the Japanese must preserve their distinctive sense of aesthetics, which he defined as *shin-zen-bi* (truth, goodness, and beauty). Miyake's concept of *shin-zen-bi* has striking similarity with India's Vedānta philosophy which characterizes the human spirit as '*satyam, śivam, sundaram,*' but it is not known if Miyake was aware of it.

The renewed interest in India resulted in the commencement of courses, which though Buddhism-oriented, led to the establishment of departments of Sanskrit, Buddhism, and Indian Philosophy in the Japanese Universities. In 1885, two Buddhist scholars, namcly Nanjo Bunyu (1849-1927) and Takakusu Junjiro (1886-1945),[17] who had studied under F. Max Muller at the University of Oxford, started Indian studies at the Imperial University of Tokyo. Since Buddhism as a religious sect had disappeared from the Indian soil after the advent of the Muslims, the Japanese interest in Indian culture was directed to the study of ancient India. But in the absence of any direct links with Indian scholars and academic institutions, the Japanese had not only to rely on Western scholarship; but also study in European academic centers under the guidance of European scholars.

Direct contact between the people of India and Japan began only with the arrival of an art historian Okakura Tenshin (1862-1913) in Bengal in 1901. A vociferous spokesman for Japanese art, he saw his mission, as interpreting not only Japan, but the whole Asia, to the West. He therefore played a key role in creating an awareness of Asian unity. The crowing phrase "Asia is one" with which he wrote his book, *Ideals of the East* (1903), speaks for his deep regard for Asian ideals. The book was written in English with the specific object of enlightening the British intellectuals about Asia's rich cultural heritage. Although Okakura had come with the purpose of surveying Indian art and visiting places of Buddhist interest (Bodhgaya, Benares, Sarnath, Ajanta, Ellora, and the Himalayan foothills), he used his year-long stay (November 1901-October 1902) to interact with many artists, intellectual and spiritual leaders. In Calcutta, where he spent maximum time, Okakura formed close association with Rabindranath Tagore (1861-1941) and his family, Swami Vivekananda (1863-1902) and his disciple Sister Nivedita (1867-1911). Okakura and Tagore are said to have shared an understanding of the hearts and a spiritual connection. Together, they used to contemplate the future of the Asian people. Cherishing discussions with Okakura, Tagore later recalled that he came to know about Japan and Asia only from Okakura.

The Indian political scenario was in turmoil at the time of Okakura's visit. A wave of despair and anger had engulfed the Indian people after their appeals for a representative government were turned down by the colonial masters. To express solidarity with the Indian cause, Okakura wrote a book, *The Awakening of Japan* (1904), in which he made a fervent appeal to the Indian youth to unite and work for the revival of Asia in the strength of its past religious and cultural unity derived from Indian influences, which had reached as far as China and Japan. Okakura felt anguished to notice a sense of despondency among the Indians, but he bore no contempt. Rather, he empathized with them and defended them by saying that Indian culture was imbued with traditional pacifism, which left them unprepared to deal with the aggressive nature of foreign rule.[18] The first hand observation and an objective understanding of the Indian situation alleviated some of the earlier negativism in Japanese thinking on India.

The formation of Japan-India Association in 1902 was an important step towards promoting interaction between the people of the two countries. A prominent statesman Ōkuma Shigenobu (1838-1922), who became its President in 1906 and served until his death in 1922, made it an important forum for promoting Japan-India cultural and economic links. In 1907, Ōkuma set up a study circle (*Indo gakkai*) on the campus of Waseda University to promote Indian studies and stimulate interest in Indian affairs. Japan at that time was bound to Great Britain with a treaty signed in 1902, renewed in 1907, and again in 1911. Despite constraints of the Anglo-Japanese alliance, Ōkuma openly sympathized with the Indian cause and in several of his speeches urged the British to grant self-government to India. A shrewd politician, he also exhorted the Indians that if they wanted self-government, they must learn lessons from Japan and "strive and improve themselves." If the Indians reform themselves, Great Britain would surely see the fact and grant self-government to the Indians, like Canada, Australia, and other nations.[19]

The renewal of Anglo-Japanese Alliance in 1907 had added coverage for India, thus making Japan a watchman of British interests in India and East Asia. This infuriated Ōkawa Shūmel (1886-1923), a graduate of Indian philosophy from the Tokyo University's Department of Philosophy. After studying India's classical age, Ōkawa's inquisitive mind turned to contemporary India. The idealized image of India was shattered in 1913 when he read Henry Cotton's *New India.*[20] In 1916, Ōkawa wrote several articles exposing the exploitative nature of British rule and denounced the presence of Great Britain as a source of misery in Asia. He remonstrated against the continuance of the Anglo-Japanese alliance, which he saw as a deterrent for the Japanese in fostering better understanding with the Indians. Therefore, he pleaded with his government to cultivate friendly relations with the Indians and help them in their struggle for freedom.[21] Most Japanese, including Miyake Setsurei and Ōkawa Shumei, wanted to help India out of respect for India being a land of Buddha and its long cultural tradition. Their interest in India was however limited to the withdrawal of Western colonialism.

Thus by the turn of the 19th century, the Japanese had discovered various facets of India, the mystique land of Buddha which they had been worshipping from afar. The process of discovery was by no means complete, yet efforts had been initiated to know India, and understand its past and present.

Indian Discovery of Japan

The Indians, on the other hand, remained completely oblivious of the existence of Japanese islands as late as 19th century. Several Indian monks had succeeded in making their way into Japan, but none of them returned or left any records of their impressions of Japan. In absence of any kind of feed-back from these Indians visiting Japan, the Japanese awareness of India remained a one-sided affair. There are historical evidences suggesting journeys undertaken by several Japanese devotees of Buddhism to India, but they all ended up either in China or in obscurity. China, on the other hand, was very well known to India and one can find references of direct contacts in several ancient Indian texts. The Indian epics *Mahābhārata*[22] (4th century BC) and the *Rāmāyaṇa* (3rd century BC) refer to China as *Cina,*[23] and Kauṭilya's *Arthasāstra* (3rd century BC) points to a flourishing trade between the Maurya Empire and the land of *Cina* for *Cinapatta* (Chinese silk).[24] Later, as Buddhism spread to China around 1st century AD, contacts between India and China increased.[25] Between 4th and 5th century, several Indian monks traveled to China and Korea, for instance Kumārajīva (343-413) and Buddhabhadra (359-429) to China, and Malānanda to Korea in 384 AD. The historical records indicate the presence of Indians in many Southeast Asian countries as early as 1st century, but none seem to have crossed over to Japanese shores. As a result, there is absolutely nothing to throw light on the Indian awareness of Japanese islands, and this ignorance lasted for several centuries until the advent of Europeans into Indian subcontinent.

Despite its colonial nature, there is no denying the fact that British rule played a crucial role in opening up the floodgates for knowledge to come into India. The year 1780 saw the emergence of Asia's first weekly newspaper, James Hicky's *Bengal Gazette,* published in Calcutta, and by the early 19th century, many vernacular newspapers had started in different parts of the country. So, by the second half of the 19th century, India's urban elites were well aware of what was happening in other parts of Asia, including Japan. The leading British newspapers like *The Times* and *The Daily Mail* also carried descriptions of Japan. Japan's swift modernization and its ability to withstand the Western menace exerted a great impact on the minds of educated Indians who were trying to organize their political struggle against the British. Direct observations made by Indian sojourners voyaging via Japan constituted another source of information. At a time when most of Asia had come under colonial rule, Japan had acquired a reputation for having successfully preserved its independence and embarked on a course towards becoming an economic and military power.

After the founding of the Indian National Congress in 1885, as the Indian struggle picked speed, the patriotic leaders began seeking ways and means to throw off the yoke of British imperialism. Enthused by Japan's remarkable progress, several Indians from divergent background visited Japan to know the secrets of its success. Among these early visitors were, P.C. Moozomdar and Swami Vivekananda, both of whom were closely associated with the new religious and spiritual movements in Bengal. While nothing is known about Moozomdar's views, Vivekananda left records of his impressions in his many letters and speeches. In 1893, Vivekananda made a brief stop over in Japan on way to the Chicago Congress of World Religions. He was profoundly impressed by the sense of dignity and honour, cleanliness, etiquettes and manners, and the industrious nature of Japanese people. A man filled with dynamic energy and a fiery passion to push India forward, Vivekananda urged the Indian youth to look to Japan for India's development and progress. In a letter to one of his disciples written in 1901, Vivekananda expressed the hope that someday it would be possible to establish a "connection between India and Japan."[26]

It was not late when Vivekananda's dream of establishing connection between India and Japan was realized. A person who voyaged along with Vivekananda to Japan was Jamshetji Nusserwanji Tata (1839-1904), the head of the Tata business group. J.N. Tata was on way to Japan to meet Shibusawa Eiichi (1848-1931), a prominent Japanese shipping magnate of Nippon Yusen Kaisha (NYK), to explore the feasibility of establishing direct trade links with Japan. India's burgeoning textile and spinning industries had generated a lot of interest among the Japanese businessmen.[27] In 1888, Sano Tsuneki had come to India from Osaka with a team of engineers to know the technology of spinning. In 1892, 50 percent of raw cotton used by Japanese mills came from India but for transportation they had to depend on European vessels. Despite tough competition from European firms, which monopolized trade and commerce in this route, both Tata and Shibusawa succeeded in starting shipping services in their own ships to transport cotton goods. The Japanese government encouraged this Indo-Japanese venture by providing financial subsidies. The commencement of direct shipping facilities not only stimulated bilateral trade with branches in Kobe and Yokohama, it also led to the establishment of Japanese Consulate in Bombay in 1894 and in Calcutta in 1907.[28] Even though Tata later withdrew from this joint venture with Japan, the NYK continued its shipping services which besides raw cotton, also transported several other commodities, like pig iron, teak, jute, gunny bags, fertilizers from India; glassware, matches, umbrella sticks and handles etc. from Japan. The base cargo carried from Bombay was raw cotton, and that from Calcutta was pig iron. Hence these routes were known for many years as the "cotton route" and the "iron route."[29] Encouraged by the trading prospects, many of Japan's leading trading houses (*zaibatsu*), such as Mitsui and Nichimen, forged links with Indian partners and opened offices in Bombay and Calcutta.

These early trading links not only facilitated interaction with the Japanese entrepreneurs, they also gave Indians an opportunity to know the country's developmental process. Social reforms, spread of mass education, and promotion of industries were some of the areas in Japan's modernization which had the greatest impact on Indian thinking. An engineer-statesman Mokshagundam Visvesvaraya (1861-1962) visited Japan in 1898 and was impressed by the Japanese people's receptivity to new ideas and the zeal for self-improvement. Japan had made progress not only in industrial advancement but also in compulsory and girl's education. What struck him most was the emphasis on vocational education that geared to practical needs of all the people at all levels. The guideline for education in Japan, Visvesvaraya noted, was that henceforth "there shall be no community with an illiterate family, nor a family with an illiterate person," and praised the government for its efforts in promoting these reforms. He contrasted Japan's case with India where the educational facilities were restricted to only a small section of population. The purpose of the British was primarily to train loyal servants of the empire and only secondarily to enlighten the masses.[30] Visvesvaraya discovered in Japan a working model for India and was convinced that with education and planned economic development, India could also rise to Japan's level. After returning to India, he wrote his observations in *Reconstructing India:*

"Industries and trade do not grow of themselves, but have to be planned and systematically developed. In none of the advanced countries, not in England, not even in *laissez-faire* America, has the government kept aloof from the industrial activities of the people. On the contrary, the government has entered energetically into the service of commerce and industry. This is specially the case in Japan, whose industrial policy India needs to adopt as far as possible, if she desires rapid progress."[31]

The Japanese, Visvesvaraya noted, through their diplomatic missions not only try to keep in touch with the world's activities, but also strive to achieve whatever is good for their country.

The Indian people's interest in Japan enkindled further after its victory in the Russo-Japanese War of 1904-05. A small Asian country's ability to defeat a gigantic European power was hailed by all Asians as it shattered the myth of military invincibility of the West. The event had an electrifying impact on the Indians and other Asians, for it showed that any country, even outside the West, could rise to a higher position only if it did what had to be done. The Indian leaders, such as Dadabhai Naoroji, Gopal Krishna Gokhale, Lala Lajpat Rai, and Bal Gangadhar Tilak exhorted their countrymen to learn lessons from Japan, and imbibe the virtues of patriotism and spirit of sacrifice. Despite his faith in the superiority of spiritual over material force, Rabindranath Tagore found the occasion to praise Japan and celebrated Japan's victory with a bonfire in the evening amid cheers of '*banzai*'. Tagore composed three verses; one of them is as follows:[32]

"Wearing saffron robes, the Masters of religion (*dharma*)
Went to your county to teach.
Today we come to your door as disciples,
To learn the teachings of action (*karma*)."

Mohandas Karamchand Gandhi (1869-1948), who was at that time in South Africa, attributed Japan's victory to the spirit of self-respect and self-reliance. Emphasizing the need to cultivate the spirit of self-respect, he said, "Having remained in bondage for a long time like parrot, we cannot realize what honour and freedom are."[33] And to the 16-year old Jawaharlal Nehru (1889-1964), then studying at Dover, the event struck "like a thunderbolt." Recalling the impact forty years later, he wrote in his autobiography:

"Japanese victories stirred up my enthusiasm....I invested in a large number of books on Japan and tried to read some of them...Nationalistic ideas filled my mind. I mused of Indian freedom and Asiatic freedom from the thralldom of Europe...I dreamt...I would fight for India."[34]

The well-informed Indians saw in Japan a living example of a country "meeting the West with their own techniques." India too could reproduce that feat provided it was allowed to live in political freedom. Describing the mood of the people immediately after the war, D.S. Ramachandra Rao in his book *East and West* (1905) said, that the "marvelous victories of Japan" had awakened Indian national consciousness which a century of British rule had been unable to stir.[35] In the minds of educated people, words like "nationalism," patriotism," "discipline" and "self-help" became synonymous with Japan.

Inspired by Japan's daring feat, the Indian leaders intensified the demand for '*Swaraj,*'[36] and as the struggle entered the '*Swadeshi*' phase, attempts were made to displace British goods by augmenting indigenous production of goods imported into India from British factories. The Indian manufacturers saw Japan as a source from where the new equipment and machines could be obtained to increase the supply of home-made goods and displace the British goods. Funds were raised to send students to Japan to learn industrial arts and methods so that they could contribute to the production of simple goods like pencils, glass, watches, cardboard, cane-boxes, and textiles.[37] The popular mood was one of hope that Indian nationalism might eventually prevail over British imperialism if India were to follow the Japanese example and become self-reliant.

However, the enthusiasm to know more about Japan did not lead to deeper understanding of the country, because, as a British colony, India was not free to adopt the Japanese model. Politically as well as economically, the Japanese model threatened the British interests in India. The princely states, which constituted two-fifths of Indian territory, were relatively in a better position though even their policies were subject to British approval. The Nizam's State of Hyderabad sent a mission under Syed Ross Masood to study Japan's educational system. But, it was only in the princely State of Mysore in South India, which was not a British territory, that some steps were undertaken towards industrialization and the introduction of a modern education system on a free and compulsory basis.[38] This too was made possible mainly through the efforts of Visvesvaraya, who became the Diwan of Mysore State in 1912 and used his position to implement some of the ideas that had attracted him during his trips of Japan in 1898 and 1919.

Japan's participation in the First World War on behalf of Great Britain[39] created serious misgivings in the minds of some Indians who felt the need to initiate dialogue with other Asian countries. Although Asia was nothing more than a geographical description, some eminent minds both in India and Japan began searching for an Asian identity. Behind this effort was a growing consciousness that Asia was a conquered continent, Europe a conquering one. As Vivekananda said, "on the material place, Europe has mainly been the basis during modern times; but on the spiritual plane, Asia has been the basis throughout the history of the world." Such thinking about 'Asia' did not develop independently in India or Japan. In reaction to excessive adulation of Western civilization, several ideologues had initiated an intellectual movement towards discovering the 'Asian' ideal. These ideologues also formed relationships across the Asian region. Vivekandanda, for instance, visited Japan; Okakura spent a year in India. In formulating the Asian concept, Tagore said: 'it was from Okakura that we first came to know there was such a thing as an Asiatic mind.'[40]

To realize Okakura Tenshin's dream of Asian unity, Rabindranath Tagore visited Japan thrice in 1916, 1924, and 1929.[41] Tagore's *Visvabharati* University at Shantiniketan founded in 1901 was a popular haunt for the Japanese intellectuals, poets, artists, and monks visiting India. In 1913, Tagore had become the first Asian to win Nobel Prize thus contributing to India's international reputation from the world of literature. Hence, Tagore's visit aroused euphoria among the Japanese. Although Tagore's impressions on Japan can be inferred from his several lectures delivered in Japan, they were meant for specific audience. His travelogue *Japan Yatri* (Visit to Japan, 1919), on the other hand, was written for the Indian audience, and contains his observations and critiques of things both Indian and Japanese. Tagore expresses his admiration not just for Japan's economic, industrial and scientific advances, but also its social and cultural traditions and the values, such as the love for simplicity, reverence for the past, respect for the departed, regard for the family system, recognition of social obligation, and the intimate relationship between man and nature. Japan seemed to be a perfect blend between East and West, and between tradition and modernity. The Indians, Tagore said, should adopt more suitable things from Japan rather than from Europe.

But Tagore's was not the first travelogue on Japan. Muzurul Huq, a scholar from Bangladesh, has traced another travelogue *Bongomohilar Japan Jatra* (A Bengali Lady's Visit to Japan, 1912).[42] This travelogue, however, failed to catch the attention of the readers, probably because the author was an obscure and ordinary Bengali housewife, Hariprabha Takeda, from Dhaka in East Bengal. Although there is no comparison between Tagore's and Hariprabha's travelogues, either in the contents or the literary value, the latter does deserve mention for four reasons. First, it is an important historical document shedding light on direct contacts between the common people of India and Japan. Second, Hariprabha was not only the first commoner to visit Japan, her 64-pages book on Japan is probably the first written by an Indian, and probably the first by a non-Japanese Asian lady. Third, Hariprabha's aim was to meet her husband's family, not to understand the country or prove her writing skill. And yet, she felt inspired enough to record her observations which in itself deserves recognition. Fourth, despite many flaws in language and style, Hariprabha's account is lively and gives the reader a vivid description about everyday life of the Japanese people,[43] which one would not expect from the pen of a serious writer of Tagore's stature.

Not much is known about Hariprabha except that in 1906 she married a Japanese businessman, Uemon Takeda, who owned a soap factory in Dhaka. In November 1912, Hariprabha along with her husband sailed on a four-months' trip to Japan to meet her in-laws living in Niwa, Aichi prefecture. She found Japan in a state of gloom on account of the death of Emperor Meiji, during whose glorious reign Japan had become a modern world power. She visited the museum in Ueno in Tokyo where she saw the late-emperor's coffin, and then she went to the burial site at Momoyama near Kyoto, where a shrine was under construction. During her four-month stay in Japan, Hariprabha encountered many interesting experiences. Few Japanese outside the city had seen an Indian. Naturally, the sight of a *saree*-clad Indian with *sindoor,* the vermilion dot on her forehead aroused curiosity and mused the children who rushed to have a look at the *Indojin* until her father-in-law chased them away. The travelogue contains account of her impressions of the food, behaviour, and dress of the Japanese people, including a description of the *kimono.* She tried Japanese food for two weeks but then she started cooking Indian food for herself. Some of her observations show that she was contrasting Japan with her own country. She did not find Tokyo a gorgeous capital city. She was perhaps comparing it with the cosmopolitan Calcutta.

But she liked the Japanese policemen in the *kōban* (Police beat box) and found them very friendly and helpful, and not the object of fear–like the British police force.[44]

Tagore's accounts of Japanese society and everyday life are very analytical, not meant for general readers. For instance, State Shinto, he writes, lacks spiritual content, but recognizes the emperor and his ancestors as gods; therefore the authorities can use this to deepen the feeling of patriotism among citizens. The excessive kind of patriotism, he said, is destructive because it advances itself at the expense of another. Tagore also felt disturbed to note that, as in India, men adopted western dress when they went to the office, and left their Japanese clothes at home. This trend was making the world an uglier place to live in. So it were the women in their *kimonos* that caught his eye, and made him feel that they represented the true Japan. He admired Japan's "great Art" for its emphasis on aesthetics, simplicity and harmony. The Japanese people, he noted, talk less and do not waste time and energy in useless quarrels and found the Japanese character epitomized in the 17 syllable-*haiku*. A hint is enough to convey a message. The restrained expression of emotion in Japan forms a total contrast to the situation in India. He wrote in *Japan Yatri,* "If we could learn the art of living from Japan with an open mind, our homes and hearths would be cleaner, out behaviour more refined, graceful and restrained."[45] Tagore and Hariprabha's travelogues bear testimony to the fact that the Indians, while attempting to discover Japan, were also discovering themselves.

While Tagore expressed his unmitigated praise for the advances made by Japan in the field of science and technology, he was openly critical of the ferocity with which modernity was encroaching upon the traditional, and baneful effects of Western civilization were coming to the fore. A messenger of peace, Tagore felt sad at the sight of numerous war memorials raised at various places commemorating Japan's victories over China (1895) and Russia (1905). He saw in these displays an imitation of ugly aspects of Western civilization.[46] During his last visit in 1929, Tagore grew totally disillusioned with Japan. A meeting with the Korean students in Japan and the accounts of ill treatment caused Tagore many restless hours. Tagore wanted to visit Korea but could not do so due to political reasons. To boost their morale, Tagore wrote a short poem:

"In the golden age of Asia
Korea was one of its lamp bearers,
And that lamp is waiting to be lighted once again
For the illumination in the East."

The poem "*Light of the East*" assumed instant popularity and became a source of inspiration for the Koreans. A journalist Joo Yo-han immediately translated it into Korean and published in *Dong*-A daily for wider dissemination.[47] Later, after Korea's independence, the poem found a place in middle school textbooks.

With every visit, Tagore's perceptions of Japan underwent radical changes; and with every change he realized that there was a yawning gap between the real Japan and his mental picture. While Tagore admired the mobility and adaptability of Japanese minds which enabled them to learn from European civilization, he felt disturbed to note that what Japan had learnt was not the art of civilization, which heals and unites; but the science that inflicts wounds. He saw Japanese militarism as illustrating the way nationalism could mislead even a nation of great achievements and promise. The growing nationalism and the belligerent chauvinism made him uneasy. He felt sorry to see Japan going along imperialist lines of the West. To him, the dream of Asian unity now seemed remote.

Tagore did not define Asian unity in political and geographical terms, hence most Japanese failed to understand him. Tagore was aware of the cultural diversities that existed in Asia, but he formulated his conception of Asianism on the basis of certain social and spiritual values which bound humanity together. These values, Tagore thought, would lay the basis for a regenerated Asia. To the pragmatic Japanese minds, culture alone was an insufficient base to bring together the countries of Asia to face European challenge; and interpreted Asianism as 'liberation of Asia from the West' and its unification under Japanese hegemony. The nationalists in

Japan found Tagore's definition of Asianism vague and his messages lacking any concrete plan for action. Actually Tagore was misunderstood not only by the Japanese, but also by some Indians, such as Rash Behari Bose and Subhash Chandra Bose, who attracted by Japan's Asian identity and its advocacy of 'Asia for Asians' were seeking Japanese assistance to fight Great Britain and liberate India. In 1937, during Japan's war with China, Rash Behari sent a cable to Tagore seeking his approval for his efforts. Tagore promptly wrote back:

"Your cable has caused me many restless hours, for it hurts me very much to have to ignore your appeal..... I know, in making this appeal, you counted on my great regard for the Japanese. For, I did once admire and look up to Japan and did once fondly hope that in Japan Asia had at last discovered its challenge to the West, that Japan's new strength would be consecrated in safeguarding the culture of the east against alien interests. But Japan has not taken long to betray that rising hope and repudiate all that seemed significant in her wonderful, and to us symbolic, awakening, and has now become itself a worse menace to the defenceless peoples of the east."[48]

Thereafter, as Japan's war with China escalated into a full-scale war, Tagore gave up on Japan. In a letter written in 1938, Noguchi Yonejiro, a poet and an ardent admirer of Tagore, pleaded with him to change his opinion of Japan. Noguchi tried to explain Japan's position and said that Japan is fighting to create a "new world order in Asia" and the goal was still "Asia for the Asians." Tagore remained steadfast to his ideals and wrote back with bitterness that the Japan he had come to admire was not nationalistic, scheming, and aggressive, but a different Japan whose culture embodied totally opposite qualities: harmony, forbearance and benevolence. Expressing his remorse and utter sorrow, Tagore prophesized:

"I know that one day the disillusionment of your people will be complete and through laborious centuries they will have to clear the debris of their civilization wrought to ruin by their own warlords run amok. They will realize that the aggressive war on China is insignificant as compared to the destruction of the inner spirit of chivalry of Japan."[49]

Although Tagore did not live to see it, Japan did realize and at a heavy cost. Tagore admired Japan and saw its strength in her aesthetic sensibilities and not in her armies and industrial power. The Japanese novelist Kawabata Yasunari (1899-1972), the second Asian to win Nobel Prize for literature, was deeply inspired by Tagore's ideas. In his *Bi no sonzai hakken* (The existence and discovery of beauty) written in 1969, Kawabata credited Tagore for discovering Japan and helping the Japanese to know themselves. Quoting from Tagore, Kawabata remarked that "a foreigner found it easier to know what it is in Japan which is truly valuable for all mankind."[50]

Postwar period: Forming a relationship

The popular Indian perceptions of postwar-Japan were deeply influenced by the sufferings of the Japanese people caused by the atomic holocaust of Hiroshima and Nagasaki, first of its kind in human history. Since India had not experienced any kind of aggression at the hands of the Japanese troops, the Indian viewed Japan's situation with sympathy and open mind. The Indians felt a strong sense of kinship and expressed solidarity not only with Japan but all other Asian countries who were still languishing under colonial rule or devastated by the war. This was evident in the sole dissenting voice given by the Indian judge at the Tokyo trials, and Indian government's decision to sign a bilateral treaty with Japan and accord Japan the status of a sovereign state.

It does not however mean that Japan had been absolved from all its wartime deeds. There were still some in India, and many in Asia, who viewed Japan as an aggressor and enemy of Asia. In the presence of such complex attitudes, a popular world leader Jawaharlal Nehru's visit to Japan in October 1957 played a very crucial role in softening world stand. Besides, boosting the morale of the Japanese people, the visit also facilitated Japan's rehabilitation in the international community. The visit had enkindled profuse interest and admiration for India, which became evident by the publication of translation of Nehru's highly acclaimed work *Discovery of India* in Japanese language. The gift of a baby elephant *Indira* to the children of Japan had stirred the Japanese because all their big animals at Tokyo's Ueno zoo had either perished or killed during aerial bombings. *Indira* traveled all over Japan and was greeted with cheer wherever it went. All these gestures had a very positive influence in the shaping of the thinking of people in the two countries.[51] An opinion poll, conducted in Japan in mid-1950s, showed India as the "most liked and respected country."

Although by mid-twentieth century, the people of the two countries had become aware of each other, there still existed on both sides considerable ignorance about the history, language and traditions. In 1947, speaking before the delegates of Asian Relations Conference, Jawaharlal Nehru attributed European domination of Asia to the isolation of Asian countries from one another. In the ancient period, he said, India had contacts and intercourse with the neighbouring countries but they were all disrupted after India fell prey to foreign invasions.

"While the old land routes almost ceased to function, our chief window to the outer world looked out on the sea routes, while led to England. A similar process affected the other Asian countries, who for cultural and economic reasons looked to Europe and not to their own friends and neighbours from whom they had derived so much in the past."[52]

Expressing deep concern for the lack of knowledge about each other, Nehru had proposed the establishment of academies or schools for Asian studies. Nehru's ideas found expression in the Indian School of International Studies (ISIS) set up in 1955 through the pioneering efforts of Hridayanath Kunzru, K.M. Panikkar and Arjun Appadorai.[53] Following Cultural Agreement in 1956 between India and Japan, several academic fellowships and cultural exchange programmes came up offering opportunities to the people interested in knowing each other. A beginning was thus made for Japanese studies in India through the study of Japanese language and interaction with Japanese scholars and universities as well as field studies in Japan. The first generation of: Indian researchers on Japan included P.A. Narasimha Murthy (Economics), S. Seshiah (Economics), R. Prasad (Japanese literature), R.P. Dua (History) and A. Mallappa (International relations); and the Japanese researchers on India included Ara Matsuo (History), Nakane Chie (Anthropology), and Takasaki Jikido (Buddhist studies). These trained area specialists carried on the mission by setting up full-fledged study centres in their home countries.

This surge of mutual interest however proved to be short-lived, partly due to the impact of Cold War politics on the region, and partly because of the increasing tensions between India and China. The sudden death of Nehru was also an important factor. It was only through the efforts of Nakamura Hajime and Bhikshu Chaman Lal and the publications of their writings that interest was re-enkindled giving a fresh lease of life to the forgotten heritage shared by the two countries. The late 1960s saw an increase not only in Japanese studies of India and Indian studies of Japan, but also in the number of departments. All these developments have facilitated direct interaction between the scholars, thereby bringing an end to the stage when they had to rely upon the findings and materials of Western scholars to know each other. The last three decades have seen a large number of people, in business, academia, and tourism, who have overcome the language handicaps and are striving to promote mutual understanding. Although our knowledge of each other is still inadequate in many ways, there is a hope for closer understanding because the process of discovery has begun, and on a solid footing.

References

1 Charles Elliot, *Japanese Buddhism* (London: Macmillan, 1969), p. 211.

2 The philosophy of Chinese sage-philosophers came to be known as *'seidō',* meaning the 'Way of Sage'. Confucianism was seen more as a study of classics, hence it was known as *'Jūgaku'.*

3 Kibi-no-Makibi learnt Sanskrit and Devnagari from Bodhisena, a Brāhmaṇa monk who said to have come to Japan by way of China and Pai-chi in 736 AD. Kōbō Daishi studied Sanskrit in China between 804 and 806 AD from Prajña and Muniśrī, both Kashmiri *ācārya,* who were in China since early 9th century AD.

4 Takaoka Shinnō left Japan in 861, after staying for 6 months in China left for India but died in the mountains of Laos in 865.

5 Upendra Thakur, *India and Japan: A study of interaction during 5th-14th centuries AD* (New Delhi: Abhinav Publications, 1992), p. 46. The first Indian to enter Korea was Malānanda who came via Eastern Tsin in 384 AD and started the Pai-chi sect of Buddhism.

6 Gyōki is also credited for helping the Emperor Shomu for the construction of the colossal image of Buddha, and later its installation in the middle of the capital Nara, as an object of national worship. It is believed that Gyōki traveled to the shrine of the Sun Goddess at Ise carrying a holy Buddhist relic as an offering. He spent 7 days in praying, after which the Sun Goddess appeared to the emperor as a dream and conveying that the Sun and the Buddha were the same. This was in 742, and the following year an edict was issued announcing the commencement of the construction of Buddha's image. Gyōki however did not live to witness the final dedication (*kigen*) ceremony (in which eyes of an image are touched to symbolize bringing it to life) and died in 749. George B. Sansom, *Japan: A short cultural history* (Stanford: Stanford University Press, 1998), pp. 133-34.

7 S. Dutt, *Buddhism in East Asia* (New Delhi, 1966), p. 196; Upendra Thakur, p. 46.

8 Charles Elliot, *Japanese Buddhism,* p. 225.

9 Muneo Tokunaga, "Japanese Studies of Indian Philosophy and Religion" in Chie Nakane and Masao Naito, eds., *Towards Understanding Each Other: Fifty Years' History of India-Japan Mutual Studies* (Tokyo: Kyodo Printing Co. Ltd., 2000), p. 26.

10 Yamazaki Toshio, "Zen kindai Nihon no Indo kan" in Yamazaki Toshio and Takahashi Mitsuru, eds. *Nihon to Indo kōryū no rekishi* (Tokyo: Sanseido, 1993), p. 22.

11 Motoori Norinaga, *Naobi no mitama* in Yoshikawa Kojirō, ed., *Nihon no shisō,* vol. 15, (Tokyo: 1969), pp. 285-296.

12 Fukuzawa Yukichi, *An Encouragement of Learning,* tr. David A. Dilworth and Umeyo Hirano (Tokyo: Sophia University Press, 1969), p. 79.

13 Fukuzawa Yukichi, *An Outline of a Theory of Civilization,* tr. David A. Dilworth and G. Cameron Hurst (Tokyo: Sophia University Press, 1973), p. 32.

14 Fukuzawa Yukichi, *An Encouragement of Learning,* p. 79.

15 During his trips to Europe, Itagaki Taisuke (1837-1919), a leader of the Liberal Party, felt greatly irked when the Westerners referred

to Japan as 'Asian' and clubbed it along with China and Korea. Sushila Narsimhan, *Japanese Perceptions of China in the Nineteenth Century: Influence of Fukuzawa Yukichi* (New Delhi: Phoenix Pvt. Ltd., 1999), p. 119.

16 *Nihonjin,* vol. 2 (May 1889); Naito Masao, "Kindai Nihon no keisei to Ei-ryō Indo" in Yamazaki Toshio and Takahashi Mitsuru, eds. *Nihon to Indo kōryū no rekishi* (Tokyo: Sanseido, 1993), p. 40.

17 Takakusu Junjiro had also spent sometime in India.

18 Okakura Tenshin (Kakuzō), *The Ideals of the East* in *Collected English Writings of Okakura Tenshin,* vol. 1 (Tokyo: Heibonsha, 1984), p. 120.

19 K.V. Kesavan, "Indian Image of Japan," p. 20.

20 Nagasaki Nobuko, "Indo kokumingun no keisei" in Nagasaki Nobuko (ed.), *Minami Ajia no minzoku undo to Nihon* (Tokyo: Ajia Keizai kenkyujo, 1980), p. 5.

21 Foreign Department, Confidential B., External B., 1919, nos. 3-17; cited in T.R. Sareen, "India and Japan in Historical Perspective" in *India and Japan: Indian Intellectual Perspective,* ed., Rajaram Panda and Kazuo Ando (New Delhi: The Japan Foundation, 1998), p. 125.

22 *Sabhāparva* (The Court Chapter) in *Mahābhārata* (Baroda: Oriental Institute), 23.19, 47.19, 22-23, mentions that when Arjuna went to conquer Pragyajotish (Assam), Bhagdatta, the Assamese king fought with an army comprising of Chinese soldiers; Harprasad Ray, "The Southern Silk Route from China to India: An approach from India" in *China Report,* 31:2 (New Delhi: Sage Publications, 1995), p. 179 n9.

23 *The Kiṣkindhākānda* (Fourth Book of Vālmiki Rāmāyana) (Baroda: Oriental Institute, 1965), verse no. IV. 42.12; Harprasad Ray, "The Southern Silk Route," p. 179.

24 R.K. Mukherjee, *Indian Shipping* (London: Longmans, Green Co., 1912), pp. 100-15; Harprasad Ray, p. 184.

25 China sent a mission to India in 65 AD to bring some relics of Buddha and some copies of the Buddhist scriptures.

26 P.A. Narasimha Murthy, "Japan in the Indian Mirror: Changing Images of Japan in the Indian Mind" in Hiroichi Yamaguchi and Haruka Yanagisawa (eds.), *Tradition and Modernity: India and Japan Towards the Twenty-First Century* (New Delhi: Munshiram Manoharlal Pub., 1997), p. 70.

27 India's tea also evoked interest and in 1874, Tada Motokichi came to India from Shizuoka prefecture to study the production and technology of black tea.

28 K.V. Kesavan, "Indian Image of Japan: Its Historical Change" in Chie Nakane and Masao Naito, eds., *Towards Understanding Each Other,* p. 19.

29 P.A. Narasimha Murthy, *India and Japan: Dimensions of their Relations: Economic and Cultural* (New Delhi: Lancers Books, 1993), pp. 30-31.

30 *Ibid.*, pp. 24-25.

31 P.A. Narasimha Murthy, *India and Japan: Dimensions of their Relations; Historical and Political* (New Delhi: ABC Pub., 1986), pp. 24-25.

32 Stephen N. Hay, *Asian Ideas of East and West* (Cambridge, Mass.,: Harvard University Press, 1970), pp. 42-43; cited in P.A. Narasimha Murthy, *India and Japan* (1986), p. 20.

33 *Collected Works of Mahatma Gandhi,* vol. 5 (Ahmedabad: 1973), p. 43.

34 Jawaharlal Nehru, *An Autobiography* (London: The Bodley Head, 1945), p. 16.

35 P.A. Narasimha Murthy, *India and Japan* (1986), p. 21.

36 According to the British official opinion, particularly the Home Member R.H. Craddock, "it was Japan's victory that first started the idea of *Swaraj* in India." *Foreign Department Documents,* External B, Confidential B, 1919; nos. 3-17.

37 P.A. Narasimha Murthy, *India and Japan* (1986), pp. 22-23.

38 Savitri Vishwanathan, "Indian Approaches to Japanese Studies" in Harumi Befu and Josef Kreiner, eds. *Otherness of Japan: Historical and Cultural Influences on Japanese Studies in Ten Countries* (Netherlands: Deutsches Institut für Japan Studien, 1993), p. 284.

39 Under the clauses of the Anglo-Japanese Alliance, Japan was not obliged to intervene unless there was any threat from Germany to British interests in India or in the Far East.

40 Stephen N. Hay, *Asian Ideas of East and West;* cited in Anthony Milner, *'Asia' Consciousness and Asian Values* (Canberra: Faculty of Asian Studies, 1996); see www.anu.edu.au/asianstudies/ publications/html.

41 Tagore also traveled to China and many parts of Southeast Asia, establishing numerous relationships with leading thinkers in these societies. He found that ideas about the 'East' and 'Asia' met resistance in China, where such notions as the 'Middle Kingdom' and 'Southern Barbarians' influenced Chinese perceptions of, and disdain toward, other 'Asian' peoples.

42 The only surviving copy of *Bongomohilar Japan Jatra* (Dhaka, 1915), a 64-page travelogue, was retrieved recently from the India Office Library of the British Museum, and republished in 1999 as part of a series of books by women. For details, see Muzurul Huq, "The Bride from Bengal: Hariprabha Takeda in Early Taisho Japan" in *The Transactions of Asiatic Society of Japan,* Series 4, vol. 15 (2001); also, www.asjapan.org/lectures/2001/htm.

43 *Ibid.*

44 Unfortunately, nothing is known about what happened to Hariprabha and her husband after their return to India. Attempts to trace their whereabouts have been made difficult because the Brahma Samaj of Dhaka, a society of educated and forward-looking Hindus that Hariprabha and her parents belonged to, became non-existent after the partition of India in 1947 when a large numbers of Hindus moved to India. And, after Bangladesh Liberation War of 1971, the Samaj's library and office building were destroyed.

45 Sandip Tagore, *Peopled Azimuth: Reminiscence and Reflections of an Indian in Japan* (New Delhi: Inter-India Publications, 1987, p. 266.

46 P.A. Narasimha Murthy, *India and Japan* (1986), pp. 62-63.

47 Lee Jeong Ho, "Literary Contacts and Influence Between India and Korea: A Comparison between the Poetry of Rabindranath Tagore and Han Yong Woon," Paper presented in International Conference (March 27-28, 2003), Delhi University.

48 *The English Writings of Rabindranath Tagore,* ed., Sisir Kumar Das (New Delhi: Sahitya Akademi, 2002), vol. 3, pp. 823-24. The letter is dated 11 October, 1937.

49 *The English Writings of Rabindranath Tagore,* pp. 834-35. The letter is dated 27 October, 1938.

50 Kawabata Yasunari, "Bi no sonzai to hakken" in *Kawabata Yasunari Zenshu* (Collected Works of Kawabata Yasunari), vol. 15 (Tokyo: Shinchosha, 1973), p. 214.

[51] Hiroichi Yamaguchi, "Japanese Perceptions of India in Modern Times" in Hiroichi Yamaguchi and Haruka Yanagisawa (eds.), *Tradition and Modernity,* pp. 90-91.

[52] P.N. Haksar, ed., Nehru's Vision of Peace and Security in the Nuclear Age (New Delhi: Patriot Publishers, 1987); cited in Savitri Vishwanathan, "Indian Approaches to Japanese Studies," p. 285.

[53] In 1970, the school was merged with the School of International Studies (SIS), Jawaharlal Nehru University, New Delhi.

4

Bodhisena, the Brahman Bishop and Professor Hajime Nakamura

Saroj Kumar Chaudhuri

A large number of Indian monks went to China to spread the message of the dharma in ancient times. Only one Indian monk, however, made it to Japan in those early days. He is Bodhisena, better known by his title Baramon Sōjō, or Brahman Bishop. This paper will introduce Professor Hajime Nakamura's visit to the monk's grave, his epitaph, and other information preserved in Japanese records.

1. Prof. Hajime Nakamura's Visit to Bodhisena's Grave

Nakamura visited the grave of Bodhisena on a sunny winter day. He writes about his visit as follows. [1]

Bodhisena reached Dazaifu in Western Japan on the eighteenth day of the fifth month of the eighth year of the Tenpyō era (A.D. 736) along with Tajihi no Hironari, the Japanese ambassador to T'ang, and his Champa disciple Buttetsu. On his way to the capital Nara, on the eighth day of the eighth month of the same year, he met an eminent Japanese monk Gyōgi, who ushered him to the capital. He was appointed a bishop under an imperial edict. He acted as a priest in the Eye Opening Ceremony of the Great Buddha of Nara. He died on the twenty-fifth day of the second month of the fourth year of the Tenpyō Shōhō era (760).

The grave of Bodhisena is located within the precincts of the Reizanji Temple in Nara. Although the official name of the temple is Ryōzenji, it is popularly called Reizanji. The temple was given this name officially because contemporary people believed that the Indian monk had come from Gṛdhrakūṭa, which was known by the name Ryōjuzen in Japan. It was established for Bodhisena by the monk Gyōgi in the year 736 under an edict of the emperor Shōmu. Most structures of the present temple were built during the Kamakura period (1192-1333). The temple has a Buddha idol of the Hakuhō period (around 672).

There is a small stone marker with the letters 'Way to the Grave of Brahman Bishop' engraved on it at the entrance of a downhill path behind the three-story pagoda. The path leads to a structure, and a monk of the temple who accompanied Nakamura said that Bodhisena's grave was originally located by the side of this structure. The monk's impression was that the grave was shifted when the structure was constructed.

There is also an uphill path behind the three-story pagoda. This path leads to a flat piece of land containing graves of the temple parishioners. A little below these graves, there is a narrow path branching out to the right and ending in a forlorn grave. It is the grave of Bodhisena. The tombstone at present is about 90 cm high, with the top missing. There are no traces of any letters on the highly weathered tombstone. The appearance of the grave suggested that it is totally forgotten. When Nakamura asked the priests about any memento of Bodhisena in the temple, their reply was in negative.

2. Epitaph of Bodhisena

There is an epitaph of Bodhisena dated the twenty-first day of the fourth month of the fourth year of the Jingo Keiun era (773) written by his disciple Shūei. It is written in Chinese and preserved in a number of works. Nakamura has given a modern Japanese translation of the epitaph based on the version found in Dainippon Bukkyō Zensho. The title of the epitaph is *Minami Tennjiku Baramon Sōjō Hi narabini Jo*, which can be roughly translated as The Epitaph of the South Indian Brahman Bishop and Introductory Notes. The epitaph is pretty long with many allusions and eulogies, so only the information directly related to Bodhisena is given below. [2]

The name of the Bishop is Bodhisena, a Brāhmana of the Bhāradvāja gotra. His virtues were well-known in the sixteen countries of India. Ninety-five heretic sects revered his exalted appearance. It is difficult to narrate his activities in India, because India is far away, and materials related to him are lacking. He was very intelligent since his childhood, and was of very quiet disposition. We can respect his spiritual attainment, but cannot fathom it. His vast wisdom can inspire us, yet we cannot measure it. Following the great example of the Yuehchi monk Lokakṣema and the great achievements of the Parthian monk Ansekō, he reached the great country of T'ang by crossing the Himalayas and setting sail on the South Seas. He braved many dangers on the way. In T'ang, both monks and lay believers respected him highly because of his nice behaviour.

At that time, our emperor Shōmu had sent an embassy to T'ang. Seeing the reputation of Bodhisena, our ambassador Tajihi no Mabito Hironari and the scholarly student monk Rikyō requested him to accompany them to Japan. Bodhisena did not refuse as their request was very sincere. He sailed on the thirteenth day of the twelfth month of the eighteenth year of the Kaigen era (730) along with the Champa monk Buttetsu and the T'ang monk Dōsen. On the way there was a violent storm with waves reaching the sun and dark tempest obscuring the heavenly bodies. The boat was in great danger. Life and death were only a hair apart. As people on the boat were lamenting in despair, Bodhisena concentrated his mind and started meditating. He prayed to the Buddha wholeheartedly. Presently the storm subsided, and all on board praised him seeing the miracle. The party reached Dazaifu in Kyushu on the eighteenth day of the fifth month of the eighth year of the Tenpyō era (736).

Bodhisena reached Naniwa on the eighth day of the eighth month in the same year. The great monk Gyōgi was very happy to learn about the arrival of Bodhisena, and met him there. When he reached the capital Nara, the emperor lodged him in the Daianji Temple, and the ministers and nobles visited him to pay their respect. The monk Gyōgi visited him thrice in the capital along with many monks and lay believers.

Bodhisena was a strong adherent of the *Ke-gon-kyō* sūtra and always recited it. He was very well conversant with *mantras*, which his disciples are propagating even now. He was very modest in his disposition, and never showed happiness or anger in his face. He always hid the glow of his intelligence. So there was none who could fathom it. Any amount of reverential treatment failed to change his disposition. Again, no amount of pressure or strict laws could frighten him. He was appointed a bishop in the second year of the Tenpyō Shōhō era (750) under an imperial edict. With this, people renounced evil and adopted the righteous path. He passed away suddenly at night on the twenty-fifth day of the second month of the fourth year of the Tenpyō Hōji era (760). He was facing west with folded hands, as if he was meditating. There was no change in his facial expression. His mortal remains were consigned to fire on the second day of the third month of the same year. He was fifty-seven years of age at the time of his death.

At the time of his death, Bodhisena told his disciples as follows: 'I have seen pure Buddha-nature, and have instilled it within myself. Even then, I worshipped Amitābha Buddha and Kannon (Avalokiteśara). The dress and the things I will have with me at the time of my death should be sent to the Pure Land Paradise. In my lifetime, I made idols of Cintāmaṇicakra Bodhisattva in order to express my gratitude for the favours I received from my parents, people, kings and the three treasures. I thought of making and installing the idols of eight Bodhisattvas, but could not accomplish it because of my preoccupation with mundane affairs. I want you, my disciples, to fulfil my wish.' His disciples made the idols of eight Bodhisattvas to fulfil his last wish.

3. Bodhisena in Japanese Historical Records

Although a native of India, it seems that Bodhisena did not make any noteworthy impression on the contemporary Japanese. *Shokunihongi*, the second official history of Japan written in A.D. 797 mentions him only briefly. The entry for the second day of the tenth month of the eighth year of the Tenpyō era (736) says that the emperor Shōmu gave winter dress to the monk Dôsen and the Brahman monk Bodhisena.[3]

4. Academic Activities of Bodhisena

It appears that one of the problems Bodhisena faced in Japan was communication gap. The reason for this assumption is that the Japanese have written so little about him. The contrast becomes very vivid when we compare him with Ganjin, the famous contemporary monk who came from China in the year 754. It was Ganjin, and not Bodhisena, who established the altar for ordaining monks, a vitally important development in the history of Japanese Buddhism, in the Tōdaiji Temple of Nara.

One area where Bodhisena could have made a lasting contribution is Sanskrit, the language from which most of the scriptures were translated into Chinese. But the time was not ripe yet. Had he come in the hay days of Tantric Buddhism in Japan, his knowledge of Sanskrit would have been a much sought after commodity. But he came about a century too early.

When Buddhist missionaries fanned out of India to the north to spread the message of the dharma, a major policy they adopted was translating the scriptures into local languages, so that the neo-converts could read them. The missionaries followed this tradition in China also. As Sanskrit was ignored in China of that period, the Japanese also did not evince any interest in the language. However, the situation changed in China with the ascendancy of Tantric Buddhism around the eighth century. In Japan also the attitude towards Sanskrit changed with the introduction of Tantric Buddhism in the ninth century. But there was no Indian around at that time.

As for academic activities of Bodhisena, it seems that he was appointed a teacher in a college in Nara in 750, and a record says that he taught "Buddhosnisa Dhāraṇi", "Sahasrabhuja Dhārani", "Prajñāpāramitā Dhāraṇi" and "Cakravarti Cintāmaṇi Dhāraṇi" to one Hada no Kitatu. A very authentic record is the book *Shittanzō* written by the monk Annen (841 - ?). It quotes a word *Samyaksabuddha* from a book carried by Bodhisena.[4] Unfortunately, the name of the book is not given. Even then it seems that it was still there at the time of Annen. *Shittanzō*, however, deals with the contents of *Shittanshō*, a book that Bodhisena's Champa disciple Butteteu carried with him, in more detail.

5. Brahman in a Literary Work

Manyōshū, the oldest anthology containing poems up to 759 and compiled towards the end of the Nara Period (710-784), has a poem on Bodhisena. The poem is given below. The explanation of the poem given here is that given by the editors in the book.

The bird
Foraging in the Brahman's field
Is stopping on the flagpole with swollen eyes.

The meaning of the poem is that the bird that was foraging in the field of the Brahman had its eyes swollen because of his curse, and is now stopping on the flagpole. In those days, meetings for composing poems were held from time to time, in which a few words were given to the participants to compose a poem with. The words given here seem to be Brahman, garden, bird and flagpole. The poem judged to be the best in the meet is given here.

There are two opinions on the identity of the Brahman mentioned here. One is Bodhisena, and the other is the dancers who wore Brahman masks in Gigaku dance. [5]

6. Mask of Brahman in Gigaku Dance

In those days, Gigaku dances were performed in temples and the royal court. Here the dancers put on different types of masks, for example, courtier, lion, Chinese woman, drunken West Asian, and so on, while performing. One type of masks depicted the Brahman. These masks were preserved in temples like Tōdaiji and Hōryūji of Nara and its vicinity. Now they form a collection in the Tokyo National Museum. [6]

7. Bodhisena in Japanese Folk Tales

For the Japanese, Bodhisena was a very novel personality. He was a man from the land of Śākyamuni, and that also a Brahman, the highest caste in the Indian social hierarchy. So, it is natural that popular stories evolved around him with the passing of time. One such story appearing in *Konjaku Monogatari*, a thirteenth century collection of Japanese folk tales, is given below. [7]

Emperor Shōmu appointed the monk Gyōgi as a narrator in the Eye Opening Ceremony of the Great Buddha of the Tōdaiji Temple. Gyōgi told the emperor that he was not suited for the purpose. A foreigner was coming to act as the narrator. He submitted a petition to the emperor to allow him to go to receive the narrator. Gyōgi went to the port of Naniwa with one hundred monks, the official in charge of temple affairs, and musicians playing music to receive the narrator. But the person was not there. Gyōgi released a vessel full of ceremonial water in the sea. The vessel floated away towards west. The waves could not break or overturn the vessel. The vessel reached a boat and started returning. In the boat, there was a monk from South India who had come to attend the Eye Opening Ceremony at the temple. Gyōgi was there to receive his old acquaintance. The Brahman got down from the boat and the two embraced each other. Their joy knew no bound. People thought that it was a miracle for a Japanese to wait for the arrival of a man from far away India, and address him as an old acquaintance. Gyōgi addressed his guest with a poem.

Our vow in front of Śākyamuni in Gṛdhrakūṭa,

The eternal truth never withers, I now realise.

Bodhisena replied to him with another poem.

In Kapilāvastu, we took the vow together,

For that, I am seeing the face of Mañjuṣrī today.

Hearing this, all knew that Gyōgi was an incarnation of Mañjuṣrī. After this, Gyōgi came to the capital with Bodhisena. The emperor was very happy, and had the ceremony of the Tōdaiji Termple performed with Bodhisena as the narrator. He is our Brahman Bishop. He lived in the Daianji Temple.

Bodhisena belonged to Kapilāvastu of South India. He took a bow to meet Mañjuṣrī. A venerated person told him that Mañjuṣrī was in Godaizan in China. So he went from India to

Godaizan[a] in China. But an old man told him there that Mañjuṣ rī was born in Japan for guiding people. Hearing this he came to Japan to fulfil his desire. That Mañjuṣrī of Japan is none other than the monk Gyōgi. Gyōgi also came to know of his arrival and came to receive him. Bodhisena behaved as if he knew Gyōgi. Many people had doubts because they did not know this. They are all ignorant people. So the saying goes.

References

1. *Shōtoku Taishi,* Nakamura, Hajime ed., Nihon no Meicho, Chūō Kōronsha' Tokyo, pp. 461-466.
2. *Shōtoku Taishi*, pp. 461-466.
3. *Shoku Nihongi* Vol. 2, Naoki, Kōjirō, tr, Tōyō Bunko No. 489, Heibonsha Tokyo, 1998, p. 39.
4. Van Gulik, R.H., *Siddham*, Sarasvati Vihara Series, Vol. 36, International Academy of Indian Culture, Nagpur, p. 111.
5. *Manyōshū* Vol. 4, Poem No. 3856, Takagi, Ichinosuke et al. eds., Nihon Koten Bungaku Taikei Ṣūṣ n 7, Iwanami Shoten ṁā, Tokyo; 1962, p. 153.
6. Imaizumi Atsuo et al., eds, Nihon Bijutsu Zenshi Ṣūṣ, Vol. 1, Bijiutu Shuppansha, Tokyo, 1959, pp. 101-02.
7. *Konjaku Monogatari*, Vol. 3, (Book No. 11, Story No. 7), Yamada Yoshio et al., eds., Nihon Bungaku Taikei Ṣūṣ n 24, Twanami Shoten ṁā, Tokyo, 1962, pp. 70-71.

The word given for 'narrator' is *kōshi* which literally means a person delivering a lecture or a sermon.

5

Orthopraxis in Japanese Religious Tradition

Bijayananda Kar

I

Professor Hajime Nakamura has made very notable contribution in focusing Asian philosophical thought in the global perspective. His keen interest in classical Indian philosophy is well evident from his numerous writings on Indian thought, specially Buddhism and Vedānta. It is good that an International Seminar is now arranged in honour of Professor Nakamura in Delhi where there is impressive assembly of prominent Japanese, Indian and other Asian scholars as well.

He has shown, in his writings, substantial and authentic grounding on Japanese religio-philosophical tradition. I, therefore befitting to the occasion, feel interested to share of my stray thoughts over the development of Japanese religio-philosophical movement down the ages, specially keeping in mind the growth and development of Buddhism in that great country of south-east Asia. Basing upon certain textual references primarily and also hinting at certain philosophical implications, mainly at the dimension of applied ethics, an attempt will be made here to show as to how orthopraxis as well as orthodoxy have been meaningfully harmonised in the Japanese thought and which has been turned out to be highly significant from the socio-empirical standpoint.

II

So far as religion in Japan is taken into account, one interesting thing that is noticeable is: there has been all along a persistent attempt being encouraged and carried out, i.e. to expose and explore the meeting points between orthopraxis and orthodoxy. The theoretical issues concerning any religious belief or faith are not accepted with a sense of indifference or unconcern towards its practical operation and efficacy. The sharp dichotomy between monastic life and that of the lay householder is reasonably modified in practice. The monks are not closed to clerical rigidity but are engaged in social welfare of the commoners. This move is grounded on practical necessity. The advocacy of spiritual attainment in order to have some meaning at the human level must have to be operated through social dimension. In order to attain that objective radical gap between the monk and the commoner needs total transformation. Religion is, after all, for social welfare and upliftment. This vital point has been duly taken up in the Japanese religious framework in general.

It goes without saying that Confucianism, Shintoism and Buddhism are conspicuously different at the doctrinal level. They are on distinct theoretical foundations. But, all the same in Japan, there is a move for one single world-view in which the spiritual and the temporal are not completely placed apart. Rather they are integrated for the cause of social solidarity. The usual clash between orthopraxis and orthodoxy is mostly avoided in the Japanese religious tradition.

III

In this context, a religious pamphlet relating to Zen Buddhism is worth noting. According to it the presentation of Zen as religion is for peace of mind in general well-being rather than a path of meditation". Practice, which is feasible and plausible in the social front, that is given priority over theory-bound precept. Japanese mind is well conscious of the point that a moral precept of a religious belief must be operational within the social framework. And this practical need cannot just be ignored or bypassed.

Shintō is different religion. But it is also noticed that it has assimilated some Buddhist practices within its fold. So also Buddhism in Japan has accommodated within itself some form of Shintō purification rite. All such moves point to a definite direction as to how in Japan at least different religions form one single world-view. This sort of priority of practice over theory is not simply a modern development. It has its continuity throughout in the religious tradition of Japan.

IV

Buddhism in Japan faced opposition from other religions, some rationalist groups and also socio-political hostility during 1600-1868 A.D. A Shingon monk: Jiun Sonja (1718-1804), trained in the preachings of Buddhism and meditative practice, commenced a movement "Vinaya of the true Dharma" with the aim of invigorating the spirit and discipline of Buddhism. He maximised both thought and practice, i.e. morality, meditation and the learning of the texts. But, at the same time, he minimised the sectarian orthodoxy. He did not only revive monastic discipline but also moved beyond for dissemination of the precepts among the laity. To him, insight and ethical conduct are inextricably linked in Buddhism. It is clear from this as to how Buddhism in Japan has undergone certain modifications both in the order of clerk and laity to effectively meet the demands at the practical front.

The usual orthodox monastic order in Buddhism was not favourable to any form of liberalism in the life-style of the monks and the clerks. They were expected to observe strict puritanic measures. The clerks were to remain unmarried throughout. Occasional lapse in this regard was opposed on the ground that such liberal moves would undermine the distinction between the laity and the clerk. But, despite that, the general tendency in the clerical order, in Japan at least, is found to be a gradual shift to acknowledge the practical need of locating a linkage between the laity and the clerk so far as dharmic view of life is concerned. It seems that such a changed and liberal look to the clerical order is out of practical necessity. The monks are to propagate the Buddhistic message to the common people. They are supposed to give guidance for practising morality both at the individual and social levels. A true religious set up cannot override the sense of adoption of moral view of life in tune with social needs and requirements.

In that context, disallowing the clerks to move for marriage is to bring in some sort of psycho-physical oppression that would rather give rise to some sort of secret violation of the rigid prohibition and that would invite all sorts of immoral moves that upset the social stability and balance. It is, therefore, a proper pragmatic step to allow clerical marriage and that is within the moral set up.

In certain Buddhistic circle, there was the strong belief that the women were incapable of attaining enlightenment. The ground for such belief was that woman's body, being filthy, was not a dharma-receptacle. Then it was supposed that women were capable of undertaking only 'easy' practices whereas men were able to grasp the profundity of the Buddhistic wisdom. But in Japan, there is found to be a positive reaction against such unsocial and unethical prejudice and, in this connection, the authentic Buddhist source: *The Lotus Sūtra* of the Heian period (794-1185) has been usually referred to. Such citations provide the point that women are also capable of attaining enlightenment. This point clearly vindicates as to how, in the Japanese traditions, the religious faith never remains uncompromising but is distinctly flexible and amenable to the demands and expectations of human concern. By this sort of liberal outlook, the Japanese tradition rejects unhealthy as well as pernicious social discrimination based on gender inequality.

It is notable that abortion is legalised in Japan since 1948. Initially there was violent religious reaction against it. But, particularly the Buddhist order, despite opposition from certain quarters, has introduced a ritual: Kuyō on the basis of which the parents can pray for the well-being of aborted fetus in the 'beyond', i.e. in the 'realm of the gods and the Buddhas'. This shows as to how the religious faith is found to be more concerned about the practical bearing of such faith than on its abstract dogmatic stand. No religious belief can reasonably withstand the peace and stability of human beings in the mundane plane. If uncontrolled birth causes harm to human peace and welfare, then that has to be checked and for that any religious inhibition has to be reasonably modified. Because human well being is, of course, the most important concern and there is no point in ignoring that. It is definitely encouraging that religion in Japan, in general, have been found as not opposed to practical needs and have advanced a meaningful compromise in this regard. The religionists seem to have well realised that religion in the name of spiritual attainment must not bc presented as anti-human.

Here it can be noted that the religious reforms encouraged in Japan like the praying for the well-being of the aborted fetus in the relam of gods may not be that rationally convincing. But in the circle of religious faith, the meaningful change can be effectively introduced in a gradual process adopting the medium of specific religious language to which a believer is firmly conditioned. This device can be treated as half the way. It is better to move half the way than to have no movement at all.

A similar point of liberalism and free thinking is noticed in the Shinshū tradition in which the religious organisation has made itself free from all sorts of magic, taboos and unlucky days. Because of embracing such reformative measures, Shinshū is often called as "the does-not-care sect".

Despite its acknowledgement of meditation and the cultivation of self-power for the sake of enlightenment, due emphasis has been given on the inculcation of salvific powers and the practices of ethical duties. Attempt has been carried out to establish a rational linkage with venerable ancestors. A happy and peaceful life is distinctly of most important concern for such Buddhists. The basic preoccupations of the Buddhists of Japan are focused in this world and in personal happiness. On account of this, they are more interested in establishing a purposeful relational bond between them and their ancestors. The ancestors are enshrined in each family so that, it is sincerely believed, peace and happiness in the family and in the surrounding would be alive. Due to all this, it has been often remarked that Buddhism for most Japanese is a religion of death and the ancestors. The religious tradition of Japan, more or less, advocates the world of gods as the spirits of the dead, indicating thereby a close affinity between the living and the dead, so that the heritage of humanity is given a meaningful spark of moral continuity. This sort of belief is not to be construed as purely visionary in the abstract ideational sense of the term, it has remarkable sense of practical morality in the socio-empirical framework. The whole enterprise seems to be deeply humanstic.

In short, it can be observed that Japan has all along taken a very meaningful and purposeful initiative in promulgating religious reforms which have brought out not only the clergy and the laity more close to each other but also such steps have definitely moved a long way to exhibit as to how religion can have sustenance without having the rigidity of fundamentalism. Religion, in the proper sense of the term, is bound to be of social significance and also must be of contemporaneous relevance without having any disregard to the principles of applied ethics. A proper religious sense cannot afford to be unethical from the social point of view. It seems that religions in Japan, so far as practice is concerned, have set a good example.

References

1 *Religions of Japan in Practice:* (edited by) George J. Tanabe, Jr. Princeton Reading in Religions, Vol. V, Princeton University Press, 1999.

6

Zen Aesthetics as reflected in Muromachi Japan's Suiboku-ga

Anu Jindal

Suiboku-ga[1] or ink painting, practised in the Muromachi period (1333-1573) in Japan, was distinctive in that one of the most important schools of painters was that of monks belonging to the sect of Zen Buddhism, which was the established faith. As the inspiration for the visual expression was rooted in the tenets of Zen, accordingly the aesthetics of the paintings displayed specific characteristics. Discussion of this particular kind of aesthetics formulates the basis of this paper. Art through the ages, practised by a variety of people across the earth, has very often been linked with the religious or philosophical thinking of the people producing it. In the case of *suiboku-ga*, the practitioners of religion themselves became the creators of the art; thus the relationship of religion and art became exceptional and the corresponding artistic expression unique.

The making of the paintings were part of the religious experience, where the ideology of the religion became the conceptual basis for the ink paintings. As in Zen the goal of *satori* or enlightenment was to be reached through the path of contemplation so too the act of painting was akin to an act of contemplation and required the deepest concentration. Some of the Zen monks who practised this art were truly talented artists and may very well be termed as "Zen-artists", with the Zen monk Sesshū Tōyō (1420-1506) representing the epitome of this nomenclature. The artistic expression produced was typified by highly refined paintings, replete with profound meaning.

Zen Buddhism

Zen Buddhism came to Japan from China in the Kamakura period (1185-1333). Transmission of cultural influences too came along with the faith, in the form of art objects, calligraphy and literature. *Suiboku-ga,* particularly the paintings of the Chinese painters of the Sung period were much appreciated in Japan. Amply supported by the ruling Ashikaga shoguns, Zen Buddhism firmly established itself in the Muromachi period with Kyoto as its headquarters. Zen Buddhism and Chinese influences dominated intellectual life and Zen temples became great intellectual and cultural centres.

Zen rejected relic and image worship, or study of scriptures and advocated simplicity, contemplation and self-discipline. Logical debate and written literature were considered inadequate to express the spirit of Buddhism and instead oral teachings by the master to the disciple were encouraged. To appreciate the present and live accordingly was vital corresponding to a very significant point always emphasized as characteristic in Zen discipline "that one should live in the act, live in the moment itself, without worrying and disturbing oneself with thoughts of the past and the future."[2] Zen Buddhists prided themselves on going beyond the accepted forms of thinking and reasoning. The Buddha himself would transmit the deepest truth to genuine followers of the faith, not in words but directly to his soul, and this truth would be revealed in an intuitive flash of understanding, when he would achieve *satori*. Zen claimed that the potential to attain Buddhahood lay latent in every human being and the ultimate goal of *satori* could be found in the natural world itself. This could be achieved simply and primarily through *zazen* or contemplation which would allow one to look intuitively into the nature of things, rather than to analyse logically. As Prof. Hajime Nakamura says "the way of thinking that seeks for the Absolute in the phenomenal world plays an effective role in the assimilation of the Zen sect." Further he explains the phenomenalist way of thinking by quoting the Zen master, Dōgen's views: "Dōgen meant to say that the truth which people search for is in reality, nothing but the world of our daily experience. Thus he (Dōgen) says 'The real aspect is all things. All things are this aspect'"[3] Thus pursued one may be able to rise above worldly concerns of good and bad and be able to involve purely in straightforward action, irrespective of joy or grief. The practising of *zazen* would make one understand "the fundamental unity of existence underlying and pervading all particular beings and changes, which is, however, not to be sought in the external world but directly and most clearly in one's own inner heart" and "when one realizes this through training in Zen, he has absorbed the universe into himself, which amounts to identifying himself with the cosmos."[4] The simplest methodology would suffice and consequently the appreciation and practise of art and literature became an intrinsic part of Zen life and served as a means to strive towards the goal of spiritual attainment. *Suiboku-ga* was foremost among the arts favoured by the Zen clergy.

Zen and Suiboku-ga

It was not just artistic but also spiritual release that Zen monks found through the making and viewing of *suiboku-ga*. Aesthetic refinement was considered "not only as a means for the composure of mind but a natural expression of the soul deriving its poise and peace from the bosom of the universe."[5] Involvement with aesthetics could calm the mind and draw forth an expression from the inner recesses of the creator which corresponded to the inner core of nature. Chinese Ink Paintings that were imported in great numbers from China served as the role models for the Japanese monks to emulate. Chinese paintings that were "at first imported as guides to spiritual awakening, to the *satori* or 'enlightenment' of Zen soon became part of the spiritual discipline practiced by priests and served to express personal religious experience."[6] So intense was the influence of Zen "that poetry and painting have been explicitly identified with Zen in phrases such as *shizen ichimi* (poetry and Zen are one) and *gazen ichimi* (painting and Zen are one)."[7]

Zen Buddhism differed from other Buddhist sects in that in Zen there was emphasis on individual training and discipline. To the follower of Zen self-control embodied the essence of true freedom as this could release him from the struggle with mundane reality and lead towards realisation of the inner light and in Zen thinking "victories over the inner self are more true than the austere penances of the medieval hermit, who tormented his flesh instead of disciplining his mind."[8] Self-control afforded the patience and diligence to do years of disciplined practise to reach the level of virtuosity required for the execution of *suiboku-ga*, so as to successfully achieve the perfection of portrayal which imbued the work with a special life of its own. Brevity in the visual expression belied the fact that intense forethought and practise went into the making of an ink painting.

Suiboku-ga employed the minimum of visual elements and devices, as well as the least of materials and tools, thereby adhering to the principles of simplicity and frugality so strongly propagated by Zen. "In the making of a painting, the painter must combine the vocabulary and grammar of art and to understand the communicational function of a painting, it is important to understand the context of production and the context of consumption."[9] Zen's denial of logical analysis and reasoning encouraged the need to look within oneself and in nature for inspiration and direction. Preconceived notions and attachments had little meaning. By refusing all non-essential features one could arrive at an understanding of nature and its mechanisms. Translated into the artist's language, this attitude of Zen denoted total freedom; a state of being every artist yearns for. His perception of the being of things emerged directly and spontaneously from within himself independent of scholarly reasoning. This understanding was considered so powerful that the actual quick execution of an ink painting, achieved with a few deft brushstrokes could be likened to the achieving of enlightenment gained in a flash of intuitive understanding. Similarly the aesthetics of the paintings functioned in a manner so as to communicate the philosophical basis of Zen.

Minimalism, asymmetry, suggestion

Minimalism was a key factor of Zen Aesthetics. It was maintained in form, colour, content, rendering, execution and material; thereby overall in the communication in keeping with the austere character of Zen, yet the main aim of attempting to make the spirit of the object move on the paper could be uncannily and palpably felt in the compositions. Succinctness of visual content known as the "thrifty-brush tradition" encouraged the viewers' participation and involvement with the artistic work. He may wander himself in the spaces created as well as those left bare. That which was left unsaid "spoke" far more than that which was depicted allowing the viewer to formulate his own inferences. This quality is particularly well seen in the paintings of Shūbun Tensho, a monk-painter and one-time abbot of Shōkoku-ji and is the hallmark of his style.

The "one-cornered" style, as the name suggests, encouraged asymmetrical arrangement of the forms in the composition, wherein forms would be concentrated in one side of the painting and large areas of the picture space were left vacant alluding to the state of emptiness, raising the work above being merely for representational or decorative purpose; rather it conveyed austere profundity of expression. This is reflected in a Zen tenet on the state of emptiness: "In emptiness, forms are born, when one becomes empty of the assumptions, inferences, and judgements he has acquired over the years, he comes close to his original nature and is capable of conceiving original ideas and reacting freshly."[10] The unfilled spaces were in themselves replete with "visual content" and meaning, highlighting what was vital and eliminating the unnecessary.

The power of suggestion was also part of the intention of the artist and the true Zen painter portrayed only about sixty percent of the scene and left the rest to enthuse the imagination of the viewer. As Okakura opines: "beauty, or the life of things, is always deeper as hidden within than as outwardly expressed, even as the life of the universe beats always underneath incidental appearances. Not to display, but to suggest, is the secret of infinity."[11] As D.T. Suzuki describes "a simple fishing boat in the midst of the rippling waters is enough to awaken in the mind of the beholder a sense of the vastness of the sea and at the same time of peace and contentment."[12] It is as when one observes a profusion of flowers blooming in a garden, one enjoys their beauty, no doubt, but one can feel overwhelmed. On the other hand if we were to isolate a single stem of flower we would be able to appreciate its beauty in far greater depth and our mind would be able to recreate the vision of this one flower in the garden among many others. The minimum of representation has the maximum of impact. This is akin to the Zen attitude that counsels a "replacement of restless detail by quietness, which is the chief 'action' in deep meditation."[13] The symbolism of suggestion itself stirs one to an insight into the inner core of nature. Sesshū's *Winter Landscape* depicts a desolate winter scene where the world is cloaked in a blanket of snow but the mere hint of foliage foretells of the coming of spring.

It required a perceptive mind to understand that immense practise, hard work and conceptual ideating went into the making of the paintings. They were conceived intuitively and expressed spontaneously allowing no room for erasures or changes. The analogy of this practice with the Zen notion that enlightenment was achieved in a quick flash particularly appealed to the monk-painters. The *Splashed-Ink Landscape* by Sesshū in the Tokyo National Museum which appears to have been painted in the matter of a mere few seconds corresponds to this belief. This painting, an exceedingly abbreviated portrayal of a landscape so cursory as to border on the abstract, is a highly insightful statement of artistic and spiritual expression.

Rhythm of lines

Line, the first step in the rendition of an ink painting, was one of the strongest elements of the paintings. The brush was the instrument through which this was executed and the painter displayed his dexterity in employing *fude no chikara* or strength of the brush to bring forth a meaningful manifestation of his expression. The *enpitsu no kihaku* or spiritually dynamic impact of a brushstroke infused the work with the vital forces of the subject under consideration. To achieve this the painter employed an immense variety in the techniques of application of the brushstrokes e.g. thick or thin and long or short lines, broken lines, lines applied with a dry or wet brush. Infinite variety was displayed in the range of tones, depending on the quantity of water mixed with ink and the pressure of the hand. Diverse techniques helped to denote different aspects of the scenes depicted; "axe-cut" strokes were used, as the name denotes to render rugged forms e.g. mountainscape, rocks and boulders, while criss-cross lines added texture. Gently swaying curvilinear lines contrasted with rigid hard axe-cut strokes. Quality of line took from calligraphy in terms of how the stroke began and ended i.e. from thick to thin or the reverse. Tonal variations gave feeling of far and near, as for example of the mountain ranges. *Tentai* or dots peppered over the forms, emphasizing "the painter's compositional intentions by either stressing or softening the linear forms" and also served to "reinforce the invisible connections of a painting, underlining the painting's general architectonic flow."[14] Special brush techniques were used e.g. to achieve the furry effect of a rabbit or monkey's hair the bristles of the paintbrush were spread and then the ink was applied.

Ink paintings made by the truly successful painter who had the power to render *enpitsu no kihaku* represent objects from the phenomenal world and yet communicate the very essence and basic character of the forms portrayed. This vitality of the natural world is seen in Sesshû's *Autumn Landscape* and *Winter Landscape* where the lines vibrate with the power of rhythmic life force. So the hardness of rocks is clear, the organic quality of wood in the tree trunks is obvious and the gentleness of foliage is palpably felt. Even the flaky, light character of snow is felt by the viewer. If it is a gentle autumn afternoon then it looks just like that, and when it is a cold winter day that is exactly how the viewer perceives it. All of this was achieved with an economy in brushwork that corresponded to economy in words as observed in the practise of Zen.

Colour

Traditional norms of adornment rely heavily on the sensuousness of colour and most schools of paintings utilize it accordingly. The choice of the medium of *suiboku-ga* encouraged the portrayal of expression simply through black *sumi* or ink on white paper or light coloured silk as the background. The deliberate denial of colour matched with Zen values of self-denial and severity. While light touches of colour may be added in some places, largely the volume and detailing of the forms was rendered through a myriad range of rich grey tones made by mixing *sumi* with varying amounts of water to give washes. This also suited the Zen emphasis on the power of suggestion as opposed to that of being obvious. At first glance it may appear that the artist has abstracted the subject, through portraying sceneries devoid of colour, but on further appraisal "one is reminded of the Zen saying that 'many colours blind your vision'."[15] As the viewer progressively builds up his relationship with the painting, he notices the subtle indications given by tones and textures, till a point emerges where the painting shimmers with all the iridescence and emotions that colours communicate in the actual scenes in the visible world. To interpret the colourful world in black and white and yet remain "colourful" rather than "colourless" was indeed an achievement of the Zen monk as an artist.

Further the paintings delve into the cryptic depths of human psyche to unravel the nature and meaning of existence. The practitioner of Zen endeavoured through Zen contemplation to reach a state of total calmness where he is able to observe and understand the world with complete insight. This state of serenity allowed no emotions or attachments, dissolved the individuality and transported one into nothingness. From this standpoint of penetration into the heart of nature, no colour or embellishment seemed necessary and the world could be portrayed without the physical aid of coloured pigmentation. Rather solely through the finest nuances of tones he was able to imbue his painting with a soul rising above mere realism. The very rejection of colour allowed the painting to reveal, without any diversions, the depths of nature.[16]

If we look at Sesshū's *Autumn Landscape* the atmosphere is suffused with the warmth of a mild autumn day, the plants and trees have all the richness and feeling of vegetation minus the advantage of a representation in green hues. Strong dark lines emphasize the ruggedness of the rocky hills in the foreground with soft washes providing the gentler modulations of the boulders. Even softer tonal washes effectively signify the mountains in the far distance, with all of this contrasted with gently lapping water. Thus the beauty of every aspect of natural scenery is communicated to the viewer; an ideal setting for reflection and communion with nature.

Form

Forms from the real world constitute the vehicle of communication of the ink paintings. Natural landscapes are the principal subject matter observed and some key forms recur: mountains, rocks, waterfalls, rivers, trees, forests, vegetation all balanced against the vastness of space. Man is an intrinsic component, yet is a small cog in the giant wheel of nature. To give the appearance of the magnitude of nature and how man is an infinitely small part of the whole wondrous cycle, proportion was skilfully utilized. A popular figure is that of the *bunjin* or scholar, walking or often riding on a donkey with a helper boy accompanying him, wandering in the wilderness, walking up a mountain path, crossing a bridge or sitting in a simple hut nestled among gigantic trees and huge mountain ranges. Fishermen sailing in small boats in vast water bodies, monks involved in mundane tasks of sweeping floor with a broom, mending clothes, fishing with a fish net or gazing admiringly at the beauty of nature were other oft repeated forms.

While these forms are taken from the visible world yet in *suiboku-ga* there was no place for objective reality. The following lines by Dōgen, exemplify this:

"'When you paint spring, do not paint willows, plums, peaches or apricots—just paint spring. To paint willows, plums, peaches or apricots is to paint willows, plums, peaches or apricots. It is not yet painting spring.'

by Dōgen from his 'Plum Blossoms' in Treasury of the True Dharma Eye."[17]

Each form is carefully chosen for its beauty and is worthy of its assigned place in nature, but the primary value for the Zen monk-painter is in each form's symbolism. So the *bunjin* and the monks engaged in pragmatic tasks echo the Zen philosophy of the need for a simplistic and controlled life aimed at living in harmonious communion with nature and within this simplicity itself, the truth would be revealed to the true seeker.

Zen influence on Subject Matter

With Zen influence and the popularity of the technique of ink painting, the subject matter of the paintings concentrated on particular themes. The main subjects dealt with were *chinsō* which were portraits of Zen priests or eccentric figures drawn from Zen or Taoist legend, *kachō-ga* were paintings of birds and flowers while *jimbutsu-ga* were paintings depicting people and things including animals, plants, fruits and vegetables, *shigajiku* were poem-and-picture scrolls where poetry and painting both described the same theme. Most popular were the *sansui-ga* or landscape painting where panoramic views of idealized landscapes depicting Chinese sceneries became commonplace. Done on different formats either scrolls or on sliding doors these ink paintings were displayed in the interiors of Zen temples and monasteries and in the living quarters of Zen abbots and were considered conducive to introspection and a quiet, simplistic life.

The life of the Zen monks involved attending to routine and mundane tasks, both manual and menial, rather than scholarship. They listened to the master's sermons that were invariably short and enigmatic and debate if any was in the form of exchanging *koan*. *Koan* was a kind of cryptic riddle, the answer to which was often peculiar and unfathomable, and was quite frequently accompanied by direct action. A subject not commonly dealt with in *suiboku-ga* was the illustration of a *koan*, exemplified in *Catching a Catfish with a Gourd* by the Zen monk-painter Josetsu, in the collection of the Taizōin sub-temple in Myōshinji, Kyoto. The scene depicts a man involved in the unlikely task of attempting to catch a slippery catfish in the tiny scooped out mouth of a gourd. In the upper part of the work some thirty monks have written poems trying to interpret the same paradoxical theme.

The fact that landscape painting found particular favour with the monks reveals that they had a fascination and deep involvement with the subject of natural surroundings. Zen monasteries were often situated in or near the mountains among natural surroundings. Though monastic life itself could often be busy and noisy, yet living in or near such surroundings in close touch with nature encouraged the Zen monks to keenly observe mountains, rocks, rivers, animals and vegetation and these observations deeply affected their philosophy. They were able to appreciate natural phenomena in the deepest sense so as to relate it to their inner being. In *suiboku-ga* this observation is not merely naturalism, but it is as if the artist has penetrated into the very life of the objects he has depicted and the painting serves to reflect the spirit of the object.

Drawing attention to the simple lifestyle of the monks was a very popular form of painting made in the *shigajiku* or poem-and-picture scroll format. The upper part of the scroll had poems composed by monks, while the lower portion painted by a monk-painter was devoted to illustrating the scholar's study eulogising on the need to facilitate an appropriate atmosphere for contemplation and harmonious cohabitation with nature, away from the noisy, mundane world; a kind of retreat into a tranquil environment where a monk could devote himself to the four gentlemanly pursuits of poetry, painting, music and calligraphy. Monks presented these kinds of paintings to other monk friends within the temple, as a celebration of the building of the friend's new study or in the hope that such a wish may be realised. Such a retreat was often merely an idealized place, existing only in the minds of the Zen monks and painted as gifts to fellow monks in recognition of mutual spiritual goals. Thus the paintings of the scholar's study created an imaginary world as an expression of the aspiration for peace and tranquillity. This was the Zen way to realise the ideal world in this world—a kind of delusion, an economical way to change one's mind to change one's view of the world.

The Zen monk-painter Shūbun's painting *Reading in a Bamboo Grove Retreat* (c.1446) a National Treasure in the collection of the Tokyo National Museum is an example of this genre. In this painting Shūbun has employed exquisite, simplified brushwork to depict an ideal of natural harmony through the scene of a man sitting quietly reading in a rustic hut, in tranquil natural surroundings while in the foreground a visitor is crossing a bridge. Two twisting pine trees dominate the picture. A feeling of serenity and otherworldliness pervades the painting. Several eulogistic poems have been written by other priests in the upper part of the scroll, admiring nature and corroborating the yearning to have a retreat in such surroundings. Shūbun's talent invested his paintings with a wide range of delicate ink tones. His depictions created an atmospheric softness and almost floating quality through the expansive and spacious, mist-shrouded landscapes, due to the gentle ink washes and large areas of picture space left empty. Typical of his style was to contrast varying elements like defined foreground forms and huge mountain faces with misty backdrops and vast unpainted areas, in a deliberate attempt to create ambiguity, which conforms to the precept that much can be said without saying too much and what is left unsaid is often more evocative. Other landscapes of Shūbun are equally expressive, the mystery created by his handling of space imbuing the painting with a spiritual message of an idealized world.

Harmony with Nature

Zen sensitises one to appreciate the wondrous beauty of nature in a way that perhaps one has not felt earlier. Nature has a serene balance and perfect harmony as shown through the changing seasons that we can learn from. Zen teaches that one must attempt to live with it, rather than to fight against it. This understanding of nature influenced *suiboku-ga* in its perception and expression. Nature remained the vital fountainhead of inspiration. Just as in Zen the ideal was enlightenment achieved through contemplation, so too the aesthetic approach of the artist banked solely on contemplation. It was imperative to strive for an intuitive insight into the nature of things as opposed to a logical analysis of it. The creative process was akin to a spiritual experience, wherein the painter developed the closest possible affinity with his subject to the point of becoming one with it. Once he was able to reach the state of "oneness" with the subject, he negated the apparent, the obvious to appreciate the inner meaning. To achieve a complete understanding of universal nature and thereby to find the ultimate reality remained the final goal of the creator.[18]

This emphasis on naturalness and appreciating the greatness and sublime beauty of nature underlined the essential need of man to live in harmony with nature. Being imbued with this sense of affinity, the follower of Zen found it but natural to portray human life in comparison with nature e.g. "a mind clear as moonlight, a person free as clouds and waters, the soul itself enigmatic as the dragon in thick clouds, and so on."[19] This absorption of the purity and serenity pervading the universe resulted in the state of a 'mood' or 'air-rhythm' (*fū in*), as it was called. This mood had the sentiment and temper of transcendental calmness and found its expressions primarily in poetry and then painting.

Sesshū's magnum opus, *Landscape of the Four Seasons (Long Landscape Scroll)* in the Mōri collection exemplifies this spiritual experience perfectly. In Sesshū's long landscape scroll a rhythmic continuity is maintained throughout the exceptionally long narrative. It follows the four seasons, and accordingly there are variations in the depictions, but the continuity is achieved through the repeat of certain idioms such as the *bunjin*, and the path meandering through the mountainscapes, forests and flatlands. "*Kachi kachi ai de* or here is an ideal world for the *bunjin* to escape from the ordinary world."[20] Sesshū has created a serene journey of man's wanderings in breathtakingly beautiful natural surroundings, which reveals the understanding and acceptance of the truth of oneness of man with nature.

An oft repeated theme within *sansui-ga* was of the four seasons, extremely popular in Japanese art, in many other schools of painters. When painted by the Zen monks it emphasized the need to understand the evanescence of nature and life and that "the fluid aspect of impermanence is in itself the absolute state. The changeable character of the phenomenal world is of absolute significance for Dōgen"[21] Sesshū's *Autumn Landscape* and *Winter Landscape*[22] are examples of four-seasons paintings. *Autumn Landscape* features a rocky terrain comprising of gentle hills, with a fair degree of vegetation. The roofs of fishermen's huts and their sailboats with gently lapping water can be seen in the foreground while two men are sitting in this idyllic setting conversing with each other with a temple complex in the background. As was the norm with *suiboku-ga* about one-third of the upper portion is devoid of forms alluding to suggestive space. The coldest season of the year is shown in the *Winter Landscape* through the depiction of a rather barren landscape featuring huge, craggy rock faces contrasted with snow clad mountains. A lone figure ambles up a diagonally winding path, which cuts through the rock face, towards a temple complex, which nestles amongst the mountains in the middle ground, seeming to be a warm sanctuary amidst the chill of winter. Perhaps the most forceful and striking aspect in the *Winter Landscape* is the unfinished vertical line of the rock, which is almost like a gash, yet facilitates the feeling of infinite space.

The minimalism of *suiboku-ga* is apparent in these works. Sesshū has limited himself to the use of an uncompromising black of the ink strongly contrasted against the white of the paper, and brushed in some choice tones for the rendering. No excess of forms clutter the pictorial space and the detailing is minimal. Both paintings convey the same message - the desire of man to live in harmony with nature. In both paintings man is not subdued by the gigantic grandeur of nature rather nature displays magnanimity towards man, allowing room for man to live peacefully in its lap.

Ki'in seido (spiritual vitality)

To paint from the soul was the highest achievement that the Zen monk-painter strove for. To achieve this objective he had to initiate the mental process by the Zen method of contemplation. He would do so to such an intense point as to feel one with the subject and feel it reverberate in his own being, allowing him to perceive the subject's intuitive character. This would give him the irresistible power to transmit by the physical means of his brushwork to bring alive the forms on the material body of the paper. Japanese painters frequently repeated this precept:

"*Waga kokoro waga te wo yaku;*

Waga te waga kokoro ni ozuru.

Our spirit must make our hand its servitor;

Our hand must respond to each behest of our spirit."[23]

The meaning of this precept was intensified for the Zen monk-painters as rather than painting a representation of the visible world it was essentially the essence of the subject that they wished to invoke so as to truly infuse the painting with *ki'in seido* or spiritual vitality. *Ki'in* may be described as that intangible quality which affords an elevated sentiment, a nobility of spirit, to the painting. Bowie explains "this quality, this manifestation of the spirit, can neither be imparted nor acquired. It must be innate. It is, so to say, a divine seed implanted in the soul by the Creator"[24]. *Seido* is that quality without which the painting would be lifeless, simply an arrangement of lines, tones, dots, without the vital life-force coursing through it.

Conclusion

A supreme and abstruse aesthetic refinement characterised *suiboku-ga*. All the elements and principles of art functioned at the behest of Zen norms as the creators were the followers of the religion. The process of creative production corresponded to the act of contemplation where body and mind attempted to merge with the spirit, with intuition as the guiding factor. Just as painters of the works were a highly specialised sect, that of Zen monks, so too the viewers had to be attuned to this rarefied visual communication. Only a select few could attempt to unravel the mysteries evoked by the emphasis on minimalism, suggestion, and subtlety. A surface scrutiny of the paintings showed a portrayal easily identifiable with realistic objects from the phenomenal world, but the monk-painters aimed at discovering a far deeper meaning, that of the truth of nature hidden within the seemingly simple but in actuality complex realms of the ink paintings, leading to distinctive artistic fundamentals developed to bear fruition to this expression. With such a philosophical basis *suiboku-ga* emerged as a highly profound and refined artistic expression.

References

[1] Literally translates to ink-and-water painting. The term applies broadly speaking to the ink paintings that were made in the Kamakura and Muromachi period.

[2] Rahula, Walpola. *Zen and the Taming of the Bull*. The Gordon Fraser Gallery Ltd., London, 1978. p. 18.

[3] Nakamura, Hajime. *Ways of Thinking of Eastern Peoples: India-China-Tibet-Japan*. Edited by Wiener, Philip P. University of Hawaii Press, Honolulu, 1985. pp. 351-352.

[4] Anesaki, Masaharu. *History of Japanese Religion: With Special Reference to the Social and Moral Life of the Nation*. Charles E. Tuttle Company, Rutland, Vermont & Tokyo, Japan, 1963. pp. 208-209.

[5] Ibid. p.214.

[6] Saito, Ryukyu. *Suiboku: Studies in Ink Painting*. Kodansha International Ltd., Tokyo, 1965. p.10

[7] Awakawa, Yasuichi. *Zen Painting*. Translated by Bester, John. Kodansha International Ltd., Tokyo & Palo Alto, 1970. p.9.

[8] Okakura, Kakuzo. *The Ideals of the East: With special reference to the Art of Japan*. Charles E. Tuttle Co., Inc., Rutland, Vermont & Tokyo, 1970. p.175.

[9] Kishi, Fumikazu Prof. "Art as Communication" as narrated to author. 1998.

[10] Holmes, Stewart W. & Horioka, Chimyo. *Zen Art for Meditation*. Charles E. Tuttle Co., Rutland, Vermont & Tokyo, 1996. p.66.

[11] Okakura, Kakuzo. *The Ideals of the East: With special reference to the Art of Japan*. Charles E. Tuttle Co., Inc., Rutland, Vermont & Tokyo, 1970. pp.176-177.

[12] Suzuki, D.T. *Zen and Japanese Culture*. Charles E. Tuttle Company, Inc., Rutland, Vermont and Tokyo, first published 1959, this printing 1997. p.22.

[13] Wood, Ernest. *Zen Dictionary*. Charles E. Tuttle Co., Rutland, Vermont & Tokyo, 1957. p.7.

[14] Briessen, Fritz Van. *The Way of the Brush: Painting Techniques of China and Japan*. Charles E. Tuttle Company, Rutland, Vermont & Tokyo, Japan, 1990. p.56.

[15] Paine, Robert Treat and Soper, Alexander. *Art and Architecture of Japan*. Pelican History of Art, Pelican Books, London, 1964. p. 161.

[16] Jindal, Anu. "Impact of Zen Buddhism on Suiboku-ga", International Conference on "India and East Asia: Learning from Each Other", Department of Chinese and Japanese Studies, University of Delhi, 2003.

[17] Tanahashi, Kazuaki and Schneider, Tensho David. *Essential Zen*. Harper Collins Pulishers Inc., San Francisco, 1995. p. 106.

[18] Jindal, Anu. *Nature in Japanese Art: Suiboku-ga of the Muromachi Period with special reference to Sesshū Tōyō*. Ph.D. Thesis, National Museum Institute of History of Art, Conservation & Museology, New Delhi, 2000.

[19] Anesaki, Masaharu. *History of Japanese Religion: With Special Reference to the Social and Moral Life of the Nation*. Charles E. Tuttle Company, Rutland, Vermont & Tokyo, Japan, 1963. p.213.

[20] Ota, Takahiko Prof. (Dr.). As narrated to author. 1998.

[21] Nakamura, Hajime. *Ways of Thinking of Eastern Peoples: India-China-Tibet-Japan*. Edited by Wiener, Philip P., University of Hawaii Press, Honolulu, 1985. p. 352.

[22] Originally from a set of four scrolls of the four seasons, the spring and summer season scrolls are now lost.

[23] Bowie, Henry P. *On the Laws of Japanese Painting*. New York: Dover Publications, Inc., Ist published 1911, this ed. 1952.

[24] *Ibid*.

7

The Characteristics of Korean Buddhism

Geo-lyong Lee

I

Introductory Remarks

Buddhism was introduced to the Korean peninsula from China in the era of the Korean Three Kingdoms around the fourth century A.D.[1] The close relationship of Korea with China was one of the factors that it accepted Buddhism easily from China. However, some historical documents, such as *Records of the Noble Masters of Yang Dynasty* and *Records of The Noble Buddhist Masters in the East*, give suggestions that the transmission of Buddhism can be actually dated even earlier than the fourth century A.D. [2]

Also, there is a legend concerning the transmission of Buddhism to Gaya, a tiny Kingdom located at the southern end of the Korean peninsula, by sea and directly from India. According to a document called *Records of Three Kingdoms* (Book iii, Chapter 4), there remains a replica of a stupa in Hogye Temple of current Kimhae, which was carried in by ship when an Indian princess to be married to King Suro (the founder of the Gaya Kingdom) was travelling from her country, Ayuta in eastern India.[3] Unlike the major Three Kingdoms which accepted Buddhism indirectly from China, this small Gaya Kingdom stands apart for its introduction of Buddhism by a sea route. Considering the Buddhist performances of King Suro who died in 199, it is assumed that the introduction of Buddhism into the Korean peninsula was about 2 centuries earlier than A.D. 372.

Therefore, the introduction of Buddhism into Korea can be categorized in terms of Chinese and Indian, even though no official historical documents have been found to corroborate the legend concerning the Gaya Kingdom. Because of the absence of documents on Gaya Buddhism, we can not identify the features and inclination of Gaya Buddhism.

Nevertheless, it can be said that the main stream of Korean Buddhism has been Mahāyāna Buddhism which was introduced to the Korean peninsula from China. From start to finish, Korean Buddhism has been developed based on the philosophical thought of Mahāyāna Buddhism, and it comes under the culture using Chinese character and depends on the sūtras in Chinese character.

II

Individual Identity of Korean Buddhism

As mentioned above, Korean Buddhist thought is closely related to the philosophical thinking of Chinese Buddhism. Therefore the initial Buddhism to be introduced was directly or indirectly Chinese. However, this does not mean that Korean Buddhism is an imitator of Chinese Buddhism. It was a form of Buddhism different from Chinese Buddhism, even though some of the basic ideas were Chinese in origin. It was the new research done by Korean masters who created what came to be called Korean Buddhism.

There are a lot of instances showing that Korean Buddhism has established its own individual identity from the era of the Three Kingdoms. In Koguryo, Master Sungnang's research on the three treatises becomes the basis of the Chinese Three Treatises sect (San-lun-tsung).[4]

Another example of individual development is to be seen in Shilla Vijñānamātravāda which also developed apart from the teachings in China. Thus Vijñānamātravāda followed the teachings of Shilla Master Woncheok who established a different view from his colleague, Chinese Master K'uei-chi. In case of Baekje Vinaya thought, Baekje Master Kyomik had already introduced the original Indian Vinayas in five parts one century earlier than the foundation of Chinese Vinaya

School during the T'ang Dynasty. The Vinaya texts were translated in Baekje and published in 72 volumes, so that an individual Vinaya thought, one suited to the Baekje social system, was established. Shilla Master Euisang's Avatamsa thought is also very different from his Chinese Dharma friend Master Fa-tsang. Whereas Master Fa-tsang attached weight to the philosophical understanding of Avatamsa doctrine, Master Euisang emphasized the practical parts of Avatamsa thought, without any Chinese influence.

In this way we can say that Korean Buddhist thought, in close connection with Chinese Buddhist thought, has firmly established its own individual identity.

Looking at Korean Buddhist culture and thought, in fact, we find that there are certain attributes which make it very different from the Buddhism found anywhere else. Throughout its long history, Korean Buddhism has developed certain attributes. These distinctive features are divided into the following three areas.

III

Generosity of Accepting Indigenous Culture

In Korea Buddhism has demonstrated the great tolerance, the ability to accept the indigenous culture. When Buddhism was transmitted to the Korean peninsula, it was definitely a foreign religion. However, no Korean person thinks of Buddhism as something foreign today. That is because Buddhism has been perfectly adjusted to the emotions and sentiments of the Korean people and homogeneously mixed with them. Buddhism comprehended the primitive thinking of Shamanism and so developed traditional thinking. Concepts such as karma, cause and occasion, transmigration, etc., had roots fastened deep into the Korean people.

The reciprocal relationship between Buddhism and Korean culture was very peaceful from the beginning. Buddhism developed along the direction of accepting the traditional Korean culture on the one hand, and bestowing new meaning and value upon the culture on the other hand. Accordingly, traditional Korean culture was enhanced in meaning and value by its assimilation with Buddhism. In the process, Buddhism became absorbed and adapted more naturally and harmoniously. It was, of course, because of the naturally tolerant nature of Buddhism. With central teachings regarding selflessness and no feelings of superiority, Buddhism was able to take an inclusive attitude towards Koreans who, in their turn, could properly graft Buddhism on the already existing Korean culture.

Therefore, the absorption of Buddhism into Korea does not mean that there was exclusion of either of the elements. It was a process of mutual union and harmony, in which a homogeneous entity was established by reciprocal negotiation. In that sense, the universal, liberal character of Korean Buddhism is said to present an ideal model to any country or people in solving the problems raised between cultures.

Buddhism in Korea played an important part not only as a religion but also as an embryo of Korean cultural phenomenon as in the cases of China and Japan due to its comprehensive culture-rich characteristics.

IV

Protecting the Nation and the People

Korean Buddhism offered a mental framework and ideology which corresponded to each phase of social development in the historical process. All the Three Kingdoms made Buddhist thought their central ideology. Korean Buddhism, in the process of searching for its religious goals and ideologies, was always concerned with national development and harmony. Moreover, Korean Buddhism played a tangible role in offering a refuge in times of trouble. For this reason, Korean Buddhism is often called 'nation-protecting'

This particular characteristic of Korean Buddhism, as a spiritual tradition contributing to the development of the nation and the society, is found right back at the very beginning of its introduction. When Buddhism was first brought, Korea was changing its political system from a tribal federation to a centralized national system and Buddhism played a major role in solidifying the sovereign power and in establishing a national system. As the centralization became stronger, the quality of 'nation-protecting' became more and more evident. From an ideological point of view, the people were given a brighter outlook and the monks helped to protect the nation in times of invasion. These are only two of the many positive influences which Buddhism had on Korea.

The fact that monks became soldiers and rose up to protect the nation from invasion during the 15th century is a result of the unique position of Korea, one constantly invaded by powerful neighbors. But the protecting role of Buddhism goes much deeper. Faced with any dangerous crisis, Korean Buddhists constantly looked to Buddhism for solutions. They sought an ideology of development in Buddhism and so the monks' army was merely a manifestation of the traditional and positive nature of the nation-protecting status which Buddhism had acquired.

Needless to say the righteousness of this military dimension of Buddhism has been sorely criticized and especially from the point of methodology. But considering the character of the movement and the fact that it was carried out in the light of national development and the welfare of the people, it finally appears to have had a positive influence. For, though it was nationalism or extreme patriotism, it should be recognized as the result of a beneficial ideology of mutual aid between a religion and the nation.

V

Pursuit of Harmonization

The pursuit of harmony and unification were constant focal points of Korean Buddhism. This is the most noteworthy aspect of Korean Buddhism throughout the process of the historical development of Korean Buddhism. Korean Buddhism has pursued the perfect overcoming of any philosophical confrontation between the different ideas and schools of Korean Buddhism and the harmonization of theory and practice. For this reason, Korean Buddhism is often referred as 'Tong-bul-kyo', which means 'whole Buddhist harmonization'.

Such a harmonious characteristic of Korean Buddhism has been developed by all the great Korean Buddhist thinkers and implemented by practical leaders. Among them, Shilla Master Wonhyo's Buddhist thought was the earliest and the most outstanding form of Whole Buddhist Harmonization in the history of Korean Buddhism; it was the starting point and conclusion of the harmonization of Korean Buddhism. His whole thinking is centered on the idea of reconciliation. Through his creative theory, he harmonized the two different types of categories of Buddhist values which had been considered a problem. Also, he brought together the concept of the 'void' of Mādhyamika philosophy and that of 'existence' of Vijüānamātravāda philosophy – a subject of argument in Indian and Chinese studies – in the structure of his concept of the 'One Mind.'

This characteristic of harmonization and unification is also seen in Vijüānamātravāda thought of Master Woncheok and the Avatamsa thought of Euisang. Even more so, we find this dimension in the writings of Master Euicheon whose theory of dual practice of study and meditation aimed at the harmonization of doctrinal theories and actual practice, and so the unification of Meditation and Study which were in great conflict at that time. Chinul's Seon[5] thought is the same.[6] He boldly accepted Study, especially Avatamsa, which had been denied by the Meditation Schools and by that act he brought Meditation and Study together. Once again in the Seon thought of Master Sosan, during the Choson Dynasty when Buddhism was been persecuted, Confucianism, Taoism and Buddhism were brought together. This characteristic of harmonization and unification, though being most distinct, does not only have its meaning and value in the field of Korean Buddhism alone.

These trends of liberality of accepting indigenous culture, nation-protecting, and pursue of harmonization continue today. With 16 centuries of history behind it, Korean Buddhism now has a big responsibility to continue in the same vein. Korean Buddhist thought and culture is the ideological foundation of the Korean people and the driving force behind the development of the country. Today as much as ever, Korean Buddhism is now being strongly urged to once again bring a fresh philosophical ideology and way of practice applicable to modern society.

References

1 The officially transmitted year is regarded as the second year of Goguryo King Sosurim (A.D. 372), as it is since then that native Korean documents are first recorded.

2 According to these two documents, a Chinese Buddhist monk called Jisundorim (A.D. 314-366) from Dong-jin had sent a letter to a Taoist monk in Goguryo.

3 No official historical documents have been found to corroborate the legend concerning the Gaya Kingdom.

4 San-lun refers to the three treatises upon which this sect is based, namely the *Chung-lun*, the *Shih-erh-men-lun*, and the *Pai-lun*, the first two attributed to Nāgārjuna and the third attributed to Āryadeva. The sect was first transmitted to China by the great translator Kumārajïva in the early 5th century.

5 Buddhist meditation in Korea is called 'Seon' or 'Chamseon', which corresponds to Ch'an in China and Zen in Japan.

6 Shilla masters introduced Zen Dharma from various Chinese Zen schools, but they never proclaimed to belong to those schools. Instead, they earlier founded their own or joined the already existing Korean Nine Mountains of Zen and so held on to the Korean Zen tradition. This tendency is also seen in the Zen thought of Master Chinul in the Middle Koryo Period.

Bibliography

1. Bong-choon Lee, "Buddhism from India to Korea", *The History and Culture of Buddhism in Korea*, The Korean Buddhist Research Institute, Seoul, 1993.
2. Yi-beom Won & Byeong-ho Lim, *A History of Korean Buddhist Culture and Some Essays*, Seoul; Jip Moon Dang, 1992.
3. Korean Buddhist Chogye Order, What is Korean Buddhism?, Seoul, 2000.

8

Is *Avisamvādakatva* Inconsistent to *Kṣaṇikatva?*

Raghunath Ghosh

I

The present paper deals with the problem whether the property of being uncontradicted (*avisamvādakatva*) is inconsistent to the phenomenon of momentariness admitted by the Buddhists. One may raise a question that an uncontradicted experience cannot be known within a moment. Hence to admit cognition as uncontradicted is to accept its non-momentary character. In this paper an effort will be made that there is no such contradiction so far as the Buddhist theory is concerned.

II

To the Buddhists the valid cognition (*pramā*) is defined as a cognition corresponding to the reality (*avisamvādakam jñānam)*.[1] The term *samvāda* means one to one correspondence or transparent to the reality. Whatever is in one's cognition must correspond to what really exists in the external world for being a valid cognition. It there is a successful communication between a speaker and a hearer, it is also called *samvāda* in the sense of dialogue. In such case also there is transparency in correspondence. If a hearer understands what the speaker says and the vice-versa, we may describe it as correspondence (*samvāda* or *avisamvāda*). The Buddhists have preferred to the usage of the term—*avisamvādaka* i.e., cognition which does not have an unsuccessful or failing correspondence as found in the case of illusion, doubt etc. The originated cognition capable of apprehending the real object is also the means of cognition (*pramāna*).[2]

To the Buddhists a source of knowledge (*pramāṇa*) is not different from the valid cognition itself (*pramā*), because the valid cognition of an entity depends on its external feature or form. The form which is in an object of valid cognition becomes the source of its knowing and both *pramā* and *pramāṇa* having the same form must be identical. In this case the object of valid cognition is the form of an object, which becomes at the same time the source of it.[3] Moreover, both *pramā* and *pramāṇa* must be originated simultaneously without any temporal gap, as such gap is not permissible in their philosophy due to the acceptance of the theory of momentariness. Hence they are to be taken as non-different. As *pramā* here is different from illusion, doubt etc, the *pramāṇa* is also the same. A valid cognition is the presentation of an object what it really is while illusion represents an object as what it really is not (*atattvānubhava*) e.g. water in mirage etc. In the same way doubt is taken as an uncertain cognition (*anavadhāraṇātmaka-jñāna*), as it bears cognition of uncertain object e.g. a man or a post (*sthāṇnurvā puruṣo veti*). And hence such cognition cannot be taken as a valid one. In other words, this is the general definition of *pramāṇa* given by Dharmakīrti in his *Pramāṇavārttika*. Right cognition is uncontradicted in the sense that it does not mislead one, i.e. an object indicated by the right knowledge or *pramāṇa* in a particular place and a particular time could actually attained by one. In common discussion also an individual is said to be a 'dependable guide' if his informations correspond to the actual state of being *(samvādaka)*. In the like manner, *pramāṇa* is to be understood. *Pramāṇa* only reveals the true nature of an object and it can lead correctly an individual to the attainment of the object. The false cognition, which is not *pramāṇa*, is contradicted by experience. To them the validity of *pramāṇa* cannot be doubted, since the nature of an object as revealed by it is in conformity of the actual order of things. Hence the Buddhists have defined valid cognition as an uncontradicted experience (*avisamvādakajñāna*).

An objection may be raised by the opponents in the following way. A valid cognition remains in an agent *(pramātā)* and an object of the cognition is the thing known *(Prameya)*, which remains outside the *pramātā*. It is not correct to call valid cognition *pramāṇa* if it cannot lead an individual to attain the object i.e. *prameya*. Due to the non-availability of the real object in the practical field (*aprāpakatvāt*) it cannot be said as *pramāṇa*. In reply, the Buddhists are of the opinion that the cognition or valid cognition cannot compel an individual to perform some activity or to attain object compulsorily, because it depends on the agent's will. But with the help of *pramāṇa* he ascertains the exact nature or essential nature of an object as such and such type (*evambhūtamidam vastusvarūpam*), but not otherwise (*nānyathā*). *Pramāṇa* provides an individual with such certainty. If there is any necessity, a person can utilise his valid cognition by way of attaining the object in the external world, otherwise not. One is having certain knowledge about an object which he may encash or may not. If it is utilised, it proves the uncontradictory nature of *pramāṇa*. The generation of the sense of certitude regarding cognition is the mark of *pramāṇa*.[4]

It may again be argued that the fact of unfailing correspondence is confirmed through the real attainment of the object seen (*dṛṣṭārthapāpaṇa*). What is seen or perceived cannot be attained due to the continuous change of the nature of an object as per the theory of momentariness. The external form of an object which is seen is not touched, because the object seen has been lost in the continuous flow of time. How can the validity of cognition be established in terms of its uncontradicted nature ?

The Buddhists reply this problem in the following way. To them it is true that the object seen cannot be attained due to the effect of momentariness. Though a different object is apprehended altogether yet we have a strong and definite cognition (*adhyavasāya*) in the form—'the object which is perceived is apprehended' (*dṛṣtameva prāptam*). It is the case of the attainment of what has been perceived *(pratītaprāpaṇa)*, but not the attainment of the unperceived. When there is the cognition of water in the case of mirage, it is the case of the attainment of the unperceived, because the perceived object is mirage and attained object is water. In fact, there is no capability of attaining the perceived i.e. the real nature of an object (*aprāpaṇayogya*).[5]

The problem does not come to an end here. In fact, whether an object is capable of causing us to attain an object seen earlier or not cannot be determined until its causal efficacy is known (*arthakriyāprāpti*). In other words, whether an object is really water or mirage is known through its causal efficacy i.e. quenching thirst, which is not possible in the same moment. It cannot also be said that the distinction between a valid and an invalid cognition is known at the point of its origination, because the causal efficacy of it cannot be known at this moment. How can it be known as right cognition? In response to the above-mentioned charge the Buddhists argue that, though it is very difficult to know the distinction between valid and invalid cognition at the time of its origination in general, the distinction of one from another can be known through the acquaintance with the specific cognition of the features of the object (*jñānaviśeṣodayāt*). A less intelligent person cannot apprehend the validity or invalidity of cognition of an object at the time of origination due to the absence of the knowledge of its unfailing correspondence (*avisamvādakatva*) or failing correspondence (*visamvādakatva*). Though it is true, the same individual can apprehend the validity of the same through the causal efficacy of an entity, (e.g. water) in the forms of bathing, washing, drinking etc. In the same way, he can know the validity of fire through the perception of burning, cooking etc. or by the emergence of smoke from a distance.

There is another type of man having sharp intellect who can realise the validity of cognition though his keen observation or matured perception (*paṭutara pratyakṣa*). From this it follows that one can know the unfailing character of the cognition or uncontradicted cognition within a moment with the help of one's matured perception—without depending on the fact of its causal efficacy (*na tu arthakriyāprāptyā*).[6]

It may be again be argued that the auditory perception does not enable an individual i.e., hearer to attain the object he knows. If uncontradicted experience is the mark of valid cognition, how is such cognition proved to be valid?

In reply the Buddhists are of the opinion that the validity of cognition lies on the apprehension of the real nature of an object *(arthasvarūpapratīti)*. Such encounter with reality does not always need confirmation through the attainment of the causal efficacy in the external object.[7] This view is subscribed by Dharmakirti also in his *Pramānavārttika* (1.1)-*"Pramānam avisamvādi jñānam arthakriyāsthitiḥ avisamvādanam"* [8]. That is, valid cognition is uncontradicted cognition and uncontradiction means the realisation of causal efficacy in an object. To Dharmakīrti the knowledge of the essential quality of an object is accepted as the causal efficacy. In the case of sound of a word the hearing is the causal efficacy, because the purpose of sound is served if it is heard. In the like manner, the purpose of Sun, Moon, Sky etc. is served if it is seen. The simple act of seeing is their causal efficacy. The essential nature of the object is its causal efficacy (*jñeyasvarūpasamvittiḥ iṣṭā tatra kriyāsthitiḥ*). If such nature of an object is known, it is to be known as valid. This exact nature of the object is its causal efficacy, which is different in different object. Due to the differentiation of the causal efficacy a jar is treated as different from a cloth. When a child looks at the jar, it is not of same type, but it is of different type due to meeting diverse needs. As it serves different purpose in different time, it is called momentary. For this reason the causal efficacy is nothing but the realisation of the true nature of an object *(jneyasvarūpabodha)*.

To the Buddhists a wise man comes to know of an object by means of clearer perception (*paṭutara pratyakṣa*). As soon as it is attained, he comes to know of its causal efficacy at the same moment. But the blunt persons come to know of the causal efficacy of an object through inference. Hence the validity of perception is intrinsic to the Buddhists having clearer perception. But others having less intelligence can know of its validity by other cognition i.e., inference. This is applicable to the persons who fail to ascertain its causal efficacy at the initial moment.[10] Bhāsarvajña puts the Buddhists rejoinder in justifying their position. The Buddhists say that the same *santāna* (continuity), which was perceived, is to be determined (*ya eva santānaḥ, pratyakṣena dṛṣṭah, sa evādhyavasīyate*).[11] Dharmottara has explained it in a clearer manner. To him the same *santāna* of existence which is to be determined (*adhyavaseya*) as non-difference is the object of action of fulfilling a human purpose.[12]

III

From the above we may draw the conclusion that Dharmakīrti and others believe that if perception is 'perfect', it can reveal both the object and its causal efficacy within a single moment. In this connection a question may be raised: how do the revelation of the object and its causal efficacy arise within a single moment? In normal viewing the object is known first and then its causal efficacy. If it is a habitual knowledge (*abhyāsadaśotpanna jñāna*), the cognition of an object may quickly be followed by its causal efficacy, which may be described as '*Śatapatrabhedanyāya*'. Just as a pin can prick hundred of petals, a particular cognition of an object may be followed by its causal efficacy swiftly. However minutest it may be there has to be accepted a temporal gap. In the same way, the thesis that the same *santāna*, which is perceived, is to be determined can be rejected. Bhāsarvajüa rejects this in the above-mentioned manner. To him without the moment (*kṣaṇa*) there is no *santāna* in reality (*kṣaṇavyatirekena santānasyāpi vastuto'sambhavāt*).[13] If there is at all any *santāna*, it is to be taken as existing in different moment.[14]

It is to be pondered how do the Buddhists understand by the word-*paṭutara pratyakṣa* (clearer or matured perception)? They have opined in favour of two types of perception - one by the wise persons and another by the blunts. The above-mentioned objections may be raised by the second category of people. So far as the former is concerned, they have clearer perception (*paṭutara pratyaksa*). Is it a normal viewing? I thing it is a kind of *samyagdṛṣṭi* (right vision) which is connected with our intuition (*prajñā*). This type of perception being intuitive in character can reveal both the object and its causal efficacy within a moment just like a flash of light. Without accepting a transcendental or *yogic* element in viewing the Buddhists position it cannot be explained. If an individual possesses such vision, he will have vision to see the object and its causal efficacy within a moment, because it is a kind of subtle perception revealing both. The momentary nature of an entity is to be understood by intuitive introspection *(samvedana)*. For, the intuitive introspection indicates that sensation is only a 'momentary flash' and that it is nothing but the reflex of a momentary thing. What a momentary sensation grasps is only the thing that corresponds to the sensation. The sensation of a blue colour apprehends the blue colour and the present moment, but not that which precedes or follows before or after. The external objects are nothing but sense data and corresponding sensation confined in the single moment. This pure sensation points to the instantaneous nature of elements.[15] The entities, even held to be momentary cannot exercise causal efficacy whether in succession or in simultaneity and hence it is just a futile attempt to take refuge in the doctrine of continual flux for them.[16]

In reply Śāntarakṣita says that though several factors of production of the sprout do not have any action on one another at the initial stage or at any stage of production yet they cooperate with each other in the matter of producing a 'self-same effect'. For though they do not have mutual interaction, they are not the same or similar entities as before, they, on each one of them, though momentary, having derived its peculiar causal efficiency from its own proper cause, severally contribute to the production of the second set of efficient factors.[17] The idea behind all that has been said above is that without the help of the subsidiaries the fact of the sprout arising out of seed cannot be accounted for. But the difficulty is that, under the doctrine of momentariness, there is no room for mutual assistance amongst the several factors involved in the production of the sprout. It is contended that the seed and all other factors severally derive their causal efficacies from the proper causes of their own. And distinct causal entities thus born of these factors at the second stage are severally endowed with the efficacy to bring out the ultimate cause viz, the sprout.

What follows, therefore, is that in the event of each being causally efficient to produce the ultimate effect, there should be no room for so many factors getting involved in the process. In order to understand this one should have a right vision.

Hence a person having such right vision has matured perception *(paṭutarapratyaksa),* which can reveal both the object and its causal efficacy within a single moment. Hence there is no inconsistency in their thought.

References

1 *Bauddhatarkabhāṣā* of Mokṣākaragupta, Edited by Dr. Raghunath Giri, Prachya Prakashan, Varanasi, 1969, p. 2. Henceforth-*Tarkabhāṣā.*

Nyāyabindu of Dharmakīrti, Edted by Mrinal Kanti Gangopadhyaya, Indian Studies, Calcutta, 1971, p.4.

2 *Tarkabhāṣā,* p. 2.

3 *Ibid.*, p.1.

4 *Ibid.*, pp. 2-3.

5 *Ibid.*, p.5.

6 *Ibid.*, pp.4-5.

7 *Ibid.*, p.5

8 *Pramāṇavārttika*-1/1.

9 *Ibid.*

10 *Ibid.*, p. 6.

11 *Nyāyabhūṣaṇa*, 55/20-21, Edited by Swami Yogindrananada, Varanasi, 1968.

12 *Pramāṇaviniścayatīkā* by Dharmottara in Tibetan, p. 5727.

13 *Nyāyabhūṣaṇa*, 57/21-58, 3.

14 Shoryu Katsura: *Dharmakīrti's thought and Its impact on Indian and Tibetan Philosophy*, Wien, 1999, pp. 450-455.

15 Stcherbatsky: *Buddhist Logic*, Vol.1, p. 87, Munshiram Manoharlal, New Delhi, 1984.

16 *Tattvasamgrahapañjikā,* Verse No. 82, Edited by B. Bhattacharya, Gaekwad Oriental Series, Gaekwad, 1925.

17 *Ibid.*, Verse nos.86-87

9

My Maitreya Buddha, The Late Professor Hajime Nakamura

Yong-kil Cho

I

I would like to offer boundless respect and gratitude to the spirit of Professor Hajime Nakamura. My name is Yong-kil Cho and as a professor I am teaching early Buddhist ideas at Dongguk University, one of Buddhist universities in Seoul, Korea.

My recognition of Professor Nakamura Hajime's noble personality and endless love for Buddha has been unchanged for 35 years. I could understand the early Buddhist ideas broadly transcending the times, absolutely thanks to two teachers, Korean Dong-hwa Kim and Japanese Nakamura Hajime.

Overwhelmed by Mahāyāna Buddhism and Zen Buddhism, primitive Korean Buddhism was not appreciated rightly. Through Dong-hwa Kim's primitive Buddhism considerably hard to understand at that time I could grasp only its outline as original Buddhism. In the meanwhile, I came to read *Primitive Buddhism: its Ideas and Life* published in March 1970 by Nakamura and understood Buddhism easily through both his background explanation of Buddha's contemporary times approaching historical truth and his teaching of religious background, which had been thought to be very difficult.

His wide analysis and explanation of races, nations and cities in India as a social basis, formation and change of caste and all the thoughts of various philosophers gave me a great chance to face up to the reality of living in the 20th and 21st centuries. And then it made me awakened to transcend times and history. Under the American influence of Catholicism or Christianity, which regarded Śākyamuni Buddha as a mythicized and mystified object, or even shaman, superstition, or idol, not as a person who had existed in history, in Korea general circumstances of Buddhism got criticized socially and nationally. Its situation was very different from Japan's. In other words, unlike Korea, Japan continued to develop inherited history and society without a radical change in ruler or ruling group.

It can be said that Nakamura Hajime's teaching and review on Śākyamuni Buddha's humanity, historicity, and social point of view were the beginning of the newest discovery in East Asian countries like Japan and China, especially in Korea where the radical change took place. That is because it was a work to take away opposing aspects of Hīnayāna and Mahāyāna which were divided, separated and furthermore bisected in the stream of times. Nakamura who explored 8 sacred places for Buddhist pilgrims through excavating the Buddhist relics by many scholars and showed the dignity of Śākyamuni, Gautama-Siddhārtha to this world, Korean, Japanese and world Buddhism, can be said rightly to make a new Maitreya Buddha appear in this world. He is also another Maitreya Buddha to me.

I believe that the objective evaluation of Śākyamuni's character and philosophy not as a mythical god or a mysterious person but as a person who had existed in this world was a strong foundation for Mahāyāna Buddhism to uplift nobility of all the lives by spreading completeness of Buddha-nature universally. It was Nakamura who opened a way for Buddhism to be distinguished in the world history of thought beyond the limit of the East and the West. In doing so, he focused on original Buddhism in confusion of a theory that Mahāyāna Buddhism is not Buddhism and overcame the boundaries of Southeast Asia as well as Japan, China, and Korea. Not only do his lifetime masterpieces like *History of Ancient India* (I,II), *Gautama Buddha* (Life of Śākyamuni), *Establishment of*

Primitive Buddhism, *Thought of Primitive Buddhism* (I,II), and *Morality of the Life in Primitive Buddhism* have a great influence on my basic thought of general Buddhism, but also his original teaching is delivered to many people that I am instructing. Therefore, the fact that Buddha's mind is handed down to his mind, his mind to me and then to Korean people is an evidence that he lives forever.

He wrote down at a preface to *Primitive Buddhism: its Ideas and Life* in March 1970, "I'll be happy if ideas and morality in life of simple and realistic primitive Buddhism is known to general people by going back to the origin of a spirit flowing consistently at the bottom of the whole history of Buddhism." His words take place as a unforgettable guiding principle for all human beings as well as for Japanese and Korean people.

II

As an opinion on the birth and working period of Śākyamuni, Nakamura's clear explanation of young Gautama's seeking after truth and preaching, the later part of his life, his entering *Nirvāṇa*, and finally compilation of *sūtra* is an important guideline to younger scholars. He arranged a basic standpoint of primitive Buddhism as a theoretical basis on which Buddhism could be contended to be the most distinguished philosophical system among many conflicting theories in the world.

He points out that various philosophical theories are conflicting and competing that are essentially incompatible in human society. Every philosopher contends that only his theory is an absolute truth and other philosophies are false and wrong. All the philosophies are comparative and unilateral in that they are conflicting and competing one another. He also points out clearly that any philosophical theory can not avoid a fate of comparativeness. He thinks that Gautama Buddha observed closely this fatal contradiction deeply rooted in the basic structure of man's philosophical thinking.

He points out that this aspect is discussed repeatedly in early Buddhist *sūtra*. "Scholars in this world hold fast to their own views and discuss things in many ways, adhering to different opinions and professing themselves to be masters. A person who knows this is aware of a truth. A person who criticizes this is not perfect yet."(Sn.818).

The philosophers contend that only their theories are absolutely true and perfect, but others are false. "He preaches only his theory has purity but many other theories don't have it. Like this, those who preach different theories are tenacious to adhere to their ways firmly"(Sn.892). "The opinion said to be a truth or a fact by some people is said to be false or vain. Like this, they argue with different and tenacious opinions. Why do many masters say the same thing?"(Sn.883)

"Some people say a teaching is the best, but others say the same teaching is mean and poor. Which one is true? They call themselves persons who reach a truth, saying their teachings are perfect but the others are mean and poor. They argue with different and tenacious opinions, and each of them insists that his hypothesis is a truth. If a teaching is treated poorly because of others' criticism, there will be no excellent one out of many teachings. That's because all the people in the world think highly of their own theories and preach other teachings are poor."(Sn.903-905).

They themselves think their philosophical theories are perfect and admit themselves to be 'perfect persons' in mind. When it comes to a basis of their standpoints, they are necessarily the same but have dispute in common. He said, "Regardless of any opinions, inherited knowledge, precepts, pledges, or thoughts, they say gladly 'Objectors are fools and don't master a truth', depending on those things, ignoring other thoughts and justifying their theories"(Sn.887). But, "Truth is one and there isn't the second truth"(Sn.884). Which one on earth is true? Those who are seeking a solution to metaphysical problems can't help being embarrassed with this fact. "They dispute with different and tenacious opinions and say 'Others are fools and they aren't the persons who master a truth." All of them think and say they are the right ones who master the truth, yet who are saying a truth?"(Sn.879)

III

Gautama Buddha was critiçal that philosophers argue with one another "because they are indulged in their opinions and polluted." "How can a person, who is caught with desire because of greed, overcome his opinion?"(Sn.781)

All the philosophers are caught with their own theories. "Some of many schools besides Buddhism depend on all the philosophical opinions"(Therig.184). However, they are all wrong.

"They don't know dharma." Since they argue about the metaphysical problems that can't be solved with man's thinking, they get into a firm tenacity. As a result of it, they themselves lose their ways as men and commit vice unwillingly. "They discuss in their strong ways, so who can be thought to be foolish out of them? If one preaches the other teachings are foolish and they aren't pure, He will bring about strong tenacity himself"(Sn.893). He points out that a person can't reach an ultimate goal of Vimutti with this dispute.

Gautama thought that argument is meaningless and hoped not to join it. His teaching transcends all the philosophical opinions. Therefore, he is said to 'transcend a variety of arguments' or he keeps away from the arguments. He is in a position that "If man throw away all the (philosophical) conclusions, he never sticks to anything in the world."(Sn.894)

Since his goal is to 'wipe off wickedness', he does not try to establish a certain metaphysical theory. "To me, there is nothing like 'I'm preaching the following'. While I certainly knew tenacity for various things is tenacity itself and reflected without being stubborn despite faults of many opinions, I saw Nirvana in me"(Sn.837).

Accordingly, early Buddhism refused to answer the metaphysical problems disputed at that time. He who listened to the famous figuration of a poisoned arrow and realized its meaning is often compared to a doctor (MN. NO.63, Vol.I°, pp.429-430, *Majjhima-nikāya* vol. 16, Cula Malunka Sutta.). According to Buddha, man is suffering from a mental disease and the role of Buddha himself is that of a doctor.

IV

Through above mentioned examinations, Nakamura presents two outstanding characteristics in early Buddhism. First, do not discuss meaningless and unnecessary matters.

Second, we should not make an argument if we do not have an obvious and definite basis. He teaches that we can enter Nirvana at last, by getting rid of delusions. It encourages reasonable thinking.

Nakamura's points displayed on this basis of it open new horizons of Buddhism reborn into realistic Buddhism, practical Buddhism, and Buddhism in life covering all the religions, philosophies, and ethics in the 20th and the 21st centuries, which Buddha originally had aimed at. He rightly defined the concepts of *duḥkṇa*, *anitya, anātman,* non-self, *nirvāṇa*, and *samsāra*, and empathized that man should be equipped with quality of generosity and refinement through boundless compassion. He suggested an alternative for modern people to relieve uneasiness, solitude, *kleśa*, and delusion.

He showed the early religious body in detail, opened endless horizons of ethical and moral Buddhism in life, and set up a place for Buddhism as a morality in life. It was he who taught to solve such difficult problems easily in the present world as sexual morality and marriage, morality of married couple, man and wife, morality of family, relatives, parents, children, and relations between labor and capital. It was he, an incarnate Maitreya in this world who established practical Buddhism in life of morality, settling philosophical and religious problems like morality of monk, morality of friend, dignity of ascetic spiritual world, economical idea of the middle way, and problem of production.

Any statement can not describe Nakamura's moral influence upon this world. I, Professor Yong-kil Cho from Korea, promise to spread the thought of Nakamura, who succeeded to Buddha's wisdom, with all my heart. Also, I hope him to come again in a light and light up the global village of *avidyā* as Buddha's light was emitted in the world.

My forever Maitreya! I faithfully depend on Maitreya Mahāsattva!

10

Tribute to Late Professor Hajime Nakamura

(living in a physical world, he blossomed in a symbolic universe)

Lokesh Chandra

Friendship with Professor Hajime Nakamura extends to two generations, to my father and me. My father Raghu Vira used to teach Japanese in 1935 to Indians, the British thought he was a Japanese agent, and they imprisoned him. This stirred the Japanese intellectuals, besides the Buddhist scholars of Japan, who wondered why an Indian had been imprisoned for teaching Japanese. This made him so famous throughout the intelligentsia of Japan that many of the leading Japanese scholars, not only of Buddhism, but of several other disciplines, came to be his friends. Nakamura happened to be one. When once he came to Delhi and was to address a Conference in which the-then Vice-President Radhakrishnan was to preside. He came to my father and asked him the language in which he should speak. My father said, of course, Sanskrit. Nakamura spoke in Sanskrit. Radhakrishnan spoke in English. It was the beginning of a deep friendship between Nakamura and Radhakrishnan. Radhakrishanan realized for the first time, that very few European scholars could speak Sanskrit.

Nakamura was one of the rare East Asian scholars who could speak and write Sanskrit and one of his works in on "Modern Sanskrit", as to how it has evolved over the last sixty years. I used to send him Sanskrit newspapers, Sanskrit magazines and modern Sanskrit writings. His interest was not only classical Sanskrit and Buddhist Sanskrit, but contemporary Sanskrit as well. I went to Japan for the first time in 1970. Nakamura came to receive me at the hotel. I said: 'I want to visit your house'. He said: 'yes, welcome'. 'How should I come to your residence?' He used to live far away from the city of Tokyo. He said: 'I will come to fetch you'. He came. We were coming down the lift, it was so silent. I said: 'Professor Nakamura, Zen Buddhism has invaded the lift. You have silent monks and noiseless machines.' He thought that I am a bit of a naughty person. When we reached his residence, he put me on a very small chair in the shape of a palm of the hand. 'Professor, what is this chair?' He said: 'this is the hand of Lord Śākyamuni'. 'Why do you put me in Lord Śākyamuni's hand?' He said: 'once Hanumāna was creating uproar in Heaven. Lord Buddha said: 'I hold you in my palm so that you won't be naughty; you won't create havoc'. I asked Nakamura: 'Am I the naughty Hanumāna?'. He was silent. In this way Nakamura was referring to a great event in Chinese Buddhist history: the visit of Hsuan-tsang to India. He is supposed to have been accompanied by a monkey who was his constant companion. In the popular mind, in the psycho-history of the Buddhist tradition in East Asia, the monkey is a venerable companion of the Chinese pilgrim-scholar. When seated, Nakamura asked me: 'How do you see Japan?' I said: 'As a child in 1936, the first lesson that I read in Japanese was *"saita, saita, sakura ga saita"*, (the cherry blossoms have blossomed, they are blossoming). They represent *anityatā* or impermanence. They are the supreme Void and at the same time they are enshrined in Japanese painting, and a vast amount of Japanese poetry has been written on them. It is the *paramitā,* the perfection of Japanese culture. Japan is not 'sword and chrysanthemum', but in it are three categories. They are the three Buddhist concepts of *śunyatā, anityatā* and *paramitā*. Thus began our conversation, sitting on the Hanumāna chair: 'Professor Nakamura, if I am Hanumāna, you are Hsuan-tsang. I want to go inside and see your library. Do you have a Japanese book on Buddhist logic.'

He showed me a huge commentary on Buddhist logic. I had the feeling that Buddhist logic was not studied in the East Asian languages. For the first time I saw such a commentary, was so delighted that I requested Nakamura to translate it because it could have a bearing on the linguistic culture of the East Asian people.

Nakamura asked me another question as to why Indian concepts are negative like non-violence, non-alignment? The Monkey had to answer the questions of the great Chinese scholar-pilgrim. I was still on the monkey chair, and the conversation was on. 'Professor Nakamura whether they are negations or whether they are super-positives is a matter of discussion. Perhaps, these negations come from the Buddhist tradition. In the Mūla-mādhyamaka-kārikā of Nāgārjuna the very first stanza speaks of the eight negations. The negatives of contemporary India can come from this tradition. The Mūla-mādhyamaka-kārikā begins:

neither non-extinction nor non-origination,

neither non-ephermeral nor non-permanence,

neither non-identity, nor non-differentiation,

neither non-coming into being nor non-going out of being.

These eight categories on which inter-dependent origination is based are negatives. We have to consider as to who contributes to the negative conceptualizations of India's contemporary polity. Negative expressions like non-alignment and non-violence are parallel to the Buddhist philosophic formulations where Buddha does not accept the permanent, the eternal, the *śāsvata,* but at the same time he does not accept the ephemeral. He believes in the non-ephemeral and the non-eternal.

Then we were discussing *ahimsā*. Nakamura asked me 'how do you explain *ahimsā*?' I said: 'we have two words: *śakti* and *himsā; śakti* is power, *himsā* is violence. Buddhism went to China on horses. The Chinese saw these horses not only as mounts of the monks, but they envisioned them as power and virtue. The horses went to the imperial cavalry of the Han Emperors, and the monks to the monasteries. In

China, Buddhism was an expression both of power and virtue. For the first time, power and virtue became convergent in the political thought of China. The Buddhist tradition distinguishes between power and violence. Violence is with vice, power is with virtue. In the Indo-centric traditions there is no God or Goddess of Non-violence, but the Hindu tradition has *Śakti* the Goddess of Power. Power and Virtue coexist with *Ahimsā*.

The foundation of the Japanese state was linked to Buddhism during the period of Shotoku Taishi. Buddhism did not tolerate foreign intervention. Shintoism stepped into the political conceptualization of Japan, when the 'black ships' invaded Japan at the end of the 18th century under Commodore Perry. Shintoism was used to replace Buddhism. We had a long discussion, as Nakamura besides being a great scholar of Buddhism was also a contemporary person. Nakamura was a link between India and the Japanese intelligentsia.

His contribution to Buddhism is tremendous. The role of Buddhism as a polycentric expression of the human mind can have global implications. His understanding of the deeper processes of Hindu-Buddhist tradition becomes crucial in our 21st century, when we seek new horizons. Frontiers are fast fading out. The horizons are important, as have to share. It is a world which is moving towards a shared rather than a unified earth. We have to be citizens of this earth sharing with each other. Here Nakamura's work becomes crucial, to comprehend how sharing has taken place in different periods of history between various countries.

The interaction of Buddhism with Confucianism, Taoism, and Hinduism, as well as the role of Upaniṣadic thought in the evolution of Buddhism evoked lively discussions with Nakamura. When he was working on pre-Śankara Vedānta, writing his Japanese text, we had long discussions. I would go to him in the evenings or he would come to the hotel to discuss these questions. He was a great mind not only in the convergences, but also in divergences. The divergences are important because they characterize different nationalities, different periods of history, and territorial imperatives have a role to play. Talking of universalism, we have to keep in mind territorial distinctions, expressed in modern parlance as globalization and localization. Nakamura's work is classical and contemporary at the same time and that is why we celebrate him today. There are rare insights in the long historic traditions of Asia of sharing and also of seeing not only convergences but also conflicts, and in them we might find a new vision for a world which is gradually moving into a new direction that is coming closer to Asian thought. Asia does not propagate its ideals, but the West itself is studying the East to understand how Asia has managed its affairs for the last five thousand years. The Chinese State has existed for five thousand years, the Japanese State has been in existence for two thousand five hundred years, and of course, we are also an ancient nation. All these nations have to pool their experiences to give a bright and brilliant future and here Nakamura comes in. Hajime means the *Ādi* or *Ādya*. Like the *Ādya Śankarācārya* he is *Ādya Nakamura*.

My tributes to Nakamura who loved India as much as his own country. When I first met him in Japan in 1970, he had established the Eastern Institute, and took me to bless the Institute. I said: 'how can I bless the Institute in your presence? You are my senior'. He said: 'you come from India; you have to bless it'. I asked him 'why have you established this Institute'. As Miki pointed out the students at the routine institutions were in turmoil; research and thought could not flourish in these turbulences. He had to create a place of silence. Buddhist thought developed in remote forests. In Zen paintings, we see mountains and streams (*sansui*) where there is nothing of material life, they all transcend materiality. His Eastern Institute is the new *sansui* of the mind.

He loved Buddhism in a deep way. He was one of the great scholars of his generation who saw in Buddhism the 'Being' of his country. He said: 'India is the mother of our culture and we are the daughter of India, so far as culture is concerned.' All his life he strove to see that Sanskrit studies flourish. He loved to speak Sanskrit and used to read Sanskrit journals. I was sending him a number of these journals. Ultimately he wrote a book on contemporary Sanskrit vocabulary and grammar published by Motilal Banarsidass from Delhi. Besides his academic pursuits, he was keen that India and Japan collaborate to understand each other's culture. He came here a number of times. From his general ambience, I could sense that he regretted that we do not study Japanese culture in India, nor Japanese Buddhism. Had we studied, we might have enriched the understanding of Japanese Buddhism itself.

Some times we would sit down and read a Sanskrit text of Buddhism. For example, we read the first chapter of The Lotus Sūtra. He was interested in my understanding of this Sūtra, with my background of Hinduism and Buddhism, because of his interest in the relationship between Upaniṣads and Buddhist thought in its original form, or what he called Original Buddhism, This Seminar fulfils one of his wishes wherein we understand the great contributions of Nakamura, while on the other hand, we hope that a Nakamura Chair for Buddhist Studies will be established for the study of Japanese Buddhism. To understand the Upaniṣadic tradition, some times it becomes important to look into Chinese, Japanese, and Korean scholarship on Buddhist thought for the last two millennia. I used to say to Nakamura: 'we sent a bride to you and you have adorned her with such grace. See the Buddhist paintings and sculptures. She was a tiny girl, now she is a charming lady'. He would smile. I said: 'what you have done to Buddhism is beyond our comprehension, and what you are personally contributing to the understanding of Buddhism is again of magnitude. You are understanding Buddhism not in isolation but in the total context of Upaniṣadic thought. Upaniṣ adic thought was primarily a concern of the kṣatriyas, who depart from *karmakāṇḍa* and go deep into *jñānakāṇḍa*. Lord Buddha was a kṣatriya. Nakamura has pointed out the role of Upaniṣads in the early formation of Buddhism. This Seminar brings to the forefront India's understanding of the contribution of Japanese scholarship to their own tradition as well as to our tradition.

We have looked too much to the West and too little to the East. Language is a barrier. We have to overcome this communication gap. Many Indians are studying Chinese, Japanese and Korean. It is time that we look deeply into the classical traditions of Japan. We celebrate Nakamura as an eminent Buddhist scholar, and we admire him as a prominent Japanese intellectual. He was close to the Japanese Imperial family. The Emperor and Empress sent special flowers at his funeral ceremonies. He straddles across the Asian mindscape as a towering figure and summons us to look once again to our neighbours. Whenever I met him, I was reminded of poet Saigyo 'Had I not been told, never would I have known that hidden deep within the root lies a flower.'

Nakamura was the roots and the flower. Buddhism originated in India, but we have lost it. Today we seek the roots and their flowering in the country of Nakamura, with his incredible simplicity and spontaneity. He was the eyes of culture. I used to point out 'ours is a culture of the mind, and yours is a culture of the eyes and the hands. Whatever you create is done with sensitive beauty. You have given to Buddhism a new persona, a new life, a life so poetic and so artistic'. Nakamura's memory is part of that noble tradition. Bodhisena went to Japan, but very few Japanese came to India in ancient times. From the writings of Takakusu, we may surmise that one or two Japanese could have come in ancient times. The way they describe India is very realistic, this cannot be done just on hearsay. Nakamura continued the tradition of great Chinese scholars, like Fa-hsien, Hsuan-tsang and I-tsing who brought luster to the inter-cultural contacts between India and East Asia.

I will always remember Nakamura for all the kindness that he showed me in Japan. Whenever I went to Japan, he would come with a big board with my name. I had no problem in finding him. His affection lives so long as I live. He will be in the Ganga by his ashes. An year ago a Japanese lady passed away, her ashes were brought for being immersed into the Ganga by her sister. She said, "I want to put these ashes into the Ganga, please bless them." I recited the Buddhist Dhāraṇi of Usnisavijaya, the very first Dhāraṇi that was used by Shotoku Taishi.

The role of Sarnath is important in the life of the Japanese. One day Prime Minister Mrs. Indira Gandhi sent a Japanese to me. He had got a stone from Sarnath. He had asked our Prime Minister: 'did Lord Buddha's feet touch this stone?' Mrs. Gandhi was moved by this question. She directed him to me. He came, and would not sit, but repeated the question. I said: 'yes, Lord Buddha's feet must have touched this stone because you have picked it up. There is a connection between you and the stone'. Without waiting, he ran away from my place. I did not get his card, which is unusual for a Japanese. He was delighted like a child. The same sentiments must have been in the mind of Nakamura, when he saw the great image of Sarnath. It is here that the Dharma was declared, the sanctum of *Dharma-cakra-pravartana*, the most sacred spot of the Buddhist world. His photograph with this image is evocative spontaneity. When we pay him homage, we are paying tribute to the last fifteen hundred years of our contacts with Japan, as we are uplifted in earthly events and winged into a spiritual order.

11

The Late Professor Hajime Nakamura's Works in Japanese

Sengaku Mayeda

It is a real pleasure and honour for me to have been given this opportunity to participate in this International Seminar and talk about the Late Professor Hajime Nakamura's Works in Japanese.

I. Brief Life of Nakamura

Our esteemed Guru, Nakamura, was born on November 28, 1912 in Matsue City in the western part of Japan. In the following year his family moved to Tokyo. In 1936 he graduated from the Department of Indian Philosophy and Sanskrit Literature in the Faculty of Letters, the University of Tokyo. In 1943 at an exceptionally young age he was appointed Associate Professor at the same university and in 1954 promoted to full Professorship. From 1964 to 1966 he served as Dean of the Faculty of Letters. In March 1973, having reached the mandatory retirement age, he left the University of Tokyo. In the same year he was appointed Professor Emeritus of the University of Tokyo, and from 1984 he was a member of the Japan Academy.

Now, four and a half years have already passed since Nakamura peacefully breathed his last at 10:45 AM on October 10, 1999 at the age of 86, surrounded by all his children and under the tender care of his wife Mrs. Rakuko Nakamura, a medical doctor.

Even though he eventually became bed-ridden and was reduced to a condition where he could not utter even a word, he would occasionally raise the wrist of his right hand a little, and when provided with a magic pen his hand moved automatically as though writing a document on a piece of paper. It seemed that his right hand remembered the habit of writing he had acquired all through his life until his very last moment. Without his being aware, the right hand would move spontaneously. With that single right hand Nakamura turned out more than 1000 books and articles both in Japanese and in the European languages, (those written in European languages numbering more than 200). He was indeed an author of unprecedented greatness, and here I can touch upon no more than a small segment of his achievement.

II. Nakamura's field of research

Nakamura's field of research was exceedingly vast, encompassing Indian philosophy, Buddhist studies, historical studies, Japanese thought, comparative thought, etc., with reference not only to Japan, India, China, Europe and America but also extending to the Eurasian continent. Timewise his scholarship also stretched from the ancient to the modern. Moreover, with regard to every field, he undertook research that was novel, original, and pioneering, and the number and quantity of his publications were astonishingly large.

The scholastic world of Nakamura sprouted with vigor and continued to expand boundlessly like a banyan tree that granted people respite and tranquility. The banyan tree possesses numerous enormous trunks, which have their roots firmly embedded in the soil, and at a casual glance one gets the impression that each trunk is an individual tree.

There is a book entitled "*The World of Nakamura Hajime*" (Seidosha,1985). This book which was published when Nakamura was 72 years old, was jointly authored by 5 specialists in 5 different trunks of the banyan tree, i.e. (1) comparative philosophy, (2) Indian philosophy, (3) Early Buddhism, (4) Mahāyāna Buddhism, and (5) Japanese Thought. The contributors were H. Mineshima, specialist in comparative philosophy, S. Mayeda, myself, specialist in Indian philosophy, J. Abe, specialist in Early Buddhism, Sh. Kawasaki, in Mahāyāna Buddhism, F. Sueki, in Japanese Thoughts. Even these five scholars are not enough to cover the entire range of Prof. Nakamura's scholarship. They could not deal with the history of world philosophy, Indian and Western logic, Indian and Buddhist arts, and the like.

In the present volume five Japanese scholars discuss Nakamura's contributions to the studies in the 5 fields only. (1) Nara discusses Nakamura's contributions to the study of Buddhism, (2) Yajima to the study of Jainism, (3) Motegi to the study of Sāmkhya, (4) Hino to the study of Vedānta, and (5) Wada to the study of logic. They have been able to touch only upon small tips of the gigantic iceberg.

However, upon closer observation one notices that all the trees constitute one immense cosmos-like formation, with a single tree in the center constituting the axis and all the others securely attached to it. In the case of Nakamura, I personally am of the opinion that the tree that constituted the central axis, was none other than Indian philosophy.

III. The Starting Point of His Scholarship

With the above in mind, among his many scholastic achievements we have first of all to mention *A History of Early Vedānta Philosophy* written in Japanese. It was with this doctoral dissertation that he started his career as an established scholar of the 20th century in the field of Indian Philosophy.

This doctoral dissertation was submitted to the University of Tokyo in 1942 and published by the Iwanami Shoten Publishing Co., Tokyo, 1943-56 in 4 bulky volumes. It was a philological, historical, and philosophical reconstruction of the history of nearly a thousand years of pre-Śankaran Vedāntic philosophy, which was until then almost entirely unknown. In 1957 this doctoral dissertation, which is in fact an epoch-making research earned him the imperial award of the Japan Academy, the highest award given to scholars in Japan.

Through the efforts of the late Professor D. H. Ḣ. Ingalls, Harvard University, U.S.A. he was able to obtain some financial support from the Enchin Research Center of Harvard University. Thereupon, in 1967 he began the English translation of the work, and finally in 1982 the first volume was published under the title, A History of Early Vedānta Philosophy, Part I, tr. by Trevor Leggett, Sengaku Mayeda,

Taitetz Unno, and others (Delhi.: Motilal Banarasidass). It was very regrettable that Part II was published two years after his death as The Dr. Nakamura Hajime 2nd Anniversary Special Issue of the Toho, the Journal of the Eastern Institute, in Tokyo in 2001; I said "regrettable" for he was very eager to see its publication while he was on his sick bed.

To these four volumes of *A History of Early Vedānta Philosophy*, The Thought of Śankara, which is still in Japanese only, was added as a fifth volume in 850 pages by Nakamura himself in 1989, thus completing the five volumes of the series entitled Indian Philosophical Thought in more than 3000 pages in total. These 5 volumes were in fact the basis of the further development of Nakamura's scholarship.

IV. The Authorized Edition of *The Selected Works of Hajime Nakamura*

A. Outline of the History of Indian Thought (The First 32 Volumes)

It was in July 1999, three months prior to his death, when the authorized edition of *The Selected Works of Hajime Nakamura* (Shunjusha) was finally completed. This series consists of 32 volumes and additional 8 volumes which together make up a total of 40 volumes. Here, one might be able to view this entire body of selected works as sequel to the series mentioned above and Nakamura regards the first 32 volumes as his Outline of the History of Indian Thought.

It is really regrettable to us that *The Selected Works of Hajime Nakamura* in 40 volumes is entirely in Japanese and that these important contributions of Nakamura to Indian philosophy and culture are not well known to Indian scholars. I introduced and explained the contents of each volume of the Selected Works to Indian scholars on the two occasions of the birth centenary of T.R.V. Murti held in Varanasi in December, 2003 and the 6th Indo-Japanese Symposium on "Fifty Years of India-Japan Relations" held in New Delhi in January, 2003 for academic exchange between India and Japan by the Indian Council of Social Science Research, which is the nodal agency of Indo-Japan Academic Exchange Committee of India. To my great pleasure, S.R. Bhatt was a member of the participants in the Symposium.

In addition to them, *The Grand Comprehensive Dictionary of Buddhist Terms: Enlarged and Revised Edition* in 4 volumes, *The Illustrated Dictionary of Buddhist Terms* in 1 volume and *The Structure of Logic* in 2 volumes show what superhuman contribution the late Nakamura made to philosophy and culture of the world as well as of India.

First of all, I would like to briefly explain *The Selected Works of Hajime Nakamura* in 40 volumes.

The Introduction

The first four volumes of these *Selected Works* include those which propelled Nakamura into international prominence, namely *Ways of Thinking of Eastern Peoples* (Tokyo: Misuzushobo, 1949), which was first got translated into English by the UNESCO in 1960 and later as *Ways of Thinking of Eastern Peoples: India, China, Tibet, Japan* (Honolulu: East-West Center Press, 1964). I still remember clearly hearing a male announcer commenting the character and ways of thinking of the Chinese people, quoting the name of Nakamura, during the Indo-China War in 1962, when I first visited India.

According to Nakamura these works play the role of an introduction to the entire series, newly including in the fourth volume the section entitled "Ways of Thinking of the Korean People" which until then was missing.

Volumes 5 to 7 are three works on the ancient history of India and make up the introduction to what follows, the main discourse. This fact reveals his intellectual perspective which sees the importance of Indian history in the formation of Indian thought.

The Outline of Indian Philosophy

The remaining volumes 8 to 32 are distributed in accordance with the historical evolution of Indian thought. Hence, volumes 8 and 9 are dedicated to a detailed exposition of thoughts as seen in the 4 Samhitās and the Upaniṣads. In volume 10, the teachings of the anti-Vedic independent thinkers (*śramaṇa*) who appeared in the 6th and the 5th century B.C.E. has been expounded upon, including the teachings of the well known Jainas.

The volumes 11 to 18 contain results of Nakamura's many years of energetic research in early Buddhism based on a solid methodology. Volume 19 is concerned with the exchange of thoughts between India and western world, based upon the Milindapañha in Pali and Chinese.

The next 4 volumes, from volumes 20 to 23, deal with Mahāyāna Buddhism. The four volumes that comprise volumes 24 to 29 of the *Selected Works* focus upon the six philosophical systems of India. The two following volumes 30 and 31 are a Japanese translation of *The Compendium of All Philosophical Systems* by the renowned savant Madhava of the 14th century. This work by Nakamura happens to be the world's first complete translation of the entire text.

The next volume 30 is concerned with Hinduism and the Epics, and the remaining two volumes 31 and 32 are Modern Indian Philosophy and Contemporary Indian Philosophy respectively.

The above 32 volumes in total constitute the main body of Nakamura's *Outlines of Indian Philosophy*. As far as I know, this publication is the largest, most detailed, and most comprehensive *Outlines of Indian Philosophy* covering the entire history of Indian Philosophy from the Vedic thoughts to the Contemporary thoughts, except the Islamic and Christian thoughts in India.

B. Additional Volumes

The above main body of his Selected Works has 8 additional volumes in which Nakamura moves beyond India and looks towards Japan and the other parts of the world.

1. History of World Thought

The first four volumes entitled *History of World Thought* comprise of additional volume 1 *Ancient Thought*, volume 2 *Universal Thought*, volume 3 *Medieval Though*t, and volume 4 *Modern Thought*. This work takes a "problem approach," which was used in western philosophical studies, e.g., by Wilhelm Windelband, *Lehrbuch der Geschichte der Philosophie* (Tuebingen, 1921) and not what might be called an "-isms approach" (Hinduism, Buddhism, etc.) .

The English versions of these four volumes are available today under the titles, *Parallel Developments* and *A Comparative History of Ideas*. The English draft of four public lectures, which Dr. Nakamura delivered in 1963 at Harvard University were later compiled by Professor Ronald Burr of California University, and in 1975 was first published in English as *Parallel Developments: A Comparative History of Ideas* (New York and Tokyo: Kodansha International-Harper). When this book was sold out and went out of print, its revised edition entitled *A Comparative History of Ideas* was published (London and New York, Kegan Paul International, 1986).

In the Preface of the second edition of *A Comparative History of Ideas* Nakamura says:

"We are living in the age when things should be viewed and discussed on a global scale. No event is isolated from other events.

We are in need of a kind of global history of ideas in which the developments of ideas should be viewed in the global scope, and yet we are afraid that no work to the effect has been brought about. Of course, there have been published a number of authoritative works, such as History of Philosophy : Eastern and Western or History of World Religions and so on. But in these works separate courses of development of ideas in various cultural areas were set forth in different chapters by different scholars from different angles, and the final outcomes seem too disparate, providing us with no conformity in the purpose and the style.

I thought that in order to keep conformity, developments of ideas in various cultural areas should be viewed by a single author and then the details should be corrected by other scholars specializing in various aspects of human intellect or in different traditions.

To this end I have toiled presumptuously to write a comparative history of ideas covering various traditions in global scope. In launching this project I tried to avoid elaborate theorizing and allow the data to speak for themselves, as a glance at the following pages will show. Some theoretical considerations are, of course, unavoidable, but whatever theories emerge in this work do not wander far from the problems that emerge from the data of intellectual history."(p.· v)

While describing the aim of the work in the same book (pp. 3-4), Nakamura says:

By "parallel developments" I refer to the fact that in different areas of the world similar problems, even if not similar concepts, emerged at certain stages of cultural development. In other words, it appears that certain intellectual problems are characteristic of certain stages in the history of culture, I do not mean, of course, that similar problems occurred at precisely the same time, but hopefully the following discussions will show that the history of ideas in each cultural area has undergone a similar development with respect to intellectual problems.

In the Editor's Preface, Donald Burr comments as follows:

Nakamura's book represents an effort to discuss the history of ideas primarily from the perspective of Asian thought, though perhaps sometimes with an Indian emphasis. As a result, it presents problems in intellectual history from quite a different perspective than most European and American historians of ideas, who view the history of philosophy using European thought as a norm of criterion. This is part of the genius of the work; but it must not be overly stressed because it is based on the *differences* in traditions. For it becomes clear as one works through Professor Nakamura's book that the old East-West dichotomy in many respects is simply inadequate. Certain common intellectual problems have surfaced wherever man has appeared; and methods must be found for getting beyond the East-West preoccupation if significant intellectual progress is to be made with respect to understanding the history of ideas. At the same time, however —and this is the paradox of Professor Nakamura's book—it become clear in the end that many of the problems of what is called "modern thought" (by Western philosophers) did not manifest themselves in India, China, and Japan before the period of "Westernization" except in scattered and tentative ways. In place of the Western scientific orientation, however, very human ethical considerations were often emphasized." (p. ix)

Charles Morris, University of Florida, says in his Preface:

"*Parallel Developments—A comparative History of Ideas* is a remarkable book by a remarkable man, Nakamura. It is the most interesting and most worthwhile book I have read in many years. It indeed sets a new standard for dealing with the history of thought across many cultures, especially India, China, Japan and the European West.

These cultures are not treated separately, one after another, as is usually done in histories of thought. Rather the emphasis is upon such problems as the concept of God, the question of immortality, the controversy over universals, the nature of orthodoxy and heterodoxy, the problem of moral values, and many others. The thought of the various cultures is then collected around such problems. ....

Nakamura believes that all the intellectual problems which a given culture faces are problems found in all great cultures, and that the order they are dealt with is about the same in all cultures and reflects the general order of human social development. But in stressing the similarities Nakamura is equally aware of the subtle differences found in the various cultures.

Nakamura is indeed a world-citizen. While he has spent much of his life on Indian and Buddhist thought, he is not concerned with showing the superiority of the thought of any specific culture. He has lived long in Europe and the United States even though his homeland is Japan.

This is a time in which many persons are showing a concern for the whole of mankind, Nakamura's book meets in an eminent way this interest. As a remarkable book by a remarkable man it deserves a wide and varied circle of readers."

2. Japanese Thought

In the following set of volumes, the author discusses various aspects of Japanese thought from his own viewpoint of history of world thought.

The additional volume 5 entitled, *The Inter-change of the Cultures of the East and the West*, may also be regarded as an introduction to Japanese thought in the volumes to follow.

Additional volume 6 entitled *Prince Shotoku* or the founder of Japanese Buddhism deals with the source of Japanese Buddhism. Then follows additional volume 7 entitled *The Critical Spirit of Modern Japan*, wherein he discusses the thought of Shosan Suzuki(1579-1655), a Buddhist monk who did not stick to the established teachings and propagated a Buddhism which is in conformity with the secular professional life, and Nakamoto Tominaga (1715-1746), who conducted a comparative study of Buddhist texts and was severely attacked by Buddhists. Finally, in additional volume 7 entitled *The Modernism of Japanese Religion* he discusses the modernism of Japanese religion prior to the arrival of western civilization.

Herewith I would like to come to an end of my explanation of his Selected Works. However, my explanation has not yet touched the entire body of Nakamura's works but the works SELECTED by himself only.

V. Two Kinds of Buddhist Dictionaries

Now, I would like to proceed to explain another of Nakamura's most important contributions to the study of Buddhism and Indian philosophy, i.e. a compilation of his two kinds of "timeless" dictionaries, which are not included in *The Selected Works of Nakamura Hajime*. One is *The Grand Dictionary of Buddhist Terms* and the other is *The Illustrated Dictionary of Buddhist Terms*. The former was completed in 1975 in 3 volumes and its completely revised and enlarged edition entitled *The Grand Comprehensive Dictionary of Buddhist Terms: Enlarged and Revised Edition* was published in 4 volumes, in 2001 by the Tokyo Shoseki Publishers.The same publisher published the latter work, 760 pages in length, in 1988 as a sequel to the former work.

A. *The Grand Comprehensive Dictionary of Buddhist Terms*

Firstly I would like to explain *The Grand Comprehensive Dictionary of Buddhist Terms: Enlarged and Revised Edition*. The author began to conceive in his head to compile such a dictionary when he was appointed Associate Professor of the Tokyo Imperial University at the age of 30 during the Pacific

War (1941-1945) in 1943. He started to study how Japanese writers and monks translated Chinese Buddhist terms into their own language. In Japan it has been customary since the time of the introduction of Buddhism into Japan in the 6th century A.D. that Japanese Buddhists have been using Chinese Buddhist terms without making any special effort to translate them into their own Japanese words. As you know, Japan imported Chinese characters and even now we use a lot of them in our daily life. This must at least be one of the reasons why Japanese Buddhists did not think it necessary for them to translate Chinese Buddhist terms into their own Japanese words.

However, there were some Buddhists who tried to translate them into daily Japanese words in order for them to make good use of Buddhist thought in their daily life. Nakamura intended to collect and arrange those efforts of the past Buddhists and compile them into a dictionary. His efforts resulted in a dictionary entitled *A Dictionary of Buddhist terms translated into Japanese* in 1947.

This was his first step toward another larger and fuller dictionary. The author began to undertake his great enterprise in 1948. After 19 years of his hard works he finally completed his manuscripts of about 30,000 Buddhist terms in 1967 and handed them over to a publisher in Tokyo.

Then a tragedy, which many people still remember even now, took place. His entire manuscripts of the dictionary were lost due to unknown causes by the publisher. The publisher searched for them but alas, in vain! The result of the author's 20-years hard work disappeared without any trace. I guess everybody here can imagine how deeply dismayed and helpless the author felt.

However, being not defeated by such a misfortune, to the great surprise, Nakamura rose up again from such a deep despair and resumed the enormous task of editing again one month after the totally unexpected and disappointing event. The author wrote in his postscript of the Dictionary, vol. 3, as follows:

"There were some people who said to me that the lost manuscripts, which were prepared more than 20 years ago, must have already been outdated, but such kind of works do not necessarily become outdated. Even now those old works can still be utilized. The loss of the manuscripts was a severe blow to me and it was in fact restarted from nothing."

It was in 1975 after the lapse of 8 years that the author finally succeeded in publishing *The Grand Dictionary of Buddhist Terms* in 3 volumes from the Tokyo Shoseki Publishers. The volume one consists of 800 pages, the volume 2, of 669 pages, and the volume 3, Index, of 392 pages. It consists of 1861 pages in total.

It was a matter of course that many scholars and students supported and cooperated with him in many ways, directly or indirectly. But this dictionary is not stated as "Edited by Hajime Nakamura" but as "Authored by Hajime Nakamura." He explains the reasons at the end of his postscript attached to volume 3. When he examined the manuscripts of Buddhist terms prepared by many different hands, he found out that those manuscripts are not homogenous in quality, not consistent in contents and sometimes wrong due to cooperators' misunderstandings of Chinese Buddhist terms used in other Buddhist dictionaries which they used for preparing their manuscripts for Nakamura's dictionary.

Then, in 1969 the author began to collect Buddhist terms directly from Buddhist texts and to write the items by himself without depending on the assistance of others. And at the last stage he himself decomposed and reorganized the entire manuscripts and rewrote them after examining all of them. For this reason Nakamura made himself the author of this dictionary in order to make clear the person who is responsible for this dictionary. Judging from his incredible effort and the importance of his role which he played in the compilation of the Dictionary, Nakamura is really the author and not the editor.

In editing this dictionary the author selected in principle common nouns only directly from about 400 chief Buddhist texts composed in India, China and Japan and tried his best to explain meanings of Buddhist terms clearly and briefly in current plain Japanese without using Chinese Buddhist terms as was the case with other Buddhist dictionaries compiled in Japan. In case there exist original texts in Sanskrit, Pali, and Tibetan he went back to the original words of Buddhist terms and aimed at the accuracy and exactitude of the explanations of the Buddhist terms. In addition the author gave the sources for the Buddhist terms as much as possible in order for the users of the Dictionary to go back to the original texts for further examinations. In this sense this dictionary can serve as a kind of Sanskrit and Pali Dictionary as well. In this way the Grand Dictionary of Buddhist Terms in two volumes was published in 1975 along with an additional volume which contains (1) A list of the abbreviations of the sources, (2) An Index to the Number of Strokes of Chinese Characters, (3) A Japanese Syllabary Index to the Buddhist Terms, (4) A Tibetan Index, (5) An Index to Pali, Sanskrit, and the like and (6) Postscript. Winning the highest praise, this Dictionary earned him the Mainichi Publications Cultural Award as well as the Society for the Promotion of Buddhism Cultural Award in 1975. About 30 years had elapsed since the author started this great enterprise.

However, the author was not satisfied with this Dictionary. It was really surprising to us that soon after its publication the author further proceeded to take cards of Buddhist terms for the large-scale enlargement and finally made up his mind to revise the Dictionary in December, 1994. At that time the number of the cards taken by him was more than 100,000. Based on them, 10,000 items among the 45,000 items contained in the Dictionary were revised and about 8000 new ones were added to it. In this way the revised and enlarged versions containing 53,000 items and consisting of 3 volumes and 1 additional one in 2288 pages in total was completed and published after the passing of the author who could see only its first proof.

B. *The Illustrated Dictionary of Buddhist Terms*

Now, I would like to touch upon the second dictionary entitled *The Illustrated Dictionary of Buddhist Terms* in one volume and 760 pages, published by the same Tokyo Shoseki Publisher in 1988. Soon after the publication of the former dictionary, Nakamura, the author and compiler, set about this new big project. As the title shows well, it not only explains the meanings of Buddhist terms in Buddhist texts by words but also elucidates them visually in a straightforward manner with the support of many illustrations, pictures, and photographs. This is not a dictionary for arts and archeology but for the purpose of showing in what concrete forms abstract ideas and thoughts are expressed. This happens to be the one and only illustrated dictionary existing at present, which encompasses not only Buddhism but also Hinduism and the Indian civilization.

These twin dictionaries are truly a great human monument constructed by him during the period that spanned 58 years in total in the 20th century.

VI. *The Structure of Logic*

Here I would like to introduce Nakamura's very important book entitled *The Structure of Logic* in two volumes consisting of 539 pp. and 604 pp. respectively (Tokyo: Seidosha, 2000) which was published in book form after his death. In this book he tried to create a new logic which is truly universal in such a globalized world and equally applicable to both of Eastern and Western logic which are necessarily limited historically and socially, although logic should be universal. As far as I know, this is the first venture to bridge the Eastern and Western logic in the world. I hope that this book will be translated into English in the near future by a scholar who is not only versed in logic, Indian and western, but also with a good command of Japanese and English.

VII. Nakamura's Eastern Institute and Sincerest Wish

Apart from his important publications, I would like to take this opportunity to explain our Eastern Institute which is one of the great achievements attained by the late Nakamura.

In 1970 Nakamura established a non-profit organization Eastern Institute for the purpose of cultivating young scholars, promoting researches mainly in the fields of Indian and

Buddhist studies, and disseminating Eastern thought. In 1973 upon his retirement from the University of Tokyo, he realized what had long been an ideal of his, namely the creation of a community for the guidance of the individuals by starting the Eastern Institute. In so doing he was actualizing something that was impossible for him at the university. His retirement from the University of Tokyo was thus an opportunity for him to fulfill this dream. In this Institute the quest for truth was the primary objective. Here he opened the doors wide to all those who possess a sincere zeal for study without any encumbrance by factors such as a person's academic career, age, occupation, nationality, and gender. Nakamura served as the Institute's director and devoted his efforts towards the guidance of numerous individuals without secluding himself within an ivory tower.

In accordance with his own wishes the funeral was sponsored by the Eastern Institute and on November 6, 1999, from four o'clock in the afternoon, it was solemnly planned and executed. His majesty the Emperor dispatched as an offering a sum of money to cover part of the funeral expenses. A bouquet of flowers arrived from both the Emperor and Empress and condolence messages from other members of the royal family. Since the day was blessed with good weather, the mourners numbered more than 1200. In keeping with the wishes of Nakamura who was not attached to any Buddhist sect, the *Triśaraṇagamana*, the Prajñāpāramitahṛdayasūtra (*Heart Sūtra*), the *Four Great Bodhisattva Vows* and the *Creed of Life* were recited prior to the traditional segment of the funeral service began. The mourners all recited them with deep devotion while cherishing the memories of this illustrious figure.

Nakamura has made a lasting contribution not only within Japan but in scholarly gatherings all over the world. That he has been highly acclaimed for these activities is obvious from the fact that within Japan he has received decorations such as the Medal of Culture and the First Order of the Sacred Treasure among others. He has also received numerous awards from abroad, including an honorary doctorate from the president of India. Please let me quote a part of the memorial writing from the former Indian President K.R. Narayanan,

"Nakamura was well known in India as an outstanding and eminent scholar, and true friend of our country. For more than half a century, Nakamura put to use his deep knowledge and extraordinary intellectual abilities, to make accessible to contemporary generations rich heritage of humankind's ideas, particularly, of the civilizations of Asia. The results of his prodigious endeavors not only inspired scholars all over the world, but also helped to acquaint a larger popular audience with the world of the intellect. Nakamura was thus a vital symbol of our common pursuit of knowledge, embodying a commitment transcending national boundaries, and encompassing major world civilizations.

Nakamura's friendship with India was reflected not only in his personal contacts with individuals and institutions in this country, but also in the dedication with which he interpreted Indian thought to the outside world, as part of his larger endeavors."

In the end I would like to inform you that portion of the ashes of the late Nakamura was scattered into the Holy Ganga river by his family after a Hindu puja on December 20, 2002.

The tomb of the Family Nakamura and a gravestone on its side was constructed in the suburbs of Tokyo before his death. On the gravestone was inscribed the following Buddha's words of compassion:

May all creatures always abound in happiness and peace; May all be always blessed with peace.

Let none cajole or despise his fellows anywhere; let none wish others harm.

Keep on this compassion with all your might.

Nakamura himself translated these words from a Pali Buddhist text "Mettāsutta" of the *Suttanipāta* (145-151) and Mrs. Nakamura wrote them down with a writing brush. These words must be the last and sincerest wish for the human kind that Nakamura had in common with Mrs. Nakamura.

12

Professor Hajime Nakamura's Contribution to the Buddhist Studies

Yasuaki Nara

1. Introduction

'Professor Hajime Nakamura's contribution to the Buddhist studies' is the topic I am asked to write on. No gainsaying the fact that this is the greatest honour for a former student of Nakamura—but at the same time I am well aware of my limitations.

A cursory look at his works will make the reader realize that he covered as vast an arena of academics as Indian history and philosophies; Indian, Chinese and Japanese religions; comparative studies in the History of the Ideas and the ways of thinking of the Asian people. Nakamura's publications vouchsafe the fact that the broad area of Indian studies including Buddhism was his first love. Out of his 40 collective works, 13 (volumes 11 to 23) are devoted to Indian Buddhism, viz.

Volume 11 : Gautama Buddha I (1992)
Volume 12 : Gautama Buddha II (1992)
Volume 13 : Lives of Gautama Buddha's Disciples (1991)
Volume 14 : The Formation of Early Buddhism (1992)
Volume 15 : The Thoughts of Early Buddhism I (1993)
Volume 16 : The Thoughts of Early Buddhism II (1994)
Volume 17 : Early Buddhistic Ethics for Living (1995)
Volume 18 : Social Ideas of Early Buddhism (1993)

Volume 19	:	Exchange of Thoughts between India and Western World (1998)
Volume 20	:	From Early Buddhism to Mahāyāna Buddhism (Mahāyāna Buddhism I) (1994)
Volume 21	:	The Thought of Mahāyāna Buddhism (Mahāyāna Buddhism Il) (1995)
Volume 22	:	The Logic of Śūnya (Mahāyāna Buddhism III)
Volume 23	:	The Thought of the Buddhist Art (Mahāyāna Buddhism IV)

Academic world is grateful to Sengaku Mayeda for bringing out a very useful and precise summary of all these works.

Before I take up the issue of analyzing the content of these works, I would like to give a brief summary thereof.

Gautama Buddha's life is dealt with in Volume 11 and 12 of the collected works. In this monumental work Nakamura has analyzed and interpreted a huge volume of data at his disposal and constructed a, more or less, complete and authentic life history of Śākyamuni Buddha. I shall take up this volume for discussion later in this essay.

Vol. 13 details the names and life histories of three hundred odd disciples of Buddha. To compile this work, the author has made use of a huge number of Buddhist texts from India, China, Tibet and even Japan.

Vol.14 traces the evolution of Early Buddhism.

So far as the study of the religious teachings and the evolution thereof is concerned, Volumes 15 and 16 can be considered the most important ones.

Whereas the 17th volume discusses the Buddhist way of life, the next one details the social, political and economic ideas of Buddhism. The 18th volume has an appendix which gives an overview of the research of Early Buddhist thought and texts.

Vol.19 analyzes Milindapajña, a famous Buddhist text. In this volume, Nakamura conducts a comparative study of Indian and Western thought.

The next four volumes, viz. 20, 21, 22 and 23 are devoted to Mahāyāna Buddhism.

This brief survey of the works of Nakamura amply shows that there is hardly any area of Indian Buddhism which he did not touch.

His comprehensive outlook and deep understanding of the history of Indian philosophy, religion and social ideas, and foolproof research tools enabled Nakamura to have insights and reach inviolable conclusions.

Nakamura Methodology

While conceiving the format of this essay, I grappled with the problem on how to approach such a vast subject? Should I summarize what Nakamura wrote about Buddhism? If yes, should I do it book wise or chapter wise? Frankly speaking, it is well nigh impossible at least in a research paper that needs to be completed in a limited space and time! Therefore, I propose to introduce the basic methodology on which his academism hinges. This methodology runs like a silver streak in all of his works. After giving an outline of his methodology, I would also add suitable illustrations showing its application and how it led tó the conclusions he has drawn.

The works of Nakamura I am considering, as we have seen above, are just a small part of his complete works. An analysis thereof will be used in two ways; firstly, to outline his methodology, and secondly, to highlight his unique discoveries on the life and thought of the Buddha.

One word about his presentation. Rather than using technical terms or jargon, he gives very simple and descriptive headings to the chapters of his works. This practice underlines his consideration for the general reader, a reader who is not trained in or used to the technical terms of academic discourse. Without compromising on the front of academic excellence, he made his thought and works on Buddhism accessible to as many people as possible. This explains why his works are read not only by scholars but also by general intelligentsia in Japan.

2. Is Indian Studies another case of Egyptology?

Before going into Nakamura's methodology, I would like to relate an incident that occurred at the time of his retirement from Tokyo University.

Nakamura's last lecture in the university was titled "Is the Indian Studies another case of Egyptology?"[2] In his illuminating lecture he observed that to almost all scholars of the ancient Egyptian studies, the ancient Egyptian culture is, more or less, a dead tradition. According to them the Egyptian thought has nothing to do with the ways of their *living* regardless of their being Christian, Jews or others. Nakamura said that these scholars get fellowships or grants from some foundations, go to Egypt, excavate pyramids and sphinxes and, return to their study rooms with lot of data. Sitting in their armchairs and sinking their ankles into a thick carpet (he himself said so), and smoking a pipe they read the excavated documents in hieroglyphics and try to construct the lost history of ancient Egypt. In their eyes the Egyptian tradition is no more than an objective and inanimate target to study and analyze in purely scientific terms. There is hardly any *sympathy* accorded to the life and thought of the people who had given birth to and maintained the rich civilization.

In the course of his lecture, he said, "Are our Indian and Buddhist studies the same with the Egyptian tradition?" He himself answers, "Hindu culture is a living tradition from the times immemorial. A life current that has been flowing uninterrupted till today! The stream that includes the lives of Indian people is characterized by the concerns about sorrow and pleasure, spiritual angst and Śā*nti*, peace of the mind and so on. Not only that, Buddhist thought and practice which took root in India has also been handed down to many Asian countries including Japan, and continues inspiring them to get rid of ignorance and sufferings."

Therefore, he concluded that Indian Studies is, by no means, a dead or inanimate object to handle, but a living subject to be approached with sympathy for those who have created and developed a *living* Indian tradition. He was categorical in saying that to study the thought of a civilization is "to listen to the groaning" of the people. He says that the change and development of the thought take place in the premises of the actual human life with mental conflicts.

This comment is the guiding principle of his methodology with which he approached Indian studies. That is "listening to the groaning of the people in the mental conflicts". This explains why he gave so much importance to the relationship between the thought and the actual life and to trace the evolution of Buddhist thoughts.

3. On the criteria of the formation of the Early Buddhist Texts

Now I would like to introduce Nakamura's idea of "the criteria of the formation of the early Buddhist texts". To me, his ultimate aim was to trace the history of world thought. In fact, four volumes of his collection "The Selected Works" bear the title "The History of World Thought." When did he begin thinking on these lines, we cannot say, but it seems to me that from the very beginning of his research career he was more interested in the process of the *development* of Buddhist thought than in the study of the Buddhist doctrine as such. It was as early as the year of 1956 when he brought out the result of his study in which he established the path breaking criteria of segregating the old and new content of the Buddhist texts.

What I am going to introduce now is a revised version of this study which is given at the end of volume 14 (pp. 573 to 732).

As is well known the Buddhist sūtras and the vinayas were formulated over a span of centuries. Therefore, each text is often a jumble of the old core content and new additions. The new and old elements are inextricably intertwined with each other. In his study under discussion, he says that the long and tedious academic endeavours of a bunch of competent and outstanding scholars before him could give information about the process of the compilation of the texts. They however did not shed any light on the historicity of the content, i.e., which part of a given text was old or let us say original, and which one was new or interpolated. Nakamura's concern was to accurately determine which part, section or verse was old or original and which one was a later addition. For this purpose, he established some objective criteria and discussed them in four sections, viz.

the philological study	(vol.14, pp.585-607)
the quotations in the texts	(pp.607-624)
the linguistic proofs and	(pp.625-652)
the historical-cultural evidences.	(pp.653-729)

As for the philological analysis of the texts for the reliable criteria, Nakamura first discusses the verse/prose problems. He says that the metrical portion in the Pali Tripiṭaka has been studied by our predecessors to represent the earlier strata than the prose, and he summaries the five reasons suggested by them. First, the linguistic features, especially the remnants of the Vedic and the Magadhi language. The second reason why the metrical portions are supposed to be old is known that the way of life of the *bhikkhus* depicted in the verses is primitive and the doctrinal theories are not so much systematized as we now know them. The third, when compared with Pali as well as Chinese translations, the prose portions are, in most of the cases merely the supplementary expositions of what is said in the preceding verses. Furthermore, some names of the *vaggas* and chapters, like those in the Dhammapada or Suttanipāta are quoted and exposed in the prose portion and this shows that some collections of verses did exist earlier as a kind of authentic texts. The fifth, some prose portions are definitely the paraphrasing of the verses, not vice versa.

To the above-mentioned evidence Nakamura added the following three points. The first is that there is no dearth of phrases in the verse that remind us of the phrases and the thoughts of the Upaniṣads. He further asserts that some of these Buddhist phrases seem to have been closely connected with the phrases of the Upaniṣads. The prose portions are far removed from the Upaniṣad. Secondly the same can be seen in relation to the Jaina texts. Some phrases in Dhammapada and Suttanipāta are very similar or in many cases the same as those used in early Jaina texts like Āyārāṇga, Sūyagadanga, Uttarajhayana, Isibhāsiyaim and others. Furthermore there are some Jainistic expressions that are not used in the later Buddhist tradition. The way of enumerating delusions are sometimes close to those of Jainas than to the Abhidhamma texts. Finally Nakamura says that in the verse portion of the early Buddhist texts there are none of the Buddhist doctrinal terms which became very common in the later phase of Tipiṭaka.

In this way Nakamura asserts the precedence of the metrical portions to the prose, which can be one of the criterion of the text formation. He also says that some verses are the metrical summary of the prose and hence posterior.

Nakamura cross-checks the quotations and the references to other texts or chapters. One example is illustrated here.

Samyutta Nikāya, XX, 7 tells us about a prediction of the Śākyamuni Buddha to the disciples that the *bhikkhus* in the future age will not listen to the Tathāgata's *suttantas* which are deep, profound, *lokottara* and the teachings of *Śunya*. They would like to listen to those *suttantas* that are studded with ornate and poetical expressions coming from the heretics. According to Nakamura this story shows that the Buddhists in later age are more interested in the philosophical discourses given in poetry rather than in the teachings. He concludes that we can presume three stages in the formation of the Buddhist texts. First the Buddha and disciples talked with each other in a colloquial language (perhaps some forms of old Magadhi). In the second stage teachings were told mainly in the form of verses and the use of the stock phrases were liked which sometimes had been expressed in flowery language. Hence, this is the stage in which verses were composed. And finally, in the third stage the "deep meanings" are elucidated in the form of philosophical discussion. Most of the prose portions belonging to the early Buddhist texts correspond roughly to this stage. This stage is the forunner of the Abhiddharma philosophy.[3]

The comparative study of various recensions of the Dhammapda like the Pāli Dhammapada, Gāndhāri Dharmapada, Udāna-vagga, four Chinese translations and a Tibetan translation are helpful to get at the original form of this text.

Nakamura also discussed and found the merits of the Chinese translations which are often not so faithful renderings of the original texts, and this bias itself is useful to discern the comparatively new and old portions of the texts.

Another important criteria that Nakamura takes into account is about the linguistic feature of the words. Many scholars have already studied the irregular usages of Pali words in terms of pronunciation and orthography, forms of nominal declension and verbal conjugation. Based on those linguistic data, Nakamura closely examines the verses in the early texts like Suttanipāta, Dhammapada, Udāna and some portions of the Jatāka which are said to be old and pointed out the irregular usage of Pali. He did not step into the controversy of the original language of Buddhism, i.e. in what language the Buddha preached, nor did he pay any attention to the problem of the home place of Pāli. He restrains himself simply by saying that the Buddha might have spoken in some form of Māgadhi dialect and therefore some Māgadhi elements remained when his teachings were rendered into Pāli. He makes a brief comment that the Pāli language might be a dialect from Western India. Therefore the verses keeping these Vedic or Māgadhian elements belong to the old tradition.

Nakamura is however cautious to say that the verses keeping the old forms of the Ṛg-Veda or of the Māgadhian elements may be old but in some cases new elements after Aśoka period are found together. He emphasizes the need to conduct a careful study of the linguistic aspects including the problem of what the original language of the Buddhist texts really was.

Historical-cum-Cultural Evidences

What Nakamura was very keen about is not the *static* study of the doctrine but the history of thought which is closely related to the socio-cultural change of the society. In

Nakamura's lecture mentioned above he says that the history of thought is to know the dynamics of human thinking and emotions, and to hear the growning of the people. Accordingly he was always aware to underline the close relation between the thought reflected in the words and the social changes of the times.

We illustrate this concern of Nakamura by citing an example. He observed a tendency with increasing frequency to add more sacredness to the word *cakravartin-rājā* in and after the Maurya dynasty. He says the idea of the ruler of all India, *Jambsandassa issaro* (Theragāthā 914), first of all appear in the Buddhist texts definitely under the influence of the rise of the Maurya dynasty, the first empire to rule the whole India. There is a word *samrāj* in the Brahmana texts but it was not regarded so sacred at that time as it was in the later ages. Nakamura opines that the sacredness of the word *cakravartin* must have depended on the actual rise of the powerful empire in Magadha. In Suttanipāta 553 and 553, Sela, a brahmin, requests the Buddha to rule the world. But in the prose portion prefaced to the verses is mentioned what Sela thought in his mind that since this man is equipped with the thirty two mahā-puruṣa-lakṣaṇas he would be the *cakravartin* if he remained in the mundane world and if he renounced the world he would become the Buddha. Here the secular great king is compared with the most exalted religious personality. Furthermore, in Suttanipāta 554 the Buddha calls himself as "*Dhammarājā anuttaro*", the best *Dhammarājā*. In the prose section of the same text, (p.106) the *cakravārtin* is called as *Dhammiko dhammarājā* Nakamura observes this as a token of the shift of authority from religion to the secular.

In this way Nakamura picked up 64 words or synonymous word-groups which had got currency in the society or in accordance with the social changes had got additional meanings attached to them. He discussed these words or phrases under 13 headings. These word-groups are closely related to:

1. the rise of the great kingdom
2. the period after the kūṣānas

3. the changes and developments of society
4. the way of life of the śramaṇas (*bhikkhus*)
5. the Vedas
6. the Dharmasūtras
7. the common features with Jainism
8. the teaching of the Brahmin *parivrājakas*
9. the ideal personality
10. the philosophical terms and expressions
11. the expressions of the Aśoka inscription
12. Sanskritization
13. the art.

Nakamura is not directly concerned with studying the formation of the early Buddhist texts. He is keen to finding some criteria that might help in judging whether the phrases, clauses and sentences he is examining are anterior or posterior than others in terms of the development of thoughts.

As conclusion of this section he summarizes what he could find out particularly in the earliest phases of the Buddha's thought and his order. There is some novel information that I must introduce. But he illustrates almost the same conclusion in more detail in the earlier section of the same vol.14. He took them up especially in relation to his unique idea of the "Original Buddhism". He proposes it to show the earliest phase of the Early Buddhism. We will come back to this point after examining the proposal of his Original Buddhism.

4. The Original Buddhism and the Early Buddhism

Nakamura uses the term "the Early Buddhism" but this is too wide to differentiate what the Buddha himself taught and what have been developed later. This is the reason why some scholars proposed the term the "Original Buddhism" Owing however to the difficulty to show what this term really meant, or what thought or texts it represented, it has not been in use among scholars. Nakamura however has been successful to make clear, to a certain extent, the unique characteristic of Gautama's teachings. Therefore he felt the necessity to distinguish the earliest and the later phases of Buddhism.

As a result, Nakamura discusses the development of the Early Buddhism in two stages of "the Original Buddhism" and "the Early Buddhism."[4] He defines that the Original Buddhism as the Buddhism in the earliest period and it is known only from the older portions of the Pāli Tripiṭaka. The text criticism shows as mentioned above that some gāthās and some stock phrases found in the Suttanipāta, the Sāgatha-vagga in SN, Itivuttaka, Dhammapada, and some portions of the Jatākas are old. This stage may be understood as prior to king Aśoka.

On the other hand the Early Buddhism is a much wider term to be known from the most prose portion, with which the Sanskrit and Chinese Āgamas are common. Though some old elements are included in it, the Early Buddhist canon as we now see it must have been compiled after the period of King Aśoka.

The Original Buddhism as per Nakamura's term is important because it reflects the original characteristics of the Buddha's teachings and practices. They are the starting point from which the whole history of Buddhism has developed. He summarizes seven important features of the Original Buddhism as follows.

1. The words, phrases or terms which scholars have so far regarded as uniquely Buddhist are very rare in the old gāthās.

2. Any doctrine that deserves the name of a doctrine is hardly taught. Any dogma or *diṭṭha* is rejected regardless of the religious sects. Such sceptic attitude to the doctrine is rather near to that of the philosophy of Sañjaya and the early Jainas.

3. Instead of the doctrinal views particular to the later Buddhism, a large number of words and phrases of the Ājivikas and Jainism are used. Some of them are similar to the vocabulary of Aśokan Inscriptions and this fact supports the idea that most prose sentences in the Pāli canon are compiled after the reign of King Aśoka.

4. The practitioners in the earliest stages of Buddhism were ascetics rather than monks because they led solitary life in the woods or caves. There were a few however, who lived

with fellow practitioners (*sabrahmacārin*, *sadhivihārin*) but there is hardly any trace of a community life of monks in the viharas as we see in the later age.

5. These practitioners are called *ṛṣi, rishi*, and their ways of life seem to be like the hermit, or the recluses depicted in the epics of the Rāmāyaṇa and the Mahābhārata. They lived practicing meditation in the forests (*vanavāsin*) or the graveyard or cremation ground (śmaśāna). These *ṛṣis* were later on replaced by *bhikkus* in the prose that paraphrases the verses. The usage of the word *bhikkhu* in the Theravada tradition in the Southeast Asia comes from this stage.

6. There were no nuns in the earliest time. But since Megasthenes, a Greek historian, speaks of the lady philosophers, nuns must have existed before the period of Aśoka.

7. In the earliest stage of the development of Buddhism, there was no term or word unique to Buddhism. They borrowed words and phrases from other religious traditions and incorporated them in the form of Buddhist doctrine.

8. Śākyamuni Buddha was not the only Buddha. There were many other Buddhas. In Jaina tradition too, any one who perfected the spiritual practice is called a Buddha and this seems to be a general practice of these times. Buddhism just borrowed and adopted it. Names of the sages like Uddālaka, Yājñavalkya and some sages from the Epics are enumerated in the Isibhāsiyaim. The word 'Buddha' in the Suttanipāta, 513, 517, 523, 622, 643, 646 and so on does not mean anything more than an 'excellent practitioner.'

We can not say that the Original Buddhism as propounded by Nakamura stands the reason. But the reason and basis of why he had to differentiate the Original Buddhism from the Early Buddhism in general can be understood and justified. (To this point I would like to come back at the end of this article.)

5. Not-self (*Fei-wo*) and Non-self (*Wu-wo*)

Let me now introduce Nakamura's unique interpretation of the term *anātman* in the stage of the Original Buddhism, just as an illustration of how he applied his methodology mentioned above to the theoretical studies.

Ātman is of course one of the main themes of Indian philosophy and religion. Buddha is said to have preached *anātman* (Pāli *an-attan*). In fact Buddhism is known as the "*Nairātmyavāda*" and "*sabbe dhammā anattā*". It is onc of the three characteristics of Buddhism to distinguish it from other religious traditions in India.

Anātman is translated into Chinese as *Wu-wo*, which is in Japanese pronounced as *Mu-ga*, which literally means "Non-*ātman*" implying the negation of the existence of *ātman*. For the Japanese Buddhist scholars, and perhaps for the Chinese scholars too, *Mu-ga* or *Wu-wo* has been understood in the sense of the opposite idea to the Upaniṣādic idea of *Ātma-vāda*. Nakamura however pointed out that the term should be investigated carefully because it could have various meanings according to the context.

Nakamura, first of all, says that the Original Buddhism, so often calls upon human beings to get rid of the idea of "mine" or the idea of "belonging to the self". If a man does not think in terms of "This is mine" or "That belongs to others", or he does not suffer from any idea of *mamatva*, he will not grieve with the thought of "I do not have".(Sn.951)

Nakamura points out that this very idea was not alien to the Ājivikas, Jainism or to the Vedic texts. Not only this word was used exactly in the same sense, but sometimes even the identical term or sentence was also used.

This coincides with giving up the idea of possession, *parigraha*, which is also emphasized and Nakamura points out that this is the spirit of *aparigraha*, the fifth and the last precepts of the Jainas. He quotes:

Sorrow, lamentation and misery never leave those who are attached to what they think as "mine" (*mamāyita*). Hence the sages giving up objects of grasping (*aparigraha*) wander about with insight into tranquility (*khemanibbāna*) (Sn.809)

The same ethic is admitted in the Brahmanic tradition too and Nakamura dares to say that as long as we read from the oldest sources, the Original Buddhism, without establishing any unique teaching, seems to teach only the practical way of how to become real *Brāhmin* or *samana*.[5]

He further discusses the Original Buddhism and rejects to see what is not the self as *ātman*. For all of us our own body, family, wealth, position and others are so important as to often identify them with the self. But they are never the self, *ātman*, as is often emphasized in the Upaniṣads and the Vedānta philosophy. He quotes as one of the examples Sn.756.

In this world, inclusive of its gods, what is not self (*anattāni*) is taken as the self (*attānam*) and they are tied to their psycho-physical beings (*nāma-rūpa*,). Attachment to the *nāma-rūpa* is to grasp the self objectively that lead us to lose the real self.

Nakamura finds here again the influence of the Upaniṣads on the earliest phase of Buddhism.[6] (479-481)

Summarising the instances seen above, he clearly says that it is wrong, at least in almost all the cases in the Original Buddhism, to translate *anattan* as "Non the self" (Non-self). He shows that it should be interpreted as "Not the self" (Not-self). In fact the "Non the self" or "Not the self" is my translation of the Chinese *Muga* and *Higa* (Chinese, *Fei-wo*) respectively. The popular term *Muga* means that the Self or *ātman* does not exist; and the literal meanings of *Hi-ga* is Not-the-self. Implication of this term is very clear that there is nothing in this world which can be grasped as 'I' or as 'it is mine'. Therefore Not-self is rather practical ethic to give up "attachment" than the philosophical negation of the *ātman*. He found actually in the Chinese Āgama texts the case of *Higa* to *anattan* in the original text.

Nakamura also brings out his idea why the usual and customary rendering of *anattan* to the Chinese term *Muga*, or the understanding of *anattan* in the same sense that *ātman* does not exist, is quite inappropriate.

He says this term easily incurs an unnecessary misunderstanding that Buddhism neglects the existence of the self as an ethical actor. He examines such expressions as *attānam gaveseti* (to look into the self) (Vinaya, Mahāvagga, 1 ,13, p.25), *attanārakkhita*, (self guarded), *atta-piya* (to love the self), *attānam himsam* (to hurt oneself) (Sn.583), *hanti attānam* (to destroy the self by desires to the wealth) (Dp.355) etc. all of these phrases underline the importance of the self as an actor.

After studying *anātman* in this way Nakamura concludes that in the stage of the Original Buddhism the idea of *anātman* is almost identical with the old Upaniṣads, Jainism and in the philosophy of the Ājivikas. No unique and new theories or thought is mentioned. This coincides with the general attitude of the earliest Buddhists not to oppose or compete with other religious and philosophical theories. As for the idea of "*ātman*" is concerned no intention is found to reject other's thoughts. Nakamura stresses that right here we can see the important characteristic of the Buddhist view of *ātman*. In spite of teaching to find the real self in the practical living, they do not give even a hint of any metaphysical explanation or theoretical discourse on what *ātman* really is or what it is like. In contrast to other religions this stance is unique to Śākyamuni Buddha himself and to what Nakamura calls the Original Buddhism. A little later on texts of the early Buddhism began to participate in philosophical discussion and to criticize the so called Atmavāda. They did not negate the existence of *ātman* but rejected the idea of the self as an eternal entity.

6. The Content of the Buddha's Realization

As the second illustration of Nakamura's methodology I would like to discuss some points of his contribution to the biographical research of the Buddha. They are not only the new finds but also the great contribution to our understanding of what the essential character of Buddhism really is.

As for the descriptions of the life of the Buddha, i.e, the intended biography of the Buddha, we have to wait till the Mahāparinibbāna- suttanta or the Nidānakathā in the Jātakas which are supposed to belong to the Aśokan time or even later. The content mentioned in those works of Buddhist canon however belongs to much earlier times. But the fragmentary sources that might have been used in the later biographies of the Buddha are found in various records of his preachings and life. At present we have an enormous collection of materials on every incidents of his life, which are written in Pali, Sanskrit, Buddhist Sanskrit, Tibetan and Chinese, and cover all periods from the time of the Buddha himself to much later period of the late Mahāyāna age, roughly the sixth and seventh century A.D.

Here is an important factor which we should give due consideration to the biographical description. It is the strong tendency of the mytholization. Owing to various reasons the life incidents of Śākyamuni Buddha became modified toward a superhuman and very dignified being.

A legend of his mother Māyā's conception that Gautama came down from the Tuṣita Heaven in a form of a white elephant is very old, perhaps the earliest instance of the super humanization of Gautama Buddha. But in the later descriptions he was depicted as shining with gold and splendour

Devadatta was a serious and perhaps a strict type of a practitioner. He strongly requested to the Buddha to restore the monastic life of the order back to the original śramaṇistic wandering life. He became however in the later tradition to be contemporary to the Buddha to compete for wife, regarded him as rival and tried to kill him with the result that he fell deep into the *Ananta* Hell being wrapped by the fire.[7]

All these accounts, including the ones full of contradictions and mythologization, are found in abundance.

Nakamura perhaps is the first successful scholar to restore the historical figure of the Buddha as possible as the materials allow, removing later additions and modifications. Based on his criteria of the text I introduced before, he took a very tedious job to compare all the versions available to find out the core part of each legend. They are of course a great contribution to the study of the Buddha's life itself but, at the same time, help us to reveal the central essence of Buddhist thought.

Let me introduce the discussion and the conclusion of Nakamura on the issue of the content of Śākyamuni Buddha's realization.[8]

One of the most popular and perhaps the oldest traditions is the story of how the Buddha entered Ultimate Realization after examining the dvādaśa-pratītya-samutpāda (the twelve linked chain of dependent origination). The story is found in the Udāna 1-3 and also Vinayapiṭaka, Mahāvagga, I,1,1-7 with slight differences. The portion that are common to both must be the core. Nakamura did a word-by-word comparison of both texts along with the Catuṣpriṣatsūtra[9], the Sanghabhedanavastu in the Mūlasarvāstivāda Vinaya, the Vinaya in the Tibetan Canon and *Wu-fen-lU*, the Vinaya in Chinese. He could successfully take out the core of the story. Even the oldest versions of the Udāna and the Vinaya consist of both gāthās and prose, and the core is taken from the verse portion. It is very simple and straight in style and coherent even without the help of the prose.

The Buddha is mentioned as a Brāhmana in the verse portion whereas in the prose he is addressed as '*bhagavat*'. The *dvādaśāṇga-pratītya-samutpāda* is narrated only in the prose in the same formula as we have it now. Consulting also with the Tibetan and the Chinese texts Nakamura asserts that Buddha examines the formula after his realization. The text describes the results of his thought rather than the process of how he reached the final goal of his practice and hence, Nakamura concludes that no essential link is found between the so-called *dvādaśāṇga-pratītya-samutpāda* and his realization.

Of course Nakamura does not deny that during the time of his practices prior to the realization, there must be in him a kind of rough ideas of where from the suffering comes, how it begins to function as suffering, and how it could be overcome etc. which are the main theme of the *dvādaśāṇga-pratītya-samutpāda*, but they remained as fragmented ideas without being integrated into a fixed theory. In fact he found some descriptions of it in the old texts like Suttanipāta and made it clear how they used them as material for the fixed theory as we know it as *the dvādaśāṇga-pratītya-samutpāda*[10]. If it is the later development, the portion of our texts now investigating is no more than the later interpolation.

Then again it comes down to the problem of what he realized. Nakamura further studied all descriptions that touch upon the theme. Some texts says the Buddha has got his realization after looking into the nature of the delusion of objects of the senses (SN.XXXV,13: 14). The same is said of each of the *pañcaskandha* (five components of things), and also of the *pañcabala* (five powers necessary to practice, i.e. faith, endeavour, sati, meditation and wisdom) SN.XLVIII,21; Japanese. There is another text which says he saw the cause of the sufferings in the old age, disease and death (MN. No.26). Another one insists of the four supernatural powers whereas still another insists of realization by the Four *dhyānas*.

These various opinions seem to have been compromised, Nakamura opines, in the Nidānakathā of the Jātaka as follows

The Buddha got the knowledge of the past lives in the beginning of the night, purified his Heavenly Eyes in the middle of the night and got the insight into the *pratītya-samutpāda* in the last part of the night.[11]

Having studied in this way Nakamura concludes as follows:

As for the realization, there is a great difference in each text. What was the real one? Was the realization of the Buddha so vague and not final to be easily miscomprehended and handed down variously by the compilors of the texts? Was the teaching of the Buddha not established? Yes, that is true. Right in this point that the content of the realization, the starting point of Buddhism, was told of in various ways, we see the important meanings and the characteristic of Buddhism.

He says[12], first of all, Buddhism, i.e. the Original Buddhism, had no particular doctrines of its own. Gautama Buddha did not want to tell what he had realized in any fixed formula. He preaches it differently according to the occasions and the persons to whom he was teaching. Therefore the content of his realization was told of in a variety of ways and therefore accepted differently according to those who listened to him respectively.

Secondly, that having no particular doctrine does not mean Buddha had no unique thought of his own. Though different in content they converge after all into one and the same reality. The Buddha looked into the real nature of man *as-it-is* and got the peace of the mind. It is to manifest the Dharma on him through practice.

As the third point, Nakamura says that, although not explicitly mentioned in any text, Gautama Buddha admitted that the Dharma is not something fixed. It is the crucial basis that works in various ways according to each person with a concrete expression. He is free to admit the change and development of the expressions of the Dharma as long as it is not twisted or misunderstood. As a practical philosophy this stance has made it possible the limitless development of thought entailing the appearance of so many thoughts in full varieties in the later age. In the history of World Thought we have often observed that the religious dogmas have become impediments to the free expression of reality and religious faiths but Gautama's stance as seen above allows the free thought to develop with no harming to the human spirit. This seems to have determined the future characteristic of Buddhism and in its history we seldom observe any clash between religion and rationalism, or religion and science. (GB 417-8)

Discussing the most fundamental attitude of the Buddha towards reality and freedom of thought he then begins to discuss how the Dharma he found in his realization is universal and absolute as the authority of religious faith. (GB 420-1)[13] (Due to lack of space, I would not elaborate on this issue.)

7. On his "Original Buddhism"

Nakamura's enthusiasm to look for the original thought of the Buddha and trace the process of the development in the Early Buddhism have led him to find out some characteristic features in the earliest stage of Buddhism.

It is not the case that all that Nakamura discussed is unique or new. The fact of the influence of the Vedic thought was already known to the academic world. The similarity in the thought of the Jainas, the Ājivikas and others has been and still a subject of discussion of many scholars.

But by means of these data which he freely made good use of, and of his outstanding power of insight he could have found their meaning as the unique characteristics of the earliest phase of Buddhism.

They are definitely different from our traditional and usual understanding of what the Early Buddhism was. These ideas being novel and unique, Nakamura must have thought of the necessity to discuss them separately. This is what he called "the Original Buddhism".

But can the Original Buddhism be treated as an independent subject or as one of the stages of the Buddhist development? Is it possible to say that Buddhism has developed from the Original Buddhism to the Early Buddhism? Or, does it have the substantial content of thoughts and texts to characterize it as such?

The answer is rather negative. I am almost sure that Nakamura did not intend to create a new independent stage of Buddhism. As far as my knowledge goes, he had not written any article to propose the new stage. The "Original Buddhism" (which I am talking about now) is discussed only in a chapter of the book "The Formation of Early Buddhism".

By the Original Buddhism, Nakamura might have meant for the characteristics of the earliest phase of what he called the Early Buddhism.

But his contribution has remained in that he could cull out some fragmented ideas and locate them in the process of development of Buddhism. In this sense we can understand how he was tempted to use the new word of "Original Buddhism", and his intension is justified and successfully achieved.

References

1. This is the Japanese translation of the slightly revised edition of his "*Indian Buddhism*, A Survey with Bibliographical Notes", Delhi, 1980, pp.61-89.
2. His lecture is published (in Japanese) in "Shunju", Shunjusha Publ. Co. Tokyo,1973.4, pp. 22f.
3. Vol. 14, pp. 607-609
4. Vol. 14, pp. 66-76, 77-79
5. Vol. 15, p. 474
6. Vol. 15, pp. 479-481
7. Nakamura discusses in detail the problem of Devadatta. Vol.14, pp. 509-571
8. Vol.11, pp. 392ff.
9. E.Waldschmidt's edition, pp.102f.
10. Vol.16, pp. 387f.
11. Jātaka, I, p. 75
12. Vol.11. pp. 417-8
13. Vol.11, pp. 420 f.

Abbreviation

SN. Samyutta Nikāya
SN. Suttanipāta
MN. Majjhima Nikāya
Dhp. Dhammapada

13

Professor Hajime Nakamura's Understanding on the Influence of Mahāyāna Buddhism on Gauḍapāda's Philosophy

Sun-keun, Kim

Introduction

The purpose of the present work is a study of Professor Hajime Nakamura's understanding on the influence of Mahāyāna Buddhism on Gauḍapāda's philosophy. Gauḍapāda (A.D. 640-690?) has based his philosophy on '*Prasthāna-traya*' or the three basic works of Vedānta and Mahāyāna Buddhism – Śūnyavāda of Nāgārjuna and Vijñānavāda of Vasubandhu. His philosophy is presented in the Gauḍapāda-Kārikā or the Māṇḍūkya-Kārikā. The Māṇḍūkya-Kārikā or the Gauḍapāda-Kārikā is the first available systematic treatise on Advaita Vedānta. Gauḍāpāda-Kārikā is divided into four chapters. It is treated as a treasure by the aspirants for *mokṣa*.

Let us now proceed to examine what are the fundamental philosophical doctrines expounded by Gauḍapāda.

Hajime Nakamura's Understanding on the Influence of Śūnyavāda of Nāgārjuna on Ajātivāda of Gauḍapāda

The fundamental philosophical doctrine of Gauḍapāda is ajātivāda or the doctrine of No-origination. In the third chapter of his Kārikā, Gauḍapāda has explained his famous ajātivāda. Ajātivāda is a denial of jāti or real creation; the world of plurality is an appearance. The phenomenal world of plurality is declared to be mere appearance due to *avidyā*.

Ātman is said to be the only Reality, the eternal and non-dual Self. According to C. Sharma's interpretation. "Negatively, it means that the world, being only an appearance, is in fact never created. Positively, it means that the Absolute, being self-existent, is never created (*aja*)."[1]

Gauḍapāda was influenced by Śūnyavāda of Nāgārjuna in maintaining that origination, from *paramārtha-satya* (absolute truth) is an impossibility. He says that whatever exists from the perspective of the other-dependent (*paratantra*), does not exist from the standpoint of absolute truth (IV. 73). Gauḍapāda is here speaking and adopting the discourse of the Madhyamaka-from two levels; the empirical (*samvṛti*) and the absolute (*paramārtha*). According to Gauḍapāda, things do exist empirically, but they do not so exist from the perspective of absolute truth. He examines the various theories of creation and rejects them all. From the absolute truth there is neither birth nor death, neither appearance nor disappearance, neither production nor destruction, neither liberation nor bondage; there is neither the aspirant nor the liberated—this is the highest truth.[2]

Gauḍapāda talks of creation only from the empirical standpoint. From the standpoint of *samvṛti* or empirical truth, the Unborn appears to be born only through *avidyā*. Through its beginningless and indescribable power called *avidyā*, the Real appears as many. Gauḍapāda begins with a detailed exposition of No-origination (*ajāti*) by means of a dialectical critique of causation. He has established *ajātivāda* by proving the falsity of the world through *Śruti* and by showing that it is an appearance of the non-dual eternal *Ātman*.[3] In the fourth chapter, in 19 Kātikās he has proved that the Bauddhas have elucidated *ajāti* by giving the following three arguments: (1) absence of energy in the cause to produce the effect (*aśakti*), (2) absence of knowledge of any relation between cause and effect (*aparijñāna*), and (3) incompatibility of the order of succession (*karma-kopa*). And in the twenty-second verse he concludes like Nāgārjuna, that nothing can originate either from itself or from other than itself; neither the real nor the unreal nor both real and unreal can be produced.[4] The real is unborn and eternal and so cannot be produced. It is called 'Unborn' (*aja*) from relative truth only. From the absolute truth, it cannot be called even 'Unborn' for it is really indescribable by intellect.[5] Thus Gauḍapāda's own presentation about the nature of absolute truth, as stated in II. 31-32, may well have been inspired by what he found in Mahāyāna literature. The idea that there are two levels of reality would not itself have been new to Gauḍapāda.

Before concluding our discussion of Gauḍapāda and Nāgārjuna there is a further resemblance which should be remarked upon, and that is between some expressions of Nāgārjuna and the Māṇḍūkya Upaniṣad itself. In the two introductory verses of the Mūlamādhyamakakārikā Nāgārjuna characterizes Dependent Origination as "the cessation of phenomena" (*prapañcopaśama*) and as "auspicious" (*śiva*). In Māṇḍūkya Upaniṣad 7, *Turīya-Ātman* is also referred to in the very same words: "The fourth is... where there is the cessation of the phenomenal world (*prapañcopaśama*), it is peaceful, auspicious (*śiva*) and non-dual." Perhaps the Māndūkya is here influenced by the Mahāyāna.

Hajime Nakamura is of the opinion that the Māndūkya Upaniṣad seems to have been influened by "the thought of Śūnyatā of Mahāyāna Buddhism and he estimates the composition of the Māṇḍūkya as between the beginning of the common era and 200 CE.[6] Nakamura's discussion of this point is that the Māṇḍūkya has taken the expression directly from Nāgārjuna.[7] We can follow him when he says: "the concept of the fourth realm (*caturtha*) was perhaps influenced by the *Śūnyatā* of the early Mahāyāna Sūtras in the formation of the Māṇḍūkya.[8] The ācārya, like Nāgārjuna, believes that Reality is beyond the four categories of thought (*catuṣkoṭi-vimirmukta*). Ācārya Gauḍapāda says: Only an unintelligent person covers the Real with existence, non-existence, both and neither. These are the four categories of thought with which the Real appears to be covered, but, in fact, it is untouched by them; he who realized this Lord (*Bhagavān*) himself becomes the omniscient Real.[9] The ācārya talks of creation only from the relative standpoint which is a means to realize that goal of *ajāti* or *advaita* and preaches *karma* (action) and *upāsanā* (devotion, meditation) for the common people to lead them slowly to transcendent knowledge (*jñāna*).[10]

Hajime Nakamura's Understanding on the Influence of Vijñānavāda of Vasubandhu on Reality as Pure Consciousness in Gauḍapāda

Gauḍapāda was influenced by Vijñānavāda of Vasbandhu in maintaining that Reality is Pure Consciousness which manifests itself as, and ultimately transcends, the subject-object duality. Consciousness is the only reality and it is never related to any external object, neither in the past, nor in the present, nor in the future.[11] According to ācārya Gauḍapāda, the Real is ātman, the Absolute, *Turīya* and Pure Consciousness. Gauḍapāda accepts the arguments of Vimśatīkā of Vasubandhu to prove the unreality of the external objects.[12] From the absolute truth, perception and practical utility are invalid arguments to prove the reality of the world.[13] The external world is unreal because it does not exist always, as Reality must do. It is also unreal because the relations which constitute it are all unreal; because space, time and causality are impossible. It is also unreal because it consists of objects and whatever can be presented as an object is unreal. Reality is the Pure Self which is Pure Consciousness and which is at the background of everything.[14]

Gauḍapāda was influenced by Trimśikā of Vasubandhu in maintaining that the individual subjects, the mental states and the external objects are appearance of pure *Vijñāna* due to beginningless *avidyā* which projects the illusion of subject-object duality. Gauḍapāda also says that just as a moving fire-brand appears as straight or curved, similarly consciousness, when it moves, appears as the subject-object duality.[15]

Thus Gauḍapāda utilizes ideas from the Vijñānavāda of Vasubandhu to show that the world is an appearance of Consciousness and is not something that exists apart from Consciousness. He also accepts the arguments of the

Vijñānavāda of Vasubandhu to prove the unreality of the external objects. Concerning the fourth chapter, Nakamura maintains:

The fourth chapter accepts the non-self theory and abandons the traditional *ātman* theory of the orthodox Vedānta school. The fourth chapter does not refer to *Brahman* or *Ātman* at all. Here, non-self, emptiness and the non-differentiated Consciousness-only constitute the basic doctrines.[16] In the fourth chapter, especially, though occassionally in the other chapters as well, Gauḍapāda presents Advaita Vedānta using Buddhist terms. But he uses them in such of a way that they can conform to the fundamental Vedāntic understanding of Consciousness.

Conclusion

Thus we see that ācārya Gauḍapāda's Kārikā is not only the first available systematic exposition of Advaita Vedānta, but also the first available work which brings out a correct realtionship between Advaita Vedānta and Mahāyāna Buddhism.[17] T.R.V. Murti has offered the opinion that; "Gauḍapāda appears to us as the Brahmanical thinker boldly reformulating the Upaniṣadic ideal in the light of the Mādhyamika and Vijñānavāda dialectic. But there was more borrowing of techniques than tenet.[18]

Thus Nakamura draws the conclusion that Gauḍapāda's philosophy has been borrowed from the Mahāyāna.[19] I think that Gauḍapāda has adapted ideas from Mahāyāna Buddhism to suit his own perspective. I would prefer to say that Gauḍapāda "stated" the Upaniṣadic teachings under the inspiration of some of ideas of the Madhyamaka and the Vijñānavāda.

References

1 C. Sharma, *A Critical Survey of Indian Philosophy,* p. 242.

2 *Māṇḍūkya-Kārikā,* II, 32.

3 *Ibid,* II. 31-35; III. 17-23; 27-31.

4 C. Sharma, *The Advaita Tradition in Indian Philosophy,* p. 148.

5 *Māṇḍūkya-Kārikā,* IV, 74.

6 H. Nakamura, *A History of Early Vedānta Philosophy* (Delhi: Motilal Banarsidass, 1983), p. 30; 42.

7 *Ibid,* p. 298.

8 *Ibid,* p. 34, note 37.

9 *Māṇḍūkya-Kārikā,* IV, 83-84.

10 *Ibid,* III, 15-16; C. Sharma, *The Advaita Tradition in Indian Philosophy,* p. 150.

11 *Ibid,* IV, 25-27.

12 *Ibid,* IV, 27.

13 *Ibid,* IV, 42.

14 C. Sharma, *A Critical Survey of Indian Philosophy,* p. 246.

15 *Māṇḍūkya-Kārikā,* IV, 47.

16 H. Nakamura, "The Vijñanavāda Theory as Presented in the Fourth Chapter of the Māṇḍūkya-Kārikā", in V. Raghavan (ed.), *Proceedings of the First International Sanskrit Conference,* March 26-31, 1972. Delhi: Ministry of Education and Social Welfare, 1981, Vol. 4, p. 196.

17 C. Sharma, *The Advaita Tradition in India Philosophy,* p. 163.

18 T.R.V. Murti, *The Central Philosophy of Buddhism* (London: George Allen and Unwin, 1974), p. 13.

19 H. Nakamura, *A History of Early Vedānta Philosophy* (Delhi: Motilal Banarsidass, 1983), p. 42 and 298.

14

Professor Hajime Nakamura's Contribution to Vedānta Studies

Shoun Hino

Professor Hajime Nakamura's work on Vedānta, a research conducted in Japan was not only pioneering, but a huge step forward. Nakamura was initiated into Vedānta by his guru, Hakuju Ui. Here we find a guru-śiṣya-paramparā in Vedānta studies at the University of Tokyo. Ui-Nakamura-Mayeda form a triad in this line, and of course under Mayeda's influence much has been achieved by the department of philosophy of the University of Tokyo.

Nakamura's *magnum opus* is, needless to say, the four volumes of *The History of Early Vedānta Philosophy*. [Sometimes we talk of five volumes, to include *The Thought of Śankara* published over two decades later.]

4/5 Serial Publications	English Edition
1. *The Early Vedānta Philosophy* (Shoki no Vedānta Tetugaku)	*A History of Early Vedānta Philosophy*, Part One (1983)
2. *The Philosophy of Brahma-sūtra* (Burahuma-Sutora no Tetugaku)	–do–
3. *The Development of Vedānta* (Vedānta Tetugaku no Hatten)	*ibid*, Part Two(2001)
4. *The Metaphysics of Words* (Kotoba no Keijijougaku) (1. to 4. in 1950-1956)	–do–
5. *The Thought of Śankara* (Śankara no Shisou) (1989)	not translated

This four-volume publication was composed at an initial stage of his academic career, but is a masterpiece. It was produced when he was only in his twenties! These volumes were invaluable to Japanese students of Vedānta, but unfortunately it was long before an English version was prepared.

The first volume of 1983 (Part One), comprising 1 and 2, was published by Motilal Banarsidass due to the endeavors of Mayeda and others, while Part Two, comprising 3 and 4, under the auspices of the Eastern Institute (Tokyo), appeared more than ten years later, in 2001. Though this was released after Nakamura's demise it fulfilled his last ardent wish. Mayeda reported[1] that P. Hacker had wanted to have an English translation while he was studying with him between 1963 and 1964. With the financial aid of the Eichin Research Center of Harvard University (due to D.H.H. Ingalls), the first volume was published in 1983, a quarter of a century after the completion of the four-volume publication.

Despite the forty-year gap between the study and the English version its academic value remains unchanged. Because the original work was in Japanese, its excellence was not so widely known in the earlier days.

Nakamura started his doctorate thesis on *The History of Early Vedānta Philosophy* in 1937, was awarded a Doctor of Literature degree from the University of Tokyo in 1943 and in the same year at the age of thirty, obtained the office of Associate Professor of the University of Tokyo.[2] It was this dissertation which became the four volumes brought out by Iwanami Shoten Publishers between 1950 and 1956.[3] Meanwhile the author became Professor of the University of Tokyo in 1954. In 1957, this work was awarded an Imperial Award.[4] Of course the war and post-war austerities brought great hardship to academia and cultural activities. Nakamura had to take great care even just to keep his manuscript from loss.[5]

In 1957 Pt. Jawaharlal Nehru visited Japan. In that year he had a chance to talk with envoys and suggest the promotion of cultural exchanges between Japan and India. This was the first contact which later culminated in the Indo-Japan Cultural Association in 1958. (For this reason also it is quite significant to have such a seminar like this to commemorate Prof. Nakamura.)[6]

According to D.H.H. Ingalls, there have been three types of methodology regarding research on Śankara and Advaita Vedānta:[7] These are (i)the traditional method, (ii)the philosophical method and (iii)the historical and philological method. The traditional method is time-aged and may be said to be of a religious purpose rather than research. In the purely philosophical method we should mention Eliot Deutsch, Rudolf Otto and others, and George Thibaut and Paul Deussen etc. for philosophical studies with a philological background. Deussen is particularly outstanding and therefore is said to have established the philosophical method. He studied Śankara's thought as a philosophy and maintained him to be the greatest philosopher of India. The first and second methods lack a historical point of view and therefore it was problematic to evaluate Sankara in the history of Vedānta.

Nakamura's teacher, Hakuju Ui, followed R. Garbe, who did his research on Indian philosophy from the historical and philological view-points. Furthermore Ui's study was based on a word-by-word understanding of quite a number of original texts in Chinese and Tibetan as well as Sanskrit. Under the influence of his academic attitude, he was not satisfied with Deussen's methodology and interpretation which was prevalent in those days, and endeavored to develop his own new methodology.[8] Nakamura, as a disciple of Ui, naturally followed this method and always took recourse to evidence obtained from original texts in every possible language. This historical and philological methodology led to the present-day study of the History of Indian Philosophy.

This evidence-based research methodology made Nakamura's scholarship unique and outstanding. His set of four volumes is no exception. In the Preface to the first volume[9] he explains that by examining much evidence of

Vedānta philosophical thought, he is attempting to describe the history of the early Vedānta schools collectively and historically as much as possible. To that end, he collected fragments elaborately and entirely from many original texts in India and Buddhist works in Tibetan and Chinese translation and reconstructed the early Vedānta philosophy from the philological and philosophical view-points.[10] This set of volumes has shed light on a dark part of the history of Vedānta philosophy, and is an epoch-making study in the research history of Vedānta philosophy.

The first volume, entitled *The Early Vedānta Philosophy,* consists of two parts, viz. 'The Significance of the Early Vedānta Philosophy' and 'The Early Vedānta Philosophy Seen from Indian Schools of Philosophy'. His evidence-based methodology enabled him to discuss and solve various important philological and philosophical problems such as the age of the Upaniṣad and the dates of Śankara and other ācāryas of his time. Moreover original Abhidharma and Mahāyāna Buddhist literature, Jaina literature, Vedānta philosophy found in orthodox Brāhmanic literature, Vedānta thoughts introduced by the classical Greek—all these are translated and examined.[11] By taking an instance I would like to illustrate his unparalleled greatness.

The dates of Śaṅkara are an important matter for discussion, for they influence the history of Indian thought. Scholars traditionally followed K.B. Pathak's assertion of 788-820 in 1881. Unfortunately this assertion was not backed by any evidence. To the contrary, Nakamura insisted on 700-750, taking recourse to philological evidence. This has been supported by L. Ronou and D.H.H. Ingalls. [Later K.K. Raja insisted on 'around the end of the 8th century'.][12]

The second volume, taking recourse to the *Brahma sūtra*, discusses people and ideas before the establishment of this *sūtra,* translates it and analyzes its thought. Earlier scholars like P. Deussen interpreted the *Brahma sūtra* by taking recourse to Śankara's Bhāṣya (the oldest of the 56 commentaries on it), and regarded Śankara's ideas here as the original intention of the *Brahma Sūtra*. Of course this is wrong and people have gradually come to understand that the intention of the *Brahma sūtra* is one thing and Śankara's thought is another. Under the circumstances the study of the *Brahma sūtra* itself was an urgent necessity.

Nakamura used the method of comparing the three oldest commentaries of Śaṅkara, Rāmānuja and Bhāskara. This was a painstaking philological way but the only one to reveal the original meaning of the Brahma *sūtra*. It was not in India, nor in the West, but in Japan that the original meaning was clarified and accepted. This is another epoch-making achievement in the history of Vedānta studies.[13]

The third volume, called *The Development of Vedānta Philosophy,* consists of two parts. This book handles the post-*Brahma sūtra* but pre-Śankara period. The first part refers to thirteen ·ācaryas of the post-*Brahma sūtra* period. Their fragments, found in various sources, are properly arranged and their personalities, works and thoughts are proposed. The latter part is devoted to the study of the Māṇduyakārikā by Gauḍapāda, who was Śankara's guru's guru.

Regarding part one, Bhartṛprapañca is a pre-Śankara Vedānta philosopher who left no works available to us in any written form. Should one wish to reconstruct his philosophy, one has to collect scattered references to him in others' works. We have quite a few references in Sureśvara's Vārtika on the *Bṛhadāraṇakopaniṣad* and some in Śankara's Bhāṣya on the same. Nakamura performed the task of collecting materials from scattered sources.[14] This means that he read the whole of Sureśvara's Vārtika, but he frankly abandoned the deeper studies of Bhartṛprapañca and Sureśvara. I confess that I myself have spent more than 20 years studying them. I believe that it is significant to have Nakamura's Foreword to my serial publication of Sureśvara's Vārtika.[15]

Regarding part two, the Māṇdukya kārikā is somehow Buddhistic and shows the initial appearance of the Advaitic thought that the world is false and that the *Brahman* is identical with the *Ātman*.

This work was completed around 1940 and published in 1955. At the same time Vidhushekhara Bhattacharyya studied the same work of Gauḍapāda and published the results in 1943, under the title Āgamaśāstra of Gauḍapāda (Calcutta University).[16] Let me introduce an episode related to these two books, the one in Japanese and the other in English. In the initial semester of my studying at the University of Poona, I happened to attend a Vedānta class for MA which prescribed two texts, Māṇḍūyakārikā and Brahma sūtra Śāṅkara Bhāṣ ya. When our teacher K.P. Jog (my guiding teacher at a later time) found a Japanese student using Nakamura's book on the Māṇḍūyakārikā, he immediately decided to incorporate Nakamura's explanation into his lecture. Since then in the class he has referred to Nakamura's translation and annotation. He rightly evaluated the excellence of Nakamura's work. Nakamura's achievement is far more excellent for he was conversant with Buddhism, and the world would have been surprised if it had been published in English.[17]

The fourth volume is devoted to the study of Bhartṛhari and entitled *The Metaphysics of Words*. Only after the 1960's did we begin to have good printed texts and translations or research books. It was 20 years before that he was working. Mayeda rightly says that he was a scholar beyond compare.[18]

At the end of his four books of History of Early Vedānta Philosophy Nakamura presents his conclusions after a long and vast study. [This is confirmed with a slight alteration in the last portion of vol. 5, viz. *The Thought of* Śan*kara*.] It would be better to have his own words on this point:

"It is generally recognized that the representative philosophy in the history of Indian thought is Vedānta and that its most well-known philosopher is Śaṅkara. The high esteem for Śaṅkara may be ascribed to two factors.....He [=Paul Deussen] went to extremes in praising Śaṅkara and regarded him as one of the three greatest philosophers in history,....The scholars of Indian philosophy who followed him also considered Śaṅkara to be the most important figure in Indian philosophy.....Śaṅkara is known today as the greatest philosopher in the history of Indian thought.[19].........From the above examination it becomes clear that all of these characteristics were advocated by someone before Śaṅkara. According to various previous scholars' ideas, he completed such a great achievement....Therefore it follows ..that there are few original ideas of Śaṅkara himself. He was the person who synthesized the Advaitavāda which had previously existed before him. The academic position of Śaṅkara himself was completely conservative....Śaṅkara, therefore, was not an original philosopher who advocated a radically new theory; rather, he was a synthesizer of existing Advaita and the rejuvenator, as well as a defender, of ancient learning.....Śaṅkara's greatness was not that of an original thinker but that of an unequalled commentator. [20] ....As a result of our investigation of early Vedānta philosophy, therefore, we must revise the traditional evaluation concerning Śaṅkara which has been generally accepted."[21]

The fifth volume was published later in 1989 and is separate from the above four-volume set. For it is called *The Thought of Śaṅkara* and is obviously distinguished from the early Vedānta philosophy. According to tradition quite a few works are ascribed to Śaṅkara himself. They are classified into three groups; (1) Bhāṣyas, (2) Prakaraṇa-granthas, and (3) Stotras. His usual text- and- evidence- based academic attitude confirms for him that (2) and (3) are of rather doubtful authenticity. This might have led to Mayeda's serial publications on the authenticity of Bhāṣyas traditionally ascribed to Śaṅkara.[22] Mayeda carried out his study under Paul Hacker as well as Nakamura. [Hacker made his contribution to the study of post-Śaṅkara Advaita with the same methodology as Nakamura's as mentioned above.] Mayeda maintains that the most important thing for the study of Śaṅkara is to clarify the reality of his philosophy. By concentrating on Śaṅkara's real and independent work, i.e. Upadeśaṣāhasrī, he has succeeded in this task in his triad of publications: Śaṅ*kara's upadeśasāhasrī, A Thousand Teachings* and *upadeśasāhasrī* (in Japanese).[23] These are textual critique based on the historical method and English and Japanese translations.

Nakamura covers every possible problematic discussion of Śaṅkara's Advaita in the main part of his volume. He also refers to *bhakti* and 'grace' here, which we are likely to overlook in Advaita studies although the word is a key to Hinduism.

Besides the five volumes, we have vols. 27 and 30 of *The Selected Works of Nakamura Hajime [the authorized edition]*, in which his Vedānta study is included. In vol. 27 (entitled *The Development of Vedānta Thought*) we have collected papers and the *Vedānta Sāra* [originally an independent book], and in vol. 30 (entitled *Hinduism and Epics*) we have *The History of Hinduism* [originally an independent book] (part one) and Two Epics and Purāṇas (part two).

The *Vedānta Sāra* (vol. 27, chapter 2) was originally published in 1962 under the title *Text and Translation: the Vedānta Sāra* .[24] It is explanatory and educative and therefore useful for beginners in Vedānta. He said that it was prepared for students of the University of Tokyo in those days as a text for a tutorial course. It is a beneficial and popular work.

In chapter 1 he discusses the post-Śaṅkara Vedānta such as Rāmānuja, Madhva and Nimbārka. He has not overlooked the topic of the Schools of Vadgalai and Tengalai, which occupy an important place as far as the bhakti movement is concerned. Moreover he discusses in detail Madhva and Vallabha in chapters 8 and 9 respectively. Both are quite distant from Advaita Vedānta. Madhva upholds Dvaita, the opposite of Śaṅkara's Advaita. Vallabha maintains that the world is real, which is again the opposite of Śaṅkara's position.

He also reports his visits to Śaṅkara's Matha in Śringeri, Kañcīpuram, and Puri in chapter 11. His contacts with present Śankaracāryas as well inform us about the present-day living Vedānta. These papers are quite fresh and stimulating. We have felt the necessity of a socio-anthropological study of Vedānta today[25] and its relation to Hinduism.

Though vol. 30 is devoted to Hinduism. Let me give some space to it here, for Vedānta and Hinduism are closely connected. Part one, viz. *A History of Hinduism,* was originally published in 1979.[26] Unlike other books on Hinduism, he tried to describe Hinduism historically and the result was a success. He opines that it is problematic whether Hinduism deserves a history, for the ancient form is alive even today and there is a scarcity of textual sources which can be dated. His historical description with its text-and- evidence-based methodology makes for a unique book on Hinduism. In the case of Hindu manners and customs we come to know some which are unchanged and some which have changed in the course of time. This academic attitude influenced following studies like pūjā *and samskāra,*[27] in which actual performances are described with photos but, by means of taking recourse to the original Sanskrit texts, historical changes and regional differences are also taken into consideration.

Part two, viz. Epics and Mythology, handles Mahābhārata, Rāmāyaṇa, Bhagavadgītā and Purāṇas. These literatures are sources of Hinduism and it is therefore essential to have detailed knowledge of each while talking about India. This part overwhelms with historical and evidence-based information. We can confirm that the Hindu gods of Vedic or Paurāṇic origin are enriched in the mythology of Purāṇas.

Besides the five volumes of the History of Early Vedānta and two books from *The Selected Works,* we have many a paper regarding Vedānta, but I must summarize his contribution to Vedānta studies before closing my presentation.

(a) It is most significant that he produced the four volumes of *A History of Early Vedānta* and *The Thought of Śaṅkara* (five volumes altogether), which threw a light on a dark period of Vedānta studies.

(b) In this five volume set he established a new methodology for Vedānta studies, i.e. a text- and- evidence-based one; and he maintains a fresh evaluation of Śaṅkara, i.e. that Śaṅkara was not the greatest philosopher but a synthesizer of a past tradition of Vedāntic thought.

(c) Besides his pre-Śaṅkara and Śaṅkara works, he made many contributions and encouraged succeeding Vedānta students to proceed yet deeper in their studies. Sengaku Mayeda was among his students and is his real successor in Vedānta studies.

References

1 S. Mayeda "Prof Nakamura Hajime and Indian Philosophy," *The World of Nakamura Hajime*. Tokyo, Seidosha, 1985, p.88. (in Japanese) I am much indebted to this article while preparing for this presentation and therefore I cordially thank S. Mayeda for it.

2 "The Chronicle of Doctor Nakamura Hajime," *Toho*, vol. 15, p.6. (in Japanese)

3 "The Publication Catalogue of Doctor Nakamura Hajime," *Toho*, vol. 15, pp.31-32. (in Japanese)

4 "The Chronicle.,p.7.

5 "Prof Nakamura., p.86.

6 "The Chronicle., p.7.

7 S. Mayeda, *The Philosophy of Vedānta,* p.3 (in Japanese); originally *Annals of Bhandarkar Oriental Research Institute,* vol. XXXIII, 1952, pp.1-4; for more detailed information, S. Mayeda, "Past and Future of the study of Śaṅkara," *Mountains of Academism*. pp.20-36, JSPS,1993. (in Japanese)

8 "Prof Nakamura.," pp.70-71.

9 *The Early Vedānta Philosophy.* Tokyo, Iwanami Shoten Publishers, 1981[1950]. p. 3.

10 "Prof Nakamura.," p. 76.

11 *Ibid.*, p. 77.

12 For this I referred to my notebook for Mayeda's intensive course work on "*Upadeśasāhasrī* of Śaṅkara" held at the University of Nagoya in the fall semester of 1974.

13 "Prof Nakamura.," pp.80-81.

14 *The Development of Vedānta*. Tokyo, Iwanami Shoten Publishers, 1981[1955], pp.153ff.

15 Foreword by Hajime Nakamura to my books on Sureśvara's Vārtika in the serial publications called Advaita Tradition Series vols.5-11 (Motilal Banarsidass, 1993-2001). When I sent a complimentary copy of vol. 1 of the same, i.e. Sureśvara's Vārtika on Yājñavalkya-Maitreyi Dialogue, in 1982, he replied that this study of Suresvara's Vārtika on the *Bṛhad*āraṇyakopaniṣad is tough and will be the work of a century, and thus encouraged me to continue it.

16 *Ibid.*, p. 82.

[17] *Op.cit.*

[18] I found his phrase 'fuseishutu-no-gakusha' for the first time in *The Asahi* (a leading Japanese newspaper) on the 11th of October reporting Prof. Nakamura's sad demise.

[19] *A History of Early Vedānta Philosophy Part Two. Toho (Nakamura Hajime 2nd Anniversary Special Issue).* Tokyo, The Eastern Institute, 2001, p. 671. During this Seminar a new edition of the same was declared to have been released from Motilal Banarsidass.

[20] *Ibid.*, pp. 678-679.

[21] *Ibid.*, p. 680.

[22] See "Past and..," p. 35 note(3).

[23] (i) *Śaṅkara's Upadeśasāhasrī Critically Edited with Introduction and Indices.* Tokyo, The Hokuseido Press, 1973.

(ii) *A Thousand Teachings: The Upadeśasāhasrī of Śaṅkara, Translated with Introduction and Notes.* Tokyo, The University of Tokyo Press, 1979.

(iii) *Upadeśasāhasrī Quest after the Real Nature of the Self.* Tokyo, Iwanami Shoten Publishers, 1988. (in Japanese)

[24] The publisher was Heirakuji-shoten in Kyoto.

[25] For example, Y. Sawai, *The Faith of Ascetics and Lay Smārtas A Study of the Śankaran Tradition of* Śringeri. Vienna, Sammlung De Nobili, 1992.

[26] It was released from Yamakawa-shuppansha, Tokyo. (in Japanese)

[27] By M.Tachikawa, S.Hino and L.Deodhar (Delhi, Motilal Banarsidass, 2001).

Bibliography

English

Hajime Nakamura: *A History of Early Vedānta Philosophy, Part One.* Delhi, Motilal Banarsidass, 1990[1983]; and *Part Two.* Delhi, Motilal Banarsidass, 2004 [originally in *Toho (Nakamura Hajime 2nd Anniversary Special Issue)*, The Eastern Institute, 2001.]

Japanese

Hajime Nakamura: *The Early Vedānta Philosophy.* Tokyo, Iwanami Shoten Publishers, 1981[1950].

-do- *The Philosophy of Brahma*-sūtra. Tokyo, Iwanami Shoten Publishers, 1981[1951].

-do- *The Development of Vedānta*. Tokyo, Iwanami Shoten Publishers, 1981[1955].

-do- *The Metaphysics of Words*. Tokyo, Iwanami Shoten Publishers, 1981[1956].

-do- *The Thought of Śaṅkara*. Tokyo, Iwanami Shoten Publishers, 1981[1989].

-do- *The Development of Vedānta Thought. The Selected Works of Nakamura Hajime* [*the authorized eidition*]. vol. 27, Tokyo, Shunjusha, 1996.

-do- *Hinduism and Epics. The Selected Works of Nakamura Hajime* [*the authorized edition*]. vol. 30, Tokyo, Shunjusha, 1996.

Sengaku Mayeda: *The Philosophy of Vedānta*. Kyoto, Heirakuji-shoten, 1980.

Toho vol. 15 (Nakamura Hajime Commemoration Volume). Tokyo, The Eastern Institute, 1999.

15

Professor Hajime Nakamura's Contributions to the study of Eastern Philosophy and Culture

S. Shyamkishore Singh

I

Professor Hajime Nakamura was an internationally renowned scholar who had made lasting contributions to the Indian and Buddhist studies. He was an erudite scholar of vast learning. He had deep knowledge of the ancient Indian tradition, especially the development of Vedāntic thought from the Upaniṣads to the Vedāntic system of philosophy, as well as Buddhist philosophy, religion and cultural tradition.

In his "A History of Early Vedantic Philosophy" he has delved deep into the obstruse knowledge of early Vedāntic thought by dint of his profound knowledge of Sanskrit language and Indian philosophy. In this book, he has not only traced the development of Vedāntic thought from the Upaniṣ ads to the Vedāntic system of Śamkara and other commentators of the Brahmasutra, but has brought to light hitherto unknown facts about ancient Indian thought and culture. He has marvelously constructed the pre-Śamkara Vedānta spanning over a long period of about one thousand years. His approach to the research in this field and the methodology which he adopted are quite innovative and path-breaking. His linguistic, psychological and sociological analyses and observations are profound and logical. He has given a panoramic view of Indian philosophy and has observed that the representative thought of India is Vedānta philosophy. He writes:

"The attempt.....to define some common characteristic of all shades of Indian philosophy, so called, is nothing more than a general descriptive term to cover variegated, heterogeneous systems of thought, a historical product of countless thinkers of various racial and cultural origins advocating mutually opposing views, criticising each other and sometimes synthesizing diverse strands of thought. It is almost impossible to reach a final decision on what constitutes 'Indian philosophy'.

In spite of this complexity which defies any easy summarizing of its major presuppositions, if we were asked to name the representative thought of India, we would not hesitate even for a moment to assert that it is Vedānta philosophy".[1]

The reason which he has given for this contention is that Hindu religious sects, the common faith of Indian populace looked to Vedānta philosophy for the theoretical foundation of their theology. Besides, the influence of Vedānta is prominent in the sacred Āgamas and Tantras. Moreover, the founders and leading scholars of many sects of Hinduism had written commentaries on the Brahmasūtra, which is the fundamental scripture of Vedānta. Nakamura maintains that "Vedānta has had a determining effect on the ways of thinking of all Indians transcending racial distinction, class status, degree of education, and so forth'. And the outstanding characteristic of the history of Indian philosophy is the fact that Vedānta has been such a powerful and predominant intellectual force".[2]

Regarding the importance of the study of Early Vedānta philosophy he maintains that "However well one studies the history of thought after Śaṅkara, the results will be very incomplete if its relationship to pre-Śaṅkara Vedānta philosophy is neglected".[3] He has added that the history of philosophy after Śaṅkara will be incomplete if the pre-Śaṅkara period were to be discarded because the proper evaluation of the later thought can be made only when it is viewed in the light off the developments in the past.

Nakamura is of the view that there is no conflict between the two interpretations of the word "Vedānta"—as 'the end of the Vedas' and as 'the ultimate meaning or ultimate truth of the Vedas'. He says that "Upaniṣad, as the title of the literature, has sometimes been translated in Japan as 'the inner doctrine writings' or okugi-sho, but there is no such translation in the Chinese version of the Buddhist canon. The word 'upaniṣad' signifies that the Upaniṣads are "the records of secret teachings given at a meeting in private, with master and disciple sitting facing each other".[4]

On the issue of the relationship between the Vedānta school and other systems of philosophy, Nakamura maintains that in the course of its long development Vedānta became engaged in logical disputes with the contemporary schools of thought, and in the process of interaction it was also influenced by the doctrines of other schools. Thus, for example, scholars have frequently referred to the remarkable influence, in particular of the philosophy of Mahāyāna Buddhism on the Advaita school of the early period, that of the Sāmkhya school on the Rāmānuja school, the Nimbārka school, the Vallabha school and the later Advaita school".[5] He has maintained that "since the Vedānta school itself split up into numerous ramified schools and adopted ideas from other schools, the history of Vedānta philosophy is really something like a miniature copy or reflection of the entire history of Indian philosophy".[6]

Nakamura follows a two-pronged approach in tracing the development of early Vedānta—on the one hand, drawing materials from the outside, i.e., the classical works of the other thought systems, and on the other, from within, i.e., through the study of the classical works of the pre-Śaṅkara Vedānta. Regarding the first approach, he takes up the classical works of Buddhism and Jainism for scrutiny. What impresses us in this respect is the systematic way in which Nakamura looks at the issue. Along with minute study of the texts, he discusses the issue from two angles, namely (a) Vedānta philosophy as seen by the Buddhists of ancient China and Japan, and (b) Vedānta philosophy as seen by the Jainas. In so far as, the so-called internal evidences, particularly from the Brahmanical literatures, are concerned, Nakamura has discussed three extant classical works, namely (i) Brahma-Sūtra, (ii) Māndūkya Kārikā of Gauḍapāda, and (iii) Vākyapadīya of Bhatṛhari. According to him, these three along with some great Upaniṣads, such as, the Bṛhadāraṇyaka, the Chāndogya, etc., throw great light on the development of early Vedānta philosophy.

Nakamura's observation on the contribution of the *Brāhmins* to the development of Brāhmanical literature and the preservation of the Vedānta tradition, especially his sociological analysis of the role of the *Brāhmin* caste in Indian society and culture, is quite interesting and deserves attention of the scholars who study Indian history and culture. He writes: "Indian culture developed and attained maturity centering chiefly around the priestly caste of Brāhmins. In India for three thousand years from the ancient past to the present, the major industry has been agriculture, and almost all the inhabitants have been farmers living in small villages throughout the country, following an economic life isolated and feudalistic. The leaders at the centre of this farming culture were in fact the Brāhmins".[7] One of the reasons for this contention is that "The dependence on the course of nature for the livelihood of the people was particularly great, and incantations of the Brāhmins were essential in cultivation of the land and avoiding disasters of famine and epidemics....The close connection between the farmers and the Brāhmins was firm and unshakable for over three thousand years..."[8]

Nakamura recognizes the contributions of other castes of society, but gives his observations as follows: No small part of the noble culture which arose in India in the past was from the hands of those outside the Brāhmin caste, but it has no stability as a social tradition, and immediately vanished. The weakness of the cultural tradition of the warriors is an example. In the past there existed a brilliant warrior culture in India but practically none of it survived. For instance, it is an indubitable historical fact that in very ancient past the martial arts were actively studied, but the classics on the martial arts were all lost, and all that has survived is fragments annexed to religious works of the Brāhmins".[9]

Nakamura's findings are mostly based on the evidences from the historical facts, the reading and interpretation of scriptural texts, the Dharmaśāstras, etc., as well as the study of accounts by the foreign travelers in the ancient days. He says that "the works of foreigners traveling throughout India, living there for some time, and actually seeing first hand the life of the ancient Indian people, are particularly valuable" for constructing the socio-cultural history of ancient India.[10]

II

Nakamura's scholarly contributions to the Buddhistic studies have been well known. Mention may be made of some of his books, such as, *Indian Buddhism—A Survey with Bibliographical Notes, Buddhism in Comparative Light, Ways of thinking of Eastern Peoples*, etc. Of these, the last one is quite a challenging work which has thrown great light on the culture and tradition of the people of Asia. He has referred to a number of facts which are not known to many people about the ways of thinking of these people. He has referred to the history of Buddhism for his evidences. Buddhism, as everyone knows, is a world religion, whose basic principles are universal, transcending social and national distinctions, a religion accepted and welcomed by the people of different countries beyond its own Indian homeland. Nakamura has pointed out that as Buddhism passed from one Asian country to another it was in each case modified "according to the features peculiar to the ways of each recipient nation". Taking Buddhism as the common denominator, he has wonderfully analysed the ways of thinking of the Indian, Chinese, Japanese and Tibetan people. He says that "even in times past, when communication between peoples in different cultural areas was much more difficult than it is today, the human mind has been occupied with much the same problems. Approaches and concepts appear in different contexts, but we have nevertheless comparable histories with comparable diagnosis of the human situation with comparable, if variable, responses".[11]

Nakamura discusses the history of Buddhism in India, and the Chinese, the Japanese and the Tibetan responses to

Buddhism. He finds clues to certain fundamental and persisting characteristics of their different modes of thought. These characteristics in turn help to explain their fundamental historical and cultural differences one from another and their variant responses to western culture in our time. He has cast a wide net in the course of his study. Over and above a serious and in-depth study of the philosophico-religious literature in the subject, he has combed folk literature, prayers and scriptures of popular cults, collection of the proverbs, descriptions of everyday life and the accounts of foreign travelers. Regarding the method which he follows, Nakamura writes: "In order to accomplish the study systematically, I adopt the following methods. When possible, I aimed to isolate the characteristic features of the ways of thinking of each people in the form of expression of judgments and the inferences. I intend to proceed with investigations of concrete cultural phenomena which also reflect the ways of thinking and the thought process of each people. To clarify the particular ways in which Buddhism and Indian logic were introduced from India into China, Japan and Tibet, that is, how a universal religion and logic has modified itself according to the native characteristics of each people was the special focus of my research. I, therefore, applied the same methods in investigating the ways of thinking of each people". [12]

According to Nakamura, 'ways of thinking' (Denkweise) refer to any individual's thinking in which the characteristic feature of the thinking habits of the group to which he belongs is revealed. It involves the thinking about concrete empirical questions, which may also involve value judgments and questions of value.[13]

III

Nakamura has considered the special features of the ways of thinking of the Indians. Let me briefly put them as follows:

1. Nakamura observes that the Indian thinkers tend to lay stress on the universal rather than the particular. Indian people are inclined to consider the universal seriously in their thinking process. He refers to the verbal usage in Sanskrit in which

abstract nouns are formed adding *tā* (f.) or *tva* (n.) suffix to the root. Such kind of practice is followed in European languages also. But the difference is that the European languages express the individual by its attribute or quality realized concretely by the individual itself, while the Sanskrit expresses the individual only as one of the instances belonging to the abstract universal.[14]

2. Another feature is mentioned as the fondness for the negative expression. This will be evident when we give attention to the use of noun with the negative in the Sanskrit language. "For example, the Indians say 'victory or non-victory' (*jayājayou*) instead of victory or defeat' in English, Japanese, etc. The word composed with the negative has not only negative meaning but it has a positive meaning. According to Nakamura, in the Indian mind 'non-idleness' (*apramāda*), non-grudge' (*avera*), non-violence (*ahimsā*), etc., appeal as the more positive morality than exertion, tolerance, peace, etc. To the Europeans such a negative expression of these virtues appeals less than a positive expression as for the practical meaning.

3. Disregard for the individual and the particular is also regarded as another characteristic. Nakamura observes that "Ancient Indian languages had no pronouns equivalent to 'each' and 'every' which was distinguished by 'all'. So they used the singular form of "*sarva*" (all) to express 'each' and every'. The pronoun "*sarva*" means "all" in the plural form, and in singular it means 'each' or 'every'. Therefore the Indians thought that the individual is only the limited one by the universal through all things".[15]

4. The concept of the unity of all things has also been mentioned. Nakamura says, "From a very early age, the Indians held a strong tendency to think that the multifarious phenomena of this world are self expressions of one absolute being. The main current of Indian metaphysics is a thoroughgoing monism. A primitive form of this monistic view was expressed in the hymns of the world creation in the Ṛgveda. And it took a more clearly defined form in the Upaniṣads".[16]

5. Nakamura refers to Sanskrit again, and maintains that Indians characterise action attributively, whereas the Western people comprehend action through its changing aspects. This way of thinking influenced the construction of concepts and influenced their thought process. He writes: "The thought process which the existence at the back of phenomenal world has been regarded as important than phenomenal world itself naturally results in paralised state of concept of time, especially of concept of difference in time, which is employed in expressing concrete facts of experience. This has led to the contemplative nature of the Indians".[17]

6. Nakamura has pointed out that in Indian thinking the supremacy of the universal self over the individual self has been emphasized. He writes: "The Indian people concern themselves only about the unobstructed extension of one's self from the point of view of their languages; however, it is an undeniable fact that they never ignore the existence of others' personality. They have a high regard for others. It is often stated in the writings of early Buddhism and other teachings that one should pay regard to others, and that one should not neglect others. It has been the ideal of the Indians to attain the non-discrimination between the self and the other. They assume that the existence of the Universal Self is known directly from the existence of the individual self. In the Upaniṣ ads they teach, "All this thou art', or "I am thou". And those statements form the core of their ethics'.[18]

7. Subservence to the power of the universal law is another point mentioned by Nakamura. He says, "For Indians it is a matter of the greatest moral and religious importance to know the Universal Law and to submit themselves to it. And this feature of Indian thought can be observed also in their concept of 'faith'. '*Śraddhā*' is the Sanskrit word that is usually translated in the Western languages by 'fides', 'grauba' or 'faith'. But what Indians mean by the word is not exactly the same as the faith of Western religions. *Śraddhā* means to believe in and rely upon a man of superior wisdom and at the same time it indicates wholehearted acceptance of the doctrine that man professes. Indians, refusing to place faith in a

particular person or saint, hope to submit themselves to the Universal Law that stands above individuals".[19]

Nakamura remarks that "Indians are a religious and, at the same time, philosophical people". But he has contrasted Indian religion to Greek religion. The points that he brings out will be of some interest. He writes: "In Greece, the religion of the polis required every citizen to sacrifice himself in the interest of the thing greater than oneself– in the interest of the aggregation called polis. And it should be noted that this Greek self-sacrifice was done to meet the practical needs of the men in the polis as 'a sacrifice to the fraternity. The Indian religion, on the other hand, attached little importance to secular social organizations. Its primary concern was the quest for the universal Law. Here the Indian religion differs essentially from the Greek".[20]

Nakamura is of the opinion that "A sense of unity as a nation or a race was not nourished among the early Indians. Alexander the Great, during his invasion of India, notwithstanding some resistance of local lords was never harassed by a defence put up by the Indians as a whole".[21]

8. A point raised by Nakamura about Indian thinking is 'lack of historical consciousness'. He said that "all Indian books are tinged with a fantastic and legendary colour. They are not products of historical science, but rather works of art".[22]

In addition to the characteristics of Indian thinking mentioned above, Nakamura has also made the observation that "Indian thought is introspective in character", that it is by and large "metaphysical", and also that there is "spirit of tolerance and reconciliation".

Some of the features of Indian thinking mentioned by Nakamura need serious consideration. In respect of some others, it appears that the generalizations that he has made are too sweeping. He, however, as a serious scholar makes effort to justify his contentions with evidences and arguments. I shall not elaborate on this matter.

IV

Regarding the ways of thinking of the Chinese people, Nakamura has based his study on various cultural phenomena, particularly on the process of accepting Buddhism. He says that the Chinese did not accept Buddhism in its Indian form. After it was introduced into China it was modified under the influence of the traditional ways of thinking of the Chinese people. Chinese Buddhism has diverged from Indian Buddhism to a very great degree. He maintains that the following facts have influenced the nature and extent of these divergences:[23]

1. The Chinese made complete translation of the Buddhist scriptures into their own language. They did not use Sanskrit or Prakrit as a sacred language of the Buddhist Church.

2. In translating, the Chinese Buddhist scholars and exegetes were not in a position to refer to or understand the original Indian texts.

3. Later Chinese Buddhist scholars, with few exceptions, were not in a position to refer to or understand the original Indian texts.

4. Many texts of Chinese Buddhism developed along with lines entirely different from the doctrines of Indian schools.

5. The exegetical techniques of the Chinese Buddhists are entirely different from those of the Indians.

Let me briefly refer to some of the points given by Nakamura as the ways of thinking of the Chinese:

(a) Emphasis on the perception of the concrete—Referring, for example, to the pictorial or heliographic Chinese scripts, Nakamura maintains that the Chinese way of expressing concepts is concrete.

(b) Again, referring to the Chinese language, Nakamura has mentioned of the lack of development of abstract thought.

(c) Emphasis on the particular—Regarding this point, Nakamura writes: "the tendency to value and to devote attention to the particular rather than the universal is observable in many different aspects of Chinese culture. The

Five Classics which are works of the highest authority regarded as providing the norms for human life contain, for most part, descriptions of particular incidents and statements of particular facts. They do not state general principles of human behaviour".[24]

(d) Another feature is stated to be conservation expressed in exaltation of antiquity, i.e., to the ancient tradition and custom.

(e) "Fondness for complex multiplicity expressed in concrete form", has also been mentioned as a characteristic of Chinese thinking.

(f) Nakamura also says that "The Chinese regarded certain old classics as absolute authorities, and it was only on these that they composed their commentaries and explanations. They never looked at the classics from historical origin, or criticized them...They attached great importance to formal conformity".[25]

(g) Nakamura also makes special mention of the Chinese tendency towards practicality. He says that the Chinese are very practical people. Mention also has been made of their reconciling and harmonizing tendencies.[26]

V

Let me now briefly dwell on that part of Nakamura's book which is devoted to the features of the Japanese way of thinking. He refers to "Characteristics of Japanese ways of thinking as revealed in various cultural phenomena, particularly in the process of accepting Buddhism". He writes:

"The Japanese of the past were in the habit of expressing abstract notions through the medium of the Chinese script. The influence of the Chinese script upon Japanese patterns of thought was tremendous. It will be remembered that it was through the *sūtras* written in Chinese that the Japanese first came in contact with Buddhism and Indian thought".[27]

Nakamura, however, maintains that although Buddhism came to Japan from China, the Japanese did not simply copy the Chinese culture and tradition. Japanese people in the past, adopted Buddhism with firm faith in its teachings as interpreted according to their traditional wisdom, and as such, Buddhism as the Japanese follow it maintains its own identity. According to Nakamura, Chinese thought was not received by the Japanese in its original form.

The following points given by Nakamura deserve special mention:

(a) The Japanese have a tendency to respect the natural feelings of man. They attach importance to the rules of propriety which are based upon human relationship.

(b) Subjective relationships are given special attention and actions are taken on the basis of mutual understandings and trust among subjects. Further, the expressive forms of Japanese sentences put more emphasis upon emotive factors than on cognitive factors.

(c) Stressing upon the Japanese acceptance of actuality of the phenomenal world, Nakamura writes: "According to the general view of the Indians, it is desirable to be delivered from this world. But in Japan, while accepting the theory of the transmigration of the soul on the one hand, they wish, on the other hand, to be reborn into this world".[28] Nakamura also says, "While the religions of the world very often tend to regard this world, as the land of impurity and the other world, as the blessed land of purity, where one seeks the Heaven of eternal happiness, primitive Shintoism of Japan recognizes the intrinsic value here in this world".[29] Nakamura has also written about some other features of the Japanese way of thinking with special reference to the practice of Buddhism.

VI

In his book herein referred to, Nakamura has also dealt with the Tibetan ways of thinking. But in this paper, I have not discussed his views about the Tibetan ways of thinking in general and the way in which the Tibetans adopted Buddhism. To conclude this brief account of Nakamura's contributions to Eastern thought, it will be quite appropriate to refer to the following points presented in his own words:

"Thus we must acknowledge the fact that there exists no single 'Eastern' feature but rather that there exist diverse ways of thinking in East Asia, characteristic of certain peoples but not of the whole of East Asia. This can be affirmed by way of comparison between the cultures of the East Asian nations, and by noting the fact that Buddhism was received by various nations of East Asia according to the character of the recipient; this clearly testifies to the reality of this view-point. It other words, Buddhism whose basic principle is universality and transcendency has been taken in with certain modifications, modifications which were made according to the features of the ways of thinking of each recipient nation".[30]

Nakamura's researches in the field of Indian philosophy and culture as well as Buddhism are of very high order. He has deep knowledge and understanding of both the Eastern and the Western thoughts. Moreover, his attempt to understand the minds of various peoples is singular and unique in the sense that hardly any scholar of his calibre has followed the method that he followed. He not only treads on the usual path of studying the scriptural texts and giving interpretations to them, but also studies how people belonging to various cultural backgrounds follow a particular religion, namely Buddhism, and maintains their respective cultural identities. He has accepted the reality of cultural pluralism. He has also demonstrated how in the midst of diversity there can be sympathetic understanding among people through cross-cultural interaction and dialogue. For this purpose what is needed is to understand other peoples' culture as one understands one's own culture. The methodology followed by Nakamura may profitably be pursued by the scholars for a better understanding of Indian thought and culture.

References

1 H. Nakamura, A History of Early Vedānta Philosophy, p. 2.
2 *Ibid.*, p. 4.
3 *Ibid.*, p. 5.
4 *Ibid.*, p. 102.
5 *Ibid.*, p. 113.
6 *Ibid.*, p. 114.
7 *Ibid.*, p. 296.
8 *Op. cit.*
9 *Ibid.*, p. 297.
10 *Ibid.*, p. 359.
11 Buddhism in Comparative Light, p. 176.
12 The Ways of Thinking of Eastern peoples; Introduction.
13 *Ibid.*, p. 3.
14 *Ibid.*, p. 16.
15 *Ibid.*, p. 34.
16 *Ibid*, p. 39.
17 *Ibid.*, p. 48.
18 *Ibid.*, p. 81.
19 *Ibid.*, p. 96.
20 *Ibid.*, p. 101.
21 *Op. cit.*
22 *Ibid.*, p. 115.
23 *Ibid.*, p. 166.
24 *Ibid.*, p. 187.
25 *Ibid.*, p. 219.
26 *Ibid.*, p. 462.
27. *Ibid.*, p. 299.
28. *Ibid.*, p. 549.
29. *Ibid.*, p. 541.
30. *Ibid.*, p. 633.

16

The Contribution of Professor Hajime Nakamura to the Study of Nyāya-Vaiśeṣika and Indian Logic

Toshihiro Wada

1. Introduction

The late Professor Hajime Nakamura left a great mark on the study of Indian philosophies in general and Vedānta and Buddhism in particular as well as the comparative history of thought, and his works on these subjects have been published and widely read in English. He has also left a great heritage in the study of Nyāya and Vaiśeṣika philosophies and Indian logic, but unfortunately most of his works in these fields are written in Japanese and so are inaccessible to a greater audience overseas.

Here, I will mainly introduce one volume of the Hajime Nakamura Selected Works, i.e., the 25th volume, which is devoted to the study of Nyāya and Vaiśeṣika philosophies and Indian logic. This volume is a good guide not only for readers unfamiliar with these philosophies, but also for those who wish to obtain more information about them. The section-notes of the volume refer to 459 papers written in Japanese and 542 papers written in other languages, or 1001 papers in all. I do not know any other book in Japan or abroad that contains such a large number of references. Moreover, I wonder how Nakamura collected this vast number of papers. His friends may have presented him with papers and books, but it is also true that he went through the major journals and meticulously collected publications both in Japan and abroad.

Not included in this volume are Nakamura's Japanese translations of the *Padārthadharmasaṃgraha*, or the *Praśastapādabhāṣya*, Dharmakīrti's *Nyāyabindu*, or his "A Glossary of Indian Logical Terms". These three works accelerated the trend of using plain Japanese in the study of the Nyāya and Vaiśeṣika schools and in the translation of their texts. Of the three I will refer to the glossary to a larger extent in the following sections.

Since I am not able to speak about the whole volume, I will restrict myself to Nakamura's contributions to philological and comparative studies. The second section of the present paper is devoted first to information about his philological studies of Nyāya and Vaiśeṣika and then to some examples of his comparative studies on Vaiśeṣika and Greek philosophy. The third section deals with his method of comparing Indian logic with Western logic. In addition, I will briefly introduce his book, *The Structure of Logic*, which presents the final form of his comparative studies on the above types of logic.

2. Nyāya-Vaiśeṣika

2.1 Translation

2.1.1: Nakamura translated the *Nyāyasūtra* with the first Adhyāya of the *Nyāyabhāṣya* into Japanese. In translating, he used Walter Ruben's edition of the *Nyāyasūtra*[1] and the *Nyāyabhāṣya*, the first Adhyāya being included in Ānanda-āśrama Sanskrit Series No. 21. He referred to preceding translations of the two Sanskrit texts: Yushō Miyasaka's Japanese translation,[2] Debiprasad Chattopadhyaya and Mrinalkanti Gangopadhyaya's English translation,[3] Keśava Śāstrī's English translation,[4] and Ganganath Jha's English translation.[5] Nakamura provided English or German renderings of the technical terms of Nyāya in the notes to his translation in order to promote a clear understanding of these terms among his readers. This was an important undertaking, because he wanted to change the custom of utilizing classical Chinese renderings of technical terms in translating Sanskrit texts. He emphasized the use of modern Japanese to translate Sanskrit technical terms as a way to allow the average reader easier access to Indian philosophy.

2.1.2: Nakamura translated the *Vaiśeṣikasūtra* into Japanese using the sūtra numbers given to the text edited with the commentary of Śaṅkara Miśra, i.e., the *Upaskāra*.[6] He of course knew that the *Vaiśeṣikasūtra* presented with the *Upaskāra* caused many textual problems, but he made use of the sūtra numbers of this edition for two reasons: (1) Since preceding research on the *Vaiśeṣikasūtra* almost always referred to the sūtra numbers of that edition, it was convenient to refer to the same edition; (2) It would be impossible to make a perfect critical edition. Nakamura knew that there were two more editions available: those by Jambuvijaya and Anantalal Thakur.[7] He explained implicitly why he did not use the sūtra numbers of the editions by these two eminent scholars. That is, Jambuvijaya's edition had already been translated by Enshō Kanakura into Japanese, and Thakur's edition was not looked upon as prevailing. However, in writing notes to his translation of the *Vaiśeṣikasūtra*, Nakamura often mentioned the differences in readings among the above three editions.

2.1.3: A Japanese translation of the *Padārthadharmasaṃgraha* was published in 1978 by Nakamura as part of a paper entitled "Japanese Translation of the Vaiseṣika Texts and the Padārthadharmasaṃgraha".[8] Enshō Kanakura [1971] had previously translated the same text and the *Vaiśeṣikasūtra* into Japanese, but it is not easy for young students to read Kanakura's translation because it is full of classical Chinese renderings of the technical terms of Vaiśeṣika. I hope that Nakamura's translation of the *Padārthadharma saṃgraha* will be published in book form on the earliest possible occasion.

2.2 Comparative Studies

2.2.1: An important characteristic of the 25th Volume is its clarification of the features of Vaiśeṣika philosophy by means of a comparison with the philosophies of Plato and Aristotle. Nakamura focuses on the concept of the universal (*sāmānya, jāti*) and particular (*viśeṣa*) in Vaiśeṣika and the idea, or *eidos*, in Plato's and Aristotle's philosophies. In his comparison, he refers occasionally to Chinese philosophers, but in the present paper these references are negligible. I would like to look at how he compares the two philosophies.

2.2.2: Before dealing with Plato, Nakamura compares the concepts of the universal in Vaiśeṣika and Aristotle's philosophy and points to a correspondence between them. We should note that there is a difference between Plato and Aristotle on the universal: Plato held that a universal is an essence behind things, while Aristotle held that a universal is an essence in things. To identify a universal or an individual thing, Aristotle uses a set of concepts: genus and species. 'Genus' means a division/classification, while 'species' means a sub-division/sub-classification. For example, if the mammal is a genus, then the human being is a species. It follows that if we classify human beings, the human being is a genus while Indians and Japanese are species. Nakamura states that the genus and the species correspond to the universals in Vaiśeṣ ika, and that the essence of an individual entity corresponds to a final particular (*antyaviśeṣa*) in Vaiśeṣika. According to Aristotle, the highest universal is spirit; according to Vaiśeṣ ika, it is beingness (*sattā*) residing in substances (*dravya*), qualities (*guṇa*), and actions (*karman*). In this regard Nakamura claims that the universal in Vaiśeṣika is more physical than Aristotle's universal.

To continue the discussion of 'genus' and 'species', Nakamura mentions Porphyrios' tree. In this model, the entities in the world are classified into the corporeal and the incorporeal, the corporeal into the animate and the inanimate. The animate are living beings. The animate are further classified into the sensible and the insensible, and the sensible are animals. The sensible are classified into the rational and the irrational; the rational are classified into the mortal and the immortal. The mortal are human beings; they are Socrates, Plato, Aristotle, etc. Thus, by using 'genus' and 'species', we can arrive at an individual person. This method of classification is represented as a tree, which is called 'Porphyrios' tree'.

We can represent the relation among the universals and the particulars as in the case of Porphyrios' tree, but Nakamura states that the method of classification represented by Porphyrios' tree is not effective in classical India, because classical India placed no importance on the classification of beings by means of the universal and particular, which correspond to 'genus' and 'species' respectively, and did not develop a taxonomy of plants and animals. This assumption implies that the universal and the particular in Vaiśeṣika did not help to establish a taxonomy of plants and animals in classical India and that these Vaiśeṣika concepts have less connection with nature than 'genus' and 'species' in Greek philosophy. This implication, however, seems contradictory to Nakamura's previous claim that the universal in Vaiśeṣika is more physical than Aristotle's universal.

2.2.3: On the logical significance of Plato's idea, Nakamura agrees with Bertrand Russell that the word 'cat' refers to something and not to an individual cat, that it is not true that when a cat is born, the thing meant by 'cat' is born, that even when one cat dies, the thing meant by 'cat' does not die, and that thing meant by 'cat' is not restricted by time and space, and is eternal. This claim is also applicable to the Vaiśeṣ ika concept of universal. Nakamura holds both Plato's idea and the Vaiśeṣika universal in high esteem, because they were the first to offer a device to make individuals belong to one class.

Nakamura then presents another aspect of Plato's philosophy: that the idea is aesthetically perfect and valuable. For example, the idea of beauty is beautiful, and the idea of human being is perfect, even though living human beings are imperfect reflections of this idea. This shows that the idea involves valueness, and Nakamura states that Plato mixed two different aspects, logical and non-logical values, into the idea. On the other hand, Vaiśeṣika did not attribute non-logical value, i.e., ethical or aesthetical value, to the universals. Ethical value is confined to merit (*dharma*) and demerit (*adharma*), two of the twenty-four qualities (*guṇa*). To be precise, merit and demerit respectively possess meritness (*dharmatva*) and demeritness (*adharmatva*), which are universals. We can assume that these two universals bear upon ethical value.

2.2.4: Parmenides criticized Plato's idea by asking whether an individual is connected to its whole idea or to part of the idea.[9] If to its whole, that individual occupies many places through the idea. If to part of the idea, the idea becomes divisible. Neither case is true. Similar criticism is directed at the Vaiśeṣika universal. Nakamura considers that the Vaiśeṣ ika universal is exempt from this criticism, the reason being that a universal becomes a particular with reference to a higher universal. I personally do not understand how this reason can solve the above problem. He further states that the universals in Vaiśeṣika are not metaphysical entities, but logical entities.

If we define metaphysics as an inquiry into the substance of the world or the universe and into the entities transcending human sensation, the Vaiśeṣika universals are metaphysical. They are logical and objective as well. Nakamura's word 'logical' is problematic, because logical entities do not necessarily warrant reality in the outer world. Vaiśeṣika, on the other hand, takes the view that the universals exist independently of cognition, and that they, residing individuals, can be perceived by the sense organs. When we say that the Vaiśeṣika universals are logical, we should say that they are objective as well.

2.2.5: Another criticism of Parmenides pertains to an idea which connects an individual to its idea. Where an individual is concerned in its idea, another idea, which connects that idea and that individual, is required. Moreover, a third idea, which connects the second idea and the first idea, is also required; thus to establish the relation between the individual and its idea, we will fall in infinite regress. Nakamura states that the Vaiśeṣika universals do not have this fault, because a universal and its individuals are connected by the relation of inherence (samavāya), which does not require a further relation to connect itself to a universal and an individual. However, it is well known that the concept of inherence was criticized by Buddhists, Vedāntins, Mīmāṃsakas, and Jainas, and we, like Nakamura, know that the concept of inherence does not solve all problems of the universals.

2.2.6: Nakamura speaks about number: according to Plato, number is an idea, and the entities in the universe move in regulation of number. Number is beyond perception. On the other hand, the Vaiśeṣika number is a quality of things and is perceived by the sense organs. All numbers except one which resides in eternal single entities such as time (*kāla*), space (*ākāśa*), and atoms (*paramāṇu*) are non-eternal. It is significant that Vaiśeṣika holds that numbers are not universals but accidental to things. Nakamura points out that this feature of the Vaiśeṣika number indicates why it did not lead to mathematical rationale, which explains the structure of the physical world as in the West.

2.2.7: Nakamura proceeds to Aristotle's universal. 'Universal' means the possessor of a property indicated by the predicate of the subject, and an individual does not become what the predicate indicates. Proper nouns such as 'Plato' and 'Aristotle' mean individuals, and non-proper nouns such as 'cow' and 'flower' and adjectives indicate universals. Aristotle called an individual a substance and considered that no general/universal term, i.e., non-proper nouns and adjectives, can be the indices of substances. It follows that a general term cannot be the subject of a sentence. Nakamura, however, criticizes this view and gives as a counterexample a sentence in which a general term is the subject: "A cherry tree is a tree". The subject 'cherry tree' and the predicate 'tree' are general terms. He surmises that Aristotle excluded sentences in which the subject is a general term from his analysis, because this played an important role in collecting information on individuals in Greece, and that it was beyond the reach of the Greek people/scientists to give the status of subject to the universal and assert something about the universal. Accordingly, the Greeks directed their attention to making a sentence in which a proper noun is the subject.

It is interesting that Nakamura cited the above view of Aristotle for comparison of the Vaiśeṣika and his concepts of universal. There must be reason(s) for Aristotle's claim. The above reason presented by Nakamura is not persuasive, for the Greek people must have examined how the meanings of general terms such as 'rational', 'human being', 'animal', etc. are related. On the contrary, it is a fact, as Nakamura mentions, that the Vaiśeṣika philosophers did not give importance to a sentence in which a proper noun attains the status of subject.

2.2.8: After explaining the differences between the Vaiśeṣ ika and the Greek universals, Nakamura points out a similarity. Aristotle offered ten categories: substance, quantity, quality, relation, place, time, position, state, activity, and passivity, all of which are reflections of the grammatical classification of words in Greek. Some of the Vaiśeṣika categories too show that they are from grammatical classification in Sanskrit, for example, substance (*dravya*) from a noun, quality (*guṇa*) from an adjective, and action (*karman*) from a verb. The other three categories in Vaiśeṣika, i.e., universal (*sāmānya, jāti*), particular (*viśeṣa*), and inherence (*samavāya*), are not derived from grammatical consideration. The seventh category, i.e., absence or non-being, is the result of the grammatical consideration of the negative particle and the negative prefixes. Nakamura considers that among these seven, the categories of universal and particular play a particularly important role in Vaiśeṣika, and that the Vaiśeṣika philosophers did not regard the investigation of the relationship among individuals as important. On the other hand, Aristotle placed importance on the relationship among individuals and universals. Nakamura concludes that the Vaiśeṣika categories are metaphysical and logical, while Aristotle's categories are physical, and that this disparity in categorical systems clearly shows the difference between Indian and Greek ways of thinking.

3. Indian Logic

3.1 A Glossary of Technical Terms in Indian Logic

3.1.1: Nakamura's "Some Approaches to Understand Indian Logic: (II) A Glossary of Indian Logical Terms" [*sic*] (1983) is an epoch-making dictionary of technical terms used in Indian logic in three senses: (1) Nakamura collected terms not only from Sanskrit texts on Buddhist logic but also from those on Hindu logic, (2) he attempted to present modern Japanese renderings of the terms, and (3) he placed Sanskrit terms in the Sanskrit alphabetical order.

First, I will explain the features of the Sanskrit texts referred to in this glossary. We have an excellent dictionary of Indian logic, i.e., *Nyāyakośa*, which is written in Sanskrit and collects terms from many Sanskrit texts of Nyāya, Vaiśeṣika, Mīmāṃsā, and Vedānta, but not from Buddhist texts. The average Japanese need a dictionary of Indian logic like this written in Japanese and including Buddhist terms. To answer this need, Nakamura chose terms not only from Buddhist Sanskrit texts but also from non-Buddhist texts: the *Carakasaṃhitā*, the *Nyāyabindu* of Dharmakīrti, the *Nyāyabinduṭīkā* of Dharmottara, the *Nyāyasūtra*, the *Nyāyabhāṣya*, the *Nyāyapraveśa* of Śaṅkarasvāmin, the *Padārthadharmasaṃgraha*, the *Sarvadarśanasaṃgraha*, the *Sarvasiddhāntasaṃgraha*, the *Tarkabhāṣā* of Keśava Miśra, the *Tarkasaṃgraha* and the *Tarkadīpikā* of Annaṃbhaṭṭa, the *Vaiśeṣikasūtra*, and the *Yogasūtravivaraṇa* of Śaṅkara.

Regarding the second point, as I have stated, Japanese scholars often used classical Chinese renderings of terms, which forced students of Indian philosophy to spend long hours trying to decipher the meanings. In this glossary Nakamura sometimes provides English, German, or French renderings, which are helpful in grasping the meaning of modern Japanese renderings when they are not necessarily clear. To obtain renderings in other languages, he used the books and papers of J.M. Bochneski [1970], E. Frauwallner [1955], A. Foucher [1949], Maheśa Candra Nyāyaratna [1891], Th. Stcherbatsky [1924][1926][1932], N.J. Shah [1981], W. Ruben [1928], Chattopadhyaya and Gangopadhyaya [1967/1968/1972/ 1973/1976], G. Jha [1919], and Leggett [1981]. From these names it is apparent that Nakamura attempted to invoke the great inheritance of his predecessors even when rendering a small technical term.

With reference to the third point, i.e., the arrangement of terms in alphabetical order, Nakamura explains its convenience by providing the following examples. The term '*ānumānika*' is placed immediately after the term '*anumāna*', and the term '*śābda*' comes immediately after the term '*śabda*'. This method of arrangement is convenient in consulting a term and its derivatives and comparing their meanings.

3.2 Method of Research in Indian Logic

3.2.1: Nakamura presents three methods of research in Indian logic: (1) tradition-based interpretation, (2) chronological introduction of the texts of Indian logic, and (3) historical interpretation. He gives the highest value to the third method. The first one is to clarify the views on logic by analyzing the main text, with the help of its commentary/commentaries and the sub-commentary/sub-commentaries. For example, in order to read the *Nyāyasūtra*, its commentary, the *Nyāyabhāṣya* is used; further its sub-commentary, the *Nyāyavārttika*, is utilized. He expresses doubt as to whether or not we are allowed to adopt interpretations offered in later times when interpreting the main text. I agree with him on this point. However, if we use commentaries and sub-commentaries to investigate the historical development of logical theories from those presented in the main text, we may be successful.

The second method is to chronologically introduce Sanskrit texts and their contents dealing with logical theories. Nakamura is aware of the significance of this method, but he does not attach much importance to it. This is probably because the simple enumeration of Sanskrit texts and presentation of their brief summaries is of no direct consequence in studying logic, and because such enumeration and presentation do not lead to a proper evaluation of Indian logic.

The third method, i.e., historical interpretation, consists of presenting a logical system/theory by means of comparison with the preceding or ensuing systems/theories. This method seems similar to the first one, but it tells us that to understand some text, we do not always need to read its commentaries and sub-commentaries. In some cases we have to read other texts of the school to which that text belongs; in still other cases we have to look into texts of other schools which seem to bear upon that text. This method is universally accepted and consciously or unconsciously adopted by modern scholars. Of course, I do not mean that this method was discovered by Nakamura. He may be one of those who examined methodology of research and articulated the above three methods much earlier.[10]

Here, I would like to say that we can include the first method in the third one. In the first we focus on how to interpret the main text and read its commentaries regarded as authentic in the Indian tradition. If we assume that reading the commentaries is elucidating the historical development of a key concept/theory, we are conducting research on the concept/theory with the third method. In this sense the difference between these two methods is not as great as it appears. The difference may lie in the consciousness of the scholars who are facing texts: tradition-directed or tradition-free.

3.2.2: Nakamura states that Indian logic did not attach an independent status to the theories of notion and proposition, or to the law of contradiction. It should be noted here that he does not say that Indian logic ignored those theories and law. Aristotle prescribed that notion should be defined and that definition is formulated by means of a genus and a species, while Indian philosophers dealt with the theories of notion as those of objects. For example, when Greek philosophers define 'cow', they analyzed the notion of 'cow'. Indian philosophers, on the other hand, held that they analyzed an animal called 'cow', and they regarded a distinguishing feature of a cow as a defining character (*lakṣaṇa*). In Indian philosophy, the analysis of a proposition/sentence is made in the section of verbal understanding (*śābdabodha, śābdajñāna*), and the law of contradiction is strictly observed in the discussion of any philosophical topic. To answer his question "Why did Indian logicians discuss notion and proposition dependently of the theories of inference or verbal understanding?", Nakamura quotes Sueki's words as follows:

In general, Indian thought takes liberation (*mokṣa, mukti*) as the final goal, and liberation is nothing other than the direct experience or intuition of the highest reality, which cannot be expressed in the form of a proposition. Hence, a proposition is not a final goal but simply an aid used to arrive at liberation. If one is satisfied with understanding the meaning of a proposition, grasps things in the framework of analyticality, and insists on taking such a proposition as true, then one cannot achieve liberation. Buddhism calls a cognition, derived from a proposition, a bad cognition (*vikalpa*) and applies a negative value to it. Other schools of Indian philosophy took the same attitude as Buddhism toward a bad cognition. We can say that all the schools held that a proposition does not deserve to be analyzed solely. Thus, the anomalous system of logic, which deals with inference but not with a proposition, was established. Indian logicians did not abstract the law of contradiction nor did they express it in the form of a proposition.[11]

Nakamura agrees with Sueki's view. It is interesting that they both attempted to find the difference between Indian and Western logic and arrived at a common answer.

3.2.3: Interestingly, Nakamura discusses the problem of induction in Indian logic and points out the relationship between this problem and the development of modern science. Indian logicians were well aware of the importance of the examples (*dṛṣṭānta*) given in the syllogism to establish the relation of pervasion or invariable concomitance (*vyāpti*). If we can say that wherever *A* exists *B* also exists but cannot demonstrate an example in which both *A* and *B* are present, we cannot claim that it is true that wherever *A* exists *B* also exists. To put it another way, the example given in the Indian syllogism warrants the validity of the relation of invariable concomitance (*vyāpti*) between *A* and *B*. It follows that Indian logicians were clearly aware of the method of induction, and that by observing some examples, we can establish the universal relation between two concepts. This fact leads us to two questions: (1) Why didn't Indian logic give birth to modern science? and (2) Can those who are not aware of the importance of examples establish logic or not? Nakamura answers the first question by saying that Indian logicians were enthusiastic about clarifying the relationship among the universals and did not formulate the relationship among individual things, facts, or experiences. He answers the second question by saying that the scholars in East Asian countries who translated the technical terms of Indian logic into classical Chinese were interested in Indian logic but did not understand the different function of simile or metaphor, and the example in the syllogism. He goes on to say that this fact may be associated with the fact that those countries did not develop logic.

3.3 The Book *The Structure of Logic*

3.3.1: Here I will briefly refer to Nakamura's *The Structure of Logic*, 2 Vols. Volume 1 is of 547 pages, and volume 2 is of 604 pages. This book is like a summit that we have reached through the comparison of Western logic and Indian logic. Nakamura seems to have attempted to build a new system of logic which includes Indian logic, although precisely speaking, he dealt with the thinking of Chinese, Tibetan, and Japanese peoples as well. The first volume contains "Chapter 1: Logic and Studies of logic", "Chapter 2: Problems of Perception", "Chapter 3: The Examination of Notion", "Chapter 4: The Systems of Category", and "Chapter 5: The Principles of Thinking". The second volume contains "Chapter 6: What is Judgment?" and "Chapter 7: The Examination of Inference". The contents of this book are so far-reaching that I cannot summarize and review it properly here. We can say at least that he aimed at 'universal' logic, which is applied to both Indian and Western systems of logic.

4. Conclusion

4.1: Nakamura insisted that we should render Sanskrit technical terms in modern Japanese and not rely on classical Chinese. This seems reasonable, and most people will accept this as an important suggestion. Japan has a long tradition of Buddhism dating back to the seventh century A.D., and Japanese people still use many terms found in the Chinese translation of the Buddhist cannons. It saved time for Japanese scholars of Indian philosophy to employ Chinese translations of the terms. But nowadays we have lost a good command of classical Chinese and do not readily understand the meaning of the Chinese translation. It is undoubtedly time for us to create new translations of the terms.

Let me speak about myself. Fortunately or unfortunately, my main subject is Navya-nyāya, and in this field almost no Chinese translation of the Sanskrit terms is available. This means that I have to create renderings of the technical terms. Nakamura's translation of the *Nyāyasūtra*, the *Nyāyabhāṣya*, and the *Vaiśeṣikasūtra*, and his glossary always inspires me to make efforts to use modern Japanese.

4.2: As Nakamura's comparative studies of Vaiśeṣika and Greek philosophy, I have focused on his study on the Vaiśeṣika and Greek concepts of universal. He not only points out similarities and differences but also attempts to examine whether they lead to explaining important facts in classical Indian and Greece. It is interesting that he discusses the features of the Vaiśeṣika universal and number and concludes that they did not develop modern science and mathematics in classical India. Nakamura's inquires, such as why classical India did not develop mathematics, are possible only when a wider perspective is taken into account. We should not forget viewing particular thought from a wider perspective like his viewpoint of the history of human thought.

4.3: With regard to his comparative studies of logic, Nakamura took the view that Indian logic does not deal with notions and propositions independently of inference, and that it does not provide the most fundamental status to the law of contradiction. This view is an outcome of his efforts to compare Indian logic and Western logic, and furnishes a base for comparative studies of the two different types of logic. He attempted to ascribe the reasons for the lower important status of the theories of notion and proposition and the law of contradiction to Indian mysticism or intuition.

Now we have much more information about Indian logic, and more translations and studies of Sanskrit texts have been conducted in that area. It may be time for us to reconsider whether his ascription holds true or not. We have to inquire into why the theories of notion and proposition are not given a major place in the Nyāya-Vaiśeṣika system. To answer this question, Nakamura focused on liberation (*mokṣa*); but we may arrive at a different answer using the method of comparison which he established.

Nakamura wanted to find a 'universal' logic common to Western logic and Indian logic. There may be another view that 'logic' means only Western logic, which is universal. Since Nakamura made efforts to explain Indian logic through the framework of Western logic, he appears to have followed that view. I believe that he did so to make Indian logic understandable to those who were familiar with Western logic or who developed unconsciously under the influence of Western logic. As the first step to his goal, Nakamura attempted to compare the two systems of logic. We can discuss the similarities and differences between them and produce an endless number of papers on the subject. But if we do not ask ourselves why we write papers on these topics, we will be abdicating our responsibility in the long run. Of course, there are many reasons for writing papers. Nakamura's reason may be the most sublime of all.

References

1 Ruben [1928].

2 Miyasaka [1956].

3 Chattopadhyaya and Gangopadhyaya [1967/1968/1972/1973/1976].

4 Sastri [1877/1878].

5 Jha [1912-1919] [1919].

6 Sāstrī [1923].

7 Jambuvijaya [1961] and Thakur [1957].

8 Nakamura [1979].

9 Sueki [1970: 44]. This criticism is raised in Plato's Parmenides. Parmenides (ca. B.C. 515-450) died before Plato (B.C. 428/427-348/347) was born. Hence, it is not a fact that he criticized Plato.

[10] According to Mayeda [1980: 3] [1992], Ingalls [1952: 1-4] also presents three methods of investigating Śankara's thought. We may say that Nakamura's three methods may 'roughly' correspond to those of Ingalls.

[11] Sueki [1970: 44]. Sueki was Nakamura's colleague at the University of Tokyo who specialized in Western philosophy.

* I wish to thank Brian Burk-Gaffney, Nagasaki Institute of Applied Science for correcting my English.

Bibliography

Bochenski, J.M.

1970 *Formal Logik*, Freiburg/München: Verlag Karl Alber.

Chattopadhyaya, Debiprasad and Mrinalkanti Gangopadhyaya

1967/1968/1972/1973/1976 *Nyāya Philosophy: Literal Translation of Gautama's Nyāyasūtra and Vātsyāyana's Bhāṣya along with a Free and Abridged Translation of the Elucidation by Mahāmahopadhyāya Phaṇībhuṣaṇa Tarkavāgīśa*, Part 1 (1967), Calcutta: Indian Studies Past and Present; Part 2 (1968); Part 3 by Mrinalkanti Gangopadhyaya (1972); Part 4 (1973); Part 5 (1976).

Foucher, A.

1949 *Le compendium des topiques (Tarka-saṃgraha) d'Annambhaṭ ṭa*, avec des extrais de trios commentaires indiens (Texte et traduction) et un commentaire, Paris: Adrien-Maisonneuve.

Frauwallner, Erich

1955 "Candramati und Daśapadārthaśāstram: Ein Beitrag zur Geschichte des Vaiśeṣika", Studia Indologica, Festschrift für Willibald Kirfel, Selbstverlag des Orientalischen Seminars der Universität Bonn.

Ingalls, D.H.H.

1952 "The Study of Śaṅkarācārya", Annals of the Bhandarkar Oriental Research Institute 33: 1-4.

Jambuvijaya (ed.)

1961 *Vaiśeṣikasutra of Kanāda with the Commentary of Candrānanda*, Gaekwad Oriental Series 136, Baroda: Oriental Institute.

Jha, Ganganath

1912-1919 *Indian Thought* 4-11.

1919 *The Nyāyasūtra of Gautama with Vātsyāyana's Bhāṣya and Uddyotakara's Vārttika Transltated into English*, 4 Vols., Delhi: Motilal Banarsidass.

Kanakura, Enshō

1971 *Indo no Shizen Tetsugaku* (Natural Philosophy in India), Kyōto: Heirakujishoten. (in Japanese)

Leggett, Trevor

1981 *Śaṅkara on the Yogasūtras: The Vivaraṇa Sub-commentary to Vyāsabhāṣya on the Yogasūtras of Patañjali*: Samādhi-pāda, London: Routledge and Kegan Paul.

Mayeda, Sengaku

1980 Vedānta no Tetsugaku (The Philosophy of Vedānta), Kyōto: Heirakuji Shoten. (in Japanese)

1993 "Śankara Kenkyū no Kaiko to Tenbō" (Past and Future of the Study of Śaṣkara), Gakumon no Yamanami (Mountains of Academism), Tōkyō: Japan Society for the Promotion of Science. (in Japanese)

Miyasaka, Yushō

1956 *Niyāya-bāshuya no Ronrigaku* (Logic in the *Nyāyabhāṣ ya*), Tōkyō: Sankibōbusshorin. (in Japanese)

Nakamura, Hajime

1977/1978 "Vaisheshika Gakuha no Genten: the *Vaiśeṣikasūtra* and the *Padārthadharmasaṃgraha*" (Japanese Translation of the Vaiśeṣika Texts and the Padārthadharmasaṃgraha: II *Padārthadharmasaṃgraha* [*sic*]), *Sankōbunka Kenkyūjo Kiyō* (Annals of the Sanko Research Institute for the Studies of Buddhism) 10/11, pp. 157-316. (in Japanese)

1981 "Indo Ronrigaku no Rikai no tameni", (Some Approaches to Understand Indian Logic: (I) A New Translation of the Nyāyabindu [sic]), *Hokke-Bunka Kenkyū* (Journal of Institute for the Comprehensive Study of Lotus Sutra [sic]) 7, pp. 1-167. (in Japanese)

1983 "Indo Ronrigaku no Rikai no tameni: (II) Indo Ronrigaku Jutsugo Shūsei" (Some Approaches to Understand Indian Logic: II A Glossary of Indian Logical Terms [sic]), *Hokke-Bunka Kenkyū* (Journal of Institute for the Comprehensive Study of Lotus Sutra [sic]) 9: pp. 1-243. (in Japanese)

2000 Ronri *no Kōzō*, 2 Vols. (The Structure of Logic), Tōkyō: Seidosha. (in Japanese)

Nyāyaratna, Maheśa Candra

1891 *Brief Notes on the Modern Nyāya System of Philosophy and Its Technical Terms*, Calcutta.

Ruben, Walter

1928 *Die Nyāyasūtra's* Text, *Erläutenrung und Glossar* (herausgegehn von der Deuschen Morgenländischen Gesellschaftt 18, B and No. 2), Leipzig.

Sāstrī, Dhundhirāja (ed.)

1923 *Vaiśeṣikadarśane praśastapādabhāṣyam upaskāraś ca*, Kashi Sanskrit Series 3, Benares: Chowkhamba Sanskrit Depot.

Sastri, Kesava

1877/1878 "Text and Translation of the Nyāyasȳtra and Vātsyāyana's Nyāyabhāṣya", *The Pandit*, pp. 60-64, 109-128, 311-320, 363-380, 552-561.

Shah, N.J.

1981 "Essentials of Dharmakīrti's Theory of Knowledge: Based on the Pramāṇavārttika", *Studien zum Jainismus und Buddhismus*, Herausgegeben von Klaus Bruhn und Albrecht Wetler, Wiesbaden: Franz Steiner, pp. 251-259.

Sueki, Takehiro

1970 *Tōyō* no *Gōri-shisō* (Oriental Thought of Rationale), Tōkyō: Kōdansha. (in Japanese)

Stcherbatsky, Th.

1924 *Erkentnistheorie und Logik nach der Lehre der späteren Buddhisten (Aus dem Russischen übersetzt von Otto Strauss)*, München-Neubiberg: Verlag Oskar Schloss.

1926 *La theorie de la connaissance et la logique chez les Bouddhistes tardifs (Traduit par Madame I. de Manziarly et Paul Masson-Oursel)*, Paris: Geuthneu.

1932 *Buddhist Logic,* 2 Vols., Bibliotheca Buddhica, Leningrad: the Academy of Sciences of the USSR.

Thakur, Anantalal

1957 *Vaiśeṣikasūtra of Kanāda, with an Anonymous Commentary,* Darbhanga: Mithila Institute.

17

Contributions of Professor Hajime Nakamura to the Studies of Sāṃkhya and Yoga

Shujun Motegi

The late Professor Hajime Nakamura is known as one of the leading scholars of Indian and Buddhist thought in Japan. Even a brief glance at his works is enough to impress us with the breadth of his research interests. His wide perspective covers not only eastern thought but also western thought, not only ancient or medieval thought but also modern thought. It is as if he grasps the whole range of human thought in its entirety.

I am honoured to introduce his works on Sāṃkhya and Yoga, and to describe his achievements on this occasion before so many eminent scholars, even though this may be beyond my ability.

His works on Sāṃkhya and Yoga are presented in the 24th volume of "The Selected Works of Hajime Nakamura", 1996, Tokyo, which consist of 568 pages. This volume contains his academic achievements in these fields, namely, a general description of Sāṃkhya and Yoga as an introduction, and advanced studies for those who have an interest in Indian philosophical and religious thought. For this purpose he records in detail the history of research and arguments presented by former and contemporary scholars on almost all aspects of Sāṃkhya and Yoga.[1]

Though his interest in Indian philosophical thought led him to the study of various fields, he seems to have been primarily concerned with the Vedānta philosophy. He sometimes contrasts Sāṃkhya and Yoga with the Vedāntic Advaita philosophy. Additionally, rather than Sāṃkhya, he seems to have more interest in Yoga, which he considers to be a general method of emancipation among the Indian philosophical schools. His basic views on Sāṃkhya and Yoga are: (1) Sāṃkhya: rationalistic dualism as a counterpart to Vedānta monism, (2) Yoga: a rationalistic method of emancipation common to all Indian schools of philosophy.

Now let us examine his works on Sāṃkhya and Yoga respectively.

1. Sāṃkhya

In his book mentioned above, Nakamura provides an exhaustive explanation of Sāṃkhya. This is mainly as an introduction to those who have a general interest in Indian Philosophy. He describes the history of Sāṃkhya with detailed references to the literature of the school and to modern research. He discusses almost all the topics of Sāṃkhya on the basis of Sāṃkhyakārikā (Abbr. SK), such as *puruṣa, prakṛti, guṇa, tanmātra, vyakti, indriya-vṛtti, pratyayasarga, sūkṣmaśarīra, pramāṇa, pariṇāma, bhāva, īśvara*[2] and so on. This description presents his views on Sāṃkhya, and shows what he considered to be the characteristics of Sāṃkhya to be, as well as providing a general objective description of Sāṃkhya.

He regards Sāṃkhya thought as the philosophy of rationalism. Sāṃkhya's rationalism is seen typically in the rejection of Vedic rites as the means of emancipation. He refers to SK.2 which denies the Vedic authority as the means for final emancipation on the ground that the Vedic rites require animal sacrifice and that the result of such sacrifices is impermanent. But, he points out, Sāṃkhya does not reject the Veda as the basis of the right knowledge, accepting it as one of the trustworthy sources of knowledge.

Sāṃkhya's method of gaining emancipation stresses the achievement of discriminative knowledge of the pure and eternal soul (*puruṣa*) from material principle (*prakṛti*). Sāṃkhya, therefore, discusses the right knowledge in detail and the means to acquire the right knowledge (*pramāṇa*). According to the Sāṃkhya view, the means of right knowledge is of three kinds, direct perception (*pratyakṣa*), inference (*anumāna*) and the word of trustworty persons (*āptavacana*). The Veda is included in the third category of the right knowledge. The Veda, therefore, is denied on one hand, and accepted on the other. Nakamura points out this inconsistency in Sāṃkhya, and guesses that, although this is an apparent inconsistency from the viewpoint of western way of thinking which places importance on logic, the interpreters of the SK, a compendium of the Sāṃkhya thoughts, do not pay much attention to this inconsistency. I am not sure that his guess is correct, but what is important is that he calls attention to this contradictory attitude of Sāṃkhya toward Veda, which seems to be one of the essential problems with Sāṃkhya, that is, the birth of Sāṃkhya in the Hindu society.

In his general description of Sāṃkhya, Nakamura observes it from two unique viewpoints which are: (1) the social point of view of Sāṃkhya in Hindu society; (2) a comparison with western thought. Here we see his description of Sāṃkhya in terms of these two unique view points.

For the first viewpoint, he analyzes a dialogue between Buddhist sage Guṇamati and a Sāṃkhya sage Mādhava found in the Ta-T'ang hsi-yü-chi written by a Chinese Buddihist monk Hsüan-tsang. It is a long dialouge or debate in which Mādhava is finally defeated by Guṇamati. It is not clear what the theme of the debate is, but this episode gives us some hints about what Indian society was like at that time. Nakamura's assumptions obtained from the analysis of this episode are:

1. The governer of villages is a local lord. The lord can give a village to a *brāhmaṇa* who teaches Sāṃkhya philosophy or to a Buddhist monk.

2. The villagers are tied to the land and to its owner. If the decree of a lord causes a change in land owner, then the villagers have to transfer their allegiance to a new master,

3. People who belong to a *brāhmana* preaching Sāṃkhya philosophy have to understand it. They belong to him by the order of the local lord.

4. Sāṃkhya philosophers (for example, in this episode, Mādhava) do not place importance on debates .with the common people. They remain a part of the old system of social structure.

This description reflects one of Nakamura's views. He thinks it necessary to understand philosophical thought as an integral part of real history or society, as the result of which thoughts are more concretely understood together with their social role.

Then he continues his argument with a comparison to western philosophy. This part is his unique point of contention.

The concept of *puruṣa* is comparable with the concept of *nous* of ancient Greek philosophy. Anaxagoras, a Greek philosopher, assumes the existence of *nous* which is devoid of materiality, immovable itself and, at the same time, active everywhere. This nature is common to *puruṣa*. Aristotle insists that *nous* itself is not touched at all, but it nonetheless touches the world. This concept of *nous* is again similar to *puruṣa* which exists outside of material world.

Numenius (A. D.2), a New Pythagorean, theorizes the existence of three aspects of God. First is a principle of being, pure thinking (*nọus*), which is comparable to the concept of *puruṣa*. The second is the creator of the universe, which is almost analogous to the concept of *prakṛti*, though *prakṛti* itself does not create the world. The third is the world itself, which corresponds to *vyakta*.

Four categories of existential beings are proposed by Johanes Scotus Eriugena (A. D.9): (1) creative and not created, (2) creative and created, (3) created and not creative, (4) not created and not creative. The first category is similar to *prakṛti* or *avyakta* in Sāṃkhya. The second category corresponds to *prakṛti-vikṛti* in Sāṃkhya, that is, *buddhi*, *ahaṃkara*, *tanmātra*. The third category corresponds to *vikṛti* which are *indriya, manas, mahābhūta*. Needless to say, *puruṣ a* belongs to the fourth category of Eriugena.

The system of Sāṃkhya is based on the dualism of *puruṣa* and *prakṛti* (soul and material). From the viewpoint of dualism, Nakamura proposes a similarity to the Chinese theory of Tai Ji and also to the medieval Japanese theory of Ise Shito.

One of the specific concepts of Sāṁkhya is *guṇa*. According to Sāṃkhya, *prakṛti* consists of three elements (*guṇa*), which are responsible for not only the various events which occur in the external world, but also the psychological phenomena of human minds. They are *sattva, rajas* and *tamas*. He compares the concept of *guṇa* with the three principles of soul in Plato's theory. Plato maintains that soul consists of three parts, *philosophon* (part of love for profit), philoneikon (part of love for victory) and philokerdes (part of love for thinking), which are responsible for three kinds of pleasure, three kinds of human desire. The concept of *tamas* in Sāṁkhya is responsible for the dark aspect of human mind, which is comparable to *philosophon* in Plato. The concept *rajas* is responsible for the active aspect of human mind, which is comparable to *philoneikon*. Finally the concept of *sattva*, used to explain the brightness of the mind, is similar to *philokerdes*.[3]

These three principles of Plato belong to soul, though *guṇa* in Sāṁkhya is an element of material being. Bearing this fundamental difference in mind, we may still find something common to both triad. In this way he thinks that though the concept of three *guṇas* is seen in the scheme of Sāṁkhya philosophy, the validity of this kind of triad of the human mind can not only be applied to Sāṁkhya, but also beyond the era and the racial difference. He aims to discern a universality of human thinking in each philosophical scheme. This is the purpose of comparing thought systems from different eras and cultures.

Finally at the end of his general sketch of Sāṃkhya he refers to Sāṁkhya philosophers who were active after 16th A.D. and to whom little attention has thus been paid by Japanese scholars. This again reflects the wide range of his interests and knowledge.

1.2 Epic Sāṁkhya

Nakamura is not only interested in the philosphical thought of the higher social classes, but also in the moral concepts of the common people of ancient India. With this interest in mind he translates five stories from the Mahābhārata (abbr. MBh)[4] which convey to us the moral concepts of the common people. They admire their own occupations, denying the way of life of hermit. This study in translation by Nakamura is a long and exacting work, published under the title "The Way of Life by Layman".[5]

In this translation, we find two stories which contain the fragmentary thoughts of early Sāṁkhya and Yoga. They are (1) the discourse of Mārkaṇḍeya about Dharmavyāda (MBh. III.201-203), and (2) the dialogue between Janaka and Sulabhā, disciples of Pañcaśikha (MBh. XII.308). We shall examine these two chapters respectively with reference to Nakamura's translation.

1.2.1 Dharmavyāda

In the discourse of Mārkaṇḍeya, we encounter a rather primitive system of Sāṁkhya thought which is employed when necessary to explain the material components of the world. The story focuses upon the main theme, namely, what the real *brāhmaṇa* is. In the discourse a sort of Sāṁkhya thought appears. The verses concerning Sāṁkhya will be summarizes as follows:

After mentioning the good deed of men, Dharmavyāda, a hunter, divides the world and human being into various constituent elements, both physical and psychological. He says that this entire world, unconquarable by any means, consists of five material elements and nothing exists beyond them. These five material elements are ether, air, fire, water and earth. Sound, touch, colour, taste and smell are their properties.[6] Each of the latter elements contains the properties of the preceding elements, and each element has all the properties which exist in the three elements (*triṣu guṇeṣu*) before it.[7] Dharmavyāda continues the enumeration of the psychic elements of human beings. The sixth is consciousness, which is called mind (*manas*). The seventh must be intellect (*buddhi*). I-consciousness (*ahaṃkāra*) is higher than intellect.[8] The sense organs are five in number. In addition there exist *sattva, rajas* and *tamas* perhaps as other elements of the human mind. A lump of these seventeen previously enumerated elements is called the unmanifested (*avyakta*).[9] Being covered by all the objects, manifested or unmanifested, perceived by sense organs, the element (? *guṇa*),[10] which is composed of manifested and unmanifested, is said to be the twenty-fourth.[11] The passages of this chapter contain unclear descriptions of the usage of the term *guṇa*[12]

The hunter Dharmavyādha explains the properties of material elements in detail in the next chapter (MBh. III.202). He explains the death of human beings as the loss of balance between the moving and unmoving elements of the physical body. According to him, heaven and hell are nothing but different states of the sense organs by which man perceives the external world. If a man controls the sense organs well, he attains heaven. Otherwise he reaches hell after death. To attain heaven, man must control the sense organs by practicing *yoga* which is based on *tapas*.[13] A man who practices *yoga* is compared with a chariot that rides in a horse-drawn cart, which is a well known simile of *yoga* in the Kaṭha Upaniṣ ad.[14]

Furthermore, in the next chapter (MBh. III.203) Dharmavyāda continues his teachings. He explains three *guṇas* and their relationship not only with the nature of material elements, but also with the action of human beings. The point of his teachings is that man becomes *brāhmaṇa* by his own conduct, not by his birth. Then the hunter describes the internal process of the life of a human being. He refers to the fire in the human head which makes the vital breath (*prāṇa*) active. The vital breath is worshipped as the highest being, the light of *Brahman*. The vital breath is the highest element present in a human being. The vital breath, he continues, is the substance shared by all existing beings. The vital breath is the eternal *puruṣa*, and the mind (*manas*), the intellect (*buddhi*), the I-consiousness (*ahaṃkāra*) and finally the object of all existing beings.[15]

It is also the vital breath that controls all bodily actions such as movement, power and digestion etc. in cooperation with other winds (*samāna, apāna, udāna, vyāna*).[16] The vital breath plays the same role as the individual soul. In these chapters we come across many terms which denote the individual soul such as dehin, *kṣetrajña, jīva, ātman, parātman, bhūtātman, puruṣa* and *adhyātma*. The one responsible for usual actions is *jīva* which is a character of the individual soul (*kṣetrajña*). The individual soul, being composed of three qualities such as *sattva, rajas, tamas,* remains behind the *jīva*. On the other hand, the individual self controls himself by the practice of *yoga*. This individual self again belongs to the highest self. The highest self is the universal one that pervades all living beings. This highest self that is latent in every living beings does not appear explicitly, but it can be seen by those who perceive by the subtle and highest psychological organ, that is, *buddhi*.[17] The fact that many different terms denoting the self-concept are used here seems to be a result of a kind of composition of various fragmental passages from different contexts about the self-concept.

In order to describe the state of emanicipation the term *nirāmtan* is used, which attracts our attention. This is because this term occurs rarely, that is, only three times in the *Mokṣadharma* of MBh.[18] It should be noticed that the psychological organ used to perceive emancipated self is not the intellect (*buddhi*) but the mind *manas* unlike the theory to be found in SK.[19]

Thanks to his translation we know the primitive Sāṁkhya and Yoga views found in the teachings of Dharmavyāda. Through its assistance, we arrive at the following points:

1. The Sāṁkhya theory in the teachings of Dharmavyāda seems a composition of different concepts which prevailed at the time, and requires further study before its position in the early history of Sāṁkhya can be found.

2. As one of the characteristic features of the Sāṁkhya view found here, it can be pointed out that I-consciosness (*ahaṁkāra*) takes the highest place among the internal organs.

3. Another characteristic is that the old concept of the vital breath takes the place of the eternal soul.

4. Here the term *yoga* is used to mean the control of sense organs based on the austerity (*tapas*), and the control of the individual self in order to see the highest self. This does not mean supernatural power.

1.2.2 Pañcaśikha

In the same paper Nakamura translates Chapter 308 of the *Mokṣadharma* section of the *Śāntiparvan* of the MBh. This chapter contains a dialogue between Janaka and Sulabhā, both of whom are supposed to be disciples of the sage Pañcaśikha. In the Sāṃkhya tradition, Pañcaśikha is the third teacher of a Sāṃkhya school which was founded by Kapila and inherited by Īśvarakṛṣna, a writer of the SK, a compendium of Sāṃkhya Philosophy. It, therefore, is important to know the teachings of Pañcaśikha to construct the historical development of Sāṃkhya thought. However, because of the lack of extant material, it still remains uncertain what Pañcaśikha really teaches. In the Mokṣadharma there are several chapters in which we come across the name Pañcaśikha.[20] One of these chapters is Chapter 308 which was translated into Japanese for the first time from the Poona Critical Edition by Nakamura. This chapter is important because it shows how Pañcaśikha appears in the early history of religio-philosohical thought, or how a legendary figure is treated in later times. In this chapter, the story starts with Sulabhā's question and her curiosty about Janaka. Hearing the fame of king Janaka, Sulabhā, a yogin, wants to know whether Janaka is really emancipated or not. She therefore enteres his body through yogic power, and exchanges opinions with him inside his body. As a matter of fact, it is Sulabhā who preaches, not Pañcaśikha himself. But, as both of Sulabhā and Janaka are supposed to be disciples of Pañcaśikha, we can infer that her teachings have something to do with the thought of Pañcaśikha. The main theme of Sulabhā's discourse is the technique of eloquence which is not directly connected with Sāṃkhya. In her discourse, one of the important topics concerning Sāṃkhya is the constituent elements of living beings, both psychological and material. Sāṃkhya is known as the system that postulates the existence of twenty five principles or elements including *puruṣa* and *prakṛti*. Sulabhā enumerates thirty one elements which are called *guṇa* or *kalā*. This usage of *guṇa* is again quite peculiar for Sāṃkhya which proposes three *guṇas* of *prakṛti*. The constituent elements which she enumerated are: (1-5) five sense organs (*indriya*), (6-10) five objects of sense organs *indriya-artha*, (11) mind (*manas*), (12) intellect (*buddhi*), (13) reality (?) (*sattva*), (14) I-consciousness (*ahaṃkāra*), (15) disposition (*sāmagrya*), (16) composition (*saṃghāta*), (17) shape (*ākṛti*),[21] (18) appearance (*vyakti*), (19) unification of opposites (?) (*dvandvayoga*), (20) time (*kāla*), (21-25) five gross material elements (*mahābhūta*), (26-27) birth and death (*prabhava-apyaya*),(28) rule (*vidhi*), (29) seed (*śukra*), (30) power (*bala*) (31) unmanifest (*avyakta*) or ultimate material (*prakṛti*).[22] These thirty elements are developed from the latent state (*avyakta*), or *prakṛti*, that is, the thirty first element. These elements are classified into material elements, aspect of material elements, organs, sensations, and other categories of existence beginning with *kāla*. This enumerated list shows that this is a rather synthetic scheme which includes different elements of different levels placed in the same level. This thought is not connected with the authentic theory of the Sāṃkhya transmitted down to Īśvarakṛṣṇa. Rather it shows that this synthetic inclinement appears at the early stages and enumerates inclusive elements known in the different scheme of elements. For the present it is difficult to place the thought of Sulabhā in the history of Sāṃkhya history. However we at least have recourse to the materials provided by the Japanese translation of this difficult portion of the MBh. by Nakamura.

At the end of the paper, Nakamura explains his basic standpoint when reading ancient Sanskrit literature. He admits the importance of reconstructing the orginal form of the text. But he believes that it is more important to clarify the processes in which people of later days changed the text to suit their own purposes, as a result of which the text became widely accepted. He holds that the extant literature should be read according to original manuscripts with as few emendations as possilble. He does not like to change the readings without the support of manuscript evidence. This is true of Yogasūtrabhāṣyavivaraṇa (abbr. YSBh.) which will be referred to later. [23] So it is his firm conviction that we should read literature according to the original manuscripts because manuscripts actually existed in the historical period of interest, unlike critical editions which contain readings proposed by modern scholars.[24]

2. Yoga

In "The Selected Works of Hajime Nakamura, vol.24", Nakamura describes the general history of the Yoga school from its orgin to recent times.[25]

Nakamura begins his description of the Yoga school with the usage of the term *yoga* seen in the Ṛgveda, and then in the Upanisads.[26] He finds an earlier usage of the term *yoga* which leads to the YS. in Kaṭha Upaniṣad and Maitri Upaṇiṣad.[27] In the Kaṭha Upaniṣad we come across the famous simile of horse and cart in which body and soul are compared with the cart and chariot. He points out that in the Kaṭha Upaniṣ ad the term *yoga* means control of a horse like the mind controls the sense organs, and that the goal of *yoga* is unification with the highest God Viṣṇu. This leads to the theism found in the classical Yoga school that was systematized in the YS. In the Maitri Upaniṣad the term *yoga* appears with much greater detail though in confused contexts. He summarizes the usage of *yoga* in this Upaniṣad as follows:

1. In the sixth chapter of the Maitri Upaniṣad we come across the most detailed explanation of *yoga* (Maitri Up.6.18-30) in Upaniṣad literature. The *yoga* practice has six limbs. They are *prāṇāyāma, pratyāhāra, dhyāna,*[28] *dhāraṇā, tarka*[29] and *samādhi*. These five limbs, except *tarka*, are common to those of YS.2.29. The YS. adds the external rules, such as *yama* and *niyama*, and *āsana* to them, and as a result YS. includes eight limbs of Yoga practice (*aṣṭāṅga-yoga*). As the Maitri Upaniṣad is earlier than the YS., Nakamura infers that their

primary concern is methods of practice rather than external rules governing the lives of adherents.

2. In the first four chapters of the Maitri Upaniṣad there are three methods of practice which can be employed to attain *Brahman*, that is, *vidyā,' tapas* and *cintā* among which the term *yoga* does not occur. These three are methods of practice performed by Upaniṣad thinkers at that time.

3. The Maitri Upaniṣad must include some concepts which run counter to orthodox Hindu thought. This is because Śaṅkara, an Advaitin, does not write a commentary on it, while he writes commentaries on almost all the Upaniṣads. With this suggestion Nakamura seems to implicitly imply the non-authoritative origin of Yoga as a way of contemplation.

4. The same division of *yoga* into six limbs is again seen in the Amṛtabindu Upanidṣad,[30] one of the Yoga Upaniṣads which are composed later than the YS. The Maitri Upaniṣad shares common concepts with later Haṭh Yoga such as *kuṇḍalī*, and an explanation of *nāḍī*. This suggests the wide influence of the Maitri Upaniṣad, even though it is not accepted as an authoritative Upaniṣad.

2.2 *Yogasūtrabhāṣyavivaraṇa*

In the book mentioned above, Nakamura offers a translation of the Yogasūtra (abbr. YS), the basic text of the school, partially together with the Bhāṣya of Vyāsa (abbr. YBh), which is unlike the Sāṃkhya case. This work is designed to provide a basic or definite starting point for the further study of Yoga not only for himself but also for Japanese students interested in Yoga.[31] Among Yoga literature Nakamura seems to have special interest in the (Abbr. YSV) ascribed to Śaṅkara, the great Advaita Philospher.

In 1952 the YSV. was published in Madras.[32] Nakamura considers this text to be important to the history of Indian Philosopy for the following reasons. First, until then, the YS. had been read with the help of the sub-commentary Tattvavaiśāradī written by Vācaspatimiśra, the Vedānta philosopher. This newly published text may be an older commetary of the YBh. than the Tattvavaiśāradī, if this is really written by Śaṅkara. Secondly, even if this text cannot be ascribed to Śaṅkara, we think it important that it was long believed to be written by Śaṅkara. For those who believed that Śaṅkara was the true author of the text, the school of Vedānta was not essentially different from the school of Yoga. We are faced to re examine what is meant by the word "school" which was used mainly by western scholars.[33]

Nakamura infers that the text was written by Śaṅkara himself or at least a person close to him. The basis of this inference is: (1) the usage of terms in the YSV. is similar to that of the Brahmasūtrabhāṣya (Abbr. BSBh.) ascribed to Śaṅkara, and (2) the sources of citation or reference in the YSV. are maily the Veda and the MBh., which is very similar to those in BSBh.[34]

In the series of papers on the YSV., Nakaumura discusses and comments upon important terms in the YSV. for the purpose of a complete understanding of the text. Hereafter I shall introduce his argument concerning these terms to discover what he was interested in or exactly what was clarified by him.[35]

1. Yoga

He first focuses upon the term yoga, which is the central concept of the text. Vyāsa's interpretation of *yoga* is rather simple: *yogaḥ samādhiḥ* (ad YS.1.1). Vācaspatimiśra theorizes that *samādhi* is approved by *śruti, smṛti* and other texts to be the cause of emancipation (*niḥśreyasa*). But Śaṅkara considers the cause of emancipation to be knowledge attained by *yoga*. For him the knowledge is the cause which leads to the final purpose, that is, elimination of *kleśa*. It could be said that Śaṅkara puts more importance on knowledge than practice, which is the basic standpoint of Śaṅkara.

2. adhyāropa, or the Advaita interpretation of *puruṣa*

In the YSV. we encounter an interpretation which is reminiscent of Advaitic monism. In the Yoga tradition *puruṣa* is considered to be an enjoyer (*bhoktṛ*) of external objects. Śaṅkara takes the position that *ātman*, that is, *puruṣa*, is not an enjoyer. For Sāṃkhya, the theoritical background of Yoga, it is not a priori clear which has the function of a knower or actor within human beings, because Sāṃkhya ascribes mental functions, including recognition, to an internal organ, intellect (*buddhi*), which has its origins in the material principle *prakṛti*, even though it is non spiritual in nature. In the YSV. Śaṅkara interprets the diverse appearance of *puruṣa* using the concept of *adhyāropa* (erroneous attribution) in the analysis of YS.1.4, which is as follows.

Opponent: If *puruṣa* appears differently in accordance with the function of mind, it means that *puruṣa* changes.

Śaṅkara: *Puruṣa* appears differently as a result of the fact that the various functions of the mind are errounesly attributed to *puruṣa*. *Puruṣa* itself does not change. This happens to crystal in whose proximity something coloured is placed. (YSV.p.14.15-17)

Furthermore Śaṅkara uses the same concept of *adhyāropa* in the argument concerning the relation of *buddhi* and *puruṣa*.

These functions of *buddhi* are created by *buddhi* and exist only in buddhi. But these functions are errounesly attributed (*adhyāropyante*) to *puruṣa*. Therefore *puruṣa* is incorrectly thought to behave as a perceiver and have these functions of *buddhi*. (YSV.p.181.22-24)

It could be said that Śaṅkara solves the ambiguities of Sāṃkhya through Advaitic monism by postulating that mental functions belong to *puruṣa* but by superimposition caused by basic ignorance. This way of interpretation using *adhyāropa* suggests that YSV. inclines toward the Advaita point of view.

As another example of Advaitic interpretation seen in the YSV. Nakamura points out similarities in the term used for the explanation of *puruṣa* and that of Brahman in the BSBh. Śaṅkara interprets *puruṣa* as *nityopalabhdhisvarūpa* (one who has nature of perceiving permanently)(YSV.p.191.27, 348.23), which reminds us of the similar expression about Brahman in the BSBh.

3. Īśvara

One of the features of Sāṃkhya is atheism. But in Yoga the existence of a kind of God (*Īśvara*) is admitted as a special *puruṣa* (YS.1.24) and as the teacher (*guru*) of ancient teachers (YS.1.26). The concept of *īśvara* in the YS. is a special *puruṣ a*, that is, not an independent entity of *puruṣa* and *prakṛti*. In YS.1.27 the existence of God is referred to as being denoted by the holy syllable *oṃ* (*tasya vācakaḥ praṇavaḥ* /(YS.1.27)). The concept of God is accepted in the Vedānta school too. Śaṅkara further gives an Advaitic explanation of God as the director of deeds of origination, maintenance and end of the world (*sthiti-bhava-nidhanaprakriyānāṇāṃ vidhātā*),[36] a concept that does not accord with that of *īśvara* in the Yoga system.

There remains another problem with the concept of the all-knower (*sarvajña*). Śaṅkara seems to take a different position from Advaita in the problem of *sarvajñatā* of *īśvara*. In the YSV. Śaṅkara says that *īśvara* is not the all-knower (YSV. p.64.15), while in the BSBh. *īśvara* is considered to be the all-knower (*sarvajña*). This problem about being the all-knower, Nakamura says, needs further examination to clarify the problem of the all-knower in the Yoga school. In the description of *īśvara* in the YSV. Nakamura adds that in the YSV. *īśvara* is called *Kṛṣṇa* who appeared neither in the YS. nor in the BSBh. This fact shows that the YSV. is a step closer to the *bhakti* worship present in Hinduism.

4. citta

In the Yoga system the term *citta* is employed to denote the mind-stuff, which is not the case with Sāṃkhya. In the *Mokṣ adharma* of MBh., which contains a lot of materials concerning early Sāṃkhya and Yoga, the occurrences of the term *citta* are much fewer than other terms denoting internal organs such as *buddhi* and *manas*. It is, therefore, necessary to explain why the Yoga system employed a term not used in early Sāṃkhya and Yoga.

Nakamura argues that Śaṅkara in the YSV. considers the mind *citta* to be something pure. He quotes Śaṅkara's interpretation of YS.2.3 in which five kinds of *kleśa*, that is, *avidyā, asmitā, rāga, dveṣa,* and *abhiniveśa*, are enumerated. Śaṅkara says:

naiṣa doṣaḥ—kleśānām avṛttitvāt / na hi kleśāḥ pratyayamātrāḥ, pratyayamātrā hi vṛttayaḥ / kleśās tu cittasya malaṃ, yathā cakṣuṣtimiram / kleśamalaviyoge cittasya viparyayapratyayābhāvāt /

(Translation by Legett: There is no inconsistency (in distinguishing the class of mental process and giving the division of this illusion into five), because the taints are not mental process. For taints are not merely ideas, whereas mental processes are merely ideas. Taints are impurities of the mind, as the disease timira is of the eye. It is from absence of illusory ideas that there is freedom from the impurity of taints.(p.178))

This concept of mind is reminiscent of Mahāyāna Buddhism, which teaches that the mind is essentially pure. This hints at the close relationship between Yoga and Buddhism. This is true of the term *kleśa*. It is unique to Buddhism to use this term in the sense of taints or sin. Yoga uses this term with the same meaning, while in other schools of philosophy the term is used in the sense of pain. Śaṅkara follows the tradition of Yoga which was greatly influenced by Buddhism. But Śaṅkara's basic position allows the existence of the external things in opposition to Mahāyāna Buddhism which denies their reality. He attacks Mahāyāna Buddhists by calling them *vaināśika*[37] in the interpretation of YS.4.23 as follows:

kasmat punaḥ kāraṇāt puruṣasya cittākārāpattiḥ / tasyāṃ vā satyāṃ svabuddhisaṃvedanam / kuto vaināśikānāṃ cittam eva grāhyaṃ grāhakaṃ ceti bhrāntir ity āha — draṣṭ ṛdṛśyoparaktaṃ cittaṃ sarvārtham / (YS.4.23)

(Legett's translation: Why is it then that *Puruṣa* assumes the form of the mind? Or again, is it that it (mind) is then experiencing its own buddhi, thus giving rise to the error of the Vaināśika Buddhists, who say that it it mind (citta) alone that is both object (*grāhya*) and subject (*grāhaka*). (p.403))

Śaṅkara is influenced by the Buddhist concept but denies the Buddhist Idealism. His existentialist position is reflected in the argument of the direct perception (*pratyakṣa*) which presuppses the external object perceived through sense organs (YSV. ad YS.1.6).

5. some terms unique to Śaṅkara

Nakamura compares several YSV. terms with the terminology found in the BSBh., and states that some are unique to Śaṅkara probably to prove Śaṅkara's authorship of the text. He points out that *brahmādistambaparyantā mūrtayaḥ* found in the YSV. is reminiscent of *brahmādistambaparyanta* in the BSBh. Then Nakamura focuses upon the usage of the terms which denote the production of sound. He seems to consider the term *pratyupanīta* used in the YSV., which is used to interprete the term *upasthāpita* (made apparent) (YBh.3.17), and the term *pratyupasthāpaka* (YBh.1.6-7) unique to Śaṅkara. He considers that the term *avidyāpratyupasthāpita* in the BSBh. presupposes the occurrence of *pratyupasthāpaka* in the YSV.[38]

The verbal form *pratyāsīdatitarām* (YSV.p.52.21) is reminiscent of the one found in the BSBh., namely, *upapadyatetarām*.[39] He further points out that the term *kāryakaraṇa* (YSV.p.68.18), meaning a body, is unique to the texts written by Śaṅkara.[40]

Nakamura refers to the meaning of the term *pratyavamarśa* used in the BSBh.,[41] but he does not proceed with a further argument about the similarity to the usage found in the YSV.[42]

6. Buddhist terms, kleśa etc.

Nakamura was sufficiently well versed in Buddhist thought to find many Buddhistic terms in the YSV. which indicate the close relationship between Yoga and Buddhism.

As seen in the argument of *citta* he refers to the term *kleśa* which often appears in Buddhist literature with a specific meaning. Again, the meaning of this term in the YS. is the same as that found in Buddhist texts. In this way he sheds light upon some terms present in the YSV. which indicate the relationship between Buddhism and Yoga system of thought. In addition to *kleśa*, he discusses *āmukhīkaroti, sthiti, tadutpatti, anutpattidharma, anābhoga, pratyaya, styānam, bhūmi, khalīkāra, ābhāsa, grāhya-grāhaka, vigatatṛṣ ṇāsamucāya, nirodha* in terms of their relationship to Buddhist thought. Though it is beyond my ability to follow this detailed argument, it can be said that as a result of the examination of these terms the close link between Yoga and Buddhism becomes apparent.

7. upāsanā and siddhi

In the BSBh. Śaṅkara often refers to *upāsanā* (contemplation), as the purpose of the BSBh. is to discuss *upāsanā* in the Upaniṣads. But he also refers to *yoga* which seems to be considered synonymous to *dhyāna*. As a whole Śaṅkara seems to accept the worldly concept of *yoga* that the practice of *yoga* makes it possible for its practitioner (*yogin*) to obtain mysterious powers. For example, a *yogin* can have many bodies at the same time, or a *yogin* can reach some special place such as the sun. Śaṅkara refers again to the power resulting from *yoga* practice by which a *yogin* can pass through material things and make himself very small. He, therefore, must accept the power born from the eight *siddhis*. On the basis of the attitude of Śaṅkara towards *yoga* practice, we may infer that there is no difference between the Advaita school and the Yoga school in respect of the practice of striving towards emancipation. Śaṅkara does not need to leave the Yoga school in order to belong to the Advaita school. Perhaps this is the conclusive view of Nakamura in respect of the concept of "school" in the real traditions of Indian Philosophy. He finally refers to the followers of the present-day Śaṅkara school.[43] He says that *yogins* of Śaṅkara school seems not to believe in eight mysterious powers. They take the bus when they travel, and Śaṅkarācārya uses his own car.

8. comparison with Vācaspatimiśra

Nakamura discusses the difference between Śaṅkara and Vācaspatimiśra to clarily the standpoint of Śaṅkara towards *yoga*. As a whole there is not much difference between the two. But Nakamura points out several differencces between them. He compares the interpretation on YS.2.47-51, 55 written by both thinkers. Let me now show some differences between the two.

In the interpretation on the *anantasamāpatti* in YS.2.47, Vyāsa mentions:

ananto vā samāpannaṃ cittam āsanaṃ nirvartayati / (The posture of sitting becomes perfect when the mind is in unity with the Infinite.)

Śaṅkara adds the following points to this interpretation:

anantaṃ viśvam, anantabhāva ānantyam, tasmin samāpannaṃ vyāpya viśvabhāvaṃ sthitaṃ cittam āsanaṃ nirvartayati draḍhayati / (YSV. p.227.15-17)

(Legett's translation: The universe is infinite, and the state of being infinite is infinity. When the mind attains *samādhi* (*samāpatti*) on that which stands pervading all existence, the *posture is perfected* is made firm.

Śaṅkara takes the meaning of *ānantya* as *viśvabhāva* (all existing beings). He, therefore, seems to believe that when one is united with the Infinte, one becomes identical with all existing beings.

On the other hand Vācaspatimiśra interprets the same phrase as follows: *anatne vā nāganāyake sthiratarаphaṇāsahasrvavidhṛtaviśvabharāmaṇḍale samāpannaṃ cittam āsanaṃ nirvartayantīti* /

Vācaspati cosiders the meaning of infinite (*ananta*) in the YS. to be the Ananta, the snake king. This interpretation is apparently influenced by a religious thought. This religious influence is rather less in Śaṅkara's view compared with that of Vācaspati. This fact shows that Śaṅkara's interpretation represents an older view of Yoga than that of Vācaspatipmiśra. This is true of the interpretation of YS.2.49-50, which runs :

tasmin sati śvāsapraśvāsayor gativicchedaḥ prāṇāyāmaḥ / (YS.2.49)

bāhyābhyantarastambhavṛttir deśakālasaṃkhyābhiḥ paridṛṣ ṭā dīrghasūkṣmaḥ / (YS.2.50)

These sūtras deal with the control of breath with the practice of sitting. They explain that, when the method of sitting is properly practiced, the aspiration and inspriration (*śvāsa* and *praśvāsa*) are stopped. Vyāsa ends his interpretation by defining the words used in YS.2.49. In the same manner Śaṅkara ends his short interpretation by defining the words used in YS.2.49. But Vācaspatimiśra interprets these words by using the terms of Haṭha Yoga, that is, *recaka, pūraka, kumbhaka.*[44]

YS.2.50 explains these three kinds of breath control. Vyāsa and Śaṅkara interpret this sūtra without using Haṭha Yoga terminology. Vācaspati, on the other hand, uses again the same three terms from Haṭha Yoga and applies them to each kind of breath control. Śaṅkara perhaps considers Haṭha Yoga to be a rather peculiar way of practice compared to the traditional methods. With the term *anye*, he refers to those who use Haṭha Yoga terminology.

bāhyam anye pūraka ity ācakṣate / (YSV.p.227.30)

taṃ recaka ity ācakṣate / (YSV.p.228.13)

Śaṅkara knows the Haṭha Yogic concepts but does not use them when explaining his own views. This holds true with the interpretation of YS.2.51 which explains the fourth kind of breath control.

By means of a comparison of YSV. with the Tattvavaiśāradī of Vācaspatimiśra, Nakamura tries to clarify their resemblances and differences. Through these comparisons, he intends to place the text of YSV. in its proper position among the Yoga schools. And by discussing Buddhist terminology in the YSV., he attempts to clarify the text and its relationship to other schools, especially to Buddhism, in order to place it in its proper position in the whole spectrum of philosophical thought.

3. Sāṃkhya and Yoga criticized by Śaṅkara

One of the difficulties of the studies of Sāṃkhya and Yoga is the shortage of materials due to their antiquity. The extant literature of Sāṃkhya and Yoga are narrowly limited. Therefore it is important to collect materials from other schools which refer to Sāṃkhya and Yoga in some way. If we understand how Sāṃkhya and Yoga were regarded by other schools, this will help us to understand the characteristics of Sāṃkhya and Yoga. In this respect Nakamura's work is of importance to the study of Sāṃkhya and Yoga. He translates the BSBh. 2.1.1-2.1.3 (*smṛtyadhikaraṇa*) into Japanese with notes in which Sāṃkhya and Yoga are criticized by Śaṅkara. The topics of the argument are (1) the ultimate cause of the world, (2) the authority of the Vedic literature, (3) the pluality of *puruṣa* or *ātman*. Sāṃkhya supposes that the same entity, both material and unconscious, known as *prakṛti*, is the ultimate cause of the world and starts the process of evolution by stimulation of *puruṣa*. Therefore in the Sāṃkhya system there is no room for the world creater, Brahman or Īśvara. Śaṅkara refutes this view by quoting verses of smṛti literature such as the Manusmṛti and the MBh. which propound the existence of God. Then Sāṃkhya opposes this with the argument that there are other *smṛtis* which support Sāṃkhya view. Therefore if *smṛti* is accepted as the source of right knowledge, the *smṛti* supporting the Sāṃkhya view must be accepted as such. Śaṅkara refutes this view of Sāṃkhya with the theory that the *smṛti* quoted by Sāṃkhya is not an authentic *smṛti* that is in accordance with *śruti*, so it must be denied. The problem of the pluality of *puruṣa* is discussed in the same way that it contradicts the Veda and *smṛtis* following the Veda.

A further problem is what is the position of the Veda in the Sāṃkhya system. It could be said that Sāṃkhya's position with regard to the Veda is unequivocal. Sāṃkhya denies the Veda as the means of final emancipation , but on the other hand it accepted it as the means to attain correct knowledge which cannot be obtained by other two *pramāṇas*. But here in this portion of the BSBh. the argument hinges on the reliablity of *smṛti*, not on the position of the Veda in Sāṃkhya. Here we should understand that from Śaṅkara's point of view it is the existence of an independent material cause and the pluality of souls that must be denied as being contradictory to the statements of authentic *smṛtis*. This refutation holds true with Yoga which admits also the material cause.[45]

4. Summary

This completes my survey of the works of Nakamura in the fields of Sāṃkhya and Yoga. Although I have profited greatly from this work, I am afraid that I may not have understood him properly, and that, because of my lack of knowledge, I might have omitted some of his important contributions. Before the end of this presentation, I shall briefly summarize the features of the works of Nakamura, seen through my albeit narrow perspective.

1. I am astonished by the vast amount of his works and the wide range of his knowledge which is full of inspiration. He paves the way of research for all those who are interested in India.

2. He never fogets that, in order to understand a system of thought totally, one shoud never forget its social context. Therefore, he attempts to understand the traditional thoughts and beliefs of the common people.

3. It is his belief that classical literature should be read as it is, with constant recourse to the manuscripts which truly reflect the situation in those ancient times. To put it another way, manuscripts represent the true reality, not the opinions of modern redactors.

4. By means of literary comparisons, he strives to emphasize the universality of human nature unrestricted by cultural limits. He seems to attempt to answer the question: what did human beings think then, what do they think now, and what will they think in the future?

References

[1] Even in the independent paper, "On the Direct Perception (2)", Modern Thoughts, 13(12)1985.11, p.287-93, Nakamura discusses the concept of direct perception as propounded by the various schools. This paper is intended to introduce the basic tenets of Indian Schools of philosophy to Japanese readers who may not be acquainted with Indian philosophy. He discusses the concept of *pratyakṣa* of Vaiśeṣika, Sāṃkhya and Buddhist schools.

For the *pratyakṣa* concept of Sāṃkhya school, he referred to the Sāṃkhya Sūtra and Sāṃkhya Kārikā 5. He pointed out the fact without further argument that the concept of *pratyakṣa* was mentioned in these basic texts of the Sāṃkhya school.

2 Nakamura suggests on the basis of the views of Albrecht Wezler (cf. A. Wezler, Der Gott des Sāṃkhya: Zu Nyāyakusumañjali 1.3, IIJ. vol.12, no.4, 1970, pp. 55-262), Prof. Nakamura postulates the earlier existence of God in Sāṃkhya, though He is not a creator. This theory is validated by J. Bronkhorst with a detailed examination. (Cf. Johannes Bronkhorst, God in Sāṃkhya, WZKS. vol.27, 1983, pp.149-164.)

3 For the origin of this comparison, Nakamura quotes a passage of the Republic IX 580-581 which runs as follows:

It seems to me that these three principles and three elements correspond; also three desires and governing powers.

How do you mean? he said.

There is one principle with which, as we were saying, a man learns, another with which he is angry; the third, having many forms, has no special name, but is denoted by the general term appetitive, from the extraodinary strength and vehemence of the desires of eating and drinking and the other sensual appetites which are the main elements of it; [581] also money-loving, because such desires are generally satisfied by the help of money. (The Dialogues of PLATO, Translated by Benjamin Jowett, Great Books Of The Western World, 7. Plato, The University of Chicago, 1952, p.421.)

4 Mahābhārata, for the first time critically edited by V. S. Sukthankar, Poona, (1954f.)

5 Hajime Nakamura, The Way of Life by Layman, Hokke-Bunka Kenkyū, (Journal of Institute for the Comprehensive Study of Lotus Sutra) No.3, pp.1-97, March 1977. The summary and conclusion of this translation is contained in "The Selected Works of Hajime Nakamura", vol.30, Hinduism and Epics, pp.523-576.

6 The relevant verses run:

idaṃ viśvaṃ jagat sarvam ajayyaṃ cāpi sarvaśaḥ /

mahābhūtātmakaṃ brahman nātaḥ parataraṃ bhavet //MBh. III.201.15

mahābhūtāni khaṃ vāyur agnir āpas tathā ca bhūḥ /

śabdaḥ sparśaś ca rūpaṃ ca raso gandhaś ca tadguṇāḥ //MBh. III.201.16

7 It is not clear what is meant by three elements in MBh. XII.201.17, which runs as follows:

teṣām api guṇāḥ sarve guṇavṛttiḥ parasparam /

pūrvapūrvaguṇāḥsarve kramaśo guṇiṣu triṣu /

Nakamura translates the MBh. using the commentary written by Nīlakaṇṭha. Here Nīlakaṇṭha considers these three gunins to be *Īśa, Sūtra,* and *Virāj*. Nakamura considers this interpretation to be influenced by later Vedānta Philosophy.

8 The relevant verse is as follows:

ṣaṣṭhas tu cetanā nāma mana ity abhidhīyate /

saptamī tu bhaved buddhir ahaṃkāras tataḥ param / MBh. IIII.201.18

9 It is not clear which seventeen elements are counted. We meet in the *Mokṣadharma* of MBh. the concept that a human being is made up of seventeen elements. It is not certain that the term *avyakta* here means a human being. The relevant verse runs:

indriyāṇi ca pañcaiva rajo sattvaṃ tamas tathā /

ity eṣa saptadaśako rāśir avyaktasaṃjñakaḥ // MBh. III.201.19

10 Here there seems to be a certain confusion in the usage of the term *guṇa*. Nakamura here regards *guṇa* as objects of enjoyment, accepting Nīlakaṇṭha's interpretation, and referring to the usage of the term in Jaina and Buddhist literature. We should not discount the translation of *guṇa* as the object of enjoyment.

11 It is not clear what is meant by *saptadaśaka* and *caturviṃśaka* and what their relation might be. The verse in question is:

sarvair ihendriyārthais tu vyaktāvyaktaiḥ susamvṛtaḥ /

caturviṃśaka ity eṣa vyaktāvyaktamayo guṇaḥ /12.201.20a-d

etat te sarvam ākhyātaṃ kiṃbhūyo śrotum icchasi //12.201.20ef

12 Even the occurence of the term *guṇin* (locative plural) is rather rare.

13 The relevant verse runs:

eṣa yogavidhiḥ kṛtsno yāvad indriyadhāraṇam /

etan mūlaṃ hi tapasaḥ kṛtsnasya narakasya ca /MBh. III.202.18

14 Nakamura suggests a similarity with a simile in the Kaṭha Upaniṣ ad 3.3-17.

15 The relevant verse runs:

sa jantuḥ sarvabhūtātmā puruṣaḥ sa sanātanaḥ / MBh. III.203.16cd

mano buddhir ahaṃkāro bhūtānāṃ viṣayaś ca saḥ / MBh. III.203.16ef

16 The function of each wind is explained in detail in the following part of the same chapter(203).

17 The relevant verses are:

ātmānaṃ taṃ vijānīhi nityaṃ yogajitātmakam / MBh. III.203.30

devo yaḥ saṃsthitas tasminn abbindur iva puṣkare /

kṣetrajñaṃ taṃ vijānīhi nityaṃ tyāgajitātmakam /MBh. III.203.31

jīvātmakāni jānīhi rajo sattvam tamas tathā /

jīvam ātmaguṇaṃ viddhi tathātmānaṃ parātmakam / MBh. III.203.32

sacetanaṃ jīvaguṇaṃ vadanti sa ceṣṭate ceṣṭayate ca sarvam /

tataḥ paraṃ kṣetravido vadanti prākalpayad yo bhuvanāni sapta /MBh. III.203.33

evaṃ sarveṣu bhūteṣu bhūtātmā na prakāśate /

dṛśyate tv agryayā buddhyā sūkṣmayā jnāna vedibhiī / MBh. III.203.34

cittasya hi prasādena hanti karma śubhāśubham /

prasannātmā ātmani sthitvā sukham ānantyam aśnute / MBh. III.203.35

lakṣaṇaṃ tu prasādasya yathā tṛptaḥ sukhaṃ svapet /MBh. II.203.36ab

18 MBh. XII.192.122, 242.10, 292.37

19 The verse in question runs:

pradīpteneva dīpena manodīpena paśyati /

dṛśṭvātmānaṃ nirātmānam tadā sa tu vimucyate / MBh. III.203.38

Here it can be said that there is not a rigid distinction of the function between *manas* and *buddhi*. In the SK. it is *buddhi* that is responsible for the cognition of *puruṣa*.

20 I discussed the teachings of Pañcaśikha in Chapters 211-212 of the *Mokṣadharma*. (Cf. Shujun Motegi, The Teachings of Pañcaśikha in the Mokṣadharma, Asiatische Studien, vol. LIII.3, 1999, pp.513-535.)

21 Hopkins reads ignorance (*avidyā*) instead of *ākṛti*. (Cf. E. W. Hopkins, Great Epic of India, first published in 1901, Reprinted in 1969, p.152)

22 About the 31st element there seems to be different opinions. Hopkins thinks the 31st element as God. Nakamura does not include the 31st element in the number, counting 30 elements. Hopkins pointed out that the same number of elements is ascribed to Pāśupata. (E. W. Hopkins, Great Epic of India, p.152.)

[23] Nakamura criticizes the corrected reading *āmukhīkaroti* of *abhimukhaṃ karoti* of YBh.1.1. (YSV.p.8.3)

[24] Nakamura criticizes the following readings from Poona Edition of MBh. as having been altered without good reason, or without support of manuscript evidence:

1. *kasyādya mṛtyusenā nivekṣyate* (MBh. XII.169.14) He prefers *ko hi jānāti kasyādya mṛtyukāko bhaviṣyati* of the Bombay version of the MBh.

2. *na sa badhyate* (MBh. XII.169.25) He proposes a different reading, namely, *vadhyate* from the context.

3. *buddhyaiśvaryābhisargārthaṃ yad dhyānaṃ cātmanaḥ śubham* // (MBh. XII.234.1) He prefers *buddhyaiśvaryātisargo 'yaṃ pradhānaś Ātmanaḥ śrutam* in the Bombay version.

4. *svadhājñānakasya* (MBh. XII.235.9) He prefers the reading in the Bombay version which is *svadharmajñāpakasya*.

5. *vadhabandhavirodhena* (MBh. XII.254.39) He proposes - *nirodhena* according to manuscript evidence.

6. *saṃśliṣṭā nābhijāyante yathāpa iha vpāṃśavaḥ*(MBh. XII.308.100) He prefers *praśliṣṭaṃ ca na jānanati yathā 'pa iva pāṃśavaḥ* in the Bombay version.

7. *mahājanāt* (MBh. XII.308.143) He prefers *mahājanān* in the Bombay version and some manuscripts.

8. *rājyaduḥkhāni* (MBh. XII.308.161) He prefers *rājaduḥkhḥni* in the Bombay version , criticizing the Poona version because no evidence for it is present in the manuscripts.

[25] Nakamura classifies Yoga into several categories for the convinience of his general survey.

1. *rāja-yoga* propounded in Yoga-sūtra
2. *jñāna-yoga* propounded by Śaṅkara
3. *karma-yoga* propounded in Bhagavad Gītā, and by Tilak
4. *bhakti-yoga* proposed by Bhagavad Gītā, and by Hindu religious sects
5. *haṭha-yoga* propounded in Śakti sect of Hindu Religion
6. *mantra-yoga* propounded in Esteorogic Buddhism
7. *laya-yoga* propounded in Kuṇḍalinī
8. *vyāyāma-yoga*, which is chiefly physical training
9. *Integral yoga* postlated by Aurobindo Ghosh

26 He focuses upon the term *yogakṣema*, referring to the theories of Renou. (Cf. L. Renou, Ētudes védique, 3., Quellques termes du Ṛgveda, Journal Asiatique, 241 (Paris, 1953) p.183f. (ádhvan, bandhu, prásiti, yoga, kavi)) In the old Upaniṣads, Nakamura says, the most frequently used term near *yoga* is *upāsanā*.

27 The first appearance of the term *yoga* in Upaniṣad literature is *yoga ātmā* (concentration is his body.) (Tait. Up. II.4).

28 In relation to *dhyāna*, Nakamura comments that ancient yoga literature does not give us enough information to solve the question of whether the eyes should be kept open or not during the practice of *dhyāna*. (p.27) Perhaps the term *yoganidrā* in the Purānic texts may have attracted his attention in the same context. (p.41)

29 Nakamura presents a short argument about the meaning of *tarka*. Quoting Garbe's translation "Reflexion" and Radhakrishnan's translation "contemplative inquiry", he points out that *tarka* in this context does not have the same meaning as used in the Nyāya school of logic.

30 As an earlier explanation of *yoga*, Prof. Nakamura passingly refers to Āpastamba Dharmasūtra 1.23.5,6, which runs as follows:

krodho harṣo roṣo lobho moho dambho droho mṛṣ odyamatyāśaparīvādāvasūyā kāmamanyū anātmyam ayogas teṣ āṃ yogamūlo nirghātaḥ /5/

akrodho 'harṣo 'lobho 'moho 'dambho 'drohaḥ satyavacanam anatyāśo 'paiśunam anasūyā saṃvibhāgas tyāga ārjavaṃ mārdavaṃ śamo damaḥ sarvabhūtair avirodho yoga āryam ānṛśaṃsaṃ tuṣṭir iti sarvāśramāṇāṃ samayapadāni tāny anutiṣṭ han vidhinā sārvagāmī bhavati /6/

Here we see the list of faults which cause the torment to creatures. The eradication of these faults is said to depend on yoga. The term yoga is enumerated together with *ārjava* etc which are considered to be realized by noble persons. Therefore, the concept of *yoga* is slightly different from that of the YS.

31 The complete Japanese translation of Vyāsa Bhāṣya was thereafter published by Prof. Megumu Honda, a student of Nakamura. (Cf. Megumu Honda, Yogabhāṣya, (Japanese Translation of the YS. with Vyāsa Bhāṣya), Kyoto,1977.)

32 Patañjala-Yoga-Sūtra-Bhāṣya-Vivaraṇam, ed by T. Chandrasekharan, Madras Government Oriental Series, No. XCIV, Madras, 1952.

T. Legett translated this text into English. (Trevor Legett, Śaṅkara on the Yoga Sūtras, A Full Translation of the Newly Discovered Text. The first half of this translation was published in 1981, 1983.) Recently T. S. Rukmani published another English translation with text. (T. S. Rukmani, Yogasūtrabhāṣyavivaraṇa of Śaṅkara, 2 vols., Delhi, 2001.)

33 Nakamura refers to the view of P. Hacker. Hacker is of the opinion that Śaṅkara was at first a follower of Patañjali Yoga and later became an Advaita scholar.

34 Rukmani expressed the opposite opinion that the YSV. cannot be ascribed to Śaṅkara who is the author of BSBh. (Cf. T. S. Rukmani, *op.cit.*, Introduction p.xii)

35 Nakamura writes (at least) three papers on the YSV.

(1) Hajime Nakamura, On the Yogasūtrabhāṣyavivaraṇa ascribed to Śaṅkara, The Felicitation Volume for Prof. Jio Okuda to his 77 years old, Kyoto, pp.1219-1229, 1976.

(2) Hajime Nakamura, Śaṅkara's Yogasūtrabhāṣyavivaraṇa, Japanese Indian and Buddhist Studies, vol.25.1, pp.70-77,1976.

(3) Hajime Nakamura, Śaṅkara's Yogasūtrabhāṣyavivaraṇa, Japanese Study of Indian and Buddhist Studies, vol.26.1, pp.119-127,1977.

Based on the examination in these papers, Prof. Nakamura published a Japanese translation of (at least) the first chapter of YSV. in the Japanese journal, "Āgama".

36 So far, I have been unable to find this phrase in the YSV.

37 Nakamura points out that the term *vaināsika* is used in the BSBh. to call Buddhist schools.

38 The phrases in question here run as follows:

evaṃbhūtasya mukhyaphalatve pradhānakriyāvyavahita(vikṛṣ tāyāḥ) kriyāyā dravyaṃ dravyasya vā kriyā phalam ity anyonyapratyupasthāpakatvena pradhānaphalābhimukhīkaraṇāt phalatvopacāro na virotsyate / (YBh.1.6,7, YSV. p.22.12)

tad ekaṃ padam ekabuddhiviṣayam ekaprayatnākṣiptaṃ avibhāgam akramam avarṇātmakam antyavarṇapratyayavyāpāropasthāpitaṃ / (YBh.3.17, YSV. p.266.10)

evam ekaprayatnākṣiptaṃ varṇakramajanmapratyupanītasaṃskāranimittabhuddhiparipākābhisamīkṣayā paścimabuddhau jhaṭati parisphuritaṃ, (YBh.3.17, YSV.p.167.12)

39 Referring to Speyer's Vedische und Sanskritsyntax and Whitney's Sanskrit Grammer, holds that this verbal form is not corrupt. I came across the same kind of conjugation form in the MBh. XII.258.12.

40 Nakamura enumerates the occurences of this term in the BSBh. together with the translation by P. Deussen; die Organe des Wirkens, the organs of action.

41 The phrase in question runs as follows:

atra vadāmaḥ saty api samastavarṇapratyavamarśe yathā kramānurodhinya ev pipīlikāḥ panktibuddhim ārohanti, evaṃ kramānurodhina eva varṇāḥ padabuddhim ārokṣyanti /

42 The term *pratyavamarśa* is used in the YSV. as follows:

tad iti pūrvaprakṛtāyā avidyāyāḥ pratyavamarśaḥ /

(Legett's translation: It refers back to the Ignorance already explained.

Rukmini's translation: tad=this recalls *avidyā* which was mentioned earlier.)

43 Nakamura refers to the hospital which cares for patients with a kind of *yoga* practice, and to the institute in which *yoga* practice is analyzed by the modern science. (Cf. H. Nakamura, The Selected Works, vol.24, pp.333-338.)

44 The relevant passage reads:

recakapūrakakumbhakeṣv asti śvāsapraśvāsayor gativiccheda iti prāṇāyāmasāmānyalakṣaṇam etad iti / tathā hi yatra bāhyo vāyur ācamyāntardhāryate pūrake tatrāsti śvāsapraśvāsayor gativicchedaḥ / yatrāpi koṣṭyo vāyur virecya bahir dhāryate recake tatrāsti śvāsapraśvāsayor gativicchedaḥ / evaṃ kumbhake 'pīti / (Tattvavaiśāradī ad YBh.2.49)

45 Nakamura identifies the reference to the MBh. quoted in the BSBh., which is important for an understanding of which verses are seen by Śaṅkara as reflcting Sāṃkhya and Yoga. But he numbered the verses quoted there according to the Kumbhakonam Edition of the MBh. Here I would note the numbering the verses quoted in the BSBh. 2.1.1, following the Poona Edition of the MBh. just for the convenience of readers.

Concerning the concept of *pradhāna* and *puruṣa*:

"yat tat sūkṣmam avijñeyam" (MBh. XII.321.28)

"sa hy antaratmā bhūtānāṃ kṣetrajñaś ceti kathyate" (MBh. XII.321.29)

"tasmād avyaktam utpannaṃ triguṇaṃ dvijasattama" (MBh. XII.321.29)

"avyaktaṃ puruṣe brahman nirguṇe saṃpralīyate" (MBh. XII.326.30)

"ataś ca saṃkṣepaṃ śṛṇudhvaṃ nārāyaṇaḥ sarvam idaṃ purāṇaḥ /
sa sargakāle ca karoti sarvaṃ saṃhārakāle ca tad atti bhūyaḥ /" (MBh. XII.290.110)

Concerning the plurality of puruṣa and singularity of ātman:

"bahavaḥ puruṣā brahmann utāho eka eva tu" (MBh. XII.338.1)

"bahavaḥ puruṣā rājan sāṃkhyayogavicāriṇām" (MBh. XII.338.2)

"bahūnāṃ puruṣāṇāṃ hi yathaikā yonir ucyate /
tathā taṃ puruṣaṃ viśvam ākhyāsyāmi guṇādhikam /" (MBh. XII.338.3)

"mamāntarātmā tava ca ye cānye dehasaṃsthitāḥ /
sarveṣāṃ sākṣibhūto 'sau na grāhyaḥ kenacit kvacit //" (MBh. XII.339.4)

"viśvamūrdhvā viśvabhujo viśvapādākṣināsikaḥ /
ekaś carati bhūteṣu svairacarī yathāsukam /" (MBh. XII.339.5)

18

Freedom of Thought and Jainism

Professor Hajime Nakamura's contribution to the study of Jainism

Michihiko Yajima

"Isn't it more important to understand the spirit of Jaina people who are now living in India than to read any one of a great many classics of Jaina literature?" —Hajime Nakamura—

Recollection

When Professor Hajime Nakamura was involved in research on Jainism in 1950s, the textual material and other references for studying available in Japan were extremely limited. Later, he recollected those days in his introductory remarks on Ratnacandra's *An Illustrated Ardhamāgadhī Dictionary* (5 volumes), reprinted in Japan, in 1977, as follows: "I think that the present students are very fortunate and even enviable. It was about 20 years ago that, realizing the necessity for research on Jainism, I took a photograph of all the volumes of the Dictionary and bound it. Alas! It became about 20 volumes. It was much too large to handle." (*Selected Works* [the Definitive Edition], vol. 10 [see below], p. 870)

Pioneers of Jaina Research in Japan

It is worthy of note, even astonishing, however, that, although the material was very limited, there had already been *a history* of Jaina study in Japan even before Nakamura. The first studies go back to Shigenobu Suzuki (1890-1917) who studied Jainism in the early 1910s. Though he passed away at the age of 27, his posthumous manuscripts including Japanese translations of *Kalpa-sūtra*, *Tattvārthādhigamasūtra* and *Yogaśāstra*, were edited and published by his *guru,* Junjiro Takakusu in 1920.

After Suzuki, there appeared several scholars who cultivated research work on Jainism. For convenience, I quote here an article of Atsushi Uno entitled: "Jaina Studies in Japan", *Jain Journal* 8, no.2 (1973), in which he mentioned the names of six Japanese scholars who had written books and/or articles on Jainism until then (that is, up to 1973) , namely, S. Suzuki, Hakuju Ui, Ensho Kanakura, Seiren Matsunami, Hajime Nakamura and the author himself. All of these scholars, with full use of modern philological methods, contributed to making Jainology take root in the soil of Japan and to putting the Indological and Buddhist studies there on a firm basis. Their achievements are, of course, not restricted to the field of Jainism, but nobody will oppose calling them the 'pioneers' of Jaina study in Japan. As for Nakamura, it can be said that he was not only a pioneer, but also a successor who further developed the Jaina study of his *guru* Ui.

By the way, it seems somewhat mysterious to me that, although in his paper Uno introduces most of the scholars including himself along with their writings, he mentions S. Matsunami and Nakamura only by their names and does not refer to their writings. Why did he not show any details about those two scholars? In this paper, Nakamura is given only the following sentence: "Dr. H. Nakamura, Professor of Tokyo University, has also published several treatises in some journals and referred to some points in his books." And it is more mysterious that, quite recently, only a few years after Uno's death, his paper containing little information about Nakamura's contribution to Jaina study was reprinted in the same Journal (35, no.4, 2001) *just as it was before.* In reprinting, the editor of the Journal kindly added a list of the writings of S. Matsunami, but again nothing was mentioned of Nakamura and his works.

It is delightful to the students of Indology both at home and abroad that *Kalyāna-Mitra, a Felicitation Volume to Professor Nakamura*, edited by V. N. Jha, was published from

Delhi in 1991, through which his great contribution to Indological and Buddhist studies has become more widely known to the world. A bibliography of the writings of Nakamura is also attached to the Felicitation Volume, but it may be natural that only his main writings in English are listed there.

It was thirty years ago that Nakamura discussed research activities on Jainism in his "Bibliographical Survey of Jainism," *The Journal of Intercultural Studies*, Inaugural Number, (Hirakata City, Osaka: Intercultural Research Institute. The Kansai University of Foreign Studies, 1974), pp. 52-75; in which he put exhaustive footnotes to give readers related data, including his own contributions. This survey of Nakamura, originally written in English, was revised and enlarged by himself, and recently translated into Japanese by Kenji Watanabe, a scholar of Jaina Āgama, in the 10th volume of Professor Nakamura's Selected Works:

Shiso no Jiyū to Jainakyo (Freedom of Thought and Jainism), Nakamura Hajime Senshû [Ketteiban] (Selected Works of Professor Hajime Nakamura , vol. 10 [the Definitive Edition], Tokyo: Shunjūsha (1991), pp. 773-855.

In this Volume, all of his 17 articles on Jainism, 9 in English and 8 in Japanese, are also listed at the end of the attached bibliography (pp. 857-875). Most of the articles given in the list form the main chapters of the above final version, which means that his research work on Jainism over many years has been compiled into this one book. The volume amounts to about 900 pages, including three appendices, a bibliography and two indices.

This paper is to throw light on Professor Nakamura's contribution to the study of Jainism, while touching on his writings and showing how the above 10th volume of his Selected Works has been formed.

His first contribution

By the year that Uno's *original* article was published, Nakamura had already published at least 12 articles on Jainism, 5 in Japanese and 7 in English. His first and monumental article on Jaina ethics of economy was published in 1951:

"Indo Minzoku Shihon no Seishinkozo eno Ichi-shiten. Jainakyo no Keizai-rinri"- (A Perspective for Analyzing the Mental Structure of the Indian National Capital. Economic Ethics in Jainism), *Toyo Bunka* Tokyo Daigaku Toyo Bunka Kenkyusho 1951, September, pp.1-26.

Later, this article formed a part of his *Shūkyo to Shakai Rinri* (Religion and Social Ethics), Tokyo: Iwanami Shoten (1959), and its revised and enlarged edition was also included recently in the 10th volume of his Selected Works (II.4: pp. 601-669).

He summarized the article as follows:

"Jainism is very important when we consider the significance of religions in the development of capitalism in India. A very strange phenomenon may be noted in Indian economy; that is, that it has been completely dominated for a long time by Jains, who still today occupy a predominant position in business. This position derives from the creed of Jainism, which absolutely forbids killing any living being. Therefore, those professions that may provoke the death or suffering of any kind of living being, even an insect, are forbidden to its followers. Moreover, liberty of movement is strongly limited, because by travelling one may crush insects, causing death. Consequently, Jains have had a tendency to become only sedentary merchants and money-lenders. So their rigid respect for morality and their honesty have given them a good reputation among Indians - at least in not-so-recent times, for it seems that today the decadence of their customs has rendered them less admirable. Thus, they have succeeded in acquiring a dominant position in commerce, to such a point that, in the last century, 50 per cent of the capital of the people was in their hands. And yet, this concentration of business in the hands of a restricted group of persons has not given rise to the formation of capitalism. Disdain for earthly goods forbids Jains from seeking property. Besides, they have never represented a political force, so that they have never assumed the function of a rich bourgeois city class. Jainism, as well as Brahmanism, has failed in developing capitalism in India, in spite of its prevalence among merchants."(*Bibliographical Survey of Jainism*, p. 73f.)

Buddhist material useful for Jaina study

Nakamura contributed four articles to *The Voice of Ahiṃsā*, the World Jain Mission, Aliganj, U. P., in succession :

1) "Tolerance, Peace and War. (A Buddhist Scripture Setting forth a Sermon by a Jain Ascetic)," vol.5, nos. 1-2,1955, pp. 79-82.

2) "A Jaina Influence upon the Scriptures of Early Buddhism," vol. 6, nos. 3, 4, 1956, pp. 85-86.

3) "References of Jainism in Chinese Versions of Early Buddhist Scriptures," vol. 7, no. 1, 1957, pp. 18, 19 and 30.

4) "The Sage Ṛṣabha Noticed in the Chinese Versions of Buddhist Scriptures," vol. 7, nos. 3-4, 1957, pp. 87-88.

All of these articles were written mainly by utilizing material from Chinese translations of Buddhist Canon, through which Nakamura showed the significance of referring to the Chinese versions not only for the study of Buddhism but also for that of Jainism.

As a part of his efforts to show that the references in Buddhist scriptures are very helpful in tracing the development of Jainism, Nakamura gives a further example in his next article:

5) "The Doctrine of Jainism Allegedly Introduced by Āryadeva," *Shrïmad Rājendrasūri Smāraka Grantha* (Bhilwārā, Rājasthāna, 1957), pp. 816-819.

Criteria for historical study of thought

Although Nakamura had recognized the value of past research work on the Buddhist scriptures, which had mainly focused on the age of formation of the Buddhist scriptures, he realized that a more objective standard or criterion was required for surveying the historical study of thought and the formation of the order, etc. Any words and passages to be quoted as material, he notes, must be surmised from some criterion of whether it belonged to the old stratum or not.

Otherwise, any *historical* study of thought could not be approved. And he was convinced that the criteria for the formation of early Buddhist scriptures would also be largely applicable to the study of the Jaina scriptures. (II.1.5 [in the 10th volume of Nakamura's Selected Works])

Nakamura's article on the subject, "The Criteria of Research into Formation of the Buddhist Scriptures in the Early Period" was first published in 1971, along with its small supplement, as a part of the 14th volume of his Selected Works. In this he gave detailed information concerning research on Tripiṭaka and also introduced the most advanced textual studies of European and Indian scholars at that time. It was really owing to this treatise that Japanese scholars and students came to know the situation of the textual studies abroad and were stimulated into work in this field. Nakamura extracted here the criteria valid for distinguishing the strata in both Buddhist and Jaina scriptures from the researches of such scholars like R. Otto Franke, S. Lévi, M. Winternitz, H. Lüders, H. Oldenderg, W. Geiger, W. Schubring, D. D. Kosambi, Jules Bloch, F. Edgerton, D. R. Bhandarkar, E. Waldschmidt, L. Alsdorf and others.

The article was convincing enough to understand that it is indispensable when studying Buddhism to refer to the Jaina scriptures for clarifying the difference between Buddhism and other religions, and also for making Buddhistic essence clear. Otherwise, there will be a possibility of mistaking a thing not peculiar to Buddhism as an essence of Buddhism. He actually makes it clear that in many aspects of the religion such as language, thought, moral codes, practices, etc. what have been considered to be peculiar to Buddhism are quite often said in Jainism or other religions, too.

Any category being historically formed

Nakamura always tried to take a new look at anything that was categorized in the religious traditions from the historical point of view. For example, he has found that the number 'six' in the well known six leaders of free thinkers, categorized in the Buddhist scriptures, does not go back to the earliest stratum, in which the number of the representative was not yet fixed, being counted sometimes four, and sometimes five. According to Nakamura, the person who was finally added later in a certain stage was the skeptic Sañjaya and thus the number six was completed or fixed. (I.2.2)

Keen interest in *Isibhāsiyāim*

The text of *Isibhāsiyāim*, a compilation of the sayings of the forty-five (or forty-four) ancient *ṛṣis* including Mahāvira, handed down by Jainas, was critically edited by W. Schubring and first published with his German translation in 1942. It stimulated some Japanese scholars into research in this field. Nakamura was also very interested in the text and said that it was really a treasure house for those doing research work on ancient thought in India. His deep interest in both brahmanical and non-brahmanical religions encouraged him to investigate the text and contributed the articles in some chapters being related with Sāriputta (Isi 12) and Yājñavalkya (Isi 38):

1) "Sāriputta ni daihyo sareta saishoki no Bukkyo (The Earliest Buddhism which Sāriputta Represented), *Indogaku Bukkyogaku Kenkyū* 14, no. 2 (Mar 1966), pp. 1-12.

2) "Tetsujin Yājüavalkya. Jainakyo no shoden" (A Jaina Tradition of Yājñavalkya,a Upaniṣadic philosopher), *Indogaku Bukkyogaku Kenkyu* 15, no. 1 (1966), pp.29-36;
3) "Yājñavalkya and other Upaniṣadic thinkers in a Jaina tradition," *Sanskrit and Indological Studies. Raghavan Felicitation Volume*, Delhi: Matilal Banarsidass, 1975, pp. 216-228.

The contents of these articles and other subjects related with *Isibhāsiyāim* are discussed in the following chapters (I.3.1(3): various philosophers; I.3.8: estimation of free thinkers; II,1.5: characteristics of Jainism in the earliest stage).

Humbly listening to other's opinions

The tenth volume of Nakamura's Selected Works consists of two parts. In the first part entitled "The rise of cities and the appearance of free thought", Nakamura describes both the social and philosophical situations at the time when Jainism occurred. He gives in its first chapter (I.1) an historical outline of the social movement, which is a summary of the related portions from his famous *Indo Kodaishi* (Ancient History of India, part 1), the fifth volume of the Selected Works. He discusses simply such social changes like the extension of sovereignty, the fall of brāhmana's prestige, and the appearance of new religions from the countries of republicanism and others. It is pointed out there that although the royal family came to reign over the highest social grade instead of brāhmanas, their status was not yet stabilized. In order to prove this, Nakamura shows that there are descriptions of people's rising up against a bad king, the king's banishment, etc., in the Buddhist scriptures.

In the third section (I.1.3), he deals with the development of a money economy at the time when Buddhism and Jainism occurred. He introduces the opinion of Indian scholars that the use of money was very much current from the Vedic period onwards. He points out that it has become clearer that there is a close relationship between the embossed money used in the prosperous kingdom of Magadha and the weights and measures used in the Indus civilization. Nakamura concludes that it can not be denied that there is a considerable ground for their having such opinion, at least a possibility of money being used somewhere in India at Vedic times. This is an example of Nakamura's usual attitude toward the opinions of Indian scholars. He always humbly listens to their opinions and is ready to accept it even if it has not been accepted by European authorities. The other sections mention the changes such as the collapse of the conventional social system, its tendency to become unstable, the material aspect of prosperity, the phenomenon of excessive decay of morality, etc.

Doll of Ambapālī

The second chapter (I.2) starts with an episode of a certain *gaṇikā* ('prostitute'), well known in the history of India, namely, Ambapālī. In literature, a prostitute is sometimes called 'an ornament of the city' as a symbol of decadent society. Now, Nakamura introduces as a social parallel a shocking scene occurring in Indian airports, where a half-naked doll called 'Ambapālī' is sold in the shops and many tourists from Japan purchase it. He says that it would be quite natural, in a society which respects prostitutes in some way, that the inhabitants could be no longer satisfied with the old and conventional religions. It was in such an atmosphere that various thinkers appeared who could be described as materialists, skeptics, hedonists (or epicurean), fatalists, etc., and who argued with each other; many ascetics also appeared who, feeling weariness toward pleasure-seeking lives, renounced the world and devoted themselves to meditation. Nakamura analyzes the two major types of spiritual leaders, śramaṇas and brāhmaṇas, and compares them with each other, while referring to the information of Megasthenes and others.

It is well known that Nakamura's analysis of Indian society is deeply influenced by the theories of Max Weber. In this chapter Nakamura refers to Weber's opinion that religions and philosophies in India were possessed of 'freedom' that was even almost *absolute*. Nakamura states that we could not have found anywhere in Europe such a total liberty of thought until the latest modern era.

Free thinkers

Next, he begins to analyze various ideas appearing in both the Jaina and Buddhist scriptures, while referring to the studies of his teacher Hakuju Ui and other scholars like Schrader, Vogel, Basham, etc. He also gives a comparative study of 'Six representative free thinkers' and 'sixty-two types of heretical views' expounded in the Buddhist scriptures' and '363 views' and 'four types' in Jaina scriptures successively. Of the four types, it is pointed out properly that Jainism is supposed to belong to *kriyā-vādin*.(I.3.1)

His discussion of the five free thinkers, other than Nigaṇṭ ha Nātaputta, and their philosophical positions is started with Pūraṇa who denied morality, and then he discusses successively, Pakuda who held the world-view of seven elements, Gosāla, being a famous determinist, Ajita, a materialist, and lastly the skeptic Sañjaya.(I.3.1 ~ I.3.4 / I.3.6 ~ I.3.7) In between these discussions are various descriptions of the forms of *tapas* from the scriptures.(I.3.5) The chapter ends up with introducing people's views on those free thinkers or what is called 'śramaṇas', as well as summarizing the characteristics of 'śramaṇic' thought.(I.3.8)

'Historical development' of thought of Jainism

At the very beginning of the first chapter of the main part (II.Jainism, 1. Primitive Jainism, § 1. 'What is Jainism?'), Nakamura clearly denies a popular but biased opinion that there has been neither any history nor any development in Jainism. He writes: "I thought the same when I was young, but the opinion is totally wrong" and, in order to prove it, he cites an instance based upon his own experience: "When I visited Udayagiri, an ancient Jaina site in Orissa, I could not suppress roaring with amazement; for a drawing of queen (*vidyārājñī*), is assigned to each of the twenty four Tīrthankaras, who must be *vīta-rāga*, beings that are totally free from desires and have achieved enlightenment. With no doubt, Tantricism must influence it. I think this is enough to show that there has been a history in Jainism, too."

In some other chapter (II.2.4), Nakamura reports the impression of Khandagiri similarly, but there he puts the expression in another way. He writes: through the spreading out of Tantricism in Jainism, the idea of 'salvation of all the beings'(*sarvamukti*) has become gradually popular. It is nothing but 'a Mahāyānization' of Jainism; although it is a general opinion among scholars that there was no appearance of 'a Mahāyāna' in Jainism, a similar change to be compared with the Buddhist Mahāyāna has appeared in Jainism also, when we see such phenomenon as enthusiastic worship for Jina and Tantricism.

At the end of the first section (II.1.1), Nakamura makes clear the purpose of his investigation in the following chapters: "although it is generally maintained that Jainism seems to be unrelated with Brahmanism because it denied the authority of the Vedas and also despised the Vedic religion for its bloody rituals. In fact its thought developed gradually, while succeeding the philosophical contemplation of Upaniṣad, which was purely pursuing *ātmavidyā* (true knowledge of the Self). It may be rather surprising to say so, when we bring to mind the doctrinal scholarship of the elaborate and complicated medieval Jainism. It is clear, however, that there was a strong influence of Upaniṣad on the thought of early Jainism and also that there were close similarities between the thoughts of Upaniṣad, Jainism and Buddhism in their earliest strata. Let us start to examine this point in the following chapters."

This introductory section was added to the new version by the author when he separated the portion of Jainism from his *Formation of the Primitive Buddhism* (Primitive Buddhism 2), being previously the 12th volume of his Selected Works. It seems to be very important here that Nakamura became more convinced, through the investigation of the Jaina scriptures, that the thought of Jainism in its earliest scriptures was very much influenced by the thought of Upanisad and also very close to the thought of Buddhism. To prove these points, he inserted into the previous version a number of quotations from the scriptures, especially from the first part of the *Āyāranga*, i.e., *Bambhacerāim*, one of the oldest Jaina texts.

Living traditions of Jainism

Nakamura often emphasizes in his books that the scholars should not forget that Jainism is not a vestige of a past religion, but a *living* tradition in the modern society of India. Seeing the religion as a vestige probably derived from Chinese translations of Buddhist scriptures where it had been taught that there was an old religion founded by Nigaṇṭha Nātaputta, which was denied by Buddha Sākyamuni. Even some modern writers in Japan sometimes rudely refer to Jainism in their novels as the lost ancient religion.

This is also why Nakamura has spent many lines in determining the proper way of referring to the religion(II.1.3). Some scholars like Leumann and Schubring, who rejected the term 'Jainism' and instead adopted 'der Jinismus, jinistisch,' because they thought the former word was created by some British who had visited India. Nakamura says, by comparing it with 'Buddhism', that their view would be right as long as the word formation was concerned. But, when comparing it with 'Hinduism' or 'Sikhism'(*sikkh* originally means 'disciple'), it would not be consistent with them. It is interesting that Nakamura differentiated the scholars in the Germanic cultural region into two types and pointed out that those who had often been to India and had become acquainted with Indian people used the term 'der Jainismus', but those who had not got very much acquainted with them had a tendency to stick to the term 'der Jinismus' .

"What we should think about here is", continues Nakamura, "that Jainism is a *living* religion. If it were not so, it would be all right to create such a new term like 'Jinism'. But it is living and people call their religion 'Jainism', not 'Jinism'. In modern languages of India like Hindi, it is also called 'Jain.' It is my conjecture that some scholars like R. Pandeya may have used only the expression 'the Jainas' in order to avoid any friction and some others like S. Radhakrishnan and H. v. Glasenapp may have preferred the same (e.g., the Pluralistic Realism of *the Jains*; der System *der Jainas*) in the way that a religion such as Anekānta stands aloof from any *–ism*. Anyway, my usage of the term 'Jainism' is to respect the religion of a living tradition. Studying Jainism is totally different from studying the religion of the Pharaohs in the ancient Egypt which is extinct."

Nakamura often mentions the result of his own field research. For example, in order to discuss Mahāvīra and other Jinas, he refers to the statues of three jinas that he found inside of the Temple in Pāvāpurī, the place of Mahāvīra's *nirvāṇa*, which he visited in 1986. After describing the present situation of the temple and also the look of the statues, he gives a legendary lineage of twenty-four Jinas in Jaina cosmology where it is told, except the last Jina, i.e., Mahāvīra, only Pārśvanātha, 23rd Jina, is recognized to be a historical person. What he wanted to emphasize here is that Jainism has a long cultural history from very ancient times up to the present day.

Witness

Nakamura has described what he experienced for himself in India. He witnessed in Kushīnagar a Hindu ascetic who stood for ten years, even when he was asleep (I.3.5: various austerities, p. 112). To show how Jaina lay people are pious even in the present day, he introduces the case of Mr. Jain, an old master of Motilal Banarsidass in Delhi, who began ten days of meditation in September, 1977, during which he took only one meal per day and met nobody (II.1.19: way of Laity, p. 366). He reports on a nun, whom he met somewhere in India, having a broom (*rajoharaṇa*) in her hand, and putting it on the ground, said to Nakamura: "you may touch it with your hand." It was so soft that he was convinced it would not harm even an ant (II.2.7: movement of the modern Jainism, p. 413). He also tells about a naked Jaina ascetic who acted as the chairman of a seminar held in New Delhi in 1956. When he stood up, finishing his role, he held nothing except a broom in his hand (*do.*, p. 417).; In India, it is reported alcohol is not served in any party *as a general rule*. "I have hardly seen a drunkard in India," he writes (*do.*, p.416).

A compilation of common elements

A small section dealing with the similarities between Jainism and Buddhism (II.1.4, pp. 170-172) is to be referred to along with Appendix II: "Common Elements in Early Jain and Buddhist Literature"(pp. 741-772). The latter is a Japanese translation by Kenji Watanabe of the article originally written in English and published in the *Indologica Taurinensia*, vol. 11 (Torino, 1983), pp. 303-330.

Characteristics of the earliest Jainism

In the section discussing the characteristics of the earliest Jainism(II.1.5), he focused on the problem of the contents of 'cātuyāma' described as a doctrine of Niganthas in the Buddhist canon. According to Nakamura, the nineteen verses in the 29th chapter (: Vardhamāna) of *Isibhāsiyāim* reflect faithfully the teachings of *historical* Mahāvīra and also it becomes clear that the Buddhist tradition in Pali canon gives accurate information. He emphasized the importance of comparative study, even if the problem of the date of formation of *Isibhāsiyāim* remains unsolved. He points out that some important teachings of Jainism are originated from Pārśva(Isi

31), which Vardhamāna succeeded. He says the meaning of the problematic term '*vāri*' might be not 'water', but 'abstinence', as the latter is more convincing, if the context is taken into consideration. Here he accepts the new theory of others tolerantly.

In comparing various philosophical standpoints, Mahavīra admitted from his standpoint of *Syādvāda* or *Anekāntavāda* that it was possible to state any verbal judgment and to formulate a philosophical system, unlike the skeptic Sañjaya. It could be said that by reflecting on the confrontation of various philosophical opinions at the time led to the evolution of the standpoint of Jainism(II.1.6). For example, they discussed such common metaphysical problems as whether the soul or the world is constant or not, but their ways of answering were quite different from each other. This is why Jainism came into existence. '*Andhagajanyāya*', a well-known parable among Indian philosophers, is also used by Jainas, but their usage is more affirmative than other religions.

Nakamura pointed out that, although Jainas criticized philosophers who applauded their own statements and despised those of others, later they themselves set up their own form of authoritarianism and, as an instance, he mentions a dichotomy seen in the latest stratum of Jaina scriptures, i.e., *Nandi-sutta*, etc., which divides different types of learning into right and wrong, namely, twelve Jaina angas (right ones) and Epics, Mīmāmsā and Kauṭilya, etc.(wrong ones).

From the rationalistic standpoint of Jainism, a universal truth was regarded as important. It is why they thought anybody could be of an ideal personality and could realize the truth. (I.6(3)) (Nakamura has not mentioned anywhere Jaina theory of 'capability and non-capability of attaining *mokṣa*' (*bhavyatva, abhavyatva*). A. Schweitzer offered his insight into the characteristics of religions: eastern religions are logical, but Christianity is not so. Nakamura agreed with this analysis of Schweitzer, as far as Jainism and Buddhism were concerned.

As a principle of their argument, it is pointed out by Nakamura that in Jainism they take up problems for discussion mostly from the standpoint of 'living beings'(*satta, pāṇa, bhūta, jīva*) and they theoretically give relief to such living creatures as gods and birds and beasts, but actually giving relief to human beings was the main purpose.(II. 1. 7(1)) It shows rather their narrowness, according to Nakamura, that it is thought only human beings can get salvation and moreover, only '*aryan*' can get it.

All the philosophers in India thought that life was painful. But there would be only a small number of persons who emphasized the misery and pain of this worldly life like Mahāvīra. This section (II.1.7 (2)) is full of translations from the first part of *Āyāraṅga*. The inconstancy of things was also told in Jainism as in Buddhism, but it was a big difference of the two religions that Jainas admitted constancy of the things that are changing, while Buddhists denied it totally.

It is certain that the existence of the self (*ātman*) was recognized in early Jainism. They called their view '*ātmavāda*', but Nakamura said there was still some vagueness. He investigated the problematic portion of *Āyāraṅga* (I.5.5.4) and points out that the Jaina view of *ātman* is very different depending on our way of understanding of the description; in other words it depends on whether we see many *ātman*s as different from each other or regard all of them as united as one. If they are taken to be united, the view will be quite similar to that of Upaniṣad or Vedānta. It also shows the close relationship with Upaniṣad that *ātman* is called a subject of 'cognition' (*vijñātṛ*) in the same text. Nakamura showed some contexts of protection of six types of beings and also of the ethical principle so-called '*ātmaupamya*', on which their altruism is based.(II.1.8(1)).

It is to be noticed that the argument of worldly desires or passions in early Buddhism has some points in common with that of Jainism, especially in that worldly desires or passions were seemingly recognized there as a kind of matter (II.1.8(2)). It was already expressed in the old Upaniṣad that a fundamental and impulsive desire of human beings was called *tṛṣṇā*, and it was regarded as very important in both Jainism and Buddhism. Totally inquiring into such desires, that is, to know them thoroughly (*pari*-√*jñā*) was recognized to be indispensable for religious practice. This is because it is believed in Jainism that knowing something totally produces the effect of annihilating it.

The theory of the mutual dependence of things is usually considered to be preached only in Buddhism, but this is not correct. The ways of reflection that are shown in passages describing the 'Twelve-Link Dependent Origination' can be also found in Jaina canon. Even the doctrine of Middle Path can be also traced to the earliest strata of the Jaina scriptures. Thus, Nakamura concludes that both the attitudes toward searching for the law of mutual dependence and the Middle Path originated from a world of thought that was common to the religions in ancient times, including Jainism. Keeping oneself away from two extremes, however, was not put into practice in Jainism, unlike Buddhism. Nakamura advises students not to have any prejudice before making a start on doing research; because there was, and still is, a strong tendency among Japanese scholars of Buddhism to be convinced that all that has been handed down in the scriptures is peculiar to the religion from the beginning. (II.1.8 (3))

Nakamura surveyed various accounts of *karman* from the times of *Ṛgveda* and then analyzed the theory of *karman* in Jaina scriptures. Many sentences are quoted again from *Āyāraṅga I* with their Japanese translation. The section is nothing but a full analysis of the thought of the text (II.1.8 (4)).

Nakamura's investigation of metaphysical topics as depicted in the scriptures (II.1.9) starts with an outline of 'five substances'(*pañcāstikāya*). He first deals with the concept of 'soul' (*jīva*), giving an explanation of six kinds of them, a discussion of its relationship with Animism and an investigation of its general characteristics, etc. He also discusses the remaining *astikāya*s, that is, 'matter' (*pudgala*), 'space' (*ākāśa*), 'principle of motion' (*dharma*), 'principle of rest' (*adharma*). It is well known that the atomic theory in India was first mentioned in the Jaina scriptures, like *Bhagavaī* and *Rāyapaseṇaijja*, but the formation of these texts is not so old that it is unclear if the theory was expounded in Jainism from the very beginning.

It is very important that Nakamura, in discussing the complex mechanism of *āsrava* and *bandha*, or the theory of *karman*, remarked on it as follows (II.1.10): "It is not always easy for us to understand the metaphysics of Jainism, but it is quite worthy of noting that there appeared such a complete rationalism as Jaina theory of *karman*, in comparison with the magico-religious thinking which had predominated in India until then." He agreed with the opinion that Mahāvīra himself might have been interested in the observation of natural phenomena and their theorization, and that, as the founder was a person with such interest, the atomic theory was also formed.

The thought of 'friendliness and compassion' in Buddhism might have been made popular by Sāriputta. This is not a mere conjecture of Nakamura, for he clearly shows it is attributed to Sariputta both in the Buddhist scriptures and the Jaina text.(II.1.11) (As for the latter text, it was handed down by Jainas, but not counted as one of their scriptures.) It is also pointed out by Nakamura that it was thought that the most important act of showing mercy to others was *preaching*. Entering into the order to become a mendicant was not going against the world; it was because of true love for the people that one renounced the world. Preaching was an important duty of any mendicant who belonged to the order.

Nakamura further discusses various topics in the following sections: practices of mendicants in general (II.1.12), pañca mahāvrata (II.1.13), severe ascetic practices (II.1.14), right knowledge (*samyak-jñāna*) (II.1.15), mendicant life (II.1.16), emancipation (II.1.17), various epithets of Jina , its comparison with Buddhism, and the changes of the concept (II.1.18), the life of laymen (II.1.19), the system of vratas and other regulations for laity (II.1.20), and worship for Jina (II.1.21).

After the first chapter, Nakamura put a small but newly written article as the second chapter (II.2), in which he describes the historical development of the Jaina communities and points out the close relationship between mendicants and laity. He writes: "The history of Jainism is also the history of development of the communities." Only the titles of sections are given here: the beginning of schisms in Mauryan Dynasty (II.2.1), reaching a climax of worshipping for Jinas (II.2.2), systematization of Jaina doctrine in the Gupta Period (II.2.3), Hindu influence in the period of various independent dynasties (II.2.4), development after Islamic invasion (II.2.5), modernization of Jainism (II.2.6) and tendencies in modern times (II.2.7)

Holistic but multi-layered understanding

Nakamura contributed a short article on the Ārhatadarśana, being the third chapter of Mādhava's *Sarvadarśanasaṃgraha*, to *Pratidānam: Indian, Iranian and Indo-European Studies Presented to Franciscus Bernardus Jacobus Kuiper on his Sixtieth Birthday* (The Hague: Mouton, 1968, pp. 510-515) and soon published a Japanese translation of the same chapter in *Sanko Bunka Kenkyūsho Nenpo* 3 (1970), pp. 1-40: Jainakyo Gaisetsu. Sarvadarśanasaṃgraha Dai 3 sho Honyaku" Sarvadarśanasaṃgraha–(Outline of Jainism. A Japanese Translation of the 3rd Chapter of Sarvadarśanasaṃgraha). It was an extraordinary coincidence that Atsushi Uno also published a Japanese translation of the same text in 1969, in between the publishing of the above works of Nakamura.

After 1970, he did not publish any article on Jainism for about fifteen years, except a small review on Klaus Bruhn's Iconographic Work (See below). His long silence ended in 1984, after which he started energetically to publish articles on Jaina philosophy in the Middle Ages. It was really a tremendous 'explosion' of Nakamura, who, like a *tapodhana* in the forest, cultivated his spirit as a true pioneer and produced the following articles:

1) "Chūsei Jainakyo no Shisoteki Tachiba" (Jaina Thought and its Position in the Middle Ages), Nakamura *Zuiryu Hakushi Koki-kinen Ronbunshū: Bukkyogaku Ronshū* (A

Felicitation Volume for Doctor Zuiryū Nakamura), Shunjūsha (1985), pp. 11-34. (II. 3. 1)

2) "Jainakyo no Reikonkan" (Jaina View of the Soul), *Tsuboi Shunei Hakushi Shoju Kinen: Bukkyogaku Ronko* (A Felicitation Volume for Doctor Shunei Tsubi), 1984, pp.523-548. (II. 3.2)

3) "Chūsei Jainakyo-Tetsugaku ni okeru Seishinsayo" (On Upayoga: 'Cognition' in the Medieval Jaina Philosophy), *Indotetsugaku Bukkyogaku* 1, Hokkaido Indotetsugaku Bukkyo Gakkai, 1986, pp.1-14. (II. 3.3)

4) "Chūsei Jainakyo no Jissen Ron. Gaikan" (An Outline of Practice in the Medieval Jainism), *Kumoi Shozen Hakushi Koki-kinen: Bukkyo to Ishūkyo* (A Felicitation Volume for Doctor Shozen Kumoi: Buddhism and Other Religions), Kyoto: Heirakuji Shoten 1985, pp.107-126. (II. 3.5)

5) "Chūsei Jainakyo no Gedatsu Kan" (Jaina Theory of Salvation in the Middle Ages), *Toho* (Toho Gakuin, 1985), pp.26-43. (II.3.6)

The third chapter, entitled "Jaina Thought in the Middle Age"(II.3), mainly consists of the revised versions of the above five articles . (That is why I have listed them in order of the sections of the chapter.) Only the fourth section (II. 3.4: Metaphysics—Substantialism) can not be traced back to any previous independent article. Nakamura referred to many Jaina philosophical texts in them, out of which I give here only the titles of main texts other than Mādhava's work:

1) Pūjyapāda's *Sarvārthasiddhi*,

2) Umāsvati's *Tattvārthādhigamasūtra*,

3) Nemicandra's *Davvasamgaha*,

4) Kundakunda' *Niyamasāra*,

5) Haribhadra's *Saddarśanasamuccaya*,

6) Hemacandra' *Yogaśāstra,*

7) *Sarvasiddhāntasamgraha* (Jaina Section).

Nakamura noticed in the first section (II.3.1:Result of relativism) that, although Jainism, like Buddhism and

Cārvāka, has been traditionally given a rather lower position among the various religions and philosophies in India, Indian thinkers in the Medieval Times tried to establish "the philosophy of the philosophies" or "the learning about various views of the world" and it was those Jaina scholars like Haribhadra and Rājaśekhara who took the initiative in establishing this. Nakamura says that it is very interesting to compare this with the history of the West because such a trial was never done in ancient Greece, or even in the Middle Ages in Europe. Here, to show the position that the pure rationalism finally attained to, he quotes a famous word of Haribhadra from M. Winternitz, *A History of Indian Literature*, II, p. 583: "he is not biased in favour of Mahāvīra", and said: "Is it allowed in the Middle Ages in Europe to make such a statement? Can one be alive in the modern Islamic countries, who has once expressed such an idea, without being punished?" Nakamura summarized the discussion as follows: from the position of Indian people who have their own way of understanding peculiar in its holistic but multi-layered nature, it can be said that anything which at a glance seems irrational must have a certain justification for its existence. They have never forgotten such a viewpoint. "That's why," he says as conclusion, "in India, *seeing* the truth is the real meaning of the faith and so the faith is nothing but a *samyak-jñāna* in any religion, whether it is Buddhism, or Jainism, or Brahmanism."

Introduction of Minakata's view of Jainism

Nakamura agreed with Kumagusu Minakata (1867-1941) about setting the highest valuation on Jainism over all the religions in that the ideal of having respected a life and not damaging it, that is, *ahimsā*, has been thoroughly put into practice. Even if its extreme execution does not necessarily obtain many people's approval, Minakata, as a scholar of natural history, including such microbes as *fungi*, etc., emphasized the superiority of Jainism because of its setting equality in all the living beings. According to Nakamura, Minakata might be the only person who made a definite statement on this point. (II.4.1.3: p. 611)

What is the most important?

In March 1987, when Nakamura stayed in Delhi, he obtained an illustrated book for children, written in Hindi: *Paramamuktidātā Tirthankar Bhagavān Mahāvīr* .Lekhaka: Kumārapāl Desāi. Ahmadābād: Anadā Prakāsan, 1986. He became so interested in how Jainas in modern times understand Bhagavān Mahāvīra and how they teach the life of Mahāvīra to the children. He immediately decided to translate the book into Japanese. Soon Nakamura published its Japanese translation with some analytical observations, being entitled:

"Mahāvīra no sugata. Gendai Jainakyoto no jojutsu" (A Description of Mahāvīra by Jaina People in the Modern Times), in the *Naritasan Bukkyo Kenkyusho Kiyo* 11[:Tokubetsugo Bukkyo Shisoshi Ronshu, Chiba: Naritasan Shinshoji 1988], pp.435-471.

It forms now a chapter of the tenth volume of his *Selected Works* (II.5). I quote here some words of Nakamura from its preface: "why do people still retain faith in Jainism which teaches them severe penance and extreme control of their desires? On festive occasions, children are taken by their parents or by their grandparents to Jaina temples for worship. What is taught to those children? I wanted to elucidate it and understand the mind of Jainas. Isn't it more important to understand the spirit of the people who are now living than to read one of a great many classics of Jaina literature?" These words of Nakamura, who has read a vast number of books and made great scholarly achievements, are really of profound significance.

His Pupils in the field of Jaina Studies

The scholar who has shown the most excellent achievement in the field of Jainism among the many pupils of Nakamura is no doubt Kiyoaki Okuda who studied under Ludwig Alsdorf of University of Hamburg and took the doctoral degree. His thesis on Vaṭṭakera's *Mūlācāra*, which has been published in Alt- und Neu-Indische Studien (No. 15, 1979), is perhaps the first *genuine* philological research on the Jaina Ḍigambara text by a Japanese scholar. Nakamura much praised Okuda's work.

Toho Institute has also produced some young students of Jainism. Michitoshi Manda is a lecturer of the Language department, who has often visited India to do research work on Jaina canon.

Akiko Shimizu, a research worker of the Institute, who is interested in Jaina rituals, did field work on Jaina *paryusana* in Delhi (Toho 4, 1988, pp.87-91) and at a Jaina temple in Kobe, Japan (Toho 8, 1992, pp.211-213). Her study on *paryūṣaṇa* rituals in the annual meeting of the Society for the study of Jaina Studies, 1992, was sufficiently stimulating to make Eiichi Yamaguchi, a lecturer of Ariake National College of Technology, set about his full-scale investigation of the subject. But research work on Jaina rituals has just begun in Japan.

Nakamura's contribution was recognized not only in his writings, but also in his Academy, which has promoted for many years the growth of shoots in its liberal and pleasant atmosphere. Merely a few examples have been given in the above. It may be allowed here to mention a doctoral thesis of Yutaka Kawasaki, which was recently submitted to the University of Osaka. Kawasaki thoroughly investigated the description of laymen given in the scriptures of Jaina Śvetāmbara and continued the development of this topic of research that Nakamura had initiated.

Proper Understanding of Jaina Art

Nakamura discussed Jina worship as one of the important aspects in the history of thought in Jainism (II.1.21: Jina worship; II.2.2: high tide of Jina worship in Kusāna Dynasty) and wrote a review for Bruhn's work:

"A Review of *The Jaina-Images of Deogarh* by Klaus Bruhn," *The Journal of Intercultural Studies*, no. 2, 1975, p. 83.

It seems very important that, while investigating religious practices in the life of the Jainas of the Middle Age, Nakamura stressed the significance of our proper understanding of Jaina art (II.3.5 (4): meditation) and suitably requested us to refer to J. Jain and E. Fischer's *Jaina Iconography* (2 parts, Leiden E. J. Brill, 1978). Here the authors explain that, for each iconographic theme, they have chosen a quotation from Jaina literature, irrespective of the antiquity or modernity of the text, such as they consider relevant to an understanding of the living traditions of Jainism (in Preface of part 2). Thus, Nakamura has drawn our attention to that, as meditation and worship have been very significant in the life of Jainas until today, statues and pictures of the Jina or Tïrthankara must be understood from this point of view. He gives us even a stern warning: "the scholars would miss the most important meaning, if they forgot that Jaina art was neither a decorative article nor a plaything, but rather the sacred object for meditation and worship."

Conclusion

Nakamura has discussed several times the problem of the decay or disappearance of Buddhism in the Middle Age. In the last section of *Indo Kodaishi* (Ancient History of India), part 2, he says: "we must ask why only Buddhism has disappeared from India, in spite of both Brahmanism and Jainism still surviving there." This is the starting point of his comparative study of Buddhism and other religions.

In comparison with Jainism, he points out the lack of firm organization of laity in Buddhism as a weakness, and also its not having brought various rituals and consecrations into domestic life, in contrast to Jainism. It is true that Nakamura shares the opinions of scholars like S. Stevenson, M. Winternitz, etc. on this matter, but what is the most important point here is that Nakamura has always had a sincere attitude toward Jainism and wants to listen attentively to the voices of Jainas, because it is a *living* tradition, originating from the same soil in ancient India as that of Buddhism.

19

Professor Hajime Nakamura on Understanding Dharmaśāstras

Indra Nath Choudhuri

Any discussion on Dharmaśāstras can be problematic because immediately the question will be asked about their present value and relevance and a conclusion will be arrived at soon that these texts are artifical, sacerdotal piety, wishful thinking[1] and that these law books are nothing but the fantasies of the Brahmins[2] and in the present day India their value is marginal and only symbolic. This can easily be contested. There should be no doubt that the Dharmaśāstras have had a profound impact on society at all moments of its history. Kings commissioned them to be compiled and in modern times they have been the focus of intense political and social debate.[3] And if questions are raised whether they could set up practicable ideals and rules of conduct which can be followed by the members of the present day Indian society then the obvious reply would be that texts can never set up ideals and rules of conduct. Only interpreters of texts are able to do so.

Professor Hajime Nakamura is very clear about these Dharmaśāstra texts. He says that they prescribe social systems, customs and daily activities focusing their attention upon such problems as four castes and the four stages of life from the stand point of Brahmanism. These law books compiled by the Brahmins have been regarded as the most valuable materials from which to get information about social conditions in ancient India.[4]

Nakamura has done a deep study of some of these texts[5] and the references which we find in his writings about these texts give us quite a useful information about his impression on (1) the notion of dharma, which is the locus of these law treatises and (2) the Vedānta thought as revealed in them as an aspect of the history of Vedānta philosophy.

The notion of *dharma* and the idea of Dharmaśāstra as its repository are vital ideas which were discussed and debated in every age of India including the present time when Dr. Ambedkar, E.V. Ramasami and others strongly criticised Manu Smṛti and other Dharmaśāstras as representing what is wrong with Indian society but in other circles these texts are considered to contain wisdom responsible for successful marriage, economic prosperity, religious contentment, social peace and harmony.[6] Embedded in the core of these laws as enumerated in the Dharmasastra texts is the basic truth enshrined in the term *dharma*. Prof. Nakamura has done a remarkable work in defining, analysing and explaining this core locution *dharma* which is the fundamental insight of India's socio-religio and political structure.

Nakamura makes it very clear that for Indians *dharma* is the universal law- the law that all individuals and all social organisations should follow. Coming from the root Vdhṛ it serves as the norm to support human behavior or in short "the norm of action" or "the rule of conduct". It also means duty. Referring to Dharmaśāstra Nakamura points out the four dharmas of the Brahmins:

1. to be a man of a Brāhmaṇa family;
2. to do things dignifiedly;
3. to maintain honour and
4. to lead the people

The Nakamurian explanation of *dharma* is both descriptive and prescriptive. India's long intellectual history of *dharma* and dharma literature also moves between the poles of description and prescription. What starts out as careful, detailed analysis of what is effective norm of behaviour for the realization of morals ultimately ends up by raising *dharma* to the position of the Absolute. Nakamura takes the cue from the *Upaniṣads* and says that *dharma,* as the norm that guides a man to establish and to perform moral acts, is the power that realises "Truth" in this world. Indians, Nakamura says, came to think that the *dharma* is the basis of the whole universe and that all things in the universe rest on *dharma*[7]. It is, therefore, supposed that alongwith *karmamīmāṃsā* the Vedāntic philosophy had its role in explaining the term *dharma* and dharma literature.

This idea of the eternal universal law (*dharma*) was inherited by the Jainas and the Buddhists. The Jainas, from their very rationalistic stand point, assert that there exist universal laws (*dharma*) which all mankind should observe at all times and all places. Buddhists consider that the law of causal origination is the unchangeable truth. The enlightened one (Tathāgata) is only a man who has fully perceived the true law of nature that exists eternally and it is the law controlling between the state of ignorance and the way of deliverance from it. In other words, it is the universal law that stands above individuals even if the individual is the Gautam, the Buddha. It is safe to generalize here and say that most Indians find the sanction of their morality in the law (*dharma*) which transcends the gods. This Indian concept according to Nakamura stands in striking contrast to the Western idea that places the sole source of morality in the one Lord. We are all in essence one and the same with the Absolute. The concept of the eternal and universal law prevailed in Indian thought and took root among the people. King Aśoka believed in the eternal law which should be observed by all regardless of race, religion, nationality, time or place. This law is the norm of human behaviour and Aśoka called it "dharma" or "the time-honoured rule" which is beyond any state power. Infact, state power was subordinate to *dharma*.

It is very interesting to note that following the methodology of comparative religion Nakamura says that the Indian religion which acknowledges the authority of the eternal universal law is very rationalistic in its character and it offers a striking contrast to less logical personal religions of the West.[8] Schopenhauer once said that the Indian religion which has developed from rational speculation about the world is superior to Christianity[9]. Jesus stressed a personal relationship to God, while the Buddha stressed the universal validity of his truth or *dharma*. The Buddha stated, 'He who sees not the dharma sees not me–He who sees dharma sees me.' Man, in Buddha's view point, is accountable to law and not to divine will[10]. The Buddhist motto 'Rely upon the law, not on a person" has a Greek counterpart in Heraclitus who said, "when you have listened, not to me but to the law (logos) it is wise to agree that all things are one[11]. The Western counterpart of the concept of dharma can be said to be logos. Although in the sense of "word" it occasionally corresponds with the Indian *śabda* or *vāk*. Without going into detail whether Buddha is right or Jesus is wrong one can only say that this kind of comparative analysis by Nakamura indicated the essential difference between the Indian and Christian religion.

In Indian religio speculation if faith (*śraddhā*) in God or the Buddha means faith in the law, in *dharma* then the *śraddhā* or faith becomes naturally the factor which makes all living beings do good deeds and it is, therefore, in essence acceptance of the 'the idea of traditionalism' *āstikeya buddhi* and hence one can easily conclude that in India faith and knowledge are understood to be compatible.

Consequently, as says Nakamura, the Indian religion bears a strong tinge of philosophy. It only explains that dharma is extremely subtle (*sukṣma*) and intricate (*gahana*) and deep: *"dharmasya tattvam nihitam guhāyām"* and it can be compared with Tao, the Way or path. It is a path like the bird makes in the sky–there are no foot prints left behind and hence a path which can't be seen anywhere.

While clarifying the meaning of *dharma,* the Mahābhārata gives a paradoxical explanation. On the one hand, it says that *dharma* is fundamental, immovable and eternal (*kūṭastha acala dhruvaḥ*), and that it is timeless. On the other hand, it says that it is swifter than light and moves with time and hence it is both static and dynamic and therefore dharma is relative as explained by Vyāsa in terms of *'des'a kāla pratiṣṭhitaḥ'*

Nakamura endorses this view by saying that Hindus always had distrust of any specifically formidable law applicable to all cases. Indians are distrustful of the abstract formulation of the law and wants to consider each individual case on its own merits. Nakamura further says that Buddhist *dharmas* are also not rigid and strict rules. They are flexible and adaptable to places and occasions. This is the discriminatory vision of dharma which Kṛṣṇa in the Mahābhārata calls *dharmavibhāga* and Vedic seers called it *saramadṛṣṭi*[12]. The story of sage Kauśika reveals that the honest Kauśika did not know the intricate nature of *dharma* and as a result revealed the hiding place of a man to robbers, because he took a vow to always speak the truth. As a result, robbers went there and killed the man. Similarly when Yudhiṣṭhira insulted the Gandiva, Arjuna to fulfil his vow, went to kill his brother Yudhiṣṭhira and then Kṛṣṇa rebuked him and told him that as he did not know the *dharmavibhaga* in the name of *dharma* he wanted to perform *adharma*. A discriminatory or a judicious vision gives a practical meaning to *dharma* and hence Dharmaśāstra were actually a body of wisdom which gives power of discrimination to a number of people in the community. Hence it is said that the customs of the learned (śīṣṭācāra) are the real basis for the Dharmaśāstra rules[13]. Thus the trait of Hindu and Buddhist ethics is thought to be humanistic which is modified according to the tendency of the times.

The second aspect of the study of Dharmaśāstra by Nakamura is to find out the Vedānta thought as expounded in them revealing an aspect of the history of the Vedānta philosophy. The Vedānta thought appears especially in the *Āpastamba Dharmasūtra* on which are based the various Dharmaśāstras. In 1, 8, 22 and 23 of Āpastamba Dharmasūtra a Vedānta thought is explained and this section is in particular called the *Adhyātmapaṭala*. There is also its commentary entitled *Adhyātma–paṭalavivaraṇa* ascribed to Sanskara. This *dharmasūtra* was composed in the 4th or 5th Century B.C. and one can, according to Nakamura, find here the earliest gemination of the Vedānta[14].

The *Adhyātmapaṭala* is systematically organised. In the first two *sūtras* it shows an outline of religious practice, next quotes passages from the Upaniṣads mostly from Kaṭhaka Upaniṣad which explain *ātman* and finally lists the various virtues as the prescription of practice. With regard to religious practice, it teaches the yoga of meditating on and worshipping *ātman*. It calls the states of final release "peace" (*kṣema*). It clearly admits that final release is attained in the present existence.

This section is placed, as rightly said by Nakamura, on the way of explaining the atonement for transgression in general, and the author intends to recommend the knowledge of *ātman* as the best means by which to purify the mind of those who have committed various sins[15]. It is obvious as mentioned by Nakamura that these views are the earliest germination of the Vedānta because the Vedāntic thought in its later development conceives that after the realisation of *ātman* the question of worldly benefit is of no meaning because realisation of *ātman* takes you beyond worldly gain or loss. It is, therefore, known that in the society of that time the knowledge of *ātman* was considered as capable of purifying the mind. As pointed out by Nakamua along with the Vedāntic tendency the *Karmamīmāmsā* had already been established to some extent at that time to institute the social significance of the Vedāntic thought[16]. The social significance of the Vedāntic thought which is known from the Mānava Dharmaśāstra can also be recognised in other dharma literature.

The theory that one should practice both knowledge and action (*jñānakarma samuccayavāda*) can be pointed out as one of the characteristics of the Vedānta thought which appeared throughout the law books in general and which was in sharp contrast with Śankara's thought which attached importance to knowledge (jñāna) only. In the Hārtitasmriti (VII, 10, 11) it is said that "just as the birds indeed fly with two wings, so does one attain the eternal Brahman by both knowledge and action (jñānakarma)".

Thus, one can agree with Nakamura that the law books agree in their thought with the later Vedānta philosophy to a considerable extent, but the influence of the dharma literature upon the *Vedānta* is by far greater in respect of the rules of practice in life.

It is no doubt that Nakamura gives new, enabling and vitalizing interpretations to these dharma texts to the extent that they become acceptable to and desirable for those individuals who hold the Dharmaśāstra to be valuable materials to get information about social conditions in ancient India and for knowing who we were in the past is nearly always as said by Richard W. Lariviere, useful when struggling to determine who we are now and who we will be in the future[17].

References

1 Govinda Das in his Introduction to The Vyavahāra balambhatti, Chowkhamba Sanskrit Series 41, Benares, 1914, p. 1.

2 See such works as R. Fick, Die Sociale Gliederung im nordostlichen Indien 34 Buddha's Zeit, Kiel, 1897.

3 Richard W. lariviere, "Dharmaśāstra: Its Present Value & Relevance", The perennial Tree (Eds. K. Murty & Amit Dasgupta), New Delhi, 1996, p. 177.

4 Hajime Nakamura, "The Vedāntic Thought as represented in the Dharmaśāstra and the Arthaśāstra", D.D. Kosambi Commemoration Volume, 1974', Bombay, p. 138.

5 Nakamura has discussed *dharma* in many of his books and also in the article mentioned above.

6 Papers on Dharmaśāstra in Contemporary Times, U.G.C., Delhi, 1988.

7 Hajime Nakamura, Ways of Thinking of the Eastern Peoples, Hawaii, 1964, p. 113.

8 *Ibid.*, p. 115.

9 Quoted in Albert Schweitzer, Das Christentum und die Wel religion–en (1924), p. 29.

10 Hajime Nakamura, A Comparative History of Ideas, London, 1986.

11 *Ibid.*

12 Indra Nath Choudhuri, The Genesis of Imagination, Delhi, 2001, p. 236.

13 Richard W. Lariviere, see note 3; p. 182.

14 Hajime Nakamura, "The Vedāntic thought as represented in the Dharmaśāstra and the Arthaśāstra", D.D. Kosambi commemoration volume, Bombay, p. 144.

[15] *Ibid,* p. 145.

[16] *Ibid,* p. 146.

[17] Richard W. Lariviere, "Dharmaśāstra: Its Present Value & Relevance", The Perennial Tree, (eds.) K. Murty & Amit Dasgupta, New Delhi, p. 187.

20

The Human Condition of Enlightenment: *Nakamura on the Buddhist Vision of Life*

R.C. Pradhan

In this paper I intend to give an outline of Professor Hajime Nakamura's interpretation of the Buddhist philosophy of life. Nakamura is one of the most renowned interpreters of the Buddhist philosophy[1]. He is one of the greatest exponents of Indian philosophical traditions in general. In this context, it is worthwhile to understand his views on the Buddhist concept of enlightenment or *nirvāṇa*. Nakamura has given a very balanced and sympathetic interpretation of the basic concepts of the Buddhist metaphysics and ethics. He has argued against the unsympathetic and the negative interpretation[2] of the nature of enlightenment offered by the Western scholars on Buddhism.

I

The Buddhist Metaphysics of Man

Buddhism is basically a reflection on the nature of the human condition in the world and is a search for the solution of the human predicament. The human predicament consists in the metaphysical reality of suffering arising out of the realization of the finitude, impermanence and mortality of human life. The Buddha has made suffering the primary ontological fact about the human condition in the world in view of the fact that the first noble truth[3] centers around the human condition as found in the world. The Buddhist inquiry into the human condition, according to Nakamura, is the most profound metaphysical exercise ever undertaken by philosophers of the world. Nakamura writes:

"As is well known, the Buddha's diagnosis of the human condition begins with the observation that life is suffering (dukkha); existence is pain. The Buddha was convinced that suffering overbalanced pleasure in human life so much so that it would be better never to have been born"[4] .

The fact of human suffering led the Buddha to the search for the cause of suffering and its ultimate removal. The analysis of the cause of the suffering and its ultimate removal is the most fascinating aspect of the Buddhist metaphysics. Nakamura has thrown light on this aspect in his study of the Buddhist metaphysics and ethics.

The human condition has been the main concern of the Buddhist metaphysics and ethics because it is this condition that has defied all metaphysical explanations in the past. The Buddha himself questioned all the available metaphysical explanations in the Indian traditions. He did not accept the theory that man has an immortal soul[5] and that he is destined to enjoy eternal joy in the heavenly abode. This facile optimism espoused by some philosophers did not satisfy the Buddha's explorative mind. He in fact preferred to see the human condition in its true light and diagnose the maladies that afflict man in the world. The idea of suffering that provides the broad framework of his diagnosis of the human condition is metaphysically sound, according to him, because it rules out false optimism and gives a true picture of man in the world. If man would have been eternally happy, then the struggle of existence would have been less meaningful and man's ethical endeavour would have been fruitless. Buddha's rejection of the eternal soul and its eternal happiness is predicated on the premise that there is nothing eternal in the world and that nothing is eternally real in a changing universe. Everything is transient and contingent and so suffering is the inevitable fate of man. In Nakamura's words:

"Why are we so doomed? It is because of the transiency, the impermanence of your human existence. All things pass away. On account of our fragility we are susceptible to disease and death. There is suffering because all things are transient"[6].

That is to say, the transience of the human existence makes room for suffering on the ground that that which is impermanent cannot be the source of eternal happiness. Suffering is the state of impermanence itself and not an effect of it because to be impermanent is to suffer. The human existence is subject to dissolution and death and therefore is of the nature of suffering.

II

Impermanence and Contingency:

The Buddhist Deconstruction of Essentiality and Eternity

The Buddha's metaphysical rejection of the permanent soul and the eternal essences in the universe leads to his advocacy of the no-soul theory and the theory of unmitigated contingency of the universe. The no-soul doctrine, as it is often interpreted, is not just the rejection of an eternal entity called the *ātman* but is a comprehensive theory of non-essentiality and contingency of the universe. It is a theory of the universe in flux and of the changing nature of reality. It accepts only the contingent reality without any eternal essence. Nakamura writes:

"There is no substance which abides for ever. There is only becoming, change. All matter is force; all substance is motion. The state of every individual is unstable, temporary, sure to pass away"[7] .

This theory of flux or becoming is characteristic of the Buddhist metaphysics which rejects all eternal substances including the soul in man.

What made the Buddha realize the non-eternality of the universe is the fact that both in the realm of the physical and the psychic there is continuous change leaving no scope for any thing existing for ever. The physical world, contrary to what commonsense says, is unstable and is bereft of any eternal order. This is owing to the fact that the universe is not created according to a divine plan, according to the Buddhists. Only in a divinely ordained universe there is an eternal order. This is all that the protagonists of eternity (*śāśvātavādins*) propound. The Buddha, on the contrary, maintains that the eternal order is a metaphysical imposition on the world-order which is a continuous flux.

What impresses the Buddha the most about the world-order is its causal network which is represented by the theory of dependent origination (*pratītyasamutpāda*). This theory holds that every thing that happens in the world is due to a cause. All happenings in the universe are causal happenings networked into a universal causal order. The Buddha thus does not believe in an arbitrary and chaotic universe. Such a universe even does not promise regularity in the phenomena, let alone any scientific order. Thus the Buddhistic world-view is not opposed to what the scientists in the modern sense would like to call the well-ordered universe. However, this does not concede any ground to the metaphysics of the eternal order. The Buddha is opposed to the idea of eternity and the Platonic essences rather than to order and causal law within a largely contingent universe.

The no-soul theory (*anātmavāda)* is a fallout of the Buddhist metaphysics of flux and becoming. The being of the soul (*ātman*) is replaced by the becoming of the self. The eternal Ego gives way to the non-eternal self in becoming, i. e. to the changing individual self. Nakamura gives a very rational reconstruction of the Buddhist theory of no- soul in the following words:

"—the theory of No-Ego was developed more systematically. Admitting the transitoriness of everything, Buddhists did not want to assume any metaphysical substances. They reduced substances, things, souls, to forces and functions or movements, processes, and adopted kinetic conceptions of reality. Life was nothing but a series of manifestations of becomings and extinctions. It was a stream of becoming. The Buddha repudiated the popular delusion of the individual ego"[8] .

The no-Ego theory thus demolishes the idea of eternal ego that never changes and remains the same amid all changes. Such a notion of Ego is undoubtedly an anathema to the Buddhist theory of transitoriness and change.

The doctrine of the non-existence of the soul, however, must not be construed as a repudiation of the very notion of self as applied to individual human beings. The notion of self as a non-fixed center of consciousness standing for the individual human person is the very basis of our understanding of the human condition. The human individuals are the moral agents having the will to overcome their condition. Therefore the Buddha takes the individual self as the ultimate source of the moral struggle which aims at bringing an end to suffering.

III

Overcoming the Human Condition: The Possibility of Transcendence

Buddhism is not a philosophy of resignation in the sense that it does not take the human condition as beyond redemption or beyond improvement. It is a philosophy of transcendence in the sense that it proposes to overcome the suffering which characterizes the human condition. The second, the third and the fourth noble truths[9] are precisely to underline this point, namely, that human suffering can be transcended by human effort . The Buddhist ideal of *nirvāṇa* or the cessation of suffering is precisely the idea of getting rid of suffering by the removal of the causes of suffering.

As Nakamura has rightly emphasized, the diagnosis of the human condition reveals that man is spiritually sick as long as he is trapped in the network of worldly desires that cause suffering and therefore he is in need of spiritual therapy[10]. The causes of suffering lie in the desires (*kāma*) that are caused by ignorance. The twelve-linked causes[11] depict the factors which are responsible for the fallen condition of man in the world and the consequent spiritual sickness.

If ignorance is the root cause of suffering because it causes the craving for the worldly life, then the liberation from this fallen condition is possible only by knowledge or enlightenment. The Buddha equates enlightenment with *nirvāṇa* because suffering ceases only when ignorance is removed. If ignorance would have been an inevitable state of existence, then its removal would not have been possible. This is where the Buddha, like the Upaniṣadic sages[12], rises above fatalism to press for overcoming ignorance and the *samsāra* or the worldly existence. He finds in knowledge the potent instrument of the removal of ignorance and the suffering caused by it. By knowledge he meant the knowledge of the nature of the *samsāra* and the causal chains supporting it. Only by knowing that the worldly existence is miserable and that it is impermanent that man could rise above it to aspire for a better existence which is free from suffering. *Nirvāṇa* is the negation of *samsāra* in view of the fact that the conditions responsible for misery are absent in the state of *nirvāṇa*. Nakamura explains the state of *nirvāṇa* in the following words:

"According to Buddhism, the final goal is not a paradise or a heavenly world. The central theme of Buddhism is that, by following the right Path, one can free oneself from the bondage of existence and come to the realisation of the Supreme Truth. The attainment of Enlightenment is identical with Nirvāṇa. All Buddhists agree that Enlightenment is their goal, and that it is attained by following the right Path"[13].

Freedom from bondage is the central theme of the Buddhist enlightenment, even though it is debatable whether it is a state of bliss or *ānanda* in the Upaniṣadic sense. If suffering ceases or is extinguished, it should mean positively that *nirvāṇa* is a state of bliss and calmness. Nakamura rightly argues in the above passage that *nirvāṇa* is the realization of the "Supreme Truth" which amounts to enlightenment.

The negative characterization of *nirvāṇa* as a state of emptiness or a blank state having no positive content has been there right from the beginning. The Buddha himself was not interested in much speculation and controversies because he believed in the practical application of his ideas in life rather than in purely philosophical arguments. He was more like a physician, as Nakamura points out, interested in the alleviation of the spiritual suffering of mankind than in spinning ideas like a theory builder. This attitude of the Buddha makes his philosophy more practical and result-oriented than any other philosophy of his time. *Nirvāṇa* was a moral and spiritual experience for him than a mere dogma and a doctrine.

It is in fact illogical to characterize the Buddhist *nirvāṇa* as a mere extinction of existence or mere "dying out" or a nothingness. If that would have been the real intention of the Buddhists teachings, then it would be tantamount to nihilism of the worst sort. The Buddha wanted the mankind to attain enlightenment *(bodhi)* and not a dark state of non-existence. The Buddha, the "Awakened One" did well know that his Middle Path is the path of liberation, of emancipation and of the awakening and not of death. That is why there is no reason to construe *nirvāṇa* in the negative sense. Nakamura says the following on the issue:

"Contrary to the prevalent Western opinion about Nirvāṇa, the craving for extinction in the sense of annihilation or non-existence (vibhava-tanhā) was indeed expressly repudiated by the Buddha. Buddhists search not for cessation, but for the eternal, the immortal. He who has attained Nirvāṇa is extolled as being afflicted neither by life nor by death"[14] .

The idea of immortality which underlies the Buddhist concept of *nirvāṇa* has to be reinforced because this is exactly what follows from the Buddhist moral training and enlightenment. The Upaniṣadic message of immortality beyond the sphere of birth and death is clearly visible in the Buddhist ideal of Arhatahood[15].

IV

The Individual and the Universe: Human Freedom and Autonomy

Buddhism is a philosophy of freedom and autonomy of man. It is in the individual's liberation that Buddhism finds its ultimate justification. It is the radical form of individualism that distinguishes Buddhism from other philosophical traditions in India. It denies the existence of a Supreme Godhead, except the Buddha himself, to keep the individual man's autonomy intact. The Buddha's appeal to the human reason as the ground of his emancipation from the *samsāra* is to be taken note of. The Buddha is famously reported to have said to his disciples to be the "lamps unto themselves". This is enough indication of the fact that the Buddhistic *nirvāṇa* is not a gift from God but is to be achieved by the individual man.

Buddhism inherits the theory of Karma from Hinduism and transforms it into an instrument of freedom and autonomy. The theory of Karma is not a theory of resignation even in the Hindu philosophy though it might have been given a fatalistic formulation in the popular jargon. Buddhism resists any fatalistic twist to the theory of Karma which lays down that actions determine the results. As the universal law of action and life, it does not hold that man is doomed to bondage to the past life and the past actions. If bondage would have been the ultimate fate of man, then Buddhism itself would have ceased to be relevant. That is why the Buddha showed the way out of the bondage by taking to the path of knowledge. Bondage is negated by freedom. According to him, it is within the capacity of man to rise above the karmic results of the past actions by rebuilding one's life and by initiating new actions guided by moral reason.

The Buddhist ethics is based on reason which shows that the practice of virtue like compassion and fellow feeling and following the path of moral discipline laid down in the eight-fold path would result in the removal of all the bad karmic results. This prescribes a middle path in avoiding all extremes like indulgence in worldly pleasures and the mortification of the body. This balanced view of life based on the moral principles is the most authentic form of spiritualism prescribed by Buddhism. In this sense, Buddhism reconciles rationalism with spiritualism. Nakamura observes:

"...the realization of Nirvāṇa can be explained as taking refuge in the true Self of one's own. On this point the Buddha's teaching is very similar to that of the Upaniṣhads and the Vedāṇta philosophy"[16].

The Buddhist ideal of enlightenment and arhatahood is a spiritual ideal in the sense that it aims at setting a higher goal for mankind based on knowledge and realization of truth. The Buddha was emphatic on the realization of the ultimate truth about our existence and the existence of the universe.

He believed in the ultimate freedom of man from bondage which he called nirvana. He followed the Upaniṣadic *ṛṣis* or seers in bringing an end to the misery of life and in unfolding the secrets of the transcendentally real that promises happiness and immortality[17]. The Buddha was no stranger to the Indian tradition of spirituality and the philosophy of liberation.

What is characteristic of the Buddhist world-view, however, is that here the individual man is given the maximum autonomy in his search for his own salvation and the salvation of others. Man is at the center of the Buddhist universe insofar as he is the one who alone can bring about change in his own life and also in the life of others. Man freely recreates himself and his world by virtue of his own self-will and effort. There is no ready-made system of the world into which man is condemned for ever. His own karmas and his own spirit guide in transforming himself and the world around him.

V

To Be or Not To Be?

The Buddhist Philosophy of Enlightened Existence

As already mentioned, Buddhism is not a philosophy of negation or nihilism. Nakamura depicts Buddhism in the most positive terms denigrating all the negative characterizations heaped on it. Though his comments are in the present context only regarding Buddha's own message, these carry meaning for the whole Buddhist tradition. The Buddhists in general agree that theirs is not a life-negating philosophy and religion. It is basically life-affirming in the sense that it is concerned with the spiritual enrichment of life and not with suffering *per se*. In fact it is a philosophy of life that seeks to overcome death and misery.

It is unfortunate that a philosophy which made man central to the metaphysical order was misunderstood to be anti-man and anti-life. It was wrongly associated with the doctrine of escape from life when in truth it was pro-life in the robust sense of the term. Buddhism made compassion the central principle of religion and ethics and sought to found society on these principles. The Buddhist vision of life is universal and all-inclusive. Buddhism is in this sense one of the greatest of philosophies and religions of the world. In Nakamura's words:

"...Buddhism may be described as a 'universal religion'. It may also so described with reference to the Buddhist claim that Buddhist teaching is of universal significance addressed to the spiritual and moral needs of all mankind"[18].

It is no doubt true that Buddhism has a universal message for mankind and that it is eternally appealing to mankind in view of its deep spiritual and moral message.

Buddhism is not nihilism because it does not deny the meaning of human existence; it does not accept human misery as final. It transforms human existence into an enlightened existence. It seeks to make every man a Buddha, an Awakened One. Buddhism is a philosophy of transcendence in the sense that it overcomes the suffering associated with life. For Buddhism, not only is the universe contingent, but also the suffering of man is contingent. In this sense, there is a limit to human suffering and there is a realm of non-suffering called *nirvāṇa*. Nihilism which also analyzes the human condition takes for granted that human suffering cannot be alleviated and man is condemned to the worldly existence into which he is born.

Buddhism is a philosophy of enlightened existence in the sense that it speaks of another form of existence in which man does not suffer from attachment to the world. This form of existence is not one of life-negation but of affirmation of the essential spirituality of human existence. There is reason to believe, following Nakamura, that Buddhism can be compared to all life-saving philosophies like Christianity of the West and the Vedānta of the East. This follows from the fact that Buddhism gives the call to man to rise above the rut of the worldly existence and fight out one's salvation by individual effort.

The Buddhist philosophy of becoming is not against the philosophy of being in the sense that becoming is not opposed to being, rather being is identical with becoming in view of the fact that man cannot be without becoming what he is free to choose. Freedom of choice is the hallmark of Buddhist ethics. It does not advocate determinism of the type which is popularly associated with the Karma theory. Buddhism transforms Karma theory into a theory of free choice since the human actions are the results of one's own effort. Man's will is the source of both freedom and bondage. The will leads to bondage if it is unenlightened and is not freed from the craving for the world. But if will is freed from craving, it is the source of freedom and liberation[19].

The Buddhist theory of human condition is the theory of choice and renunciation. It is the theory of choice because the future life depends on the choice made by an individual in the present. It is also the theory of renunciation because freedom lies only in the renunciation of the attachment to the world. Thus Buddhism is the philosophy of promise of happiness and the philosophy of enlightenment (*bodhi*)[20].

References

1 Hajime Nakamura, *Buddhism in Comparative Light* (Motilal Banarasidass, New Delhi, 1975; Revised Edition, 1986).

2 *Ibid.*

3 See M. Hiriyanna, *Outlines of Indian Philosophy* (Allen and Unwin, London, 1932; Seventh Impression, 1968), pp.147-154 for a discussion on the four noble truths.

4 Nakamura, *Buddhism in Comparative Light,* p.35.

5 *Ibid.*, pp. 46-52.

6 *Ibid.*, p.36.

7 *Ibid.*, p.37.

8 *Ibid.*, p.47.

9 See Hiriyanna, *Outlines of Indian Philosophy*, pp. 147-154.

10 See Nakamura, *Buddhism in Comparative Light*, Chapter IV.

11 See Hiriyanna, *Outlines of Indian Philosophy*, pp. 148-149.

12 Cf. T.R.V. Murti, *The Central Philosophy of Buddhism: A Study of the Madhyamika System* (Allen and Unwin, London, 1959; Fourth Impression, 1974), pp.14-20.

13 Nakamura, *Buddhism in Comparative Light*, p.54.

14 *Ibid.*, p.55.

15 See . S. Radhakrishnan, *Indian Philosophy*, Vol. I (Allen and Unwin, London, 1923) especially on Early Buddhism for a similar view.

16 Nakamura, *Buddhism in Comparative Light*, p. 68.

17 Cf. *Dhammapada,* 75, 87-88.

18 Nakamura, *Buddhism in Comparative Light*, p.2.

19 See T.R.V. Murti, *The Central Philosophy of Buddhism*, Chapter Ten for a comprehensive discussion on the nature of freedom in Buddhism.

20 *Ibid*.

21

Professor Hajime Nakamura on Human Existence and Self in Early Buddhism

Sabhajit Mishra

Indian philosophy is characterised by almost all the shades and forms that characterise western philosophy. There are the materialists and the spiritualists, the realists and the idealists, the theists and the atheists, the heterodox and the orthodox and so on. But it has never been divided between the 'logicians' and the 'lotus eaters' as the twentieth century western philosophy has been.[1] Investigations into the laws of logic and attempts at reaching conceptual clarity and unambiguity in language are closely related with investigations into subjective experiences and exploration of the riddles of reality. In fact the former has been conceived as an aid to the latter. The foremost concern of Indian philosophy is man's existential predicament in the world and the way-out of that predicament. Each system of Indian philosophy has its own explanation of the nature of human existence in the world. Sāmkhya philosophy, for example, sees human existence as inevitably afflicted by three-fold pain-*ādhyātmika, ādhibhautika* and *ādhidaivika.*[2] Advaita Vedānta believes that man is under the spell of beginningless ignorance, alternatively known as adhyāsa, and because of this adhyāsa there is co-mingling of self with not self and vice versa. All human activities, worldly or otherworldly, are based on adhyāsa. Based on duality as these activities are, the non-dual nature of self remains concealed during adhyāsa.[3] This co-mingling is responsible for man's ailments. According to the Vaiśeṣika philosophy man's inability to comprehend the nature of objects (*padārthas*), their similarities and dissimilarities stands in his way of knowledge. And when that knowledge arises man attains worldly as well otherworldly happiness.[4]

Buddhism has its own conception of human existence. In this essay the position of early Buddhism, as explained by Professor Hajime Nakamura, regarding the nature of human existence and self will be discussed.

I

The first basic trait of human existence discerned by the Buddha is that certain aspects of human life are characterized by pain or suffering. In his first sermon the Buddha presented his analysis of the sorrowful aspects of life: "Birth is suffering; decay is suffering; sorrow, lamentation, grief and despair are suffering; in short, the five aggregates of existence (forms, sensations, perceptions, psychic dispositions and consciousness) are suffering."[5]

The fact of suffering leading to human anxiety was revealed to the Buddha in his enlightenment. Ordinarily people do not notice this obvious truth and therefore remain unaffected by the anxiety resulting from it. "People who are busy all the time, who must always think of something, must always be doing something, are incessantly running away from this experience of the basic or original anxiety." Nakamura seems to be suggesting here that the assertion that there is suffering in human life is not a commonsense assertion. It is an assertion of a spiritually enlightened Buddha. Death overcomes all men but they are not conscious of it. This means that common man leads his existence without being existentially sensitive to, or reflective about, it. This has been very well brought out in the existentialist philosophies, particularly that of Heidegger. Death, Heidegger says, is a form of dread or anguish which characterizes the original structure of human existence. It is there before man, it is there from the very beginning. But in his everydayness man looks at death as one event among the many other events that happen in his life. He thinks that just as many things are happening to him, death will also happen. But it is not there not even as a possibility. The everyday or the average man, therefore, hides his own possibility from himself. He tries to cover up the necessity of death by its uncertainty and deludes himself into thinking that death is not certain to come.[6] Obviously ordinary men are used to leading inauthentic life. Here it must be remarked that Heidegger looks at death from the angle of individual existence. Buddha, on the contrary, is looking at death from a universal angle. Moreover, the purpose of Heidegger's analysis of death is to make man existentially sensitive to what his existence originally is. He prescribes no path to terminate the dread or anxiety caused by death. The Buddha, on the other hand, is a great prescriber. He lays down a path but he also insists that it is for the individual himself to walk over the path.

II

The cause of man's threatened existence, and this is the second feature of human existence, is man's ignorance. Ignorance is the main cause from which false desires or cravings spring. Ignorance and desires respectively are the theoretical and practical sides of one fact. "Purely from a viewpoint.", says Nakamura, "false desires are seen to be ignorance; on the other hand, the Buddha's concrete realisation of ignorance was that it is false desires."[7] In actual life they are one.

According to Nakamura New Testament Christians hold a similar belief. It is ignorance, they believe, which separates man from God. "They are darkened in their understanding, alienated from the life of God because of the ignorance that is in them, due to their hardness of heart; they have become callous and have given themselves up to licentiousness, greedy to practice of every kind of uncleanness."[8] However, the Christian ethics relies more on grace rather than knowledge to be with the "Truth." Such statements as "You will know the truth and the truth will make you free" are isolated statements in Christian ethics. Buddhism, on the contrary, believes that when knowledge is attained, the will is controlled and suffering comes to an end. This close relation between knowledge and will in Buddhism in particular, and Indian philosophy in general, believes Nakamura, has its parallel in philosophies of Socrates and Plato who hold that virtue is knowledge and knowledge is the gateway to a craft, a skill, a science, and moral excellence.

III

The third feature of human existence is that what man desires is transient and transience is one with suffering. Nakamura finds parellel thoughts in the Greek philosophy and old Christianity. Heraclitus held that "Reality is a condition of unrest." Old Testament says, "Then I considered all that my hands had done and the toil I had spent in doing it, and behold, all was vanity and striving after wind, and there was nothing to be gained under sun."[9] This idea is continued in New Testament also and it is said, "The things that are seen are transient, but the things that are unseen are real."[10] At this point Nakamura makes a noteworthy observation regarding the origin of the ideas of impermanence in Buddhism and Christianity. He writes, "The Christian origins probably go back to an inchoate Hebrew conception of the greatness of God, and later the role of insignificant human beings separated from God came to be stressed whereas in Buddhism the fragile and weak existence was first stressed and then something beyond was sought for."[11]

Greek Stoics were also aware of the transience or change and this awareness generated strong will in them. Epicterus writes, "Remember that you ought to behave in life as you would at a banquet. As something is being passed around it comes to you; stretch your hand and take a portion of it politely. It passes on, do not detain it. Or until it comes in front of you yet; do not project your desire to meet it, but wait until it comes in front of you. So act toward children, so toward a wife, so toward office, so toward wealth, and then some day you will be worthy of the banquet of Gods."[12]

The dialogue between the Buddha and Ānanda at the time when the Buddha was going to die is remarkably akin to the

Greek metaphor of banquet cited above. The Buddha instructed Ānanda: "Enough ! Ānand ! Do not let yourself be troubled; do not weep. Have I not already, on former occasions, told you that it is in the very nature of all things most near and dear unto us that we must divide ourselves from them, leaving them, severe ourselves from them? How, then, Ānand, can this be possible whereas everything whatever is born, brought into being, and organized, contains within itself the inherent necessity of dissolution,-how, than, can this be possible, that such a being should not be dissolved.....Be earnest in effort, and you too shall soon be free from the intoxicants (sensuality, individuality, delusion, and ignorance)."[13]

A similar advice has been given by Epicterus in another passage. He said, "When you see someone weeping in sorrow, either because a child has gone on a journey, or because he has lost his property, beware that you be not carried away by the impression that the man is in the midst of external ills, but straightway keep before you this thought. "It is not what has happened that distresses this man (for it does not distress another), but his judgement about it. Do not, however, hesitate to sympathise with him... ...but be careful not to groan also in the centre of your being".[14]

In this way Nakamura tries to emphasise the important point that both the Buddhist and the Greek Stoics share the view that man's sorrow lies in his own attitude. Things do not make him happy or sorrowful; attitude to things makes him so. So man should not weep. However there is a difference and Nakamura does not fail to bring this to our attention. The Buddha's advice not to weep, he says, is not individual advice but universal compassion. The sympathy advised by Epicterus in the passage quoted above retains an awareness of the distinction between individuals.[15]

IV

The concept of the individual-kinetic existence and transmigration is another important aspect of human existence according to Nakamura. So far as the doctrine of transmigration is concerned, Indian philosophy in general upholds it and Buddhism is no exception. What is exceptional about Buddhism, however, is that it believes in transmigration against the background of its belief in the impermanent nature of soul. Pythagoreans and Plato also believed in the doctrine of transmigration. But, observes Nakamura, the concept of transmigration without a permanent subject was much more difficult for the Greeks to understand. He also suggests that the Greeks might have been influenced by the Oriental thought in their belief in this doctrine. The difficulty of the king Milinda in comprehending the no-soul theory and continuation of human personality, Nakamura remarks, is indicative of this fact.

The illustrations given by Nāgasena to explain the continuity of person holds in an apparent paradoxical manner that individuality is maintained kinetically which means that one state of individual existence gives way to the next, then the next and so on. The Buddhist comparison of mundane existence to a burning fire expresses the thought that life is dynamic, vibrant and constantly in motion.

The same problem is the subject of one of the paradoxes of Heraclitus in his famous saying, "We bathe and do not bathe in the same stream. We are and yet we are not."[16] The stream is not the same but it is of the same name. Likewise the individual who enters the steam "is not" in the sense of anything permanent; but he is the individual of the same name. Heraclitus thus is in basic agreement with Buddhism in the opposition to the notion of unchanging being. But Nakamura is very careful to notice the difference between them. Heraclitus, he says, was interested in change primarily for the purpose of setting forth a cosmology; for the Buddha such a purpose could only be considered secondary to his ethical intent.[17] Furthermore, the notion of fire does not carry the same meaning for Buddhism and Heraclitus. Fire, to the Buddha, was essentially nothing but a simile, while to Heraclitus fire was the permanent substance of everything. Heraclitus believed that everything originates from fire and dissolves into it again. Fire is the ultimate principle of the universe. He has said, "Neither any God nor any man has created this world which is equal to all beings. On the contrary, it always was, and will be eternal living fire burning according to rules and vanishing according to rules. "Fire", according to Heraclitus, "is an element; everything that becomes is nothing but an interchange of fire."[18]

The Buddha employed the simile of fire to show that the world is nothing but the ceaseless flux of becoming. The seemingly unchanging flame is not the same next moment. The seeming identity is a continuity of moments. The individual is only a bundle of changing *skandhas,* changing from moment to moment, from life to life, and only *nirvāṇa* can bring about its final dissolution. The comparison of mundane existence to a burning fire, then, expresses the view that human life is transient and full of suffering.

V

Human existence is nothing but a series of manifestations of becomings and extinctions. It is a process of becoming. This feature of human existence is closely related to the theory of non-Ego or non-Soul. While discussing the Buddhist theory of non-Ego Nakamura raises the question.; Did Buddhism really deny *ātman*? While considering this question he expresses the view that Buddhism really denies the concept of 'mine' or 'my possessions' (*mama*). It means that the mendicants should not harbor the idea of possession of 'mine' and 'others'. Such a concept of renunciation is to be found in Brahmanism and Jainism also. How is this rejection of mine related to the rejection of self? According to Nakamura the early Buddhist scriptures tell us that possessions do not belong to the self for ever. Therefore one should not be attached to his own possessions. Attachment to possessions is based on the wrong comprehension of what is not self as the real self. In this context, misunderstanding of body as self is specially stressed. What the early Buddhism taught, therefore, is that whatever is not *ātman,* specially body, should not be regarded as one's own. What is suffering is non-*ātman*. What is non-*ātman* is not mine, not it is I, not it is my *ātman*. What is *ātman* then? The Buddhist answer to this is that the *ātman* cannot be comprehended objectively. Whatever principle or function is imagined to be *ātman* by people is in reality neither *ātman* nor that which belongs to the *ātman*. In the opinion of Nakamura, therefore, the early Buddhists never maintained the non-existence of *ātman*. They merely opposed the substantial view of *ātman*. As for the question whether *ātman* exists or not, the Buddha himself kept silence.

Instead of expressly denying the existence of *ātman*, early Buddhism admits *ātman* as a moral agent. It says that one should perform one's duty, or one should be conscious about his 'profit'. What is meant by profit here is neither material nor sensual profit. It means the realisation of truth. Lord Śākyamuni is said to have asked those youths who indulge themselves in amusements to seek after self. *Ātman* is desirable (*priya*); it is to be loved and protected. This easily reminds one of the teachings of Yājñavalkya.[19] Even the Jainas have called themselves *ātmavādins* and teach the purification and protection of *ātman*.[20]

This analysis of the concept of non-Ego leads Nakamura to believe that "in spite of the existence of different opinions among various religions and philosophies with regard to the essence of *ātman* as the metaphysical principle, the significance of *ātman* as the agent of actions may be assured of general admittance among the Indians. For any religion of India, the ultimate goal of emancipation is the recovering of one's self."[21]

From the foregoing discussion Nakamura concludes that the denial of Ego appeared in a later period and that the Buddha did not deny soul. Moreover, he seems to have acknowledged the true self which appears in our moral conduct as conforming to universal norms (*dharma*). It is likely, Nakamura further observes, that the Buddha admitted the true self in a higher sense. True self is the latent self as distinguished from the self accepted in ordinary life. The ordinary self has to be subdued because man has a tendency to attach linguistic entities to feelings. Such feelings are given the name of self which is nothing but ignorance. The ignorance must be overcome and the true self attained. One who conquers himself is the greatest *conquerer.* This reminds us of Loa-tzu who said, "He who conquers others is strong, he who conqures himself is almighty."[22]

The latent self, therefore, is the "lord of self". Thus the Buddhist concepts of *anātman* and the true *ātman* are not at odds with each other. On the contrary, the former is one of the aids to understand the latter. The true self, according to the Buddha, is nothing other than the unobstructed flow of the events of the phenomenal existence. This belief in true self is an expression of the Buddha's confidence that unobstructed events have the moral character of universal norms (*dharma*) and coincide perfectly with man's duty. And when one acts according to universal norms, one acts morally. And when one acts morally, the true self becomes manifest.

References

1 Wolfe Mays and S.C. Brown (ed.) Linguistic Analysis and Phenomenology, London: Macmillan, 1972, p. 1, Wolfe Mays refers to a write up in the American magazine Time (7 January, 1966) in which philosophers belonging to the school of linguistic analysis were called as 'logicians', because of their interest in logic and language, whilest those belonging to phenomenology were called 'lotus eaters' because of their concern for subjective experience.

2 The Sāmkhya Aphorisms of Kapila, 1.1, also Īśvarakṛṣṇa's Śāmkhyakārikā, I.

3 Śamkarācārya, Brahmasūtrabhāṣya, Introduction.

4 Kaṇāda, Vaiśeṣikasūtra, 1.1, 1.4.

5 Nakamura, Hajime, A Comparative History of Ideas (revised edition), London: KPI limited, 1968, p. 237.

6 Heidegger, Martin, Existence and Being, A gateway Edition, Chicago: Hentry Regency Co, 1967. Introduction by W. Brook, p. 59. "One way of obscuring the "certainty" of death in everyday Dasein results from its "indefinable" character as to its own when."

7 A Comparative History of Ideas, p. 239.

8 *Ibid.*, p. 239.

[9] *Ibid.*, p. 243.

[10] *Ibid.*, p. 243.

[11] *Ibid.*, p. 243.

[12] *Ibid.*, p. 244.

[13] Mahāparinibbāna-Sūttānta, 5, 13-4; Dīghanikāya vol. II, 143-144, Quoted in A Comparative History of Ideas, p. 244.

[14] Epicterus, Encheiridon 16, quoted in A Comparative History of Ideas, p. 245.

[15] A Comparative History of Ideas, p. 245.

[16] *Ibid.*, p. 253.

[17] *Ibid.*, p. 253. For this the Buddha relied on showing man the kinetic character of human existance. Heraclitus was able to make ethical recommendations based on his metaphysics that the fiery element being best, the dry state of soul is "wisest and best."

[18] *Ibid.*, p. 254. Quoted from Takashi Ide's Poet philosophers.

[19] Bṛhadāraṇyaka Upaniṣad, 2.4.1-7. Maitreyī puts the question to Yājñavalkya: "Shall I become immortal (i.e. attain my true self) by means of the worldly riches? "Yājñavalkya replies: "No, by means of the worldly riches you will lead a life which ordinary people (ignorant of the real nature of self) lead; everything that is dear to man is dear to him because of self. The worldly things are therefore to be renounced for realizing one's self.

[20] Nakamura, Hajime, The Ways of Thinking of Eastern Peoples (tr. Toyojin no shii hoho), Tokyo: Monbusho, Compiled by Japanese National Commission, 1960, p. 66.

[21] *Ibid.*, p. 67.

[22] A Comparative History of Ideas, p. 271.

22

Professor Hajime Nakamura and Indian Buddhism

Karunesh Shukla

I

Professor Hajime Nakamura, the great exponent of Indian culture and Buddhism in Japan in modern times, is the doyen of indologists who has analysed and interpreted Indian Buddhist thought in its core. Throughout the globe his analysis and interpretation of the comparative ideas of the Asian people, their philosophy and culture, their way of thought and living are regarded as the wholesome account of the Asian culture, the Buddhist tradition and the Indian thought in the comparative light of their Western, Christian and Greco-Roman counterpart(s). Nakamura has not only analysed the core of Indian culture, its philosophy and religion in their subtle form, but has equally traced its social context in order to give it comprehension and required orientation[1]. He has presented a wholesome view of Indian culture and Indian Buddhism in addition to the other systems of Indian thought such as the Advaita Vedānta, Jainism, the Sāṁkhya-Yoga and other traditional systems.

For Nakamura Buddhism has been a living faith which he too accepted. As such he studied in depth the tenets of Indian Buddhism and its various shades in comparison with the other living traditions of Indian thought. He studied, analysed and interpreted Buddhism in all its comprehension and compared it to other living faiths of the globe, such as Jainism, Islam, Christianity, Confucianism and Judaism. He regarded Lord

Buddha as the great preceptor whose light of knowledge as also the practical view of life and living enlightened the entire humanity and presented the truth of life as a universal model.

II

Beginning with the *life of the Buddha,* studied in a comprehensive manner and based on Pali, Sanskrit (i.e. Buddhist Sanskrit) Sino-Tibetan and Japanese sources, Nakamura observes that the original sources regarding the events of Gotama's life have been intermingled with legends which have to be cautiously cleared of the ingenuine materials[2]. One has to discern the real story of Gotama's life and its events—his detachment from the world, renunciation, wandering in search of the noble path of truth, search of a competent guru, practice of penance in its various aspects, self-mortification, and lastly resorting to the ways of contemplation penance and meditation which led him attain the bodhi[3], the superb vision of the Truth that related to the extinction and non-regeneration of the worldly defilements and realisation of the Four Noble Truths (*cattāri ariya saccāni*).

Nakamura himself presented a detailed account of the life and events of Gotama the Buddha both in the Japanese[4] and in the English languages[5]. The Japanese account related to the various aspects of Siddhartha Gotama's life, utilising the early textual materials as well as later redactions and later accounts of the life of Buddha. For this purpose he also presented a Japanese translation of the original Pali scriptures[6] relating to the Buddha's life and his search of Truth. He also translated the Pali scriptures relating to the life of the Buddha and wrote a biography of the Buddha[7], 'based on results of recent critical textual studies in which each event in his life was explained with reference to non-Buddhist materials and in relation to the social background, as well as archeological findings. To illustrate, there are twenty-two scenes presenting stories from the life of the Buddha in base-relief on the stupa railings of Bharahut. Pieces of fine arts are helpful to get the picture of sociological, topological and ideological background of the days in which the Buddha lived'[8].

III

The actual date when Siddhartha Gotama was born has been a matter of controversy among scholars for the last century[9]. Majority of the Japanese scholars maintained that the Buddha attained *Nirvāṇa* is 568 B.C.[10]. Thus the year of his birth was regarded as B.C. 648. Takakusu suggested the date of the Buddha as 566-486 B.C. The late H. Ui fixed the date of Buddha as 466-386 B.C. adopting lengends set forth in Sanskrit, Tibetan and Chinese versions of scriptures, such as the Samayabheda uparacana-cakra. Because the date of King Aśoka, the starting point for chronological investigations, should be altered in the light of recent research, Nakamura proposed that Ui's chronology should be modified to 463-383 B.C.[12]

Jacobi fixed the date of the *parinirvāṇa* of the Buddha as 484 B.C.[13]. Andre Bareau[14] and Eggermont[15] and together with them Warder[16] regard 486 B.C. to be the date of the birth of the Buddha, while the Western scholars' view-point has been moderately put by Winternitz as the sixth and the fifth centuries before Christ[15], the Southern Buddhism, particularly the Ceylonese tradition maintains 483 B.C. as the date of the Buddha's *parinirvāṇa* and B.C. 563 as the date of his birth[16]. It places reliance on the enumeration of dots put annually on the Vinaya texts on the completion of the annual recitation (*pārāyaṇa*) of the scriptures called 'Vassa'[17] both in India and in Ceylon. Nakamura doubts the authenticity and the exactness of the enumeration, which he says, leads us to the conclusion that Siddhartha Gotama's birth[18] date should be put to 463 B.C. taking into consideration the other aspects of the problem and considering other historical and archeological data. However, the usually accepted date of Buddha's *parinirvāṇa* enumerated on the basis of the dotted scriptures, comes to 483 B.C.[19]. Hence his birth year is put to 563 B.C. giving him a life span of eighty years[20]. In the Tripiṭ aka, the age at the time of his demise has been given eighty years[21], but Warder[22] doubts this reckoning of the Buddha's age and suggests that his age at the time of the *parinirvāṇa* might have been seventy-nine years[23].

The Chinese scholars[24], as quoted by Nakamura[25], maintain 390 B.C. as the date of *parinirvāṇa*, most probably under the influence of H. Ui's views[26].

Among the Japanese scholars Kanakura[27] follows the Southern Buddhist tradition, to be B.C. 484 as the date of the *parinirvāṇa*.

Midzuno doubts the authenticity of the northern legend that Aśoka appeared after one hundred years after the death of the Buddha and adopts the southern tradition[28]. A re-interpretation of Aśoka's edict found at Ahraura in Mirzapur district in Uttar Pradesh, has now been taken up by some scholars.[29]

In view of these considerations the view-point of Nakamura seems justified and should be accepted by all the traditions.

IV

Nakamura analytically presented the basic postulations of early Buddhism[30] and analysed the bases of human existence, namely suffering and its cause-ignorance avijjā (Skt. *avidyā*), impermanence of phenomena[32] (anicca, Skt. *anitya*), the theory of non-ego or no-soul (anattavādo Skt anātmavāda)[33], individual-kinetic existence and transmigration[34] and the aim of human existence[35] and the path Towards the aim (i.e. *nirvāṇa*), karma and craving (*tṛṣṇā*)[37], the true self[38] and the general principles of Ethics: the value and equality of man[39], compassion and service to others[40] and the ethical dogma[41] in addition to the other aspects of the Buddhist religion and spiritual praxis leading to the acquisition of nirvāṇa[42]. All this he analysed and evaluated on the basis of the early Buddhism, based on the basic teachings of the Buddha[43] and a comparative account of the Christian and Western religio-philosophical traditions. He refers to the Western religions and mystic tradition beginning from the Greek thinkers[44] and critically evaluates the tradition in the light of the preceding and the subsequent Indian i.e., the Vedic, the Upaniṣadic, the Buddhist and the Jaina thoughts in addition to the Sāṃkya-Yoga, Nyāya and the Vaiśeṣika and other systems and mystics of the Medieval and the Modern period[45].

Through out, he studied, analysed and interpreted Buddhism as a way of thought which was the part and parcel of our living. For him *anātma* is not a theory of Buddhist dogma, but a part of the spiritual praxis of the Buddhist tradition which is continually practised even to-day. Along with the Tibetan view of non egoity (*anātma*) and the Chinese koan Nakamura regards anything permanent or eternal as non-admissible in terms of Buddhist thought. *Anātma* for Nakamura is not only the negation of a permanent soul or self, but the praxis of non-egoity, the elimination of the very notion of me and mine, which is constituted of the five aggregates of form (*rūpa*), feeling (*vedanā*), perception (*saṃjñā*), disposition (*saṃskāra*) and consciousness (*vijñāna*)—that constitute the human personality[46]. He says[47]: "The Buddha repudiated the popular conception of the individual ego. The objects with which man identifies himself, he thought, are not the true Self. Fortune, social position, family, body and even mind are not the true Self. In this sense the Buddhist theory can be called "the theory of Non-Self", i.e., anything perceived is not the Self, In addition all the then current theories about "souls" were discussed and in this sense as well Buddha's theory can be called the theory of Non-Soul or Non-Ego".

As regards the notion of self, Nakamura observes that, 'the Non-Self theory in early Buddhism does not mean that the Buddha completely denied the existence of the self in the practical and the moral sense as the subject of actions. But the self cannot be identified with anything existing in the outside world nor grasped as some other concrete physical substance. The self can be realised when one acts according to universal norms of human existence. When one acts morally according to Buddhism, the true self becomes manifest'[48]

Nakamura[49] refers to the Buddha's teachings which contain exhortations about knowing the self[50]. The Buddha also taught in his last sermon[51] to Ananda, his disciple, "Be you lamps to yourselves. Be you a refuge to yourself. Betake yourself to no external refuge. Hold fast to the Truth as lamp. Do not look for refuge to any one besides yourself"[52]. Buddha also says at the time of his demise that I have taken refuge to myself (*kataṃ me saranam attano*)[53].

'According to the Buddha, bad actions hurt oneself, for "evil done by oneself, self-begotten, self-bred, crushes the foolish, as the diamond breaks a precious stone[54]. The foolish man bears frost to his own destruction"[55]. Therefore, 'a man's limited self should be ennobled. In Buddhism a man who is devoted to religious practice is extolled[56]. In other words, to use the word used by the Buddha himself, this self is expressed by the word '*manas*' (Pali-*mano*) also, which only indicates that the mental dispositions[57] (i.e., *manas*) are to be subdued and ennobled. 'He, thus, abstaining lives his life void of cravings, perfected, cool, in blissful enjoyment, his whole self ennobled'[58]. The Buddha did not preach the existence of an eternal individual self, as is indicated in the Mahāvagga[59] (1.14). It is, therefore, said in the Buddhist scriptures, search thyself (*attānaṃ gaveseyyātha*)[60] which only means the empirical self.

According to Nakamura[61], 'In early Buddhism two kinds of self were admitted. The one is the self of ordinary daily life, a practical distinction man is led to make by the inherited concepts of language. The other is the latent self which is to be conquered. Conquering of one's self (i.e., the latent self) is a great and difficult task. This latent self is also *manas*[62] or *citta* which is to be subduced for the suppression, annihilation or elimination of craving.'

One has to watch himself and ultimately conquer it. It is difficult to be subdued[63], Nakamura clarifies[64] that the latent self was called the "lord of self"[65]. One should be earnest to carry on his own duty, in compliance of the demand of the true self. He says that multiple usages of the terms self, facilitate explanation of Nirvāṇa as "taking refuge to the true self of one's own". One must understand that the Buddhist concepts of *anātman* and the "true Self" are not at odds with each other. On the contrary, the former is one of the Buddha's aids to understanding the latter. Through following the Buddha's path and thoroughly understanding the phenomenal nature of existence and awareness (that they are altogether empty of permanent self[66]). One finds that his true Self is nothing other than the unobstructed flow of those events. The true Self is an expression by the Buddha of his confidence that unobstructed events have the moral character of universal norms (dharma) and coincide perfectly with man's duty. This, he further points out, 'led to the development of the Mahāyāna doctrine of great Self[67]. Thus the Mahāyāna Sūtras.[68], Śāntideva[69] as well as Maitreyanātha evolve the doctrine of the true and universal self (*ātma-mahātmatā*) in these words[70]:

Saṃskāramātraṃ jagad etya buddhyā
nirātmakaṃ duhkha virūdhimātram/
Vihāya yan arthamayātmadṛṣṭim
Mahātmadṛṣtiṃ śrayatemahārthām//

(With the notion that the phenomena are merely relatively produced and mutable, with no self/essence whatsoever, containing (or grown out of) of suffering or evil (contemplating on this nature of phenomena) one, eschewing one's view altogether, regard the entire world as one's great Self, and takes refuge in the view of the great Self which is really of great aims).

This happens only when craving is eliminated and with a view of universally accepted norms (*dharma*), the universal Love towards all creatures is generated through Great compassion (*mahākaruṇā*). This view point was further developed in the Mahāyāna—the Madhyamika, the Yogācāra and the Tāntrika literature—as a common practice of the Buddhists. This theme of *mahākaruṇā* led to the realisation of *śūnyatā* (voidity), the point of spiritual potency practised at the universal plane and leading to the realisation of the essencelessness (*niḥsvabhāvatā*) of phenomenal objects[71].

When the circumference of mind is broadened with the contemplation of universal Self the Buddhas attain the greatness or universal character of their true Self (*ātmamahātmatā*)[72].

V

The entire analysis of the phenomena as evanascent and mutable by the Buddha[73] which led to the doctrine of instantaneous being (*kṣaṇabhaṅgavāda*) was based on his analysis of the human suffering, its nature, and elimination (*prahāṇa*), contemplation on the root cause of evil as *taṇhā* (Skt. *tṛṣṇā*-craving) giving rise to the suffering through the twelve-linked doctrine of causal efficacy (*pratītyasamutpāda*) and the realisation (*sākṣikarma*) of the noble eight-fold way meant to be followed for the suppression or elimination of suffering or evil (*dukkha*)[74].

Nakamura's exposition[75] of early Buddhism relates to its background both the Brahmanical and the non-Brahmanical (i.e. Ājīvaka and Jaina), the main tenets being suffering as its first problem, *aniccā*, *dukkha* and *anattā* as the principal cardinal ideas of early Buddhism and *nibbāna* (Sanskrit *nirvāṇa*) as the last goal of human life which Nakamura described and analysed as blissful state of enlightenment wherein craving.lastingly withers away and which leads to the pause of further *saṃsāra*, the conitinuum of life and death[76].

According to him, the central conception of Buddhism must be that of dharma. Buddha is one who sees dharma. Dharma denotes a norm. In Buddhism the concept of dhamma was put forth to substitute the concept of Brahman in the Upaniṣads...[77].

'Various ideas were assimilated into systems of Buddhist thought and this explains the reason why Buddhism has spread in many countries without opposition by systems of indigenous thoughts in their respective country'[78].

Thus, the contribution of Nakamura to the Indian Buddhist studies has been immense and invaluable. Not only in quantum of the studies in various aspects of Indian Buddhism and the Japanese Buddhism by him are astonishingly large, his interpretation of the various themes and tenets of Indian Buddhism, both original and developed, early, medieval and later, Theravāda, Mahāyāna and Tantrayāna has been equally admirable and extremely beneficial to a student of Buddhism. His studies and interpretations are not only based on original Pali, Prakrit, Sanskrit, Buddhist Sanskrit and Apabhraṃśa and Hindi sources, but the Sino-Tibetan and Japanese translations as well.

Nakamura has been very caucious in accepting the translations of Buddhist texts in Western languages, wherein the equivalents of some technical terms are not acceptable as they cause misunderstanding and thus are, 'misleading and desperately unintelligible'[79].

Throughout, the outlook of Nakamura has been open, unpretentious as well as unprejudiced. His outlook is universal in nature, critical and comparative, yet his expositions protect the original view-point of the systems taken up for evaluation and presentation. His evaluations are always text-based, historically and sociologically analysed and presented in the comparative light of the Confucian, Greek, Christian, Jaina, Vedānta and other thought-ferments or their off-shoots. These are honest and unprejudiced interpretations by an Asian critic whose penetration into the Buddhist thought has been inherently inscribed with intensity and leaves an impression of profundity, comprehension and thoroughness.

References

1 His view point is distinctly expressed in his own words, "I choose India as a starting-point or norm for exposition for the following reasons; (1) Indian culture provides an extensive body of data ranging from the Vedic period to the present, thus furnishing rich documentation diachronically,....; (2) Indian culture, both ancient and modern, preserves in any given period a great diversity in its religious and philosophical traditions thus furnishing synchronically a wide range of problems characteristic of a particular stage; and the religions and philosophies of India have been the primary focus of my own research over several decades, and (3) thus serve as a natural starting point in all my own reflections regarding problems in the history of ideas." *A Comparative History of Ideas* London, 1986, p. 11.

2 *Indian Buddhism*, Delhi, 1987, p. 17.

3 Cf. *Kṣayānutpadayor jñāne malānām bodhirucyate, Abhisamayālaṅkāra,* V. 19.

[4] *Gotama Buddha,* Shakuron-den (the Life of Sakyamuni, Kyoto, 1958; see also *Gotama Buddha,* Los Angeles-Tokya, 1977.

[5] *Indian Buddhism*, p. 16, fn. 1.

[6] Chikuma, Butten, I. 5-58.

[7] See, *Ibid.*, p. 5.

[8] *Indian Buddhism,* p. 17; see also, Nakamura, Preface to the work, *Bijutsu nu miru Shokuson no Shogai,* Heibonsha 1979; see also *Gotama Buddha* (Shakuson den), Kyoto, 1958.

[9] For Literature and views on the point, see, Winterniz, M., History of Indian Literature, II. 597-8; Frauwallner, History of Indian Buddhism, Notes and Bibliography to the Chapters on the Buddha and the Jina; Pandey, G.C., *Studies in the Origins of Buddhism,* p. 369 sq. and elsewhere.

[10] See, *Indian Buddhism,* pp. 12 sq. for different views.

[11] Takakusus view.

[12] See, *Indian Buddhism,* p. 14.

[13] Jacobi in SPA, XXVI, Berlin, 1930, see Nakamura, *Indian Buddhism,* p. 14, fn, 21.

[14] *Journal Asiatique,* 1953, pp. 27 sq.

[15] M. Winternitz, *History of Indian Literature,* II, 597-98.

[15a] *Chronology of the Reign of Asoka Moriya,* Leiden, 1966, pp. 138-143. sq., A.K. Warder, *Indian Buddhism,* pp. 44-45; Winternitz, *ibid*, loc cit.

[16] A.K. Warder, *Indian Buddhism,* Delhi, 1980, pp. 44-45, Nakamura, *Indian Buddhism,* pp. 13-14.

[17] Cf. Nakamura, *Indian Buddhism,* pp. 13-14, W. Pachow, *A study of the Dotted Record,* JAOS, Vol. 85, no. 3, 1965, pp. 342-49, also, Nakamura, *The Date of the Mauryan Dynasty in the THG,* no. 10, Tokyo, 1955, pp. 1 sq., also Indo Kodaishi, *Ancient History of India,* Tokyo, 1966, II. 409-37.

[18] See, Nakamura, *Indian Buddhism,* pp. 13-14.

[19] *Ibid,* loc. cit.

[20] See, Warder, *ibid,* loc. cit. Nakamura, *Indian Buddhism,* p. 14.

[21] Such as in the *Mahaparinibbāna Suttanta,* D.N. II 151, Waldschmidt, MPS, 376 sq. Nakamura, *ibid,* pp. 13-14: Warder, Indian Buddhism, p. 44.

[22] Warder, *ibid,* loc. cit.

[23] He says: In one of the early texts authenticated by several schools of Buddhists the Buddha states that he was twenty-nine years of age when he left the 'world' and that event happened more than fifty years ago. This was said immediately before the *parinirvāṇa,* perhaps on the day itself. The age attained by the Buddha is thus given as more than 79 years, and the later tradition gives him a full eighty at the moment of *parinirvāṇa*. There is some reason to doubt this figure of eighty, as a very early interpretation, since it makes it difficult to reconcile the Buddhist and Brahmanical traditions about the life of King Bimbisara of Magadha, the Buddha's contemporary. It could perhaps be reduced by upto twenty years to produce a more authentic figure..., *Ibid,* p. 44; see also, pp. 45-80 for details.

[24] Cf. Nakamura, *Indian Buddhism,* p. 14, these scholars are led by—Rev. Lin-shun.

[25] *Ibid,* loc. cit.

[26] *Ibid,* loc. cit.

[27] E. Kanakura, *Indo Kodai Seishinshi,* p. 339 sq. (quoted by Nakamura, *ibid,* loc. cit., fn. 21).

[28] Nakamura, *ibid,* pp. 14-15, see also, for references, fn. 22-24 (p. 15).

[29] See Raj Bali Pandey, *Aśoka ke Abhilekha,* pp. 130-31, A.K. Narain in *Bhāratī* (BHU), V.1., 105; V.S. Pathak, in *Bhāratī,* December, 2003 now, the prevalent view is that the Buddha's date of *parinirvāṇa* falls around 350 B.C.

[30] See, Comparative History of Ideas, (CHI), pp. 237 sq. (Ch. III-(IV).

[31] Comparative Ideas, p. 237 sq.

[32] *Ibid,* p. 239 sq.

[33] *Ibid,* p. 242-44.

[34] *Ibid,* p. 250 sq.

[35] *Ibid,* p. 256-263.

[36] *Ibid,* p. 256 sq.

[37] *Ibid,* p. 264 sq.

[38] *Ibid,* p. 269.

[39] *Ibid,* p. 273 sq.

[40] *Ibid,* p. 276-77 sq.

[41] *Ibid,* pp. 273 sq., 292 sq.

42 *Ibid,* pp. 256-62.

43 See, (CHI), Early Universal Religions Ch. III (IV).

44 *Ibid;* see also, *Buddhism in Comparative Light.*

45 See *Indian Buddhism,* pp. 61-78, 99-129, 235 sq.

46 CHI, p. 245 sq.

47 *Ibid,* loc. cit.

48 *Ibid,* p. 269.

49 *Ibid,* loc. cit.

50 *Anguttara Nikāya* (PTS), IV, 113, *Dīgha Nikāya,* III. 252 (refers to *attaññū*).

51 *Mahāparinibbāna suttanta,* II.26, *Dīgha Nikāya,* Vol. II, p. 101 (P.T.S.).

52 See, CHI, p. 233 sq.

53 *Digha Nikaya,* II, 120 (gatha).

53a *Dhammapada, gatha,* 162, 163.

54 *Ibid,* vs. 161.

55 *Ibid,* vs 164, see CHI, p. 269.

56 CHI, p. 270.

57 CHI see, *Dhammapada,* vs. 1-2.

58 CHI, p. 270.

59 *Vinaya Piṭaka,* I.23; cf. *Visuddhimagga,* para 393 (Harvard ed.).

60 Mahāvaggo, 25 (Nagari Ed. (Nālanda).

61 *Comparative History of Ideas,* (CHI), p. 269.

62 Cf. *Dhammapada,* gāthā, 14, see Cittavaggo.

63 Cf. *Bhagavadgītā,* VI. 34.

64 CHI, p. 272; cf. *Dharmmapada,* vs. 160. *Mādhyamika Kārikā,* XVIII. 5 sq.

65 *Dhammapada,* Gāthā, 160.

66 *Suññamidam attena attaniyena* vā in *Majjima Nikāya,* II.

67 CHI, p. 272.

68 *Bodhicaryāvatāra,* VIII. 88-90 and elsewhere.

69 The Mahāyāna Sūtras also refer to the mahātma-doctrine, on this point, vide our paper *Bauddhanaye nairātmyasiddhāntah* in Sāraswati *Suṣamā,* XXIV (1968).

70 *Mahāyānasūtrālaṅkāra,* XI. 17.

71 See, *Mādhyamika Kārikā* XIII, 1 sq., 8, XXIV. 18; V. 8 etc.

72 *Mahayanasutralankara,* IX. 26ed: *Buddhāḥ śuddhātmalābhitvādgatā ātmamahātmatām.*

73 Dhammapada, VS. 277.

74 *Samyutta Nikāya* (Nalanda Ed.), IV. 360-2. *Dhammapada,* VS. 190-92.

75 *Indian Buddhism,* p. 63 sq.

76 CHI, pp. 258-59.

77 *Indian Buddhism,* p. 65.

78 *Ibid,* p. 2.

79 *Ibid,* loc. cit.

23

Professor Hajime Nakamura's Observations on 'Jiriki' and 'Tariki'

A Corroborative Study

Kala Acharya

Introduction

Professor Hajime Nakamura in his work *'A comparative History of Ideas'* speaks of two types of religious thought and practice, the one characterized by self-reliance or self-power (jiriki in Japanese), the other marked by dependence on grace or other-power (tariki in Japanese). He further says, "The former is a way of "Self-saving", whereas the latter resorts to "Saving of another." In each tradition, these two concepts are discernible, and it is misleading to identify any one religion with one type only".[1]

Nakamura mentions the maxim, "Work out your salvation" and says that the Southern or so-called Hīnayāna (Theravāda) Buddhism encourages self-reliance or self power. He further observes that the Mahayana form came, in course of time, to embrace a number of different schools and sects along with the new scriptures and new interpretations of the Buddhist faith in the schools or sects of the Buddhist pure Land tradition. A remarkable development was the appearance of the type of religion, which emphasized dependence on other-power comparable with the Christian religion of grace![2]

In this paper we shall deal with observations of Nakamura on jiriki and tariki, law of karma versus faith and shall comment on the impact of these practices on Hinduism. The law of karma implies that every act good or evil produces a certain result and the doer of the act has to reap the fruit of the same except in the case of expiation for an evil act or realization of the Absolute Reality. Regarding tariki and its challenge to the law of karma Nakamura says, "The followers of the Pure Realm sects of Buddhism seek Buddhahood (i.e., enlightenment) through rebirth in Amitābha Buddha's Pure Land of the Supreme Happiness. Rebirth in the Pure Realm is attained through faith in the power of Amitābha's vows to save all beings... Since he did become the Buddha Amitabha, these vows are believed to be a power which can save human beings regardless of the law of Karma." [3]

Doctrine of Karma in Hinduism

In the Ṛgveda the word karma has occurred many times where it means exploits or religious acts such as sacrifices or gifts.

In the Brāhmaṇa literature karma, that is, an action is associated with a reward. Even immortality is linked with good action. "He who is to become immortal through knowledge and through sacred works (Karma) shall become immortal after being separated from the body".[4]

The Bṛhadāraṇyaka Upaniṣad refers to action of man and its consequences, "So truly according as he works and according as he behaves so will he be; a man of good deeds will become (be born) good, a man of evil deeds will become (be born) evil; he becomes holy by holy deeds, evil by evil deed".[5] In short one's own desire transforms into will and the will into action.

Similar is the purport of a dialogue between Yājñavalkya and Ārtabhāga in the Bṛhadāraṇyaka Upaniṣad, which confirms that a man becomes good by good works and evil by evil works.[6]

The living beings are controlled by God, that is, antaryāmin and receive the fruits of their actions through God based on their conduct.[7] The Āpastamba Dharma Sūtra says that by doing their duties the members of all *varṇas* reap happiness. Those who are engaged in evil acts reap the fruit of their actions in the hell.[8]

The law of karma can be called as jiriki, which came in conflict with the doctrine of devotion, that is, bhakti, which says that one can be liberated by Grace of Lord instantaneously irrespective of his evil actions. Thus the law of karma, which was once considered as inexorable was later on challenged by the cult of devotion in both the religions, Buddhism as well as Hinduism as the devotion had a potential of mass appeal.

The impact of devotion on karma can be seen clearly in the following instances. In the Bhagavadgītā, Lord Kṛṣṇa assures Arjuna that by offering everything to Lord, a devotee becomes free from the bondage of karma and even from the cycle of birth and death. He says, "Whatever you do, whatever you eat, whatever you offer in sacrifice, whatever you give away, whatever austerity you practice, O Kaunteya, do it as an offering to me. Thus shall you be free from the bondage of actions yielding good or bad results. With the mind firmly set in the Yoga and renunciation, being liberated, you shall come to me."[9]

Thus, in the Bhagavadgītā, the total surrender to Lord overrules the law of action, that is, karma.

Doctrine of Grace and Compassion

While elucidating the significance of the doctrine of grace and compassion in tariki, Nakamura states, "The compassion of the Buddha, like the ideal Christian, was to be offered to everyone equally. In the Lotus Sūtra Buddha's compassion is compared with rain: "All those grasses, shrubs, and trees are vivified by the cloud that both refreshes the thirsty earth and waters the herbs. In the same way... I preach with ever the same voice, constantly taking enlightenment as my text. For this is equal for all; no partiality is in it, neither hatred nor affection." And again, "I recreate the whole world like a cloud shedding its water without distinction; I have the same feeling for respectable people as for the low."[10]

This concept of the benefactor with equal attitude to all is found in the commentary on Brahmasūtra by Śankarācārya. The Sūtra says, 'No partiality and cruelty (can be charged against God) because of (His) taking other factors into consideration… Śankarācārya comments, "Just as rainfall is a common cause for the growth of paddy, barley, etc., the special reasons for the differences of paddy, barley, etc., being the individual potentiality of the respective seeds, similarly God is the common cause for the birth of gods, men, and others, while the individual fruits of works associated with the individual creatures are the uncommon causes for the creation of the differences among the gods, men, and others. Thus God is not open to the defects of partiality and cruelty, since He takes other factors into consideration."[11]

Nakamura compares this attitude of the Buddha with that in Christianity saying that God was, the ideal of compassion and love in the Christianity of this period, quoting the maxim "God is Love."[12] This can be compared to what Lord Kṛṣṇa has said in the Bhagavadgītā, "I am the same to all beings; to me there is none despicable, none dear. But those who worship me with devotion, they are in me and I also am in them."[13]

Lord Kṛṣṇa, over and again gives solace to the lowly by saying that he cares for them. He says, "Even if a man of the most sinful conduct worships Me with undeviating devotion, he must be reckoned as righteous, for he has rightly resolved."[14]

This statement of Kṛṣṇa is the forerunner of Honen's statement, "Even a bad man will be received in Buddha's land, but how much more a good man."

Lord Kṛṣṇa also assures that his devotee never perishes.[15] He also confirms that even the sinful who take refuge in him attain the supreme.[16]

Bodhisattvas and Tariki

The Mahāyāna tradition speaks of the two kinds of Bodhisattvas, namely, the earthly Bodhisattvas and the transcendental Bodhisattvas. Those who are endowed with compassion, love and altruism and strive towards the attainment of enlightenment are mentioned as the earthly Bodhisattvas, while those who have attained Buddhahood but have not yet entered complete Nirvāṇa are known as transcendental Bodhisattvas. They possess perfect wisdom and are no more bound by *samsāra*. However they appear in various forms to save all sentient-beings. Prominent among the transcendental Bodhisattvas are Avalokiteśvara, Mañjuśrī, Kṣitigarbha, Mahāsthamaprāpta, Samantabhadra and Maitreya.

In his work, *Outlines of Mahayana Buddhism* D.T. Suzuki quotes from '*A treatise on the transcendentality of Bodhicitta*', "Thus the essential nature of all Bodhisattvas is a great essential heart (*Mahā-karuṇā-citta*) and all sentient beings constitute the object of his love. They look on all beings as though victims going to slaughter. With their heart full of compassion, they work for the weal and happiness of all beings. They seek no delight in pursuing their own salvation while their brothers and sisters are steeped in misery. Instead they prefer to be the Saviour".

In the Mahāyāna tradition, two aspects of 'other power' are seen, firstly other power through direct contact and secondly 'Other Power' through indirect contact. The earthly Bodhisattvas exemplify the manifestation of 'other power' through direct contact while the transcendental Bodhisattvas exemplify 'Other Power' through indirect contact.

Lord Kṛṣṇa and Tariki

The doctrine of tariki, 'other power' or grace contemporarily, developed in India and it made its distinct appearance in the Bhakti cult or the cult of devotion. The inhabitants of Vraja, the place where Kṛṣṇa was brought up had a direct contact with the 'other power', that is, Kṛṣṇa whom they called variously as 'our child', 'our friend' and 'our lover' with utmost intimacy, depending on their relationship with him. They attained Him, the Lord, through their love and crossed the cycle of birth and death. In this context the Bhāgavata Purāṇa says, "By feeling (of love) alone, the Gopis and even unintelligent creatures like cows, deer, elephants, serpents, etc, attained to spiritual consummation in Me. They never learnt the Vedas, they never served any teacher; they practiced no austerity; but by association with holiness they attained to Me.[17]"

The statement that they never learnt the Vedas reiterates the superiority of devotion over knowledge in the course of time as the Purāṇas that form a part of Hindu scriptures propagated the doctrine of devotion on a massive scale.

Devotion, jiriki and tariki

Nārada and Śāṇḍilya, the two theoreticians on devotion, define devotion as 'the whole-hearted and supreme love of God' and 'the highest form of ever-continuing attachment to God' respectively.

The Bhāgavata Purāṇa defines devotion as, "When all the energies of the sense, including the organs of knowledge and action, which are usually engaged in knowing external objects and in works sacred and secular become concentrated as a unified mental mode directed to the Supreme Being, spontaneous like an instinct and devoid of any extraneous motives, the resulting state of mind is called Bhakti, that is, devotion. It is superior even to emancipation. Like fire it burns up the soul's sheath of ignorance".[18] The definition indicates the subservience of knowledge and action to devotion. It implies both, jiriki and tariki; the effort of withdrawal of senses and concentration form the part of the former while surrender to God forms the part of the latter. Another example of jiriki and tariki together is found in the Bhagavadgītā. It says, "An aspirant who fixes his mind on Lord, who is devoted to Him, who bows down to Him, becomes one with Him."[19]

Tariki and Chanting the name of the Benefactor

The tariki is implicit in the aspirant's firm and devout belief in the existence of the Land of Ultimate Bliss and belief in Amitābha Buddha's power of protection. The efficacy of bestowing reward exists in uttering the name of the benefactor and in remembering him. The practice in the Pure Land School consists of chanting of the name of God. The practice in the Pure Land School consists of chanting of the name of Amitābha (*Nembutsu*), visualizing him and his paradise. The Sanskrit formula 'namo *Amitābuddhāya*' is rendered in the Japanese as *'namu-amida-butsu'*. It means Adoration to Buddha of Infinite Light or Salutations to Amitā-buddha.

It has been said that he who constantly contemplates on Amitābha; he who turns his thought to enlightenment, and he who devoutly prays to be born in 'Sukhāvatī', to him Amitābha appears in the hours of death and the devotee beholds the light again in the Land of Bliss. Those who think of Amitābha with a single thought are born in the Pure Land of Amitābha, where there is no darkness, and Amitābha is continuously extolled.

Nakamura mentions Five True practices prescribed by Shan-tao a new method of Pure Land worship namely (1) chanting (2) contemplation (3) worship (4) reciting the name, and (5) praise and offering. Shan Tao counseled, "Exclusively repeat the Name of Amjda with a single-hearted devotion, whether walking, standing, sitting, or lying down, without question of the length of time, never ceasing for even one moment. This is the truly determined practice, which unfailingly results in deliverance for it is in accord with the Original Vow of Buddha."[20]

Hinduism attaches great importance to recitation of the name of Lord. The Purāṇas speak highly about the importance of the name. Miracles are associated with recitation of the name. Prahlāda, the devotee of Lord Viṣnu was thrown into fire at the behest of his father, the demon king who was full of hatred for Viṣnu. Prahlāda chanted the name of Lord that turned out to be the saviour. The legendary sinner Ajāmiḷa who was saved by emotionally calling his son Nārāyaṇa at the time of his death, though he did not want to utter the name of Lord Nārāyaṇa, best illustrates the importance of uttering the name of the Lord. It is relevant here to note the statement of the Bhāgavata Purāṇa, "Unknowingly or knowingly the chanting of the Supreme, praiseworthy Name burns away man's sin, even as fire reduces fuel to ashes."[21]

It is the name of Lord that can offer protection to the people. Saint poet Tulasidāsa says that the name of Lord is more powerful than the Lord Himself. He compares the name of Rāma with a lamp of precious stone and advises to put it on the tongue so that it may lighten both the inner and the outer body.

Gītā also says that repetition of name of God is the best form of Lord Himself.[22]

The superiority of repeating the name of God over performance of the sacrifice and other practices is explained by Śankarācārya in his commentary on the Thousand Names of Viṣṇu, that is, Viṣṇusahasranāma. He says, "What is the ground of superiority of this adoration in the form of the hymn? Its superiority over other kinds of sacrifices consists in the following points in its favor: It does not involve injury to a being in the form of sacrifice; of non-violence. For doing it, you need no collection of men, money or material, nor need you observe any particular time, place or procedure."

One can cast off this sheath of sin by uttering the Lord's Name even as one walks, stands, bends down, rests, eats or drinks. Uttering Lord's name is the expiation of all expiations. It is the thought of the Lord with His Name. The singing of His Name reduces all sins, even as fire all dross. In Kali age Name alone is the means of God realization; there is no other path.

That the devotee of Amitābha is reborn in Sukhāvatī has a parallel in Hinduism. According to the Bhāgavata Purāṇa the devotee who worships God intently and after death assumes a non material form of *śuddha sattva* (non material Pure Stuff) also known as Bhagavati Tanu and serves the Lord in the Region of Light and Bliss called as Vaikuṇṭha and becomes participant in Lord's sport.

Before the rise of Purāṇas in Hinduism the life after death was either inhabitation in the heaven or hell for a specific period or liberation, depending on the karma of an individual. As the Purāṇas were influenced by the Mahāyāna tradition we find that they are replete with references to the abodes of deities (*lokas*) where the individual enjoys the everlasting bliss. Thus the interaction between religions gave prominence to Compassion, Love and Bliss as pivot of religion, which resulted into considerable change in the religious outlook and practices. This change has introduced a new portal in the realm of Hinduism.

References

[1] Hajime Nakamura, A Comparative History of Ideas, Features of Medieval Thought, p. 370.

[2] Hajime Nakamura, A Comparative History of Ideas, Features of Medieval Thought, p. 371.

[3] Hajime Nakamura, A Comparative History of Ideas, Features of Medieval Thought, p. 385.

[4] Śatapatha Brāhmaṇa X. 4.4.9.

[5] Bṛhadāraṇyaka Upaniṣad IV. 4.5-7.

[6] Bṛhadāraṇyaka Upaniṣad III.3.13.

[7] Bṛhadāraṇyaka Upaniṣad 7.23 cf Kaushitaki Upanishad. III. 8.

[8] Āpastamba Dharma Sūtra II. 1.2.2-3, 5-6,cf Gautama Dharma Sutra. XI.29.

[9] Bhagavadgītā IX.27-28.

[10] Hajime Nakamura, A Comparative History of Ideas, p. 375.

[11] Śankarācārya's Commentary on Brahmasūtra II.i.34.

[12] Hajime Nakamura, A Comparative History of Ideas, p. 375.

[13] Bhagavadgītā IX.29.

[14] Bhagavadgītā IX 30.

[15] Bhagavadgītā IX 31.

[16] Bhagavadgītā IX 32.

[17] Bhāgavata Purāṇa XI.12.7-8.

[18] Bhāgavata Purāṇa III.25.32-33.

[19] Bhagavadgītā IX 34.

[20] Hajime Nakamura, A Comparative History of Ideas, p. 389.

[21] Bhāgavata Purāṇa VI. 2. 18.

[22] Bhagavadgītā X.25.

24

Professor Hajime Nakamura's Contribution to Sanskrit Studies

Shashiprabha Kumar

Professor Hajime Nakamura was a world-renowned philosopher, an able interpreter of Indian thought in general, Buddhism and Vedānta in particular, an ardent lover of Sanskrit language and a great exponent of its philosophical content. His contribution to Indic Studies is enormous.

The comprehensive canvas of Nakamura's writings is a clear indication of his commitment, competence and consistency to expound the richness of Indian thought for the academicians across the globe. It is also an evidence to prove the inmost bond between Indo-Japan intellectual quest, which is basically founded on Buddhism but goes farther and covers almost all aspects of Indian philosophy and culture such as: Veda, Upaniṣads, Vedānta, Sāṁkhya, Nyāya-Vaiśeṣika, Jainism and also Comparative Philosophy.

The wide range of his vision is easy to be grasped by just having a cursory glance at the titles of writings by Nakamura. The comparative history of ideas, parallels within the currents of Eastern thought and inter-cultural study of East-West concepts are the significant inherent threads discernible by a careful, critical reader. Of course, the length and breadth of his scholarship is amazing but the depth of his understanding is even more astonishing. This clearly evinces the underlying fact that such a genuine grasp could not have been facilitated without a mastery of the medium in which the original sources are written.

It is with this intention that the present paper is being written but just as a brief, sketchy outline of Nakamura's tremendously significant contribution to Sanskrit Studies. His versatile genius in Japanese, Tibetan, Chinese and English languages gets manifested in most of his writings. But his curiosity for learning and command over Sanskrit language and its usage is exhibited only through a very small book entitled *A Companion to Contemporary Sanskrit.*[1] In this introductory work, Nakamura has exhibited both his sincere interest as well as analytical ability to comprehend and convey the present status of Sanskrit as a living language in contemporary India.

It goes without saying that anybody who intends to do a serious study of Indian philosophy, culture or history—cannot do so without acquainting himself to the Sanskrit language. It is not without reason then that the cultural and political invaders of India have tried to suppress and stop this inherent source of continuity of Indian culture, but the fact remains that Sanskrit is still a living language today as it had ever been. To quote Nakamura himself:

"Sanskrit is not a dead language, but a living language and since the independence of India it has gained ground in that country. There is a strong movement to make Sanskrit the national language of India and Sanskrit education compulsory, although it has not yet been approved by others."[2]

The desire to learn Sanskrit from indigenous sources brought Nakamura in close contacts with some of the Sanskrit *pandits* and scholars in India although he had learned the classical language at home with the aid of Western works. Whenever he interacted with the *pandits* and Sanskrit scholars in India, he conversed with them in Sanskrit and while doing so, keenly observed and noticed that there are some discrepancies between this living Sanskrit and its explanation in Western works.

This brings us to the point of his intellectual integrity and approaching the most direct and immediate source for learning a language. The points that Nakamura has raised in this small book are based on his vast exposure to the Classical Sanskrit language and its content as also to the Contemporary Sanskrit and its spoken variations. To the best of my knowledge, no scholar, Eastern or Western, has attempted at describing and analysing the Contemporary Sanskrit language as Nakamura has done in this small book. To quote Prof. Satyakam Verma:

"And it is gratifying that Prof. Hajime Nakamura has taken this task in his capable hands. The present study is but a part of his wider study, which might be published in near future. Herein Prof. Nakamura has tried to point out towards the changes setting in the 'Contemporary Sanskrit'. His attempt must be taken as a pointer towards a much-needed thorough study in this connection."[3]

Evidently, Nakamura has done a pioneering job in this regard and has set the tone for further research in this field.

He has discussed briefly the following points regarding Contemporary Sanskrit:

1. Social Background

(i) In pre-independence India, only males learnt Sanskrit but in present situation girls also have started learning Sanskrit.[4]

(ii) In the ancient Indian society, Sanskrit was limited to the Brāhmins, but now-a-days there is no such restriction and non-Brāhmins are also learning it.

2. Ways of Sanskrit Education being practised

(i) As an optional subject at the primary level public schools.

(ii) As a subject in Christian missionary schools.

(iii) As a compulsory subject at private schools, like Bhāratīya Vidyā Bhavan.

3. Three Language Formula and the Present State

Sanskrit has been retained as a voluntary subject in the curriculum after the Kothari Commission report. In the words of Nakamura himself.

"There prevails a great enthusiasm to bring up the Sanskrit Education------The Akhila Bhāratiya Saṁskrita Sāhitya Sammelana commemorated its Golden Jubilee in New Delhi in October 1966 on which occasion the entire building of the Vigyan Bhavan was filled with the audience who could follow speeches in Sanskrit. This meeting was more popular than a UNESCO meeting held at the same place.

-------The knowledge of Sanskrit is gradually permeating to the people"[5]

4. Contemporary Features of Spoken Sanskrit

(i) *Difference in pronunciation:* Variation in pronunciation of Sanskrit is prevalent among various parts of India–but Nakamura says that the most genuine and clearly comprehensible form is preserved among the Brāhmins of Madras region and in the Western part of India.

(ii) *Sandhi:* In writting and printing of Sanskrit, *sandhi* is practiced but while speaking it is often avoided.

(iii) *Punctuation Marks:* The question mark, the exclamation mark and even the mark of brackets were not there in the Classical Sanskrit and have most probably been adopted from the modern Western languages in the view of Nakamura.

(iv) *The Gender:* There is a practice of using either of the genders–neutral or feminine in some cases of writing and verbalising, e.g. *Navadillī nagaram* or *Navadillī nagarī*.

(v) *The Pronoun:* The pronouns which were used to address various types of persons are also changed in Sanskrit being spoken currently.

(vi) *The Tense:* In Contemporary Sanskrit, the present perfect is expressed with a perfect passive participle.

(vii) *The Adverb:* According to Nakamura, in Contemporary Sanskrit, use of adjectives as adverbs is seen to be avoided while in ancient Sanskrit, it was much in vogue.

(viii) *Word-Order:* It is usually held that there is no fixed word-order in Sanskrit sentences, but there is a conventional preferability which is observed for word-order as recommended by the *pandits*, such as follows:

Subject ➔ Object ➔ Verb

The word-order, in which the predicate comes first and the subject comes later (e.g. *nityaḥ śabdaḥ*) is not observed in Contemporary Sanskrit.

Further, Prof. Nakamura points to a visible change in Contemporary Sanskrit regarding honorifics which were traditionally used in plural number, (*ādarārthe bahuvacanam*) but currently there is a tendency to use these words in a singular form, possibly due to the present day rationalistic way of thinking.

(ix) *Negation:* Nakamura has noted another change regarding the negative particle in ancient Sanskrit and Contemporary Sanskrit. According to him only a single word *'na'* was used in ancient philosophical treatises, while now-a-days it is *'nahi'* which may have been influenced by the Hindi word *'nahin'*. In classical Sanskrit *'nahi'* was used always at the beginning of long sentences.

(x) *Questions and Answers:* In classical Sanskrit questions would mostly begin with the word, *'api'* while in contemporary Sanskrit they are usually expressed with *'kim'*.

As far as the question of validity and continuity of the above features is concerned, it is a matter of further research but there is no denying the fact that Nakamura has suggested an area which has not yet been explored in the course of Sanskrit Studies.

Moreover, Nakamura has observed certain additional points in Contemporary Sanskrit which are explained by him as steps towards simplification of Sanskrit, they are the following:

(a) The use of *sandhi* has been minimized in speaking and writing.

(b) The dual number (*dvivacana*) which is a special feature of Sanskrit, is also disappearing from contemporary spoken Sanskrit.

(c) Various verbs are being expressed in the form of a verbal noun with the use of √*bhū* or √*kṛ* e.g. instead of *paṭ hati, paṭhanam/ pātham/karoti.* This results in minimizing the rule of conjugation only with reference to *bhū* or *kṛ*.

(d) Finite verbs are being replaced with past participles.

(e) Past tense is expressed with the indeclinable form of √*as*, i.e. *sma* alongwith the present form of verbs, e.g. *gachati sma*.

It is remarkable to note that Nakamura has not only discerned these features of spoken Sanskrit but has also explained their background in the historical perspective. He has even gone up to the extent of providing information about two writings which may prove valuable material for future studies in this regard namely:

1. *Gīrvāṇapadamañjarī* (C. 1600-1659 A.D.)
   by Varadabhatta or (or Varadarāja)
2. *Gīrvāṇavañmañjarī* (C. 1704 A.D.)
   by Ḍhunḍhirāja

Apart from the above, Nakamura, in his another work entitled *The Ways of Thinking of Eastern Peoples*[6] has outlined a number of features of thought of the Indian people as revealed through language which is also quite significant from the point of view of understanding the cultural phenomena of India from the linguistic perspective. In this analysis, he has also quoted from various Sanskrit texts and has brought out the following points about linguistic expression:

(a) Laying stress on the universals:
    Preponderance of abstract notion

(b) The negative character:
    Attraction to the unknown

(c) Disregard for the individual and the particular

(d) The concept of the Unity of all things

(e) The static quality in thought process

(f) Subjective comprehension of personality

(g) Supremacy of the universal self over the individual self

(h) Subservience to universals

(i) Alienation from the objective, natural world

(j) Introspective, and

(k) Metaphysical character

Obviously, most of the above points are based on and related to Sanskrit language and its uses in Classical as well as Contemporary sources. In fact, language not only manifests knowledge but also expresses the state of awareness in the minds of its speakers. Classical Sanskrit scholars had a strong linguistic awareness and they formulated several structures to represent their spoken language.

No doubt, Classical Sanskrit has been preserved and enriched with utmost care by the scholars writing in Sanskrit. But unfortunately the change and the revision that has taken place in its spoken form has not received the due attention of Sanskrit men of letters. It is perhaps, owing to this reason that the so-called modern academicians have dared label it a 'dead language'. Originality, spontaneity and sacredness of Sanskrit language has been overshadowed by the visibly significant stability in its outer form. But what has been missed during this whole discourse is the one most remarkable feature of Sanskrit language—i.e. its longevity and inherent creativity which have been so characteristically analysed by Nakamura in his brief book under discussion.

It is therefore, in my view, the greatest and the singlemost contribution of Nakamura to Sanskrit Studies that he has given a different direction to it by suggesting an analysis of the contemporary spoken form of Sanskrit, which has not hitherto been done.

On the basis of the above, it may be said that although Nakamura was not a scholar of Sanskrit Literature as such, yet in his basic quest for learning in general and Indian thought in particular, he has expounded an invaluable aspect of Sanskrit and made enormous service to the cause of Sanskrit studies in modern India. Therefore, as an humble student of Sanskrit, I admire his observational capacity, rational analysis as well as emotional attachment for Sanskrit.

To conclude, I would like to quote from a European Sanskritist, P.S. Filliozat who has also written a beautiful book on Sanskrit, entitled *The Sanskrit Language: An Overview.* In his words:

"A language lives by the will of the people who use it. The traditional Pandits of today are of course small in number, but they are present everywhere. Their circle continues to widen through the spirit of innovation of the milieus who claim a modern Indianness. Sanskrit is their instrument, for this language has shown itself capable of preserving itself, always adapting itself, always enriching itself."[7]

References

1 Published for the Eastern Institute, Tokyo by Motilal Banarsidas, Delhi: 1973. (74 Pages)

2 Hajime Nakamura, in his Preface to *A Companion to Contemporary Sanskrit,* p. iii.

3 *Sanskrit: A Living Tradition,* Introductory to the above, p. 1.

4 In fact, now-a-days, a greater number of girls are studying Sanskrit as compared to males.

5 *A Companion to Contemporary Sanskrit,* p. 12.

6 *The Ways of Thinking of Eastern Peoples,* Compiled by Japanese National Commission for UNESCO, Published by Greenwood Press, New York: 1960, pp. 13-159.

7 P.S. Filliozat, *The Sanskrit Language: An Overview,* (Translated from the French by T.K. Gopalan), Indica Books, Varanasi: 2000, p. 133.

25

Professor Hajime Nakamura's Concept of Asian Mind and its Essential Features

Asha Mukherjee

The dichotomies between East and West are often emphasized and mutually opposed cultural sets of values are labeled as "oriental" and "occidental". The first being characteristic of spiritual, introverted, synthetic and subjective while the second as materialistic, extroverted, analytic and objective. The question arises is it really true that there are such dichotomies? Nakamura's main concern in his book *Ways of Thinking of Eastern Peoples* is to look for answer to such questions.

The method he adopts for answering this question is to examine the claims normally made by various thinkers and then examine the Eastern peoples' way of thinking and to look for some, if there is any, peculiarities to these people, which may be characterized as "Eastern". It is well known that Asia includes several cultural areas. But the term "the East" is used as if it referred to single cultural unit which is common to all Eastern countries. This is rather unfortunate according to Nakamura. Nakamura looks for the existential basis or empirical factors, which determine or explain the characteristics of people's way of thinking.

First he examines the prime factors for the similarities and differences between the different ways of thinking that are primarily classified into five categories. He then rejects them as the sole criterion for determining the people's way of thinking.

Now, let us briefly discuss these factors.

Lineage: Can we explain the ways of thinking by referring to the blood or lineage by racial factors of nations? Nakamura argues that there is no intrinsic relationship between physiological or racial lineage and peoples way of thinking. Since Aryan race which was divided into East and West, that is to say, the Europeans and Indians, came to show different features of ways of thinking[1].

Climatic Environment: The physical environment or climatic conditions cannot decide peoples way of thinking as the same climatic environment changes its ways of thinking under influence of the thought of other nations. Rather it may help in keeping cultural products intact. The prime examples are Japan and Ceylon. Tendency of conservatism also has not much to do with climate.

Material Conditions: Can we hold material conditions or economic conditions of the people responsible for determining the way of thinking? Answering this question we are told "*The theory of the materialist view of history or economic view of history* is incapable of explaining in its entirety the fact of the different ways of thinking which vary according to the thought and culture of people."[2] This cannot be the sole factor. The materialistic view of history or the general economic view of history is dogmatic and monolithic.

Religious Ideology: It is pointed out by Max Weber that a unique religious ideology is the determining factor of the distinctiveness of the social and economic life of every nation. Religion is the most important factor in determining social, economic and ethical norms of a nation. This may be true to some extent but it is only partial truth. Indians with all different religions by this logic would have many different ways of thinking and would consequently reject the idea of "Indian way of thinking".

Language forms: It is often contended that the language, its grammar and syntax, regulate the expression forms of judgement and they do not easily change, they determine and also regulate peoples thinking. Nakamura argues, "This relationship of language to thought is by no means absolute in nature."[3]

He concludes, "There is no such thing as a single fundamental principle which determines the characteristic ways of thinking of people." Various factors related in many different ways, each influencing the other, enter into the ways of thinking of a people.

Further, Nakamura discusses in detail the various characterizations of the Ways of Thinking of East Asian Peoples.

First it is generally said and argued by Hegel, that in the East man's individual existence is not fully realized, and the individual is subordinated to the universal. Single Substance alone is true and an individual has no value in itself. While in West, for example in Christianity, the 'subject' is aware of its freedom. Nakamura argues that even in the West in the Middle Ages there was subordination for self. And to say that people of the East are *intuitive* while the West *logical* and *systematic* does not have much ground in case of India as the arguments presented in *Abhidharma* literature are logical and can never be called *intuitive*.

Secondly, Eastern peoples' way of thinking is *synthetic* and of Westerners' *analytic*. In case of China, it gives the impression that it is synthetic but this may be true before the stage of analysis in China but at the later stage it may hardly be called as synthetic. In case of India, it is not at all true. The linguistic analysis and grammar in India was most advanced in any sense of the term 'analysis'.

Thirdly, there are some people who maintain that since all major religions of the world originated in Asia, East may be said to be religious, where as, Europe is non-religious. It is true that Indian people are extremely religious but the spiritual attitude of Japanese or the Chinese cannot be termed as religious. In fact one may argue that the Western people are much more religious than the Japanese or the Chinese.

Fourthly, it is often argued that Western civilization is "materialist" while the East Asian civilization is "spiritual".

East is "internal" and "subjective", West is "external" and "objective". Again, these are nothing peculiar to the East. In Indian philosophy there is a tendency to seek transcendent substantial basis for "what is real". In Buddhism especially in Mahāyāna Buddhism, voidness is expounded which is different from nothingness. In fact Chinese and Japanese have been more non-metaphysical than the Westerners.

Fifthly, Westerners are rationalistic and East Asians are irrationalistic. In the past Japanese have shown a distaste for logical way of thinking but if we see in practice we find them much more rational in the sense that they act according to some rules. Chinese are not interested in formal logic but in the utilitarian sense they are rational. Indians are logical as well as rational. Dharmakīrti's Buddhist logic and Vaiśeṣika school of India are sufficient examples of rationality. Therefore we cannot accept that West is rationalistic and East is irrationalistic.

Sixthly, Eastern thought has a tendency toward escapism and it is rather indifferent to social and political actions. The East Asian religions teach man to shun this world but Christianity preaches the importance of practical action in this world. No doubt the religious man of the East were engaged in inner-worldly activities. The inner-worldly actions were started from this worldly action. Moreover in Japan the practices of Zen monasteries are extremely rationalistic and the social work has an important place in Japan.

Lastly, many people think that East Asians are passive. There is evidence that this has been a distinctive feature of Chinese and Indians. But Japanese are highly sensitive to the transition of things. Buddhist impact in Japan has made Japanese dynamic therefore it is impossible to sum up the ways of thinking of the East Asian *in general* as merely 'passive'. It is true that in the West the non-believers were treated harshly but in India a peaceful atmosphere has prevailed. In China, a perfect freedom of faith is preserved, in Japan although the principal of freedom of faith has not been fully realized due to the interference of the state but people in general are receptive. East Asian people by and large share the view that all men are one in essence. The Indians are prone to tolerate the co-existence of philosophical thoughts of various types of metaphysical viewpoints. With all these differences we do not find any "Asiatic" standpoint among Chinese, Japanese and Indians.

From this Nakamura concludes that there is no one *single* fundamental principle that determines the characteristic ways of thinking of people. Various factors discussed above, each contribute to and influence the ways of thinking of people. All these and many others including historical process of the nation building form a complex and determine the ways of thinking of people. He says, "The ways of thinking of a people have the double relation of being conditioned by the products of man's own creation, and, at the same time, of qualifying them in return." [4] Therefore, the paired opposites way of describing a people's way of thinking is too simplistic, as it does not capture the real complex and pluralistic picture of the way of thinking of people. A study of all the people of the East is from the practical point of view almost impossible. Consequently Nakamura only concentrates on India, China, Tibet and Japan. The reason for discussing only these four is that 'among these peoples alone there exist a study of traditional Buddhist logic, which came first from India to the other three areas, and then developed independently in each.' He also believes that by examining these four ways of thinking, in effect would provide a generalized view of the ways of thinking of Eastern people. He accepts that there are some characteristic differences in the ways of thinking of East Asian nations and also that there is a certain logical and human connection among these characteristics. He does not promise to give a total unified picture but a mere description of different traits.

He argues extensively that we find no definite trait, which can be singled out for East and West dichotomy. Still we find some similarities common to all the nations of East Asia but they cannot be regarded as "Eastern". There is no single "Eastern" feature but "there exist diverse ways of thinking in

East Asia, characteristic of certain peoples but not of the whole of East Asia. This can be affirmed by way of comparison among the cultures of the East Asian nations, and by noting the fact that Buddhism was received by various nations of East Asia according to the character of the recipients; this clearly testifies to the cogency of our viewpoint." [5] The cultures of Asia are not the same and they have important differences which are deep rooted in their languages, customs and their manners. Nakamura discusses in detail that the study of way of thinking of a people cannot be limited to their philosophies only but must cover their language-patterns and behaviour-patterns which include cultural phenomena such as songs, mythology and reaction to foreign culture, language etc. Nakamura shows that as far as all people is concerned there is a certain logical and human connection among the characteristics. He presents a detailed analysis describing the cognitive and existential basis for the different ways of thinking in the East considering Buddhism and cultural influences on it. He merely discusses in detail the different traits present in four countries India, China, Tibet and Japan.

A Critical Evaluation:

The greatest merit of Nakamura's work lies in showing that there is not one single "Eastern" culture, as it is often understood. There are very important differences rooted in different languages and behaviour of different Asian countries. Within the East itself there are many differences, their ways of thinking are not limited to their philosophies they must include other empirical issues as well. He explicitly argues that individual philosopher often follows a way that differs from the way of thinking of a people and therefore cannot be truly representative of the people's way of thinking.[6] In philosophies one finds principles and generalizations and one need not go to the real empirical data on the basis of which the generalizations are made. Frankly speaking while describing the differences in cultures Nakamura is also making generalizations within Indian culture and within Chinese culture and within Japanese culture etc. forgetting his own argument, which he had presented against generalizations. Here, I would confine my comments only to his description of Indian Ways of Thinking.

First a few general remarks. While presenting Indian ways of thinking Nakamura tells us that Indians are strongly possessed by the universal, the negative, the unity of things and the subjective and are alienated from the objective. This may be applicable to the traditional Indian culture in comparison to Chinese and Japanese culture but they are not peculiar to India as we find also among Western culture. Thus it does not represent the total thought pattern of Indian people. These characteristics are present but opposite characteristics are also present.

Nakamura, while discussing linguistic pattern of Indians concentrates only on ancient India and there too only on Sanskrit and Pali and ignores almost all other modern living languages, Indian philosophies and religions. In classical Sanskrit also he makes little use of other many important writings of Kālidasa and many others whose writings have great impact on Indian way of living. He confesses in Introduction that it is impossible to exhaust all sources and data.

Now, let us turn to his positive characterizations.

The first characteristic of Indian way of thinking as presented by Nakamura is their "stress on the universal". He says "The tendency of most Indians is to lay stress on the significance of the universal only, and they almost neglect the significance of the individual or the particular." [7] This contention presupposes that Indians are abstract-minded and he does not discuss any other forms of expression. The concepts of "*pakṣa*" and "*vyakti*" also play important role in Indian logic (Nakamura is quite aware of it [8]) and they are not abstract. As used, they are different- one is used for individual and the other for particular. Some abstract ethical forces are always distinguished from concrete persons in Indian way of thinking. It is true that Indians developed a way of thinking that could see the abstract through concrete and concrete through abstract, which is not peculiar to Indians.

This characteristic we find almost everywhere, as they are two sides of a coin.

Secondly it is shown that Indians have a preference for the negative. The three reasons presented are: fondness for negative expressions, grasping the Absolute negatively, and attraction for the unknown. First, the attraction for the unknown could also be interpreted as longing to turn the unknown into known. The negatives such as *ahimsā* (non-injury) *asteya* (non-theft), and *aparigraha* (non-acquisition) are used by Indians in philosophy as well as in practice but it does imply a preference of negatives. If there are no positive contradictories of some words in a language it only proves limitations of a language whether English or Sanskrit and it cannot represent the users way of thinking. For, grasping the Absolute negatively, the examples from Upaniṣads and Buddhism are presented. The puzzle of Being and Non-being is discussed and a reference to *neti, neti* (not this, not this) is made with reference to Absolute which is infinite and transcendent. The words such as *avidyā* (the unconscious, non-knowledge, ignorance) and *akṣara* (imperishable) are often used but these are technical terms and need to be understood with reference to positive terms. The Being is an abstract notion and to grasp it as such is the main concern. It has nothing to do with preference for negative terms and thereby leading to some generalizations about the culture. The role of individual is negated, if universal Self is conceived. The universal Self subordinates the role of finite self. But from this to draw the conclusion that individual is not given any place in Indian thought, would be in my view, too simple. In fact, in all religiously oriented philosophies we find this characteristic and it is neither Eastern nor Western.

Further, Nakamura argues that in Indian way of thinking, real is universal and universal is static and they do not have sense of time. He says that "Indian people, who have not exerted themselves to grasp the concept of time quantitatively, have rarely written historical books with accurate dates and we have indicated that this fact signifies a characteristic feature of Indian culture."[9] He further argues that for this lapse the idea of transition of life, which is transmigration, perpetual wheel of rebirths is responsible and due to these beliefs 'historical descriptions have not been made with much attention to accurate dates in India.'

For the Advaitins and Buddhists Being (*sattā*) or *śūnyatā* is real and it is true universal but they also give examples of ocean and its waves to explain its fluidity which is eternal, rather than its being static and they do not reject the everyday sense of time. Therefore the conclusion Nakamura draws, we find a bit far-fetched. There were fourteen different ways of calculating the time or era in Indian tradition, which were quite scientific. It is also true that Indians did not pay much attention to empirical history writing, but it is not because they did not have a sense of time it was some how not paid much attention. Nakamura in this context makes a distinction between subjective comprehension of personality and objective comprehension of personality, which is not clear at all. He examines the simple subject-predicate form of Sanskrit judgement where predicate as a rule is placed first and Nakamura thinks that it is due to the importance attached to the predicate, quality or attribute. From this he concludes that the "Indians' way of thinking tends to emphasize qualities as subjective rather than as objective relations."[10] I am not sure if this conclusion follows so easily and even if it does, it is contrary to the views of at least some Indian schools such as *Nyāya-Vaiśeṣika* and *Mīmāmsā*.

All the above comments are meant to understand Nakamura's valuable contributions. Nakamura was the first Asian to interpret "Asian" in a detailed manner. Even now, after more than fifty years his work remains the center for future studies.

References

1 *Ways of Thinking of Eastern Peoples*, Hajime Nakamura, East-West Center Press, Honolulu, Hawaii, 1964, p.33.

2 *Ibid.*, p.34.

3 *Ibid.*, p.37.

4 *Ibid.*, p.37.

5 *Ibid.*, p.21.

6 *Ibid.*, p.9.

7 *Ibid.*, p.47.

8 *Ibid.*, p.45.

9 *Ibid.*, p.81.

10 *Ibid.*, p.87.

26

Buddhism in Jaina Literature

Samani Chaitany Pragya

We find that much is written about Jainism in Buddhist literature as compared to Buddhism in Jaina literature. Whatever is written helps us to know the basic difference of the two systems. Most of the ideas of Buddhism available in the Jaina literature are based on the differences regarding the fundamental theories of both the systems, such as, the concept of *śiva, mukti, karma, punarjanama, ahimsā* and the real existence of the physical world etc.

No doubt we find a great similarity between Buddhism and Jainism regarding the theories postulated by both the systems. It is so because Lord Mahavira and Lord Buddha, the two spiritual personalities of India were contemporary. Both of them were related to one and the same culture i.e. Śramaṇic. Both opposed distortions in the Vedic tradition and launched a campaign against the existing conditions and situations and, thereby gave new forms to Indian religion. Both did not accept the supremacy of God as the doer or the agent or the creator. On the contrary, both believed that man himself is potentially a divine being.

Moreover, Jainism and Buddhism both have not accepted the system of priest's intervention in the domain of religion. So far as spirituality is concerned, they gave equal rights and consideration to both man and woman. Mahavira had been a pioneer in all these fields.

We also find striking similarity in the preachings of Mahavira and Buddha. The similarity has been worked out by the scholars like Muni Nagarajji, Shreechanda Ramapuriya and Mahendranatha Singha in their books *'Agama aura Tripitaka'*, *'Anguttar Nikaya'* and *'Bauddha tatha Jaina Dharma'* respectively.

Apart from the similarities we find some differences also regarding the same theories as indicated before. This is why the philosophies propounded by Mahavira and Buddha are distinguished as two different schools of thought in the world of philosophy. This has been pointed out by Dalsukha D. Malvania in his book 'Jainism: Some Essays'[1]. The purpose of this paper is to identify mainly the differences which are philosophical and mentioned in the Jaina literature. They are as follows:

The Concept of *Ātman*

Generally Buddhists are known as *Anātmavādin* i.e. ones who do not believe in soul. But according to the Jaina canons Ācārāṇga and Sūtrakṛtānga, the Buddhists are categorized as *kriyāvādins* i.e. ones who believe in the action of soul.[2] According to the canons, the Buddhists accept the existence of soul but differently. The points of difference are as follows:

First, in the Buddhist philosophy there is no concept of eternal soul as such. According to it, the fundamental realities are five viz; *rūpa, Vedanā, Samjñā, Samskāra* and *Vijñāna.*[3] All are transitory. Soul is nothing but the continuous flow of *Vijñāna* (consciousness). The Buddhists firmly believe that whatever is flux is only real. It is so because the past is passed forever and the future never exists. Permanence is mere an illusion and not reality. Whatever exists in present is real and is always in flow and is instantaneous by nature.

Second, according to the Buddhist theory of *pratītya-samutpāda*, the succeeding moment is neither identical with nor different from its preceding moment. The same applies to soul. Soul is neither identical with nor different from body or five *skandhas*.[4] Though some of the philosophers of the time of Buddha believed that soul is different from body, while some others had the view that soul and body are one, but Buddha did not accept both the views. According to him, neither the view 'Body is soul' is acceptable nor the view 'Soul and body are different' is acceptable.[5]

The intention of Buddha was that if soul is destroyed with the destruction of body then it would give rise to *Ucchedavāda* i.e. the theory of total destruction. Contrary to it, if soul does not get destroyed with the destruction of body then soul would assume the state of *nirvāṇa*. In other words, it would give rise to *Śāśvatavāda* i.e. the theory of permanence. Both the theories are not acceptable. This is the reason why soul is neither identical with nor different from the five *skandhas*.[6]

Third, according to the theory of *pratītya-samutpāda*, being neither identical nor different from its preceding moment, the present moment is neither having cause nor without cause. This is the reason why Sūtrakṛtānga refers that in the Buddhist view soul is neither having cause nor without cause.[7] In this reference the writer of *Curṇī* differs from the author of the text. Accordingly, the Buddhists who believe in skandhas accept soul as caused, while Śunyavādin Buddhists accept soul without any cause.[8] According to Acharya Mahapragya, the explanation given by the writer of *Curṇī* is based on the later traditions.[9] On the basis of Jaina canons and Tripiṭaka, the Buddhist canons, it appears that Buddha rejected both the views. Out of the rejection of the two views the theory of *pratītya-samutpāda* came into being. The reasons behind the theory as indicated before are as follows:

If soul and material world are accepted with cause then it gives rise to the theory of *Śāśvata* i.e. permanence.

To accept that there is no cause of the suffering and purity of the living being gives rise to the theory of *uccheda* i.e. impermanence.

To accept that Nature, atoms and time etc. regulate the world gives rise to Viṣamavāda i.e. the theory of anamolous causation.

To accept that the whole world is regulated by *Puruṣa* or *Prajāpati* gives rise to the theory of Vaṣavarti i.e. controller of the world.

So far as the theory of *pratītya-samutpāda* is concerned, according to the Buddhists, there is no room for all these theories in it.[10]

Praśana vyākaraṇa, one of the Jaina canons, also mentions that Śunyavādins do not accept the physical world. They also deny the existence of soul separate from five skandhas.[11]

Forth, the Buddhists do not give importance to the idea of the arrival and departure of soul.[12] They believe that it increases the inflow of the karma instead of decreasing it.

Tne Concept of *ahimśā*

Jainism and Buddhism believe in non-violence as a supreme value and lay emphasis on self-control (*sanyama*) towards every living being. Non-violence is, in fact, the higher development of human consciousness. According to the Jaina thinkers, it is in the centre of all other values.[13] All other values, whether they are social, moral religious or spiritual, spring out of it. It is the value which can preserve all the beings, right from one-sensed to five-sensed.[14] Global peace and harmony is possible only through it. This is the reason why Mahavira proclaimed that non-violence is the only eternal, everlasting and perennial religion.[15] Though Buddhism believes in non-violence right from its origin yet, non-violence has not been followed so strictly in Buddhism as in Jainism.

In the chapters first and eight of Ācāraṇga, Mahavira mentions the Buddhist view saying that there are some monks who harm the water-bodied beings in the name of drinking and bathing[16]. The text does not mention any particular sect doing so but the commentators clarify that the monks were the Buddhists.[17] The reason behind such violence is not to believe in the life of water.[18] Buddhism does not believe that water in itself possesses life. As Milindapañha clearly states:

'Neither water is living nor there is life in water.'[19]

Secondly, it has also been the firm belief of the Buddhists that attachment is the main cause of violence and not action. If there is no attachment behind any action, it is not harmful. The verse referred to in the Sūtrakṛtāṇga and the story given in Samyut-Nikāya are clear evidences of this fact.[20]

The verse clearly states that in critical situation if somebody kills his own son and eats flesh, he does not commit any mistake. The explanation of the verse is given keeping in view the story referred to in Samyuta-Nikāya. The story was told by Buddha himself in order to make the monks in front of him understand the purpose of taking food. This story also implies that in the critical circumstances one can commit even violence and yet he does not get any bondage.

The interpretation of the story given by the writer of *Cūrṇī* on is somewhat different from that of the writer of Vṛitti. According to the former, the person who kills son commits violence, while the monk to whom meat of the son is offered, does not commit violence.[21] According to the latter, both do not commit any violence.[22] In this regards, if we see the Buddhist view found in Jñātādharmakathā, another Jaina canon, it also supports eating of the flesh of son in critical situation but the thing worthy to note there is that the son should be naturally dead and not killed by anybody.[23]

According to the writer of '*Jaina Sahitya Ka Itihasa*',[24] the explanation of the verse found in Sūtrakṛtāṇga is given differently keeping in view the story referred to in Buddhacaryā. According to the story, instead of the father it was Buddha himself who ate the meat of a pig and therefore there should be the word '*potti*' in the place of the word '*Putta*' in the verse, which is the synonym of pig in place of the word 'putta: And the word '*mehavi*' in the verse stands for Buddha himself.

The thing worthy to note here is that the purpose of the story might be different, but as time passed the main purpose of it is forgotten and Buddhist devotees and even the Buddhist monks started eating meat referring to the story as evidence.[25]

To understand the Buddhist idea of non-violence in a better way the second chapter of Sūtrakṛtāṇga is important. It mentions the cause of activity technically known as '*kriyāsthāna*'.[26] The activity is twofold: benevolent and malevolent. The criterion of Jainas behind the activities is: what causes violence is malevolent, while the other is benevolent. So far as the criterion of the Buddhist philosophy is concerned, it defines any activity violent in the following conditions if all of them take place simultaneously:[27]

The killed should be a living being (*sattva*).

The feeling that 'it is a living being' should be clear in the mind of the killer.

The thought of violence should be in the mind of a killer.

Ultimately, the being should be killed.

In regard of the conditions mentioned above, the Jaina theory of '*akasmāt daṇḍa*' i.e. violence without any intention[28] and such other theories are not categorized under the violent activities according to the Buddhists.[29]

The Theory of Karma

The theory of karma plays important role in the philosophies of Mahavira and Buddha. They have accepted it as an important factor to determine the present and future conditions of the living beings. They have also rejected the intervention of supreme power to make the living beings realize the result of their own karmas. Though the form of the theory of karma found in Jainism and Buddhism seems almost the same but diving deep into the theories of both the systems we find some basic differences in them.

First, the Buddhists believe that in critical condition one does not get any bondage inspite of killing someone.[30] As it has already been made clear that according to Buddhism in certain conditions if some one kills his own son and eats his flesh, he does not commit any sin and therefore in result he does not get any bondage. According to the writer of *Cūrṇi* the layman or devotee accumulates karma but not the monk to whom the flesh is offered. According to the writer of Vṛtti both of them do not get any bondage.[31]

Second, according to the Buddhist theory of karma, it is mind which plays main role in the binding of karma. In the sixth chapter of Sūtrakṛtāṇga named *Ardrakumara,* we find a debate which took place between Ardrakumara and the followers of Buddha. The point of debate was that it is mind which causes violence.[32] If there is something related to sesame (*tila*) or mustard (*saraso*) and somebody destroys it thinking it human being, he commits violence. Contrary to it, if somebody kills any human being thinking him sesame, he commits no violence.[33] Thus, it is mind which causes karmic matter and not action.

The Concept of *punarjanma*

Jainism and Buddhism both believe in the theory of rebirth. But where as the Jaina philosophy considers it necessary to think of the arrival and departure of a soul to understand the theory of rebirth, the Buddhist philosophy totally rejects it. Though the concept of eternal soul is not found in the Buddhist philosophy yet the theory of rebirth has got important position in it. This is the reason why Mahavira says that there are some who do not know where have we come from? Whether we have come from the east or west? Does our soul take birth or not? What were we before and would be after death?[34]

Who were the people referred to here there is no clarification in the text. But according to the commentators of Ācāraṇga, the Lord was talking of particularly his contemporary Buddha's theory of *asatkāryavāda* as proved from the third chapter of the very text.[35] Majjhima-Nikāya also endorses this fact by referring to the intention of Buddha himself.[36]

The Theory of Nirvāṇa

The ultimate goal of both the philosophies is absolute release from all kinds of sufferings including the cycle of births and deaths and thereby self-enlightenment and ultimately emancipation.

Answering Ganadhara Prabhasa regarding the existence of Nirvana Mahavira mentioned the conception of Nirvana of Buddhists.[37] He said that Buddhists accept Nirvana like extinction of a lamp. After extinction lamp exists nowhere so does the soul after liberation. In this context, Mahavira said that to think that lamp extincts and exists nowhere is not true. In fact, the fire of a lamp does not extinct but changes into darkness, as milk changes into curd. The same applies to the state of Nirvana in which soul does not get destroyed but attains blissful state.[38] This is the reason why Nirvana is defined as the complete freedom from suffering.

According to Sūtrakṛtāṇga, some monks used to say that one who joins their religious order, gets liberation from all sufferings.[39] The verse is spoken keeping in view the philosophers who believe in the existence of five elements, viz. earth, water, fire, air and space and one who believe in the theory of *tajjiva-taccharira* i.e. the soul is the body. According to the author of *vṛtti,* the followers of Sāmkhya philosophy also used to say the same thing about their sect.[40] But according to the writer of the Cūrṇi, the verse indicates towards the Buddhists.[41] The same can be said about the next four verses.[42]

The Conception of the Physical World

So far as the literature of Jainism is concerned, there is no direct reference to the Buddhist view. Viśesā vaśyaka Bhāṣya indirectly refers to some Buddhist conceptions. Here Mahavira rejected the theory of Śūnyavāda and propounded independent existence of the physical elements and thereby that of the physical world.[43] The reasons given by him are as follows:[44]

(I) If there were no existence of the physical elements then there would not be any doubt about their existence like sky-flower. Doubt arises only about the objects which are subjects of any *Pramāṇa*, such as perception, inference etc. and not about those that are not the subjects of any *pramāṇa*.

(II) Secondly, doubt is also a category of knọwledge. Knowledge cannot occur in the absence of an object. If there is nothing then for what the doubt would be? Even in dream one cannot doubt about the non-existing object.

(III) Besides, the problem that would arise about the theory of Śūnyavāda is, there would be no difference between dream and awakening, truth and falsehood, imagination and reality, goal and means, cause and effect, speaker and statement, thesis and anti-thesis, etc.[45]

If Buddhists argue, in this context, that all is relative and therefore, have no independent existence. The answer is, it is not a fact. Child knows things, just after coming out of the womb into the external world, without any relational awareness. It shows that things have independent existence.[46]

In this context, the logic presented by Siddhasena Divakara to prove the existence of attributes of an object is also considerable and remarkable.[47]

Thus, there is some fundamental difference between Buddhism and Jainism. The Buddhist conceptions, which we find in the Jaina canonical literature, are direct evidences to know the basic difference of the views of Mahavira and Buddha.

References

1 p. 126-29.

2 (i) Ayaro; 1/4.

(ii) Suyagado; 1/1/51:

Ahavaram Purakkhayam kiriyavaidarishanam/

Kammachintapanatthanam dukkhakhndhavivaddhanam//

3 (i) *Ibid.*, 1/1/7.

(ii) Digha-Nikaya; 10/3/20–

Panchakkhandho-rupakkhandho, vedanakkhandho, sankharkhandho, vinjanakkhandho.

(iii) Suyagado; 1/1/17.

(iv) Churni; p. 29: na chaiteshvatma ntargatau (bhinau) va vidyate samvedya.

4 Kathavatthupali; 1/1/1,2.

...tam sariram na hevam vattavve–annyamjivan

5 *Ibid.*, Khandhesu bhijjamasesu, so the bhijjati paggalo

Uccheda bhavati ditthi, ya buddhea viva] j ita Puggalo

sassato hoti, nivvanena sama samo hi.

6 Suyagado; 1/1/17–Panch khando vayantege bala

Anno anano nevahu heuyam va aheuyam

7 Churni; 29, p. 10.

Latha skandhamatrika hetumatra miccanti bijankuravat. Ahetukam shunyavadikah

Hetu-pratyaya samagriprithak bhave sh vasambhatvat

tena tenabhilapya hi, bhavaj sarve svabhavatabl

8 Suyagado; Part 1, p. 36.

9 Vishuddimagga, Part 3, p. 1185–

Purimena sassatadinamabhavo paccimena cha padena/

Ucchedividhato dvayana paridipito naya//

10 Prashnavyakarana; 1/4–Vamalogavadi bhananti–natthi jive, no jai iha pare va loe, na ya kinccha vi phusai punnapavam natthi phalam

sukaya dukkayanam....pancha ya khandhe bhananti.

11 Ayaro.

12 ahinsa payasah palibhutani sarvavratani.

13 ahinsasawabhuyakhemankari.

14 Ayaro; esa dhamme dhue neie sasae.

15 *Ibid.*, 1/59 Kappi ne Kappi ne pacum, aduva cibhusae.

16 Acharanga Churni; p. 29.

17 *Ibid.*, p. 29–ihama cha khalu no anagaranam udayam jiva viyahiya.

18 Milindapanha; p. 253-255–na hi Maharaja! udakam jivati, natthi udae jivo.

19 Suyagado 1/155–puttam pita samarambha aharattham asanjae/ bhunjamano vi mehavi! kammuna novalippate//

20 (i) Churni; p. 38.

(ii) Jataka Atthakatha; 246 Telivada Jataka.

21 Churni; p. 28.

22 Vritti; p. 28.

23 Nayadhammakahao; 18/49.

24 Jain Sahitya ka Itihas; Part 1, p. 136.

25 (i) Vishuddhimaggo;

(ii) Shiksha Samucchaya;

26 Suyagado 1/2/

27 Churni; p. 37 : Katham Punrupachiyate? Uccyate, yadi Satvashcha bhavati, sattva sangya ch Sanchintya jivitad vyaparopanam pranatipah.

28 Suyagado;

29 Jain Sahitya.....Part 1, p. 138.

30 Suyagado; 1/1/55.

[31] (i) Churni; p. 28.

(ii) Vritti; p. 28.

[32] Suyagado; 1/1/53-56 32.

[33] *Ibid.*, 2/6/26-28.

[34] Ayaro; 1/1-3.

[35] Acharanga Churni.

[36] Majjhim-Nikaya; 21.

[37] Visheshavashyaka Bhashya; gatha 1972-4.

[38] Saundarananda; 16/28-29.

Dipo yatha nirvirimabhyapeto naivavanim gacchati nantariksham/

Disham na kanchid vidisham na kanchit snehakshayat kevalameti shantim//

Jivastatha nirvirmmabhyupeto nevavanim gacchti nantariksham/

Disham na kanchid vidisham na kanchit kleshakshayat Kevalameti shantim//

[39] Visheshavashyaka; gatha 1987-8, 91, 92.

[40] Suyagado; 1/1/19 agaramavasanta vi amnna 'va vi pawaya/

imama darisanamavanna sawadukkha vimucchanti//

[41] Vritti; p.

[42] Churni; p.

[43] Suyagado; 1/1/20-27.

[44] Vishesha....gatha

[45] *Ibid.*

[46] *Ibid.*

[47] *Ibid.*

Appendix : 1

Chronological Bio-Data of Professor Dr. Hajime Nakamura

1912	Nov. 28	born at Matsue City,
1913		The Nakamura Family moves to Tokyo, the capital
1919	April	entered Seishi Elementary School
1923		
1924		
1925	Feb.	passes the entrance examination for Shihan Teacher Training School attached Junior High School (presently Tsukuba University attached JHS)
	March	graduates from Seishi Elementary School
	April	enters Shihan Teacher Training School attached Junior High School. However, absorbed in the study of philosophy and religion; studied History.
1926	April	in the department of Art and Science
1930	March	finished his junior high school career; passed the entrance examination for Dai ichi High School, Department of Literature

	April	entered Dai ichi High School Deparment of Literature; elected the German language course.studied Logic, Psychology, and History studied German under Bruno Pertzold; attended lectures on Buddhist doctrine; read extensively in Philosophy
1933	March	graduated from Dai ichi High School Department of Literature; received honours from the German Ambassador
	April	entered Takyo Imperial University, Department of Indian Philosophy and Sanskrit studies
1936	March	graduates from Tokyo Imperial University, Department of Indian Philosophy and Sanskrit studies; graduation thesis: *"The Philosophy of Nāgārjuna",* which was a result of his research on the subject. Immediately after graduation, he wrote a book explaining 2 famous old works called [Shutteigogo] and [Okina no bun] written by Chuki Tominaga. Prof. Tetsuro Warsuji wrote the Introduction to the book. Under the title "A Critical View of Modern Japan"
	April	entered graduate school; undertook study and research on the development of Vedantic philosophy under the guidence of Professor Hakuju Utsui
1937	July 18	His father, Kiyoji, passes away at 58.
	July	entered the army and entered an army hospital, begins the writing of his graduate thesis '"The Early History of Vedāntic Philosophy"

1941	March	finished formal graduate studies at Tokyo Imperial University
1943		granted the degree of Ph.D. in Literature, based on his thesis "The Early History of Vedāntic Philosophy" (Later, this work was published in four volumes by Iwanami Publishing Co.)
	April	Tokyo Imperial University appoints him Assistant Professor (holds position until March 1954)
during 1943		participates in reserach on Buddhist technical terms The resulting research is later titled "Compilation of Buddhist terms in Japanese" Works with Kichnosuke Ito on how thought patterns differ according to culture. Both of these projects were to become two of the important areas of his future research efforts.
1947	August	first edition of "Compilation of Buddhist technical terms in Japanese" is published. Feeling dissatisfied, he modifies the compilation. Finally 20 years later it was published even though one manuscript with about 30,000 terms was lost by the publisher.
1949	Nov.	publishing of "Eastern Ways of Thinking" by Misuzu Publishing Co.
1951	Sept. 4	sails from Yokohama to San Francisco to participate for the first time at a conference on Indian and Buddhist philosophy at Stanford University. He attends as visiting professor until the end of the conference in October.

1952 spends busy year travelling: travelled around Europe; lectured at Tubingen, Germany. Then he went to India: first he visited the Bhandarkar Oriental Research Institute in Pune. Then visited the Headquarters of the Ramakrishna Mission. He also met Mahendra Pratap, a leader of the Indian independence movement.

during the year requested to direct Okurayama Educational Institution by Saburo Nakaya, head of Heibonsha Publishing Company.

1954 April re-appointed with promotion to Full Professor at Tokyo University (held position until March 1973)

1955 Feb. 14 Flies to Rangoon, Burma and participates in the "Asian Conference for Intelligentsia"

Feb. 24 goes to Calcutta, then to Dronagiri in Madhya Pradesh to attend a Jain Festival. Then he visited Shantiniketan and Visva Bharti University. He was invited to Ramakrishna Birthday Festival in the surburbs of Calcutta.

Mar. 17 returns to Japan via Bangkok

1956 becomes a member of the "Japanese Indology Buddhist Group"

Nov. 20 attends the Buddha Jayanti in Delhi from Nov. 24-Dec. 5. At the same time, he attends a general meeting of UNESCO. Furthermore, he attended the conference commemorating the 2500 Anniversary of the Birth of the Buddha. Finally he visited the famous Buddhist sites.

1957 May received Japanese Academic Honour Prize for his work "The Early History of Vedāntic Philosophy"

during the year during Nehru's visit to Japan, he strongly proposed Indo-Japanese cultural relations.

1958 Jan. 26 Indo-Japanese Cultural Association was formed through the recommendation of Prof. Otoya Tanaka, and Prof. Hisaya Doi as well as the Ambassador to India, Fujiyo Hayashi. To support this, the Indo-Japanese Cultural Agreement was made between the two countries. This cultural agreement and the activities received the support of the Japanese Government.

Sept. The International Conference on "Religious studies and History" opened at Tokyo Sankei Hall. He participated as a panel member along with Mircea Eliade.

1959 June 20 participated in the "Third East-West Philosophy Conference" at Honolulu from June 22-July 30 as a panel member. (participated in same till the Fifth Conference.) Lectured at Hawaii University on Buddhist philosophy. After that he went to Claremont College in California, returning to Japan on Sept. 2.

1960 Jan. 1 participated in an international conference on Pax Romana, held by the Catholic intelligentsia in Manila.

Jan. 5 at the invitation of the Indian Government, he toured Southern India, visiting the monastery of Sringeri and the Nagarjunakonda.

	May 10	met Paul Tillich at Christology Conference held at Tokyo's International conference Hall.
during the year		*"Ways of Thinking of Eastern Peoples"* was translated into English and published under the auspices of the Japanese branch of UNESCO. (Two years later, Hawaii's East-West Centre also Punlished a somewhat revised edition.).
1961	Feb. 9	went to USA and lectured at Colgate and Yale Universites. Then went to Florida University until June as guest lecturer on Indian and Buddhist Philosophy.
1962	Aug. 13	went to Honolulu and was appointed Senior Scholar of the East-West Centre. There he revised *"Ways of Thinking of Eastern Peoples"* and held a seminar.
1963	Aug. 18	arrived in Colombo on the 20th. He then lectured on Japanese Buddhism at Ceylon University. Then came to Madras and toured South India. He participated in an informal meeing of the Indo-Japanese Cultural Association. From there he went to Europe and to Austria.
	Sept. 11	lectured at Harvard University for one semester.
1964	March	appointed head of the Department of Literature of Tokyo University (held until March 1966)
	July 2	participated in the 4th East-West Centre Conference in Honolulu as Steering Committee member. He also lectured on Indian and Buddhist philosophy at Hawaii University.

during the year received as a memento the actual working copy of *"A Study of Shinto, the Religion of the Japanese Nation"* (Tokyo, 1926) by the author, Genchi Kato. Prof Kato died the following year. Then he contributed this precious volume to Kokugakuin University

1966 April appointed Chairman of Tokyo University Dept. of Literature Cultural Interchange Institution (held until March 1973)

May 2 participated in World Religious Co-existence Conference at Princeton University. Then visited Leiden University in the Netherlands.

May 18 arrives Kathmandu, Nepal, and at the invitation of the Nepalese Government gives a speech at the graduation ceremony of Tribhuvan University.

Sept. 25 participates in a Nehru Symposium organised by UNESCO. Then travels to Bombay and Baroda.

Oct. reeeives academic degrees: Honorary Doctorate *(Darsanavidyapati)* from Visva Bharati University; from the Indian Sanskrit Association he receives Academic Doctorate (*Vidyavacaspati*).

1967 at the request of The International Association for Promotion of Culture he publishes English version of *A History of the Development of Japanese Thought* in 2 volumes, becomes a member of the Austrian Korrenspondierendes Mitglied der Osterreichischen Akademie der Wissenschaften.

1968 Jan. with the financial aid of a friend he begins to re-write the "Dictionary of Buddhist Technical Terms" which was lost. For this purpose, he calls for a research committee. Later, this becomes Eastern Research Institute

Dec. publishing of the annual magazine "Movement of Thought" begins. (now published every year for the last 26 years)

1969 Jan. 23 at the invitation of the Indian Government, he goes to Delhi to participate in "The Gandhi Symposium".

May 26 in Hong Kong, participates in the opening meeting of Institute for Religion and Social Change

1969 July 6 becomes International Committee Member of the "East-West Conference on Philosophy". Lectures at Hawaii University on Buddhist thought. At the same time, he cooperates with Prof. Clifford Miyashiro of the East-West Centre to write "History of Comparative Thought", decides to write Dictonary of Buddhist Terms on his own without The Eastern Research Institute. Finishes in six years.

1970 May 30 participates in a symposium on religion held at Die Theologische Hochschule in West Berlin at the invitation of the school and the Government of West Berlin. Then he visited Hamburg University as well as Utrecht University.

Nov. 12 the group Eastern Research Institute changes into a formal legal body. Purpose of the group is to research oriental thought and make the results available to all. He became the Chairman of this body.

1971 June 20 at the East-West Centre, he works on the manuscript of History of Comparative Thought with Gerald Larson of the University of California at Santa Barbara.

Oct. 27 at Oriental University and at Seoul University lectures on Indian philosophy.

1972 Mar. 26 participates in the first meeting of International Conference on Sanskrit held at New Delhi.

June 11 participates in an international symposium on The History of Thought at Temple University.

Dec. 3 at the invitation of the Government of India, participates and lectures in the 100th Anniversary Symposium of Sri Aurobindo's birth.

1973 Jan. 29 gives his last lecture at Tokyo University Dept. of Literature. Topic of his talk is Indian thought and culture.

April 1 reaches retirement age and leaves Tokyo University, begins to lecture at School of Oriental Studies (TohoGakuin) and becomes President of that institution. (held until Oct. 1999)

May 15 appointed Professor Emeritus at Tokyo University

May 9 receives an honorary degree from van Han University, Saigon, Vietnam. He gives a lecture there. The same day he receives Honorary Doctor of Literature from Delhi University through the Indian Embassy.

during the year requests UNESCO to publish late Genchi Kato's work, *Research on the Development of the Shinto Religion*. However, only the section on the Middle Ages was accepted. That part was translated and published. He was thus able to introduce Genchi Kato's academic importance to the world

1974 Jan. 10 Society for Comparative Thought was founded by him, and he became the Chairman (held until 1983). At the opening ceremony he gave a lecture titled The Future Importance of Research on Comparative Thought.

Feb. 13 lectured at McGill University, Montreal, on Indian Philosophy and Buddhism

Sept. 1 lectured at the State University of New York at Buffalo for 3 months

Nov. 3 received a high award from the Emperor of Japan

1975 Jan. lectured at the Imperial Palace to the Emperor on The development of Early Buddhism

Jan. 13 gave several lectures around the United States and Canada for about 5 months

Feb. 3rd volume the "Dictionary of Buddhist Terms" is published (Tokyo Shoseki)

July 11 a ceremony celebrating the publication of The Dictionary of Buddhist Terms was held for him at Tokyo University.

during the year receivess award from Mainichi Shuppan (publisher) for The Dictionary of Buddhist Terms.

1976 Jan. 15 travels to India to help produce NHK's program "Pilgrimage to Buddhist sites" Lectures to Buddhist researchers at Delhi University.

1977 Feb. receives honorary Doctorate (*Vidyavaridhi*) from Nalanda Pali Research Institute, India

July 9 lectured at Hawaii University on Buddhist philosophy and Oriental Thought

Aug. 29 participates at conference given by Ōst Asien Institution in Bonn, participates in conference "International middle-age Philosophy". He returned to India via Greece. In India he met and talked with several Buddhist and Sanskrit researchers.

Oct. 14 lectured at the important opening of the Korean-Japanese Buddhist Research Association.

Nov. 3 received high decoration from the Government of Japan for his lifetime work.

1978 Feb. Became Honorary Fellow of the Royal Asiatic Society of Great Britain and Ireland.

during the year received a decoration from the King of Nepal (Gorkha Dakshina Bahu Order)

1979 Feb. 3 opened a seminar on *Parallel Developments* at North Carolina University. Gave lectures at Florida University and the Japan Society in New York City

Oct. 20 gave series of lectures at University of Southern 0California on Japanese Thought and Buddhist Thought.

Dec. 18 received Honorary degree (*Deshikottama*) from Visva Bharati University.

Mar. 21 lectured at Sri Aurobindo Commemorative Conference at Madras Universary at the invitation of the Indian Government.

Aug. 30 participated in UNESCO conference on *Scientific and Cultural History of Mankind* as member of the editoiral board. At the same time he was asked to create a small study group on Buddhism.

Sept. 12 participated in Peking academic conference "Interchange on Oriental thought". He was Chairman of the Japanese group. He opened and participated in the "First Conference on Buddhism" at Xian University The next day he gave a commemorative lecture on the "Influence of China on Indian Culture." He visited famous Buddhist sites in China.

1981 Mar. 7 published *"Indian Buddhism: Survey with Bibliographical Notes"*

June 9 attends a conference in Vienna (Metterlinck philosophical and theological University) on "The understanding of 'Enlightenment' between Christianity and Buddhism."

June 14 attends "International Conference on Jainism" in Strasbourg.

during the year heads conference in Cambodia to discuss ways of restoring and repairing war-damaged Buddhist documents.

1982 Feb. 12 receives Honorary degree (Doctor of Letter Honoris Causa) from Sri Lanka, Colombo Keliniya University, after which he presents a lecture.

during the year receives honorary degree from China's Peoples University.

Nov. 22 attends an "International Conference on Buddhism" in Taiwan. He presents the keynote lecture on 'The philosophical meaning of Kegon thought'.

Dec. 3 attends "International East-West Colloquium" at University del Salvador in Buenos Aires. Lecture on "The Idea of Compassion"

1983 June 25 at the 10th conference of Comparative Thought Group, he is appointed Honorary chairman. He lectures on 'From the Past to the Future of Comparative Thought.

during the year receives honorary award

Aug. 14 attends UNESCO conference in Ottawa, Canada; *International Symposium on Transcultural Universals.*

Sept. 10 Attends *"Nature, Culture, Technology: A Conference"* in Stockholm, Sweden. gives lecture.

Oct. 28 attends a conference in Korea where he lectures on the development of the worship of Amida

during the year presents 2000 volumes of a dictionary of the Cambodian language to the government as part of the work to restore the lost books of Cambodia.

1984 Jan. 2 attended *"Second International East-West Religious in Encounter Conference"* in Honolulu. Also lectures.

July narrates the program "Heart of the Orient" on Japanese national television (NHK 'Citizen's University') for two months

April 29 receives highest imperial award

Aug. 19 attends the conference *"Society for Asian and Comparative Philosophy"* in Honolulu. gives lectue on 'The Meaning of Religious Belief'

Oct. 8 attends "First International Conference on Buddhism and National Culture" in India and gives the keynote lecture on Early Buddhism.

1985 April narrates a series of programs on the Buddhist Scriptures on the national radio (NHK) running 6 months.

June 15 at the 12th meeting of the Association for Comparative Thought he speaks on the current developments in comparative thought.

Dec. 31 first issue of the magazine Toho (The East) appears. Issued by the Eastern Research Institute from the school Toho Gakuin [School of Oriental Studies]

1986 Jan. 17 visits Buddhist sites and holy places with a camera crew from NHK. The places were investigated while he explained them. The program was called "India...Journey of the Heart."

June 7 at the 13th meeting of the Society of Comparative Thought he lectures on "The progress of Comparative Thought."

Oct. 8 advises a group of 63 members of Toho Gakuin as they investigate the religious culture touring Korea.

Oct. 21 Gives keynote lecture at the conference on "East Asian culture and Korean culture" held in Seoul.

1987 Feb. 28 at the opening of the Indian International Centre he lectures at the conference *"Tradition: a Continual Renewal";* lecture title is "Development and Progress of Mahāyāna Buddhism."

June 6 at the 14th meeting of the society of Comparative Thought he lectures on "What is Tradition?"

Oct. 5 attends a conference in China called "Researches on Buddhism in China and Japan" where he gives the keynote lecture "The characteristics of Japanese Buddhism"

Oct. 13 at Peking University's conference on Chinese and Japanese Comparative Culture, he lectured on the progress of research in Asian Culture in China.

1988 April began one-year series on NHK titled "Recounting the Heart of the Orient"

May 20 attends a conference in Hanover, Germany, called *Geist and Natur.* His talk is called *"The Historically Differentiated Paradigmatic Developments"*

June 4 at the 15th meeting of the Society of Comparative Thought he lectures on Overcoming the slavery of Academics.

Dec. the authentic and authorised edition of his works is published: "The Ways of Thinking of the Eastern Peoples"

1989 June 3 at the 16th meeting of the Society of Comparative Thought he lectures on "Showing Japan to the World".

Oct. 21 at the 16th meeting (special fall session) of the Society of Comparative Thought he lectures on "The Progress of Comparative Thought in Japan".

Feb. 15 attends 100th birthday celebration of Radhakrishnan at Delhi.

Nov. 15 through the cooperation of the International Buddhist Association of Shiten no ji, he lectures at University of Vienna, then visits Frankfurt where he is introduced to the Schopenhauer Gesellschaft

1990	June 9	at the 17th meeting of the Society of Comparative Thought he lectures on "Why are We Slaves of Academics?"
	Nov. 28	attends international conference at Geneva University on "Mystery and Rationality." He gave a talk.
1991	June 4	Prof. John Carter of Colgate University leads 40 seminar students to Toho Gakuin. He gives special lectures to the scholars.
	June 20	In India a commemorative volume is published: *KALYAN MITTA: Professor Hajime Nakamura Felicitation Volume* (Indian Book Centre) At the Indian Embassy in Tokyo a commemorative gathering was held by the ambassador, Arjun Asrani.
	Nov. 2	receives 28th awarding of the prize for the best translation (*The Complete Jataka Tales,* 10 vols)
1992	Feb. 27	appointed to the German Association of Academicians (die Akademie der Wissenschaften zu Gorringen)
	Nov. 28	On his 80 birthday he is honoured by the Austrian association of Academicians.
1993	Oct. 9	at the 20th meeting of the Society of Comparative Thought he lectures on building a new world using comparative thought.
1994	Jan.	After many years a Department of Japanese Studies is established at Visva Bharati University.

	May	receives the *Dr. Bimal Charan Law Gold Medal of The Asiatic Society of Bengal* for 1993
1995	March	attends a conference at Granada, Spain. At the meeting there was discussion on the establishment of an East-West University.
1997	Oct. 19	attends the 7th Japan-China academic conference on "The Lotus Sūtra and the culture of Japan and China." His talk was on "Going beyond the Lotus Sūtra".
1999	March	received the 50th culture broadcasting award by NHK.
	July	The 40 volume set of his complete works is published (Shunju sha)
	Oct. 10	Hajime Nakamura passes away.
2002	Dec. 20	Immersion of his Ashes after a Hindu Puja by his family members.

Appendix : 2

The Late Professor Dr. Hajime Nakamura's Main Works in Japanese

I. *The Selected Works of Nakamura Hajime,* in 40 volumes (Tokyo: The Shunjusha Co., 1988-1999)

Volume 1 : *Ways of Thinking of Indian People* (1988; 10+389+17pp.)

Volume 2 : *Ways of Thinking of Chinese People* (1988; 8+380+16pp.)

Volume 3 : *Ways of Thinking of Japanese People* (1989; 6+478+16pp.)

Volume 4 : *Ways of Thinking of Tibetan and Korean People* (1989; 8+401+18pp.)

Volume 5 : *Indian History I* (1997; 22+517pp.)

Volume 6 : *Indian History II* (1997; 24+685pp.)

Volume 7 : *Indian History III* (1998; 24+625+67pp.)

Volume 8 : *The Thoughts of Veda* (1989; 24+647+28pp.)

Volume 9 : *The Philosophy of the Upaniṣads* (1990; 26+856+30pp.)

Volume 10 : *Freedom of Thought and Jainism* (1991; 28+875+43pp.)

Volume 11 : *Gotama Buddha I* (1992; 24+776pp.)

Volume 12 : *Gotama Buddha II* (1992; 18+506+51pp.)

Volume 13 : *Lives of Gotama Buddha's Disciples* (1991; 26+666+31pp.)

Volume 14 : *The Formation of Early Buddhism* (1992; 22+732+44pp.)

Volume 15 : *The Thoughts of Early Buddhism I* (1993; 28+987pp.)

Volume 16 : *The Thoughts of Early Buddhism II* (1994; 22+778+89pp.)

Volume 17 : *Early Buddhistic Ethics for Living* (1995; 18+693+47pp.)

Volume 18 : *Social Ideas of Early Buddhism* (1993; 18+735+38pp.)

Volume 19 : *Exchange of Thoughts between India and Western World* (1998; 24+638+28pp.)

Volume 20 : *From Early Buddhism to Mahāyāna Buddhism* [Mahāyāna Buddhism I] (1994; 34+900+37pp.)

Volume 21 : *The Thoughts of Mahāyāna Buddhism* [Mahāyana Buddhism I] (1995; 24+906+39pp.)

Volume 22 : *The Logic of Śūnyatā* [Mahāyāna Buddhism III] (1994; 16+745+41pp.)

Volume 23 : *Ideals Living in Buddhist Arts* [Mahāyāna Buddhism IV] (1995; 32+630+26pp., picture 8pp.)

Volume 24 : *Yoga and Sāṃkhya Philosophy* [Six Systems of Indian Philosophy I] (1996; 19+568+36pp.)

Volume 25 : *Nyāya and Vaiśeṣika philosophy* [Six Systems of Indian Philosophy II] (1996; 18+816+37pp.)

Volume 26 : *Mīmāṃsā and Vaiyākaraṇa Philosophy* [Six Systems of Indian Philosophy III] (1995; 18+594+30pp.)

Volume 27 : *Development of Vedānta Philosophy* [Six System of Indian Philosophy IV] (1996; 18+478+48pp.)

Volume 28 : *Indian Systems of Philosophy I* [Annotated Translation of Sarvadarśanasaṃgraha I] (1994; 14+399pp.)

Volume 29 : *Indian Systems of Philosophy II* [Annotated Translation of Sarvadarśanasaṃgraha II] (1995; 14+326+52pp.)

Volume 30 : *Hinduism and the Epics* (1996; 30+633+35pp.)

Volume 31 : *Modern Indian Philosophy* (1996; 18+368+28pp.)

Volume 32 : *Contemporary Indian Philosophy* (1997; 16+538+28pp.)

Additional

Volume 1 : *Ancient Thought* [History of World Thought I] (1998; 18+526+29pp.)

Volume 2 : *Universal Thought* [History of World Thought II] (1999; 24+982+47pp.)

Volume 3 : *Medieval Thought* [History of World Thought III] (1999; 16+635+32pp.)

Volume 4 : *Modern Thought* [History of World Thought IV] (1999; 16+518+22pp.)

Volume 5 : *The Interchange of the Cultures of the East and the West* [Japanese Thought I] (1998; 12+324+15pp.)

Volume 6 : *Prince Shotoku* [Japanese Thought II] (1998; 12+355+11pp.)

Volume 7 : *The Critical Spirit of Modern Japan* [Japanese Thought III] (1998; 8+391+10pp.)

Volume 8 : *The Modernism of Japanese Religion* [Japanese Thought IV] (1998; 10+341+13pp.)

II. The Grand Comprehensive Dictionary of Buddhist Terms, in 4 volumes (Tokyo Shoseki, 2001)

III. The Illustrated Dictionary of Buddhist Terms, in 1 volume (Tokyo: Tokyo Shosekhi, 1988)

IV. The Structure of Logic, in 2 volumes (Tokyo: Seidosha, 2000)

Appendix : 3

**Proceedings of Indo-Japan Seminar on
Buddhist Philosophy
With special reference to the Thoughts and Works of
Professor Hajime Nakamura
held on March 11 - 13, 2004 New Delhi**

Inaugural Session

Chairperson	**:**	**Prof. G.C. Pande**
Chief Guest	**:**	**Dr. L.M. Singhvi**
Director	**:**	**Prof. S.R.Bhatt**

S.R.BHATT: Good morning everybody. I begin with a request to the dignitaries on the dais, led by Prof. Kireet Joshiji, our honoured Chief Guest Dr. Singhviji, H.E. Mr. Y. Enoki, Ambassador of Japan to India and other esteemed luminaries to light the lamp, which is a symbol of purity and enlightenment. Through *Agni*, the Divine Fire, we invoke the presence and the blessings of divine powers to bless and guide us in our deliberations.

Hereafter we shall have the *Mangalācaraṇa* by the *Bhikṣ usamgha*. Being a believer in 'Engaged Buddhism', I do not appreciate presentation of live flowers in the form of garlands or bouquets. Instead we present the flowers of our noble thoughts and sentiments, as Udayana in his work *'Nyāya Kusumāñjali'* offered to God the flowers in the form of arguments for the existence of God. So we shall have offerings in the form of what can be called as pious wishes and sincere efforts and I request the *Bhikṣusamgha* led by Bhikshu

Satyapalji, Head of the Department of Buddhist Studies, University of Delhi, to kindly perform the *Buddha Vandanā Prayer performed*

S.R.BHATT: I would also like to recite the following two couplets from the Mūla Mādhyamika Kārikā of Nāgārjuna in which obeisance is being offered to Lord Buddha.

Yaḥ pratītyasamutpādam prapañcopaśamam śivam

Deśayāmāsa sambuddhastam vande vadatām varam. I.2

Sarvadṛṣṭiprahāṇāya yaḥ saddharmamadeśayat

Anukampāmupādāya tam namasyāmi gautamam. XXVII.30

In fact, these two couplets give us a direction as to how inter-cultural, inter-civilizational dialogues should be conducted and therefore they have relevance to the present occasion.

I would now request our friend, philosopher, and guide Prof. Kireet Joshiji, Chairman, Indian Council of Philosophical Research, to welcome all the dignitaries who are present, both on this side of the dais and also there on the other side.

KIREET JOSHI: It is a great honour for me to extend warm welcome to all of you, who have assembled in this Hall this morning to pay a tribute to Prof. Hajime Nakamura and through him to the philosophy of Buddhism. In particular, I would like to extend warmest welcome to our Chief Guest, Hon. Dr. L.M. Singhvi, who is a *karmayogi par excellence*, who has combined in himself the teachings of all religions and teachings of all that transcends religions. He is a luminary who has encompassed in his consciousness vast wisdom culled from various traditions of the world, various branches of knowledge and yet he is as tender as a flower.

I should also like to extend my warmest welcome to H.E., the Ambassador of Japan, Mr. Y. Enoki, who has just recently joined as Ambassador to India and within three days, he has won the hearts of a number of Indians. His sense of humour, his ready wits, his moving speech on Silence and Eloquence and his insights into the ethos of India and perception in India of Japan and perception of Japan in India, are the qualities that have won our hearts and I should like to extend my warmest welcome to him amidst us this morning.

My special welcome is to Prof. Lokesh Chandraji, a living embodiment of scholarship, a mind of synthesis and a heart of great illumination, who has penetrated, particularly, the heart of Buddhism and knows vividly the great contributions that Hinduism and Buddhism, coming together in this land and other lands, have produced in a kind of culture which shines throughout Asia and the world.

I should also like to extend warm welcome to Prof. Rajasekharan Pillai, the Vice-Chairman of University Grants Commission, who has taken time to be with us this morning in spite of heavy responsibilities of a Vice-Chairman of the highest body of universities, which has to look after more than 200 institutions of higher learning and more than 15,000 colleges in India.

I should also like to extent welcome to Prof. Mayeda who has come from Japan to be present with us this morning and we look forward to his valuable contributions to this important Conference.

My welcome to Prof. S.K. Kim, who has also very kindly agreed to be with us this morning and to deliver a special address on this occasion.

Prof. D.P. Chattopadhyaya, who was going to be here this morning has conveyed to me his inability because of his pre-occupations in Kolkata, but he has asked me to convey his greetings to all of us and to believe that he will be with us in our deliberations, if not physically, with all his intellectual vigour and his lively presence.

I should also like to extend welcome to distinguished scholars, who have come from Japan, China, Korea, and Vietnam and from India, who have devoted their lifetime in thinking on Buddhism and also in practicing the truths of Buddhism.

We have seven representatives from Japan, two from South Korea, two from China and two from Vietnam and that adds to richness of this Conference. I welcome them.

I should also like to welcome Prof. Bhuvneshwari Chandel, the Director of Indian Institute of Advance Studies, who has come from Shimla in order to participate in this Conference.

I shall also like to welcome the tallest figure in India in the intellectual and spiritual field, Prof. G.C. Pande, who has kindly agreed to preside over this Inaugural Session and to give us the benefit of his wisdom and his very rich, perhaps, the richest treasure of Buddhism crystallized in pure essence in his mind and spirit and we look forward to his words of wisdom as the Chairman of this Inaugural Session.

I should also like to welcome young students particularly who have taken interest in this Conference and who have come to be with us today and the next two days.

Prof. Nakamura is, perhaps, the greatest friend that India has had in the world of scholarship. His association with India, Indian universities and Indian scholars has been unequalled by any foreign scholar or leader of thought. His penetration into the understanding of Indian thought is particularly striking. His great book 'A Comparative History of Ideas' is a remarkable and unique contribution not only to the understanding of Asian thought, but to the world thought. I do not think there is any book comparable to this work. In a span of about 600 pages, he has brought into focus all the principle ideas that have grown and developed in India, in Japan, in Asia and in the West. If you turn the pages of this great book, for example, in his short note on the proofs of the existence of God in four pages he has brought together Chinese thought, Indian thought and Western thought and has tried to show in quintessence what exactly is ontological argument, cosmological argument, teleological argument and particularly Śankara's argument which he calls psychological argument. In his exposition of Bhartṛhari in regard to this in five sentences he has brought the quintessence of Bhartṛhari's argument of the existence of God as the essence of all the concepts that nobody can deny and on that basis he has proved the existence of God. I do not think in any other book you will get such a succinct account of the proofs of the existence of God as in these five pages. I would recommend to all young students to read these five pages to understand the quintessence of Thomas Aquinas, Descartes, Spinoza, Leibnitz, Kant and Indian thought, particularly Śankara's arguments on the proofs of the existence of God. This is one subject apart from all other important subjects of philosophy he has covered in this great book.

I was very happy that in 1984, when our late Prime Minister Smt. Indira Gandhi inaugurated the International Buddhist Conference in New Delhi, he was prominently present with us and personally I was privileged when he visited my own home in Delhi and we spent two hours together in debates on Buddhism and Hinduism. I remember vividly the advantage of meeting one great mind – in two hours you learn what you cannot learn in ten years.

I am very happy that today we have assembled here to remember, to study this great mind and great soul. Buddhism is one of the most prominent systems of thought in India and it is gaining ground all over the world as one of the most illuminating systems of thought, the light that Buddha shed on this earth, the experience of *Nirvāṇa* that he brought to all of us and a *Nirvāṇa* which is not aloof from the world, but a *Nirvāṇa* that is full of compassion for the world, so that as he stood on the threshold of *Parinirvāṇa*, he took a vow not to cross the threshold unless every sentient being on the earth is liberated. The Buddha, Sri Aurobindo says, is the greatest personality who ever walked on the earth.

I am very happy that we are here today to understand the illumination of Buddha, the great tradition of Buddhism, as it developed in India and elsewhere and we have with us some of the greatest scholars of Buddhism, to all of whom I extend warm welcome.

S.R.BHATT: Thank you, Prof. Kireet Joshiji, for your very warm and eloquent welcome to the distinguished scholars and dignitaries who are present here. In fact, this dialogue is in a way the continuation of and a part of the dialogue that Hon. Singhviji initiated and spearheaded and it is really a matter of good fortune for us that he is present with us to guide us.

Indian Council of Philosophical Research has been undertaking inter-cultural dialogues, international dialogues, dialogues among different nations and different cultures of those nations. We interacted with Chinese scholars; we had a dialogue with Korean scholars; we had a dialogue with Japanese scholars in the past and now we have scholars not only from Japan, but also from South Korea, China, Vietnam, Thailand and other places all together. From Japan we have Prof. Mayeda, a worthy disciple of a worthy teacher, Prof. Nara, who carries forward the legacy of Nakamura, distinguished professors like Wada, Motegi, Hino, Yajima and others. We have amongst us a profound scholar Prof. Lee from South Korea who has translated both the volumes of Indian Philosophy of Dr.Radhakrishnan, from English to Korean language and has written several books and produced documentaries on the pilgrim places of India. So, in a way, he is our cultural ambassador to Korea. Being a Korean, he is an ambassador of India in Korea. Prof. S.K. Kim is another distinguished scholar from South Korea who also has a book on Indian philosophy and on the philosophy of Mahatma Gandhi. He is heading the Department of Indian Philosophy in Dongguk University, where 120 students are studying Sanskrit, Pali and Tibetan as compulsory languages to be taught to every student. It is a unique programme like of which we do not have in any Indian university. It is something that is to be emulated by us in India. Prof. Kim is the founder of *Korean Society for Indian Philosophy.* We invited another very prominent professor of South Korea, Prof. Yong-kil Cho but because of his extremely busy schedule he could not make it. He is a towering personality in the Buddhist intellectual community of South Korea. Heading the Department of Buddhist Studies in the Dongguk University he is the Director of Brain Korea 21 project in Buddhist Studies of the Department of Education of the Government of South Korea. He has sent his scholarly paper that will be presented by Prof. Lee in the course of the seminar.

We conceived this Seminar to pay our tributes to Late Prof. Hajime Nakamura, who as Prof. Joshiji has already pointed out, was the greatest friend of India in the modern times. He has been a frequent visitor to India. He met scholars, both traditional and modern, all over the country, exchanged views and ideas with them. In fact, once he came to my Department, when I was heading the Department of Philosophy in Delhi University, with a team of camera men and wanted me to have a video film produced as to how we teach philosophy in our university systems.

Prof. H. Nakamura was honoured, both in Japan and in India. In India the Government honoured him and I would like to read out the words of Dr. K.R. Narayanan, our former President. He writes,

"Prof. Nakamura was well known in India as one of the outstanding and eminent scholars and true friend of our country. For more than half a century, Nakamura put to use his deep knowledge and extraordinary intellectual abilities to make accessible to contemporary generations, rich heritage of humankind's ideas, particularly of the civilizations of Asia."

In fact, Prof. Nakamura was very much admired by Dr. S. Radhakrishnan, another former President of India. He was greatly respected by Indian scholars. He was one of the rare intellectuals who could speak in fluent, chaste and flawless Sanskrit.

Prof. Nakamura's friendship with India was reflected not only in his personal contacts with the individuals and institutions in this country, but also in the dedication with which he interpreted Indian thought to the outside world as part of his larger endeavours.

The central axis of Prof. Nakamura's scholarship was, no doubt, Indian thought and in the preface to the book "A Comparative History of Ideas" he writes that he is mainly approaching the issues from Indian perspective. Though it is comparative and comprehensive enveloping all cultures and civilizations of the world, his main thrust is Indian. Prof. Nakumara's excellence in scholarship was, no doubt, in Indian thought which he investigated and expounded with unprecedented greatness and comprehension and with remarkable width and breadth of his philosophical perspectives and analytical acumen, but his field of research has been exceedingly vast encompassing both Eastern and Western thoughts, ancient and modern. He has a volume on Modern Indian Thought as well. In fact, he has authored more than forty volumes and they will be displayed tomorrow in the seminar Room of Indian Council of Social Science Research, a huge bulk and I am told that he has written more than 20,000 pages. It is a phenomenal contribution to world culture and civilization. I have not heard so far of any individual who might have written that much of quantity and it contains quality also. Of course, one may not agree with his analysis, with his interpretations, with his views because in philosophical enterprise, we follow the rule of the game of agreeing to disagree and there may be many points of disagreement, but the comprehension and penetration that we find there is just amazing. In every field of his research, he has been original, novel, pioneering and authoritative.

For example his book "The Structure of Logic" is a unique and marvelous synthesis of Eastern and Western logics. I do not want to take much of your time, but would like to emphasize two points. One is about the Indo-Japan relationships and other is the present day need and significance of having intensive inter-cultural and intra-cultural dialogues. India and Japan have centuries old contacts and exchanges of ideas and beliefs. It is said that Buddhism reached Japan via Korea, but my information is that Indian settlements were there in Japan even before Buddhism went there and these may be adherents of Vedic Dharma. Historical records are not available, but it is a matter of research to go into whatever scanty information is available; as in case of China also much before Buddhism went there it is believed that the Vedic Dharma was prevalent. And in one of my research papers I have quoted one Director of the Royal Asiatic Society of Shanghai, who has given evidences of the presence and the influence of Vedic Dharma on 'Taoism'. He has tried to compare the notion of 'Ṛt' with the notion of 'Tao' and argued for the influence of the concept of 'Ṛt' on the formulation of the concept of 'Tao'. I do not want to go into detail, but I want to point out that Indian contact with Japan may be pre-Buddhistic and it is a matter of research for the scholars to point out and give us the details of it. Of course, for this the historical records may not be of much help; the folklores, folk tales and the type of mythologies that are there may be taken help of. Mythologies are half-truths no doubt, but still they can give us some clues and I think it is a needed intellectual enterprise to undertake the discovery of the first Indo-Japan contacts.

But definitely once it was *officially* introduced from Korea, Buddhism had tremendous impact on Japan, and Japanese scholars, rulers and masses not only accepted and welcomed Buddhism, they renovated it; they gave it a new form so much so that as it is the case with other countries also that type of Buddhism is not the same as what we have in India and therefore we can talk of Indian Buddhism, Chinese Buddhism, Japanese Buddhism, Korean Buddhism and so forth. Among these different Buddhist formulations, there is need for exchange of ideas and thoughts because basic ideas are the same. The basic Buddhist ideas no one has negated. Say, for example, the doctrine of '*Patītyasamutpāda*' (inter-dependent origination), has various facets and various phases and various interpretations, but the doctrine itself is common to all Buddhist cultures. The four Noble Truths are commonly accepted in all Buddhist cultures. Ideas of *karma* and *samsāra* are commonly believed by all. *Nirvāṇa* as the *'sumum bonum'* of life is common to all, though in contents there may be difference. There are commonalities as well as there are distinct identities. In a dialogue we have to understand and appreciate such commonalities as well as distinct identities.

I would like to conclude by pointing out the importance of such an intellectual enterprise in contemporary times, because the insights and intuitions into the nature of life, reality and existence which Lord Buddha has given us not only entered the minds of the intellectuals, attracted the hearts of the masses, and won over the spirits of the powerful rulers but they also brought about in non-Indian Asian countries social solidarity and political integration. This has happened in Korea, in

Japan, in China and in many other countries of Asia. It was through Buddhism that cohesion was brought about and it is an established historical fact. Same Buddhist ideas and practices can again be invoked to bring about world solidarity, universal affinity and cosmic order and therefore in the modern times, when we have a sort of value entropy and value erosion and not only Asia is suffering from that, even the West is suffering from that, the Buddhist insights of '*Mahā Prajñā*' and '*Mahā Karuṇā*' and their corollaries may be of great help to us and therefore a time has come that we must have a re-look at these values and re-interpret them. It is not that we have to copy them or we have to imitate them; we have to recreate them. There is a need for creative re-interpretation of the Buddhist ideas, ideals and practices and this is more needed in Asian countries where there is a danger of uprooting of their traditional cultures. In fact, a tradition is not something a matter of the past. Tradition must continue in the present and flow into the future. Otherwise, it is not a tradition. We call it as *'paramparā'* in Sanskrit which is highly significant. A *'paramparā'* never refers to the past alone, something that is dead. It comes from the past, but has to flow down through the present and must continue in the future. Then only it is a live tradition. A genuine tradition has to be a living tradition and it is high time that we have proper understanding of our tradition, get rooted in our tradition and not uprooted. The danger of being uprooted is faced by all countries of Asia and there is a need for a common platform. The way the Vedic Dharma and the Buddhist ideas were accepted by entire Asia at one time does point out that we have a common psyche, which may be called as Asian psyche. There is something called Asian outlook. Asian mind is there which needs to be re-formulated and if we do that, then definitely we can offer to the West newer insights and newer intuitions to meet the global challenges.

In fact, in South Korea the *Society for Indian Philosophy* had the theme of the Second International Conference as 'Contemporary World Crises and Indian Philosophical Approaches'. It was a very well thought out theme. Of course, this is an Association for Indian Philosophy and therefore it is dealing with this Indian theme, but it can be the entire Asian philosophy. There is some commonality in Asia which may be called as the Asian Thought, the Asian Mind. Of course, it is diversified and that is why Nakamura has used the word 'Ways of thinking of Eastern peoples' as the title of his another very seminal work. So we have to meet on a common platform; all Asian cultures have to meet on a common platform. At present we are viewing each other, we are interfacing each other, through a *tertim quid,* through Western Orientalists and whatever they have been saying to us, we are accepting the same blindly, but they had their own particular vision; they had their own particular programme; they had their own biases and prejudices. I think it is high time that we get rid of those glasses and have a re-look at our Asian traditions by mutual discussions, mutual understanding, mutual appreciation and mutual reinforcement.

This Seminar, therefore, is significant in this context. Here, we have a limited scope in terms of geography, and also in terms of culture we are confining to the Buddhist culture which to my mind is 'a Re-formulation of the Vedic culture.' I have written substantially on this point that Buddhism is not a new culture but a continuation of the purity of the Vedic culture. There is a continuous flow of the Vedic culture in the Buddhist tradition, in the Jaina tradition, in the Sikkha tradition and in many other traditions which are there and which were there in our country.

With these words of thematic introduction, we may request H.E. the Ambassador of Japan to India, Mr. Y. Enoki, to give us words of his blessings.

Y. ENOKI: Good morning teacher and the scholar leader of India, Prof. Pande, Chief Guest, Dr. Singhviji and the distinguished participants. It is against the protocol and etiquette of Japan to take the Floor before the Chief Guest's speech. But today suddenly an appointment with a Cabinet Minister was arranged this morning and I have to leave early.

I think I am not a qualified participant; I am not a disciple of Prof. Nakamura. I did not attend his courses on Indian

Philosophy. Only one encounter was there during my university student time when I found a book just incidentally in a bookshop. This was on Buddhism written by Prof. Nakamura. I was very much inspired and my interest towards India was very much steered.

The main purpose of my today's attendance is only to express profound gratitude in organizing today's Seminar to all scholars, Dr. Singhviji, Prof. G.C. Pande, Prof. Bhatt and all participants not only from Japan and India, but other Asian countries. I notice that one of the virtues of Indian people is that they try to make best efforts to reply, to reciprocate not with mere words but in deed to the friendship or goodwill shown by others. So I hear quite often 'thank you' or 'thank you very much' after the invitation to lunch or dinner. But for more serious occasion, Indian people usually keep reticence in words towards kindness shown, and try to respond in deed. After three and half years of passing away of Prof. Nakamura, organizing such Seminar inviting all relevant Japanese professors and also the scholars from other countries, if I were Prof. Nakamura, I would have felt happiest from the heaven or from the tomb depending upon the religious adherence. It is indeed significant to commemorate and to organize a Seminar in India, which Prof. Nakamura loved the most. The daughter of Nakamura is among us and I can just imagine the feeling of the Nakamura family. Again this is showing my respect to the Indian way that is perhaps not comparable to other cultures. That is the very uniqueness of Indian people's way of paying thanks.

There is another very strong point underlying as a root combining India and Japan. A couple of weeks ago, we had here in New Delhi Bamboo Exhibition, Bamboo convention. There are many particularly North East regions of India as bamboo regions. India is also a bamboo country; as Japan is so. Quite often bamboo shoots appear over the fence between two houses, with the same underground root. So, it is very difficult to claim the belonging of bamboo over the fence.

Between India and Japan there are so many fences. Some times the geographical distance causes psychological distance, but I do recognize that under the ground there is very strong root combining India and Japan. One of my senior ambassadors who was once posted here in India mentioned that between India and Japan there is very huge reservoir of goodwill and this reservoir of goodwill is built through long history by so many contributors. Certainly we have so much historical background, Buddhism on the one hand, the Japanese respect for Mahatma Gandhiji and Nehru, and also the Indian judge Dr. Pal of the World War II War Crime Tribunal, and many stories associated with people like Subhasha Chandra Bose and others. These stories are being communicated from one generation to another. Thus all these people contributed to forming very strong underground root connecting our two countries. Likewise is the case with Prof. Nakamura. I am a layman and I am not qualified to comment upon his academic achievements, but the renowned name of Prof. Nakamura everybody knows and Prof. Nakamura should be as one of the biggest underground root connecting India with Japan. To our regret three and half years ago this root passed away but with many ramifications, root extending everywhere under the ground. So today's Seminar is just one of the eloquent examples. However, not today's Seminar alone but there may be many other undertakings combining philosophy and culture, the ways of our thinking, or as Prof. Bhatt says 'Asian ways of thinking'. All this is now flourishing on the surface of the ground just from the root that Prof. Nakamura left.

Having said so, on behalf of my Government I wish to express very profound gratitude to your goodwill demonstrated in such a manner for our greatest scholar, Prof. Nakamura. Thank you very much.

S.R.BHATT: No words can express our feeling of gratitude to H.E. Mr. Enoki. He is a very busy person having very tight schedule, but still he could spare some time for us and we sincerely thank him.

Now I have the honour of requesting a leading legal luminary, a seasoned diplomat, an intellectual giant, and a cultural and political ambassador of our country, Hon. Dr.

L.M. Singhviji to give us the benefit of his wisdom and learning. In fact, he is the wise person of the contemporary India, the wisest, I should say.

L.M. SINGHVI: Revered Rinpoche, Revered Monks, Revered Shiromanis, H.E. the Ambassador of Japan, my friend, Ambassador Enoki, whom I salute on this occasion. I greatly admire him. He has contributed to a heart-warming resurgence of India-Japan relationship at the political, economic and cultural levels. I am happy that he is here with us this forenoon. I am privileged to be with him in the Seminar. My friend Ambassador Enoki has to leave soon, but I do hope that he will help in bringing about a new phase in Indo-Japan relations which have gone through certain periods of ups and downs in the history. Though it is correct to say that geographically Japan is in Asia, but there has always been a question of how much Asia is in Japan and that is a question which was answered beautifully, effectively and forever by the Late Prof. Hajime Nakamura. He was truly the spirit of Asia in our time. He was the lining light of Asian scholarship. He was a great interpreter and that is really the task of a scholar diplomat. He was the great interpreter of cultures to cultures. He brought back that sense of the roots and the branches of Buddhism and Vedānta. Swami Vivekananda had said beautifully that the roots of Vedānta and the roots of Buddhism are common. In our own time, Prof. Nakamura carried on the legacy of Gurudev Rabindra Nath Tagore. No one, except Gurudev Tagore, did more to promote the India-Japan relationship at the level of the spirit of Asian cultures than Prof. Nakamura. I pay my respectful tribute to his cherished memory. There is a very beautiful imagery that Prof. Bhatt has used for this event, just behind the lamps. That image is of Prof. Namamura with folded hands as if in prayer, as if in a greeting of friendship, and Lord Buddha with raised hands to bless us all. This is a beautiful imagery and I am grateful that Prof. Bhatt brought these beautiful images together. I am delighted to have this opportunity to facilitate Prof. G.C. Pande Chairman of this major Indo-Japan event. Prof. Pande has made an immense contribution to the depth of scholarship on Buddhism. He is himself a poet, a fact I discovered very late after having known him for many years. I discovered his Sanskrit poetry and found it to be a treasure of Indian poetic sensitivity. It is in such beautiful poetry that you can see the poetic resonance of the philosophers, for there cannot be according to the Indian tradition a philosopher without poetry and a poet without philosophy. That is why we say "*Kavir maniṣī*". I would also like to facilitate him for the recent award, one of our apex awards in the country. That award itself was honoured because it was conferred on Prof. G.C. Pande, who is one of our living legends of scholarship. My dear friend, Prof. Kireet Joshi, has spoken so eloquently today as an interpreter of the wisdom of Sri Aurobindo and the Mother. My very distinguished friend and colleague Prof. Nara is present with us. Professor Bhatt was absolutely right when he said that Professor Nara represents the continuity of Professor Nakamura's legacy. When you speak of Buddhism, the canvas is very large as Professor Nakamura taught us. For this we are able to address issues of inter-cultural relationships and of comparative studies. Professor Nakamura studies both Christianity and Buddhism for the identities and commonalties between them as he studies Buddhism in its Vedic and Vedāntic context. His interpretations show how the spirit of humankind everywhere has something very similar to offer. He brought in his interpretations the Vedānta and I think it is important that Professor Nakamura was able to bring to us this fundamental truth about the common origins and shared outlook of Vedānta and Buddhism.

I miss the presence and participation of my friend Prof. D.P. Chattopadyaya who is not with us today. His seminal contribution to study of civilizations is very important. I would like to tell you that an Indo-Japan Seminar on Prof. Nakamura is a seminar not only of India and Japan but also a Seminar of India and Korea, of India and China, of Asia and the West and that is how, I think, we have to understand that Prof. Nakamura's greatest teaching to us is in a true sense a re-statement of the teaching of Swami Vivekananda, transcending ideological provincialism and subscribing to a universal perspective of which he spoke often and about which he wrote beautifully. He quoted Oliver Holmes to celebrate and salute Lord Buddha whose tribute is truly beautiful and elegant. Professor Nakamura's writings on Zen Buddhism and his writings on Vedānta, his writings on Modern Renaissance of India are in a sense a reminder to us of Huen tsang and others whose legacy and depth came alive in Professor Nakamura. On this occasion I should also pay my centennial tribute to Acharya Raghuvira, the distinguished father of Dr. Lokesh Chandra, who like Prof. Nakamura, really brought the culturally rich and inspiring Asian awareness back to Asia and gave to us that deeper sense of Asia of which you find an evocative poetic expansion in the writings of Gurudev Rabindra Nath Tagore.

I would like to say how delighted we are to have Dr. V.N. Rajasekharan Pillai with us on behalf of the University Grants Commission. The greatest task of the University Grants Commission is to take a fresh look and fulfill Dr. D.S. Kothari's noble legacy. For a fresh look at our education, for its re-construction, we must put an emus in universal human values and bring into this reservoir the depth and the nobility of the traditions which have enlivened us for centuries. Dr. Nigwekar the distinguished chairman was with us yesterday and spoke on a kindred theme.

Prof. Mayeda and Prof. Nara have contributed much to the civilizational dialogue within Asia and I think I should make one point just before the distinguished Ambassador of Japan leaves. Duty calls him elsewhere and having been a diplomat I know how over-riding those calls of duty are, but the point is that the image of India as the birthplace of Lord Buddha has had its ups and downs in Japan. Gurudev Tagore contributed uniquely to bring back to Japan the greatness of India, the nobility of India and the sublimity of its message. The hard truth is that some times our fortunes in terms of understanding have suffered mainly because of the image of India as a very poor country, once as a defeated country in the war China waged against us, as a country which had perhaps itself forgotten the teachings of Lord Buddha. I think it is important for us Indians and the Japanese and other Asians to begin to understand India in the true spirit.

I am glad we have Prof. Ho from China. We have also had several Chinese scholars, who spoke at the Asian civilizational dialogue which I had the privilege to convene. But when I speak of the ups and downs of Asia in Japan or of India in Japan, I speak with a civilizational sense not only of India, but of Asia itself. Edwin Arnold, surprisingly not an Indian, not an Asian, did sense this transcendent impact of Lord Buddha and wrote an epic poem, which he called "The Light of Asia". Many westerners have, in fact, brought back to us that civilizational sense of India. I remember, for instance, Sir William Jones who sat at the feet of a Sanskrit teacher in India, when he was a Judge of the East India Company's Supreme Court of India. I was delighted when my friend Dr. Lokesh Chandra said that dialogue is very important, between a teacher and a pupil. Dialogue is also important among friends, among would be friends. Like Sir William Jones, Edwin Arnold and many others tried to enter into the spirit of Asia. I wish to begin what I have to say today with a small poetic quotation from Sir Edwin Arnold, who wrote "The Light of Asia". He said of this spirit of which we have spoken:

It maketh and it saidth no wise move,

Its threads are love and life and Death and pain,

The shuttle of its loop.

And then he says :

This is its touch upon the blossom rose,

the fashion of its hand shape lotus

leaves in dark soil and the silence

of the seas, the robe of spring it weaves.

I want the civilizational dialogue to weave the robe of spring and not to undo the rainbow of our aspirations, which is what has happened around the world. It is important for us to understand that celebrating Prof. Nakamura and his life and work is to celebrate a great tradition. It is to celebrate the soul and the spirit of Asia, and of India itself, celebrating Japan, celebrating China, celebrating Korea, celebrating Vietnam, celebrating Sri Lanka and Thailand, celebrating Iran and Central Asia. In the celebration of Buddhism there is a celebration of the universal human spirit. We celebrate '*Prajñā*' and *Karuṇā*', which is the great composite holistic teaching of Lord Buddha. That is implicit in this Seminar and its worldview. It is also the celebration of the healing touch the Lord Buddha gave to the world and continues to give to the world. We celebrate Amitābha Buddha whom Professor Nakamura particularly interpreted and celebrated. The Asian civilisational dialogue and this conference are in sense the Nakamura World Conference. The Nakamura World Conference is a conference in the gust of human unity and compassion.

Professor Nakamura was one of the great interpreters of Zen Buddhism and Vedānta. "A Comparative History of Ideas", in my opinion, is one of the greatest books of our times. Arnold Toynbee and Bertrand Russell have written beautifully, but Professor Nakamura's book is a book which has at its core the very depth of the Asian point of view. The book is not only the History of Philosophy nor is it merely the History of Philosophers. Nor is it the History of Dynasties; it is an History of Ideas. The ideas which dominate Professor Nakamura's work are the ideas which we must try to understand in this Conference. Professor Nakamura says 'Tao never does, yet through it all things are done.' This Conference and the Asian Civilizational Dialogue have been done through 'Tao'. We are only the instruments of Tao. The Gītā has the same advice for Universal Man, the *Pārtha*, "*Nimittamātram bhava Savyasācin.*" I do not wish to take much more of your time knowing that there are many other speakers and I ought not to over-indulge myself. What is important for us is to re-assert Asia in Japan, to re-assert Asia in Asia itself, to understand once again Asia in the Asian context and to interpret it to ourselves, the teachings of universal significance which were encapsulated in this great work and in the life of Prof. Hajime Nakamura. These are the teachings that we need to understand in the larger global and cosmic context. For every text there has to be a context and Professor Nakamura's works and his life show that the text of his life had a very large and cosmic context and the understanding of that cosmic context is something that is Asia's and India's special legacy and gift to human kind. I should also add that Europe is geographically, historically, anthropologically and culturally an extension of Asia, Eurasia is primarily Asia. Most European religions and languages had their origin in Asia. Greece too was Asia in a basic sense. The eclipse of Asia and erosion of spirituality and values has affected world ecological harmony. Professor Nakamura brought back the basic quintessence of Asia in his own scholarly way.

There is a tremendous comparative light which Professor Nakamura throws in a comprehensive framework in which he offers ideas which were relevant yesterday, which are relevant today and which will be even more relevant tomorrow. He built bridges in space and in time as did Gurudev Tagore. I compare the two because I think there is poetry in Professor Nakamura's philosophy and in Gurudev Rabindra Nath Tagore's poetry there is profound philosophy. The Buddhist religion of Grace, for instance, is a very special interpretation of Zen Buddhism. Prof. Nakamura gives us a very special and beautiful interpretation of this type of Buddhism. It is not that Professor Nakamura discovered Buddhist mysticism, but Buddhist mysticism as interpreted by him is something that touches our hearts and universalizes it. There is a colloquial saying about two philosophers who met. One philosopher said, "I know all that the other philosopher sees." The other philosopher said, "I see all that he knows." Seeing is knowing in the Indian tradition. That is the true meaning of '*Darśana*'. The Indian Council of Philosophical Research is for *Darśana* which is not just a philosophical text, not just an intellectual exercise. It is seeing as knowing in experiential sense. *Darśana* is a word that is far more expressive than Philosophy and in my submission *Darśana* is the word which has a deeper resonance and meaning, for knowledge without experience is not fully knowledge. You cannot see unless you know and unless you experience and that is why a '*Maniṣī*' or a *Ṛṣi*' is someone who is a seer.

The great ideas of Buddhism are brought to us by Prof. Nakamura not only in their texts, which is an easier exercise, but in their context, in their universal and cosmic context, and in their Vedāntic context. Therefore, he is in a sense the man who authored a new Upaniṣad of Buddhism and in this new Upaniṣad of Buddhism he brings to us a consciousness of that universal sense, which animated ancient India and which also reached out to different parts of the world. There is a very powerful saying by Anand Bodhananda Mahasthavir, who put it in the words in which the Mahābhārata had put it long time ago and in which Mahāyāna Buddhism has expressed itself through Nāgārjuna. He says: –

What is the worship of Buddha? It is the experience of "Lokanātha pīḍā", in other words, universal empathy and compassion. A *'Lokanātha'* is a word of deep resonance in India. Lord Buddha came to be known as *Lokanātha* as personified universality of compassion. In a similar vein the great *Ṛṣi* Veda Vyāsa had said in the Mahābhārata that there is no great *'puṇya*' than doing good to your fellow beings, that is *paropakāra,* and there is nothing more sinful than oppressing other beings, that is *parapiḍanam*. The Śramaṇa tradition and the Vedic Hindu tradition are thus both rooted in reverence for life, in *ahimsā* and *karuṇā*. That is how '*prajñā'* and *'karuṇā'* are combined in a synthesis by Professor Nakamura by studying in great depth in India and in Harvard and Hawaii where he went and where he is till remembered. Prof. Nakamura is remembered not so much as a Japanese but as a great interpreter of Hinduism and Buddhism together.

Swami Vivekananda taught us that in the ultimate analysis the roots of the Vedic, Vedāntic and the Śramaṇa cultures are the same thought processes and it is in those roots that Professor Nakamura sees modern Indian renaissance. Through Raja Ram Mohan Roy, Swami Vivekananda, Mahatma Gandhi and others in that perspective he brings back to us our own renaissance a somewhat forgotten renaissance.

I do not wish to take more of your time because there is much that one can say on weaving together the poly-centric ethos of Asia, the philosophical perspectives of Asia, by way of bringing together the Confucian, the Shinto, the Dao, the Buddhist, and the Vedānta. Professor Nakamura has been one of the greatest bridge builders of our age and one of the greatest rejuvenators of our philosophy with a completing sense of universality which is what makes his philosophy so relevant to our age and time. I shall say no more except to express our gratitude to all the scholars who have come here. I see Dr. Shashagiri Rao sitting in front of me. He has been editing the Encyclopaedia of Hinduism. We are proud to have Prof. Lee, Prof. Kim, Prof. Mayeda and Prof. Nara with us and to have Indian scholars, Japanese scholars, Chinese scholars, Vietnamese and Korean scholars. What more can we ask for? Thank you Prof. Bhatt for giving us more than what we could ask for.

S.R.BHATT: Sir, we feel very much enlightened by your learned address. We thank you H.E. Mr. Enoki who is now leaving, and continue with our programme. In fact, Dr. Singhviji is a *'Kalyāṇa Mitra'* for us, to use a Buddhist terminology, and we have always been seeking inspiration and guidance from him. So, we are really grateful to him for giving us very illuminating discourse.

Now I request Prof. Lokesh Chandraji, who is a living encyclopaedia of Buddhism and Indian culture and about him, Hon. Singhviji has also spoken quite a lot. He is an illustrious son of an illustrious father. So, we welcome him and request him to bless us with his choicest words.

LOKESH CHANDRA: Respected Shri Singhviji, Respected Shri Pandeji and friends. Our friendship with Prof. Hajime Nakamura goes back to two generations, to my father's period. My father used to teach Japanese in 1935 to Indians. The British thought he was a Japanese agent, and they imprisoned him. This stirred the Japanese intellectuals, as well as the Buddhist scholars of Japan, who felt that an Indian had been imprisoned for teaching Japanese. This made him so famous throughout the scholars of the then Japan that many of the leading Japanese scholars, not only of Buddhism but of several other disciplines came to be his friends. Hajime Nakamura happened to be one. When once he came to Delhi and was to address a Conference in which the then Vice-President, Dr. Radhakrishnan was to preside, he came to my father and asked him in which language should he (Prof. Nakamura) speak? My father said, of course, Sanskrit. Prof. Hajime Nakamura spoke in Sanskrit. Prof. Radhakrishnan spoke in English. It was the beginning of a deep friendship between Prof. Hajime Nakamura and Prof. Radhakrishnan. Radhakrishnan realized for the first time that very few European scholars could speak in Sanskrit.

Hajime Nakamura was one of the rare East Asian scholars who could speak and write Sanskrit and one of his works is on "Modern Sanskrit", as to how it has evolved over the last sixty years. I used to send him Sanskrit newspapers, Sanskrit magazines, and Modern Sanskrit writings. His interest was not only classical Sanskrit or Buddhist Sanskrit, but contemporary Sanskrit as well. I went to Japan for the first time in 1970. Prof. Hajime Nakamura came to receive me at the hotel. I said; "I want to visit your house". He said; "yes, welcome". "How should I come to your residence?" I asked. He used to live far away from the city of Tokyo. He said, "I will come to fetch you". He came to fetch me. We were coming down the lift and it was so silent. I said, "Professor Hajime Nakamura, Zen Buddhism has invaded the lift. You have silent monks and noiseless machines." He thought that I am a bit of a naughty person. When we reached his residence, he put me on a very small chair in the shape of the palm of the hand. Professor what is this chair? He said; "This is the hand of Lord Śākya Muni. "Why do you put me in Lord Śākya Muni's hand? I asked. He said; "Once Hanumana was creating uproar in Heaven. Lord Buddha said, I hold you in my palm so that you won't be naughty; you won't create havoc." I asked Professor Hajime Nakamura; "Am I the naughty Hanumana". He was silent. In this way Hajime Nakamura was referring to a great event in Chinese Buddhist history; the visit of Huan-tsang to India. He is supposed to have been accompanied by a monkey who was his constant companion. In the popular mind, in thc psycho-history of the Buddhist tradition in East Asia the monkey is a venerable companion of the Chinese pilgrim scholar. I was there in the Centre. When seated, Prof. Hajime Nakamura asked me: "How do you see Japan?" I said, "As a child in 1936, the first lesson that I read in Japanese was "Saita, saita, sakuraga saita", "The cherry blossoms have blossomed, they are blossoming." They represent *anityatā* or impermanence to the Japanese spirit. They are the supreme void and at the same time, they are enshrined in Japanese painting, and a vast amount of Japanese poetry has been written on them. It is the '*pāramitā*', the perfection of the Japanese culture.

Japan is not 'sword and chrysanthemum', but in her are enshrined three categories. There is a '*śunyatā*', a void, that has to be filled by creativity. This creativity vanishes as it is '*anitya*', or impermanent. This impermanence, this constant creativity, leads to perfection. I see contemporary Japan in these three Buddhist concepts of *'śūnyatā'*, *'anityatā'* and *'pāramitā'*. Thus began our conversation sitting on the Hanumana chair. I said, "Professor Hajime Nakamura, if I am a Hanumana, you are Huan-tsang. I want to go inside and to see your library. Do you have a Japanese book on Buddhist logic?" He showed me a huge commentary on Buddhist logic. I had the feeling that Buddhist logic was not studied in the East Asian languages. For the first time I saw this commentary, was so delighted that I requested Prof. Hajime Nakamura to translate it because it could have a bearing on the linguistic culture of the East Asian people.

Prof. Hajime Nakamura asked me another question as to why Indian concepts are negative like, non-violence, non-alignment etc.? You know that the Monkey had to answer questions of the great Chinese scholar-pilgrim. I was still on the monkey chair, but the conversation was going on. I said, "Professor Hajime Nakamura whether they are negations or whether they are super positives is a matter of discussion. Perhaps, these negations come from the Buddhist tradition.

In the Mūla-mādhyamika-kārikā of Nāgārjuna the very first stanza speaks of the eight negations. The negative concepts of contemporary India may have come from the Buddhist concept of negation. The Mūla-mādhyamika-kārikā begins by saying that the reality is neither non-extinction nor non-origination, neither non-ephemeral nor non-permanence, neither non-identity nor-differentiation, neither non-coming into being nor non-going out of being. All these eight categories on which inter-dependent origination is based are negative. We have to consider as to who contributes to the negative conceptualizations of India's contemporary polity. Negative expressions like non-alignment and non-violence are parallel to the Buddhist philosophic formulations where Buddha does not accept the permanent, the eternal, the *śāśvata*, but at the same time he does not accept the ephemeral. He believes in the non-ephemeral and the non-eternal."

Then we were discussing '*ahimsā*'. Professor Hajime Nakamura asked me "How do you explain *ahimsā*?" I said, "We have two words; we have *śakti* and *himsā*, and *śakti* is power, *himsā* is violence. Buddhism went to China on horses. The Chinese saw these horses not only as mounts of the monks, but they saw them as power and virtue. The horses went to the imperial cavalry of the Han Emperors, and the monks went to the monasteries. In China, Buddhism was an expression both of power and virtue. For the first time, power and virtue became convergent in the political thought of China. The Buddhist tradition distinguishes between power and violence. Violence is with vice, power is with virtue. In the Indo-centric tradition there is no Goddess of Non-violence, but the Hindu tradition has *Śakti,* the Goddess of Power. Power and virtue coexist with *ahimsā.*"

We had a long discussion, as Prof. Hajime Nakamura in spite of his being a great scholar of Buddhism was also a very contemporary person. He was a link between India and the Japanese intelligentsia. His contribution to Buddhism is tremendous. The role of Buddhism as a polycentric expression of the human mind can have global implications. His understanding of the deeper processes of Hindu-Buddhist tradition becomes crucial in our 21st century, as it seeks new horizons. Frontiers are fast fading out. The horizons are important, as we have to share. It is a world that is fast moving towards a shared rather than a unified earth; we have to be citizens of this earth sharing with each other. Here Professor Hajime Nakamura's work becomes crucial to comprehend how sharing has taken place in different periods of history between various countries. The interaction of Buddhism with Confucianism, Taoism, and Hinduism, the role of Upaniṣadic thought in the evolution of Buddhism evoked lively discussions with Prof. Hajime Nakamura. He was a great mind not only in the convergences, but also in divergences. The divergences are important because they characterize different nationalities, different periods of history; and territorial imperatives have a role to play. Talking of universalism, we have to keep in mind territorial distinctions, expressed in modern parlance as globalization and localization. Prof. Hajime Nakamura's work is classical and contemporary at the same time and that is why we celebrate him today. There are certain insights in the long historic traditions of Asia of sharing and also of seeing not only convergences, but also conflicts, and in them we might find a new vision for a world which is fast moving into a new direction that is coming close to Asian thought. Asia need not propagate its ideals, but the West itself is studying the East to understand how Asia has managed its affairs for the last five thousand years. The Chinese State has been in existence for five thousand years, the Japanese State has been in existence for two thousand five hundred years, and of course, we are also an ancient nation. All these nations have to pool their experiences to give humankind a bright and brilliant future and that is where Prof. Hajime Nakamura comes in. Hajime means the '*Ādi or Ādya*'. Like the '*Ādya Śankaracārya*' he is 'Adya Nakamura'.

S.R.BHATT: Let me express our thanks to the Thai monks, who are now leaving, for giving us the very beautiful recital of Buddha *Vandanā* and I also express our heart felt thanks to Dr. Lokesh Chandraji. In fact, he shed a floodlight of ideas that have definitely illumined our mind, given us a lot of information about Buddhism, about Hajime Nakamuraji and about Indian and Asian cultures. Fortunately, we have with us Ambassador Aftab Seth, who was our ambassador to Japan some time ago and we would request him to share his experiences about Indo-Japan cultural relations. He has been instrumental in forging deep and strong ties with Japan in recent times and we should be benefited by his experiences.

AFTAB SETH: Thank you very much. I was asked to briefly speak on Indo-Japan cultural relations, but before I come to that I would just make one general remark about Japanese culture and that is that it has, as you know, absorbed foreign cultures over the years, refined and transformed them and has treated foreign cultures with respect, some times with awe.

Our culture through the vehicle of Buddhism was similarly treated by the Japanese. By and large, there were times when they did not react very favourably towards Buddhism but Shotoku Taishi (574-622) that great member of the Japanese imperial family was the one who was primarily responsible for bringing the message of the Buddha to Japan and spreading it all over the country.

There was another great Japanese scholar-pilgrim from Kagawa prefecture in the small island of Shikoku. His birthplace is now marked by very powerful temple called Zenkoji which possesses very ancient Buddhist relics which he obtained from China where he spent several years interacting with Indian monks and pilgrims and the flow of Buddhist thoughts and ideas actually, as we all know, came through the filter of a signified culture and a signified civilization and through Korea. That was the method by which it came. Of course, there was an interaction along the Silk Road immortalized by the great Japanese painter Eiko Hirayama, who traversed that route, I do not know how many dozens of times, and painted the most beautiful paintings contained in a temple in Nara. He has painted the walls depicting the Silk Route and the evidence of this can be seen in Japan today. India's *ikat* and 'tie and dye' designs, *shibori* as they call it in Japanese—all these things traversed either through the Silk Road or came by the sea route into Japan and became very much a living part of Japanese culture. You have to merely go to the Temple of Sanjusangendo, one of the most beautiful temples in Kyoto where a thousand gods and goddesses of Indian origin are venerated and worshipped by millions of Japanese and millions of other foreign nationals who visit Kyoto.

Then, of course, as we know about 450 years ago there was a further cultural link established between India and Japan and that was through the Jesuit missionaries of whom the famous one is St. Francis Xavier buried in Goa, but whose Memorial Church is in Kagoshima in the Island of Kyushu. During that period, there was this constant flow of people between Japan, Goa, Daman, Diu and Rome. And it were the Jesuit missionaries who were responsible for this intermingling of civilizations of the Far East, South Asia and Europe. One of the things that Japan and India share, and I think we have influenced each other through this intermingling over the years, is the inclusiveness of Japanese culture. We tend to think of them as being insular and an Island nation, but actually Japanese culture is very inclusive, very tolerant of others and I quote a small piece from the *Mahābhārata*, which epitomizes this ability to absorb, respect and tolerate: "Just as all water running from the sky and from distant streams, having gone in different places, all mingle through water in the sea so, Oh Lord, the different paths which man takes through different embassies, various though they appear crooked or straight, all lead to Thee"

Now this could easily have been said by a Japanese because that is the manner in which Japanese view religion. They marry according to Shinto rites; they live according to Confucian ethical precepts; they go to a Buddhist temple for the funeral services. This is the composite manner in which the Japanese live and this Shinto-Hindu-Buddhist tradition shares another important characteristic which is the ability to treat human and non-human nature as one and that is very beautifully described by Rabindra Nath Tagore, who had his own links with Japan, in these words: "The same stream of life that runs through my veins, night and day, runs through the world in dances in rhythmic measures. It is the same life that shoots enjoy through the dust and earth in numberless blades of grass and breaks into tumultuous waves of leaves and flowers."

So, this is something that is very characteristic of Japanese culture and of the Indo-Japan cultural story. Some of you may not know that there was another important link established in the 19th century, apart from Swami Vivekananda who, of course, came to Japan and greatly admired what he saw about the Japanese national spirit and above all, the cleanliness of the Japanese and he went to Kamakura and exchanged views with the Chief Priest of Kinkakuji Temple and they traveled in the same boat to the West Coast of America and on to Chicago in 1893. But apart from him, there was another very interesting traveler from Japan, a man called Tada Motokichi from Shizuoka province, who was sent to India six years after Meiji Restoration, that is in 1874, to study the production of black tea and Mr. Tada Motokichi – I said in the Japanese way, the surname first and the first name second, brought back technology relating to the production of black tea to Shizuoka. That was the first time that black tea was produced in that country, thanks to his sojourn in India for two-three years in Calcutta and Assam and in various tea gardens and factories. Also a few years later after Meiji Restoration, Jamshedji Tata, on his way to America, stopped in Japan to see the wonders that they have wrought in terms of industrial development and improvements in agriculture and he brought back many organizational ideas from Japan.

Of course, Dr. Singhvi mentioned Rabindra Nath Tagore. He was a great link between India and Japan indeed, with India and China and much of the South East Asia. Tagore had invited the great art historian Okakura Tenshin and the great painter Yokoyama Taikan to Shantiniketan and there they learnt and worked with Indian artists and took back with them to Japan the ideas of the Bengal renaissance which deeply influenced the *Nihonga* style of painting in Japan. It brought a certain degree of light to their painting which was absent before the sojourn of Yokoyama Taikan and Okakura Tenshin in Shantiniketan and then of course, Tagore himself went to Japan in 1916 in the middle of the First World War. He was received by Okuma Shigenobu, the founder of Waseda Univesity, a leading private university in Japan. The other leading one is Keio University, founded by Fukuzawa Yukichi. Okuma Shigenobu, also happened to be the second President of the Japan-India Association founded in 1903. The Japan-India Association celebrated its hundredth anniversary only last year. Okuma Shigenobu was the man who received Tagore much against the wishes of the British Ambassador because Tagore was thought to be a nationalist and therefore somewhat subversive. But Okuma, who was later Foreign Minister and Prime Minister, overruled the wishes of the British Ambassador and received Tagore with great honour and of course, this exchange between them continued during Tagore's two subsequent visits. We know that during and before the war, it was Rash Behari Bose who traveled to Japan, married a Japanese woman and set up the first Indian Restaurant in Tokyo, Nakamuraya, which still exists and celebrated its 75th anniversary last year. Netaji Subhash Bose, we all know, went to Japan during the war to raise the Indian National Army and after the Second World War, Radha Binod Pal, the Indian Judge, the only Judge on the 30-member War Crimes Tribunal, who had any knowledge of international law gave a dissenting judgment which held the Japanese war-time leaders as not guilty. That judgment, of course, because of American censorship, as it was during the American occupation, was unknown to the Japanese. It was only after the occupation ended in 1952 that a great publisher called Shibusawa Eichi published the entire judgment of Radha Binod Pal calling it '*Truth from the East*', because Pal quoted extensively from Hindu and Buddhist scriptures in his judgment. Shibusawa published this book and that is how the Japanese public became aware of it. The revelation had an electric effect, an effect which subsists until today. No conversation, political or otherwise in Japan begins without a mention of Radha Binod Pal's dissenting judgment which gave a sense of self-respect, restored a sense of self-esteem, to the Japanese who had been made to feel through the trials as a nation of criminals, as a nation of beasts, as a nation of cruel people and Pal's judgment restored to them a sense of self-respect and self-esteem for which they are ever grateful, as they are for the gift of *Indira*, a lovely baby elephant which Jawaharlal Nehru in 1949 presented to the children of Japan. Grieved by shortage of food, absence of clothes, lack of medicine and medical facilities on account of the carpet bombing of Tokyo city, Nehru was so moved by all this that he presented this lovable baby elephant, named after his daughter, and baby *Indira* traveled to all the cities of Japan.

So Indo-Japanese culture came to be symbolized by these two things. Pal's judgment and *Indira* and both these events, both these things, exuded one important virtue and that was compassion, the most important virtue of the Hindu and Shinto tradition, and certainly of the Buddhist tradition, and then, of course, in the post-war years we had great scholars like Hajime Nakamura, and the anthropologist and sociologist, Chie Nakane, who acted as bridges between the intellectual communities of our two countries and I am happy to say we were also able to receive great painters like Nonaka Yatsuo and Okamoto Taro in the early 1970s to come and renew the tradition of Okakura and Yokoyama Taikan and re-establish contacts with Indian painters.

I was fortunate enough to have been in Japan, when we celebrated the 20th anniversary of our diplomatic relations and we had a wonderful group from Dharangashri Ballet Group from Gwalior led by Gurubandhan, who came and performed the *Rāmāyaṇa* much to the delight of the Japanese audience and we were honoured deeply to have Prince Hitachi, then the younger son of the Emperor, now the younger brother of the Emperor, as our Chief Guest. I was also fortunate enough to be in Japan for the 50th Anniversary of our diplomatic relations which saw a great efflorescence of cultural exchanges between our two countries. We were privileged to have, thanks to the Sasakawa Foundation, great scholars in our midst including two who are gracing our platform today, Dr. Lokesh Chandra and Dr. L.M. Singhvi. We had Dr. Karan Singh, we had Bhuvanesh Chaturvedi, we had Dr. Kamla Chaudhary and we had a colleague of mine Kishan Rana—all of whom came for lectures during our 50th Anniversary celebrations in order to exchange views with Japanese intellectuals.

We were also deeply honoured and reference was made by Dr. Lokesh Chandra to the role of Hajime Nakamura in bridging the Indian Embassy and the Imperial family. We were deeply honoured in this one year to have had six members of the Imperial family attend our functions; the Emperor and Empress, who came to our Exhibition of Buddha's art appropriately enough in the National Museum in Ueno; the Crown Prince and Princess who came to a joint music concert that we organized in July, 2002 of the Indian Philharmonic orchestra and the Japanese Symphony Orchestra; and we had the Emperor's younger brother Prince Hitachi come again to a festival of ours; Prince Akishino, the younger son of the Emperor, also came. So, the presence of these six members of the Imperial family at our cultural events speaks eloquently of the respect—the deep respect—that the Japanese have for Indian culture. Dr. Singhvi quoted two Arnolds—Edwin and Methew. I will quote another Arnold this time a Toynbee to tell you what he thinks of the Hindu-Shinto-Buddhist tradition. Shintoism and Buddhism both stand for man's ethical obligation to cooperate with non-human nature. I believe that the Japanese people can lead mankind into a safer and happier path.

The Japanese have mastered modern Western technology without having lost their indigenous religious tradition. This tradition serves the right spiritual antidote to modern technologies, pollution of non-human nature and de-humanization of human life. The Japanese tradition stands for the dignity of non-human nature as well as the dignity of man. And that tradition which we share, respect for nature is well encapsulated in a beautiful poem by Ichizu Izuyachi, a great Japanese poet whose memorial museum is a five minute walk from where I lived in Tokyo housed in the compound of Waseda University. I shall conclude by reading this poem:

I stand as though only I am existing in heaven and earth,
At this solitariness canon you are smiling,
Coming stealthily who is hitting the temple bell,
It is late at night and time even for the Buddha to go into dreaming,
In the Buddha's drowsy eyes the ancient feels of Yamato
Have their hazy existence.

Thank you very much.

S.R.BHATT: We thank ambassador Seth profusely for his very interesting, illuminating and informative presentation which is seasoned with deep perspective observations about Indo-Japan relations, about Japanese culture and respect India has in Japan.

Now before I request the Doyen among intellectuals, Prof. G.C. Pandeji, I would take this opportunity to request a very important person in the field of education, who is with us today and he is Prof. Rajasekharan Pillai, Vice- Chairman of University Grants Commission, and I request him to share his ideas with us.

V.N. RAJASEKHARAN PILLAI: Prof. Pandeji, Dr. Singhviji, Prof. Kireet Joshi, Prof. Nara, Prof. Lokesh Chandra, Prof. Bhatt, Prof. Mayeda, other scholars, delegates to this Conference, brothers and sisters. First of all let me express my sincere gratitude to the organizers for extending me an invitation to the International Seminar on Buddhist Philosophy with special reference to the Thoughts and Works of Prof. Hajime Nakamura. For the last two hours it was an educational experience for me. I am a scientist and a teacher. Prof. Nakamura has identified the commonalities of the Asian countries, their mindset, thought processes and beliefs. He was a profound exponent of the concept of the Asian mind with its diverse forms of expression. He could prove that there is no radical contrast between the Eastern Thought and

Western Thought. The establishment of the Eastern Institute in Tokyo by Prof. Nakamura is a significant attempt in encompassing both Eastern and Western Thought, ancient and modern.

I understand that the number of Prof. Nakamura's publications are astonishingly large, over thousands, including several dozens of original books. Most of them are in Japanese language. It is very important that these seminal contributions to Eastern Thought and World culture are made accessible to non-Japanese and particularly Indian young scholars and students. On the materialistic side, the Japanese contributions in science and technology are widely translated and made internationally available. So there is a need to attend to the spiritual and cultural dimension also.

India and Japan have centuries old cultural contacts and exchange of ideas and beliefs. The two countries along with other Asian countries have traded, both in material goods, science and technology and in Dharma. Through the Japanese society for promotion of science, Department of Science and Technology and other organizations, there are significant efforts from the Governments for cooperation in science and technology, but some institutionalized efforts are necessary in the field of Dharma too. Japan is an important, very influential Asian country that has to serve the Asian culture, the basic tenet of which is spiritual orientation. In contemporary times, the impact of Western consumerism and materialism has been devastating in Japan as well as in India and in the entire Asian countries. There is a need for spiritual re-awakening in these countries. A renewal of cross cultural interactions will not only help and contribute in mutual understanding and mutual enrichment but it will also consolidate and revitalize our spiritual resources. This is the necessity in today's world. I was thinking about what the universities and the colleges and the University Grants Commission can do in this regard.

In our universities and colleges interest towards humanities, social sciences, philosophy and such subjects is day-by-day diminishing. Recently we had a meeting of all the Councils to consider the future of social sciences, humanities and philosophy. We prepared an Action Plan in this regard and we sincerely hope that such plans can also include some aspects of Buddhist Philosophy and Nakamura's contributions. I hope this Seminar will prepare an institutionalized mechanism by which there can be dissemination of information about Asian cultures through dialogues, discussions and extramural lectures in universities and colleges, and through their publication in Indian languages, English and Japanese. The U.G.C. would be happy to collaborate with the Eastern Institute, Tokyo, Indian Council for Philosophical Research, Indian Institute of Advance Studies, Shimla, for working out a plan for such academic activities.

The U.G.C. will also consider the institution of a Nakamura Chair on Eastern Thought and Philosophy, if a concrete proposal is emanated as a result of the deliberations of this particular Conference. Recently, you all know we had a UNESCO sponsored civilizational dialogue organized by the Ministry of Human Resource Development. It is very important that we create an Inter-University Centre for Studies of Civilisations in this country. There are several University Grants Commission maintained Inter-university Centres which are totally autonomous organizations, which provide facilities for scholars, post-graduate students and even graduate students from the colleges and universities to come and spend time, but all these Centres so far are in science and technology and there is a felt need of Inter-university Centres in humanities, social sciences and philosophy. There is a policy decision to that effect. I would be most happy that if this Seminar makes a recommendation to the University Grants Commission for the institution of these two activities, namely, the Nakamura Chair on Eastern Philosophy and Thought and Centre For the Studies in Civilizations.

S.R.BHATT: I am sure we are unanimously making that recommendation to you right now. We are really grateful for what I would call as benevolent gesture emanating from our esteemed friend, Prof. Rajasekharan Pillaiji.

C.V. RAJASEKHARAN PILLAI: I would request you to make two concrete proposals.

S.R.BHATT: That you will get definitely. I may assure you that within a week you will get that. We have a saying in Sanskrit—*Śubasya śīghram*—so we won't delay it.

Now, we have the '*Varadaputra* of Sarasvati', Prof. G.C. Pandeji, whose brilliance is multi-faceted and whose efflorescence is multi-dimensional. He is a profound scholar of Buddhism and Indian culture and also well steeped in the history of world civilizations. He is the Chairman of the Inaugural Session and we would like to listen to him for the words of wisdom and enlightenment.

G.C. PANDE: Prof. Kireet Joshi, Prof. L.M. Singhvi, Prof. Mayeda, Prof. Nara, Prof. Bhuvan Chandel and Prof. Rajasekharan Pillai, Prof. Kim and all the other gathered scholars and others in the audience

I need not repeat what has been said often in these past two hours that to commemorate the memory of Prof. Hajime Nakamura is a privilege. Many tributes have been paid to him and his work has been recalled and at the end, Prof. Rajasekharan Pillai has promised the institution of a Nakamura Chair for the promotion of the Study of Eastern Philosophies. I think that itself is a very solid outcome of this Seminar, apart from the fact that it has brought together scholars from Japan and other Asian countries and India.

I hope that this cooperation in the field of Buddhist and comparative philosophical studies will continue. I have often thought it a regrettable fact that some of the great institutions which human creativity has produced have been abused. State and society, religion and culture ought to be the means of creating human unity and furthering it, but unfortunately, the State has been used as an instrument of power and some now want to understand it as based on some ethnic nationality. Society, intended to unite mankind, is being torn apart by the emphasis being laid on class interests. Religion, even world religions, claiming to be the same for all mankind have tended to create exclusive communities and civilizations, the common enterprise of all mankind has been divided into rival civilizations. For a long time history has been a history of the conflict of states, classes, religions and civilizations, whereas it ought to have been a history of the cooperation of mankind through these institutions. In one of my books on Mahāyāna Buddhism I had argued that *Mahāyāna* is the Buddhist idea of universal religion and I think that the universality of religion is most clearly expressed in Buddhism–Aśoka was its greatest spokesman. He says in his inscriptions that it is wrong to praise one's own sect or organization and declares that what is good is universal. He identifies these sense of religion or Dharma not with specific intellectual or theological doctrines, but with morality and spirituality and conduct. These, he says, constitute the sense of all Dharma. If you look into some of the most authentic of ancient Buddhist texts, say, the *Mahāprajñāpāramitāśāstra* the view of Dharma propounded there is very similar. It begins with quotations from the 'Attha Vagga' and expounds this very doctrine of the nature of Dharma, Dharma not as a dogma, but as the transcendence of dogmas, as something which unites, which is universal.

Now this idea of a universal ethics based on spirituality was carried by Buddhist missionaries to all parts of the globe and they succeeded very well in the eastern part of the world. I believe that when Aśoka sent his missionaries to the Hellenistic Greek Kingdoms, they were effective in creating ascetic communities on the Nile a source from which Monasticism in Christianity could have been derived. Because in the earlier Semetic tradition such an ascetic emphasis is not to be found at all. A religion of love and mercy, of forgiveness, of chastity, propounded by Jesus Christ could only have been based on anticipations in these sects spread by Buddhist preachers in the West.

The great importance of Prof. Nakamura to my mind was that he was a firm believer in the unity of man, as revealed and concealed in the process of history. When I published my first book in 1957, I had sent a copy to Prof. Nakamura and I promptly received a letter written by him in his hand. It began by saying that it is a wonder. We never expected a book like that from India. Later on he reviewed the book in Japanese and sent me its cutting.

In 1958, I met Prof. Suzuki who had come to Gorakhpur. He was then over 90 years of age, but looked young and perfectly healthy. He said that he had a slight defect in hearing. I think I have a greater defect even though I am ten years his junior. One great thing about Japanese wisdom that we have known it in India from Suzuki, Nakamura and others, has been the emphasis on what we call the positive side of spirituality. In India, unfortunately, most of the scholars, ancient and modern, especially, the ancient scholars who have written on Buddhism have emphasized the negative side of Buddhism. All the great Brahmanical commentators who criticized Buddhist doctrines have interpreted them in a very negative manner. It has often occurred to me that what happens is that both the Buddhism as well as Brahmanism have a dual doctrine, say a doctrine about the world and a doctrine about what transcends the world. In criticizing the rival doctrines they identify the doctrine about the world with the main doctrine. So, when Śankarācārya criticizes 'Vijñānavāda' in the Brahmasūtra Bhāṣya, he is all the time using argument which could well be applied to him also. And in fact he senses this because at the end of the discussion he says it might be argued that we are propounding the same doctrine, but then he suddenly retracts and says, no, because Vijñānavāda believes in Vijñāna as a transient particular whereas we do not believe in that. Even Vijñapatimātṛtāsiddhi does not fully conform to this characterization. So the criticism is really based on a mislabeling of the doctrine. This duality of doctrine must be kept in mind, and also it must be noted that '*śūnyatā*' is not a doctrine or a dogma. Those who would like to consider '*śūnyatā*' itself as a doctrine or dogma, they are incurable. Of course, it is a common feature in philosophy that what the master says is elaborated in different ways by his disciples and their elaborations could not have been to the liking of the Master himself. So the Mādhyamika system also tried to develop a kind of logic later on and so much has been written now on the logic of the Mādhyamikas. But I think the essential point of Nāgārjuna has been that we have to perceive truth as trans-logical.

However, the last time I met Prof. Nakamura was in the course of International Seminar on Buddhism which had been held here in Delhi in 1984, where we stayed in the adjacent rooms in the Ashoka Hotel. He presented a copy of his book which had been translated into English from Japanese, the first part of the History of Vedānta, and wrote a dedication in Sanskrit in it.

There is another thing I would like to recall. Although Sanskrit has been studied in the West and elsewhere only a very few scholars outside India have been known for that felicity in the use of the Sanskrit language. Stcherbatsky was one such scholar and Nakamura was another. They both could speak Sanskrit fluently. That is a rare accomplishment. We differed on many points–I asked him why he was siding with the view which would put Buddha in the 4th Century B.C.? He said, my teacher said so and therefore I have reported that view. So I cut short the discussion as he appealed to the fact of *Guru bhakti*.

I was saying that one important fact of the Japanese understanding of Buddhism has been the emphasis on its positive side, the side of experience. Bodhidharma had introduced from China to Japan what came to be called the Zen School later on. I had the privilege of meeting Dr. Nishitani in Zurich. I was with him for a week or so. I asked him to teach me the practice of Zen which he did and he gave me a Koan and initiated me into it. So that is one part of the understanding of Buddhism and the other part is the idea of *śūnyatā* which has been neglected in India traditionally. It has been negatively understood. The arguments have been largely on the negativities. On the *Kūrikās* of Gauḍapāda Śankara has written a commentary. It has been disputed, I believe, by some modern scholars. Some passages in the beginning and the comments certainly are not Śankara's. But in that commentary Sankara interprets words like *śūnyatā* differently not as they ought to be interpreted. My own feeling is that although the ideas of Śankara have a profound resemblance of Mahāyānic ideas, Śankara was not too well aware of the major texts of the Mahāyāna School. He knew about them only in a general fashion or through very relatively popular handouts. Between the Upaniṣadic Vedānta and Śankara's Vedānta, there is one great difference. Creation is at the centre of Upaniṣadic Vedānta, but Śankara does not believe that real creation can take place in non-duality. In fact, at one place he says that he has no interest in speaking about this whole process of creation. This change in attitude only came about because of Buddhist criticism. This fact was most clearly realized by Buddhist masters that creation invariably implies evanescence and transience '*anityatā*' incompatible within a reality, that is, non-dual and eternal. That was absorbed by Vedānta in Śankara, but he did not throw the baby with the bath water either.

Professor Nakamura has written five volumes, on the History of Vedānta in Japanese of which only two volumes have been published in English. I had written a paper and published it, on the date of the 'Kaṭhopaniṣad' disputing Nakamura's view with regard to the dating of this Upaniṣad. There are some points in the Upaniṣad which are very reminiscent of Buddhist views, *pṛthak dharma*, for example and so on. Nevertheless, the point is that Nakamura has in a very learned fashion not only clarified many points of chronology, but also brought out interaction between Buddhism and Brahmanical thought which were otherwise not so well known to Indian scholars, about Bhartṛhari particularly. His dating of Śankara appears to me quite sound and I have largely followed his dating. His work titled "Ways of Thinking of Eastern Peoples " is a very significant contribution from the point of view of cultural historians. He has shown how in translation the meanings of words change and these represent a new kind of interpretation. That is quite true. In fact, I should say, the same thing happens even within the same tradition; words change their meanings in time as they change their meaning in space, and that is bound to happen because words are never used in a fully univocal sense. Despite that logicians define the words. Definitions would become larger and larger, more and more voluminous, but more and more difficulties and ambiguities are discovered. It is no wonder, therefore, that translations produce some difference. His last work to which reference has been made, i.e., "The Comparative History of Ideas" is, I should say, a remarkable work in the sense that it could only have been attempted by someone, who was familiar with the vast and difficult areas of Eastern thought in the Indian, Tibetan, Chinese, and Japanese Buddhist traditions, who knew these ideas from the original sources. Nobody else has written a history like that.

There have been histories of Ideas in the Western context by scholars who have been familiar with the ancient and modern European languages, but no one has done with that authenticity and familiarity with Eastern languages in the same fashion. In that sense I wish that this book received a greater publicity in the Departments of Philosophy and Cultural History. But I must say that I have not found the book being used much in any Indian University. For that matter, I do not know how it is used in Japan, may be better but I wonder if it is used at all in the West because they conform the History of Ideas with Ideas in the West only. So, I feel it is a privilege for me to be able to stand here and pay tributes to the memory of Prof. Nakamura, whom I knew personally and cherish his memory. Thinking of him and his work, we should be able to move further in our knowledge not only of Buddhism, but also of Eastern philosophies of world civilisation. It is a hope which may one day be fully realized. Prof. Rajasekharan Pillai, as promised, could help that in that case because Prof. Bhatt is enthusiastic. I hope his enthusiasm continues in this field.

With these few words, I would like to thank the earlier speakers and the audience for participating in the Conference. Thank you.

S.R.BHATT: We are really deeply obliged to Prof. G.C. Pandeji for having agreed to chair the Inaugural Session. He cancelled some of his programmes in Allahabad to enable him to come over to Delhi. In fact, he was also invited by

Singhviji, but could not make it. We are lucky to have him here.

In fact, so far as history of Buddhism and Vedānta is concerned, Prof. Pandeji's understanding and depth of vision is unparallel and he has paid rich tributes to Professor Nakamura.

When I thought of and proposed for the organization of the Seminar, our contemporary Indian professors did not know who Nakamura was. And then I had to tell them about his contributions in brief and I told them that he has written more than 20,000 pages in Japanese and I think the writings in English would be also not less than 10,000 pages.

I would like to recall incidents of his life when he was on his deathbed, his fingers were moving as if he was writing. Up to the last moment of his life, he was just thinking and behaving like writing. And other thing is, he expressed his wish that when he dies, his ashes should be immersed in the River Ganges. And that was done, I think, by the family members.

Now I request Prof. Mayeda, a worthy pupil of the worthy teacher to say something.

SENGAKU MAYEDA: Mr. Chairperson, Prof. Pande, Hon. Dr. Singhvi, Prof. Kireet Joshi, Prof. Lokesh Chandra, Prof. Kim, disinguished guests and ladies and gentlemen. I wish I could speak in Sanskrit as my Guruji did. But let me please speak in English. It is a real pleasure and honour for me to be given this opportunity to make a special address in the Inaugural Session of the Indo-Japan Seminar on Buddhist philosophy with special reference to the Thoughts and works of Prof. Hajime Nakamura in the fields of philosophy, indology and Buddhist study. Its purpose is to highlight the works and thoughts of Prof. Hajime Nakamura, the Founder of the Eastern Institute.

On behalf of Mrs. Hajime Nakamura, President of the Eastern Institute I, in the capacity of the Executive Director of the Eastern Institute as well as the Head of the Japanese delegation, would like to take this opportunity to express our deepest appreciation to Prof. S.R. Bhatt for the extraordinary trouble that he has taken to organize this Indo-Japan Seminar. Our special thanks are also due to Prof. Kireet Joshi, Dr. Mercy Helen, Mr. Shrikumaran, Mr. Mahender Chopra and all the other members of the Indian Council of Philosophical Research. Without their warm-hearted cooperation our participation in this Indo-Japan Seminar on Buddhist philosophy could not have been possible.

We also highly appreciate the generous financial support granted by the Indian Council of Philosophical Research as well as the Japan Foundation. We are also most grateful to all the honorable guests and illustrious participants, Indian and foreign, who have spared their precious time to attend this Seminar in honour of Dr. Nakamura.

Now please allow me to explain the photographs of the Buddha and Dr. Hajime Nakamura in front of us which Mrs. Miki, Dr. Nakamura's elder daughter has brought with her with great care for this function. The photograph of Buddha was taken by Mr. Isamu Maruyama, a well-known photographer. This Buddha image was excavated at Sarnath. It is a place we all know where the Buddha began to preach Dharma with his first sermon.

Mr. Maruyama visited Dr. Nakamura at the Eastern Institute in Tokyo on February 29, 1996 three years prior to his death. During that visit, Dr. Nakamura requested Mr. Maruyama to enlarge the photo of the Buddha, saying to him that "on the occasion on my funeral, which may be near, this Buddha image should be placed in front with a small photograph of me placed far behind it. I wish the mourners to worship this Buddha image, but not mine since throughout my life I have only been a servant of the Buddha." This sincere request reveals Dr. Nakamura's true character very well.

He was always modest to everyone, even to his students. Mr. Maruyama suggested that the size of the Buddha's photograph be made one meter in height. Then Dr. Nakamura consented. Without knowing the above conversation made between the two persons, at the funeral these two photographs of the Buddha and of Dr. Nakamura of equal size, that is one meter in height, were prepared and placed side by side at the altar, the funeral hall. Such an arrangement might be against his wishes, but would prove agreeable to most of the mourners. Ever since then, these two photographs have been placed in the same manner at the front of the gathering wherever any ceremony took place in his honour.

Well, the Sixth India-Japan Joint Seminar on the topic, "Fifty Years of Indo-Japanese relations" in celebration of the Fiftieth Anniversary of the establishment of Indo-Japan diplomatic relations was held from January 9–11, 2003 in New Delhi. It was jointly sponsored by the Indian Council of Social Science Research, which is the nodal organization of Indo-Japan Academic Exchange Committee of India and its Japanese counterpart, that is the Japan Committee for Japan-India Academic Exchange for which I currently serve as its Chairperson having succeeded Prof. Chi Nakane. On that occasion, Prof. Bhatt and myself also participated in that joint seminar and presented the papers.

In my paper I first gave an overview of the indological studies in Japan for the last fifty years and then took up Prof. Nakamura for discussion. He was indeed the greatest scholar in the field of indological studies in Japan for the last fifty years having introduced and explained through his chief works in Japanese language which seems to be hardly accessible to Indian scholars.

It is truly unfortunate that most of his works are written in Japanese and that his publications in English or in foreign languages represent only tip of the iceberg of enormous amount of books and articles he has published. Dr. Nakamura has also a couple of very famous English books entitled "Ways of Thinking of Eastern Peoples : India, China, Tibet and Japan" and "A Comparative History of Ideas". But he is also the author of a great number of Japanese books published under the title "The Selected Works of Hajime Nakamura in 40 volumes", "The Grand Comprehensive Dictionary of Buddhist Technical terms" in four volumes, "The Illustrated

Dictionary of Buddhist Technical Terms" in one volume, "The Structure of Logic" in two volumes and numerous others. Dr. Nakamura is not only the author of scholastic books, translations and articles for the intellectuals and specialists, but also the author of numerous popular, introductory books and publications for the general readers.

It was fortunate for me that I was present at the Session of the Sixth Indo-Japan Joint Seminar. Under that Prof. Bhatt took so keen interest in Dr. Nakamura's Thoughts and Works that he decided to organize such a large scale International Seminar to highlight the Works and Thoughts of Dr. Nakamura. In so doing, he has brought together such distinguished scholars as participants to India, the country which Prof. Nakamura always loved very deeply and admired beyond words.

Dr. Nakamura's field of research was exceedingly vast encompassing Indian philosophy, Buddhist studies, historical studies, Japanese thought, comparative thought, etc. with reference not only to Japan, India, China, Europe and America but also extending to the whole world. On this occasion five Japanese scholars who are participating in this Seminar, whom Prof. Bhatt has carefully selected, will shed light on Dr. Nakamura's deep and vast scholarship. Prof. Yasuaki Nara will take up Dr. Nakamura's contribution to the Buddhist studies for discussion. Then Prof. Shoun Hino on the studies in Vedānta, Prof. Shujun Motegi on the studies in Sāmkhya, Prof. Michihiko Yajima on the study of Jainism and Prof. Toshihiro Wada on the studies in Nyāya-Vaiśeṣika Logic. I am pleased to inform you that these five Japanese scholars are eminent specialists in their own fields. I am very grateful to them all for their whole-hearted cooperation, although they are extremely busy at their respective universities. I myself would like to introduce you to Dr. Nakamura's works in Japanese, which I have brought here with me from Japan in order to show you a portion of his great achievement. I am myself very keen to find out on this occasion how you understand Dr. Nakamura. Having presented to you this realistic portrayal of the human side as well as academic side of Dr. Nakamura I now wish to conclude my address by once again expressing my deepest appreciation to Prof. Bhatt, Indian Council of Philosophical Research and its entire staff and Japan Foundation. Thank you very much for your kind attention. *Dhanyavāda*.

S.R.BHATT: Now I request Prof. S.K. Kim from Dongguk University, South Korea, to say a few words about Prof. Nakamura. Prof. Nakamura was a very keen visitor to Korea and has written on Korean mind as well. He had several students there and Professor Cho of South Korea, who was to come, but could not come, has sent his paper and the title of the paper is "My Maitreya Buddha, The Late Professor Nakamura Hajime." Prof. Kim also is a specialist in Indian philosophy and would be sharing his thoughts with us.

S. K. KIM: *Namaskāra*, G.C. Pandeji and other great scholars, ladies and gentlemen, I would like to thank you for attending this Seminar. I am teaching Vedānta philosophy at Dongguk University in Seoul, Korea.

I am honoured to be invited here to deliver a special address at the Indo-Japan Seminar on Buddhist Philosophy with a special reference to the Thoughts and the Works of Prof. Hajime Nakamura.

I am very grateful to Prof. S.R.Bhatt for organizing this Seminar and for inviting me. As you know, Professor Nakamura had very notable contributions in focusing Asian philosophical thought in the global perspectives. His keen interest in classical Indian philosophy is well evident from his numerous writings on Indian thought, especially Vedānta and Buddhism.

Professor Nakamura's work on Vedānta was not only pioneering but also a huge step forward. It is Prof. Sengaku Mayeda, who is successor in Vedānta study as well as academic office. Originally, Prof. Nakamura was initiated into Vedānta by his Guru Prof. Hakuji Ui. Prof. Nakamura's magnanimous offer is a History of Early Vedānta Philosophy. In this work he has dived deep into the abstruse knowledge of early Vedānta Thought on the basis of his profound knowledge of Sanskrit language and Indian philosophy. In his book he has not only dealt with the development of Vedāntic thought from the Upaniṣads to the Vedāntic system of Śankara and the–commentaries on the Brahmasūtra, but has brought to light hitherto unknown facts about the ancient Indian thought and culture. He has marvelously constructed the pre-Śankara Vedānta spanning a long period of about one thousand years. His approach to research in this field and the methodology which he adopted are quite innovative and path breaking. His linguistic, psychological and sociological analyses are profound and logical. He has given a panoramic view of Indian philosophy and has observed that the representative thought of India is Vedānta philosophy. He rightly opines that Śankara is known today as the greatest philosopher in the history of Indian thought. Śankara's greatness was not only of an original thinker, but also of an unequalled commentator.

Professor Nakamura has covered every possible problematic discussion of Śankara's 'Advaita' in the main part of his volume. I think any statement cannot describe Professor Nakamura's intellectual influence upon this world. I promise to spread the thoughts of Professor Nakamura, who succeeded to Budhha's wisdom, with all my heart. In so doing, I will try to serve in universalizing, popularizing and globalizing the teachings of 'Advaita' philosophy.

I would conclude by saying that to know Brahman is to become Brahman. Professor Nakamura can be a model and hope for all. I will pray for everyone. *"Śānti, Śānti, Śānti" Dhanyavāda*.

S.R.BHATT: Thank you Prof. Kim for throwing light on the contribution of Professor Nakamura to Vedāntic thought. Now we have Prof. Bhuvan Chandel, the dynamic Director of Indian Institute of Advance Study, Shimla. She has activated the Institute. Of course, she is also a part of Indian Council of Philosophical Research and we have been receiving her cooperation in the organization of this Seminar also. So, now I request her to say a few words.

BHUVAN CHANDEL: Hon. Chairperson, Prof. Pandeji, Prof. Singhviji, Prof. Kireet Joshiji and the scholars, both on the dais as well as in the audience.

I would like to say that this is a very happy occasion for us that a scholar who devoted his entire attention, entire life time for studies of Vedānta, Buddhism, and Indian thought, is being remembered by all of us today in this hall by way of a link between the two countries, by way of academic disciplines coming together from the two countries.

I must report one thing that even when we believe that we are philosophically very rich, the West is not prepared to accept us as philosophically deep. One example of this I would like to give when about two-three years back, the World Philosophy Congress Steering Committee was meeting and our academics from India were very keen that some of the themes from Indian philosophy should be proposed by way of themes for symposia and for the sections, it was opposed tooth and nail, even though our proposal was that Buddhism should be discussed in the context of its spread in the Asian countries. The answer by the Western mind was that Buddhism is not a philosophy, it is a religion and therefore, it does not occupy any space within the structure of the thematic discussions for World Congress. In any case, our view was argued forcefully because there was a large contingent from India and Prof. Bhatt was there and we all, I think thirty of us, gathered and we did propose that it has philosophical elements and Buddhism should be discussed as a system of philosophy, not as a religion. We succeeded at Istanbul Conference; we did organize, Bhatt Sahib was again there, Prof. Kireet Joshi, Chairman of the Indian Council himself was present and we did have a large participation from Eastern countries, Japan was included and we were very happy that at least we were being heard as a philosophical voice.

So, what I have to say in this context is that the challenge is great and Indian scholars of Buddhism in particular, and Indian philosophers in general have this particular very great objective to fulfill and to prove that we exist as a philosophical community.

In this context I would like to draw your attention to the book which has been written by Prof. Pande himself. He is raising a large number of philosophical questions. In fact, I really do not understand why the Western people do not accept our arguments to be philosophically sound and deep. I would like to give some instances while remembering Prof. Hajime Nakamura.

To begin with, in the context of Buddhism I would like to say that it is for the first time in the context of history of Indian philosophy that an existential situation of man was portrayed as being foremost and being primary, that is suffering itself. '*Dukkha*' was accepted as an integral part of human existence and for the first time our attention was drawn to the fact that life has certain limitations and these limitations are no other than disease, old age, and death, which come in the way of our fulfillment of the objectives which we may like to achieve in the end and the objective in the context of Buddhism is our quest for the self-realization and fulfillment of peace. These are the higher values and if we are not paying enough attention for these limitations of life, then possibly we cannot really fulfill the aim of achieving self-realization. This is an important point to which I think we have to pay lot of attention.

Second point, which I think deserves attention, is that for the first time, Buddha evolved a particular ideal which is distinct and separate from what had been evolved by the Vedic and the Upaniṣadic traditions. In the earlier period, it was '*Ānanda*', 'Bliss', which was spoken of as the highest ideal, but Buddhism just asked for peace, that is, '*Śānti*', which should be the ideal of human endeavour. Buddha himself stood simultaneously both for knowledge as well as love, but I would like to say that his definition of knowledge itself was absolutely different from the kind of conception and definition West was giving. For improvement, human life is related to knowledge, but knowledge itself is to be seen as something of the nature of '*Sambodhi*', something which is born out of practice of '*Jñāna*' itself. I think this is a new kind of a definition and we really have to speak about its philosophical novelty also and this has to be coupled and reconciled with love, *Karuṇā*, compassion.

I think Buddhism is offering altogether a new view for all those who are seeking a fulfillment of perfection or fulfillment of human life itself. I would also like to submit that the concept of Dharma in the context of Buddhism itself, is a new kind of an interpretation because Dharma has been seen to be some kind of primarily a transcendental ideal, absolutely uprooted from '*Artha* and *Kāma*'. It is no doubt above and therefore to that extent it transcends the horizon of *Artha* and *Kāma*, but Buddhism is trying to reconcile the transcendental and the empirical status of Dharma itself and to this extent I think, the two dimensions, the two polarities, are being reconciled.

Last point which I would like to bring to your notice is that when the concept of '*Nirvāṇa*' itself is being discussed, there are very subtle questions which are being asked, for example, the metaphysical nature of *Nirvāṇa*. If this question is to be really taken very seriously, then we have to go into detail with regard to the analysis of '*Sambodhi*' itself because how *Nirvana* is to be realized, can only be answered if this kind of analysis can take place.

The third question in this context will be how *Nirvāṇa* is related to being an experience. Can it be adequately described in terms of non-being or non-experience? This is the third question which can be raised and if it is something infinite in principle, then what is its relationship with our finitude of life and with our existence itself. It is in this context that the two notions of Dharma and '*Pratītyasamutpāda*' have been given very elaborately by this great system of Buddhism. I remember in 1984 Prof. Nakamura had read a paper during the Conference and he had drawn attention to some of these problems. We had the fortune to listen to his very, very silent personality. He used to speak little, but whatever he spoke was very serious and carried lot of depth.

Now the last question in this context is who realizes '*Nirvāṇa*'. I think this is deeply philosophical. This is where Buddhism brings in the notion of '*attā*' or '*ātman*' or soul. Does it exist; or it does not exist? Buddha like a wise person was silent, he believed in non-communication and for him perhaps, the silent answer was if mind and matter do not have ultimacy, if they are themselves non-ultimate, then how can we speak of '*attā*', how can we speak of relationship of *Nirvāṇa* with soul itself. So in this context he preached middle path and I think Buddhism has to be understood by us not as a philosophy of transcendence, but as a philosophy which is deeply related to human life, which is deeply related to the basic concerns of human beings and humanity in general. As such I think, this is a great exercise.

This Seminar has a great challenge before it to discuss most of these philosophical questions in a philosophical way and to see how Professor Hajime Nakamura tried to answer these because I got a very beautiful book after the Conference was over in 1984 from Japan Foundation or it was sent by Prof. Nakamura. I have not seen another book so beautifully produced. It was an embodiment of how even publication and production matters have been mastered by the Japanese themselves. Japanese happen to be in my opinion some of the loveliest people because once when I was in Tokyo, it was their New Year. We were told that we should to go a Temple in Narita and pray there. When we went there, we also went to a restaurant. The Manager of the restaurant did not take any money from us. He said, no, it is our joint celebration. We thought this particular country which believes in keeping her indigenous values also knows how to reconcile modernity with her indigenous culture. I think this is the message that Japan gives to most of the other countries. I hope this Seminar will be a bridge between the two countries and our two countries will begin to come together along with the other countries from Asia before we can pick up the philosophical dialogue with the West. So this is I hope a small step in this direction. Thank you.

S.R.BHATT: Thank you, Prof. Chandel for raising some serious philosophical queries, which I hope we would be deliberating in the course of our discussions and these questions have been debated not only by Prof. Nakamura, but by we people also in some of our writings and we shall have an occasion to exchange ideas.

Now we come to the end of this Inaugural Session and we have a very pleasant task to perform and we request our newly joined Member-Secretary of Indian Council of Philosophical

Research—joined this week only—, and he is very kind not only to help me in the organization of this programme, but also to offer a Vote of Thanks. So, now I invite him, Prof. S.R. Vyas.

S.R. VYAS: Respected Chairman, dignitaries on the dais, learned delegates, guests, scholars and students,

The journey to the Thoughts and Works of Prof. Nakamura has already started and we have passed so many stations in that journey and as the time has come that we should break. Before this I would like to say something which to my mind is the most significant thing.

As Prof. Chandel and all other speakers, have spoken about the various dimensions of Buddhism, to my mind the basic ground for acceptance of Buddhism was the concept of suffering. As we all suffer and that is why we all must be united; we all must be in inter-personal relations to share our suffering and suffering not only at the material level or social level, but at the thought level also and at the level of values also and that is why a wide range of suffering is there and that is why we may need to come close to each other for understanding the thoughts, beliefs and other things. Prof. Nakamura might have to say a lot in this regard.

I first pay my homage to Professor Nakamura, who has done a lot and in the coming days we would be discussing his ideas and thoughts. I express my deep thanks to Japan Foundation and Eastern Institute for cooperating with us in providing financial help for this Seminar, because of that we were able to organize this event.

Secondly, I also express my deep thanks to Honourable Chief Guests, Dr. L.M. Singhavi Sahib, H.E. Mr. Y. Enoki, the Ambassador of Japan and Chairperson, Prof. G.C. Pande and others for being with us.

I would also express my deep thanks to distinguished and learned speakers Prof. Lokesh Chandra and Prof. Mayeda, Prof. S.K. Kim, Prof. V.C. Rajasekharan Pillai, the Vice-Chairman of U.G.C., Prof. Bhuvan Chandel, and Dr. Altaf Seth, the former Ambassador to Japan.

I would also like to thank the delegates, the scholars and the guests and others who are here and I would take this opportunity to express gratitude to the *Bhikshus* of the Buddhist Studies Department of Delhi University for coming over here. For a moment we were in trance when they were chanting out the *mantras* or the *Suktas*. I will take this opportunity to thank Prof. Kireet Joshi, ICPR Chairman, to be with us and for encouraging us to organize such events.

Lastly but not the least, I would also like to thank the staff of ICPR, who was with me for day and night in organizing this Seminar and the media persons also who were here and I would thank all those who directly or indirectly helped us in organizing this event very successfully.

Now I cordially invite you to lunch. Thank you.

(The Seminar adjourned to meet again.)

Proceedings of the Valedictory Session

April 13, 2004

S.R.BHATT: Now we start the Valedictory Session of the Three-day Seminar, which I believe, has been academically quite fruitful. Of course, there might be some lapses for which I seek an apology and I am also sorry that Prof. Kim was slightly indisposed, but he is here with us and he could maintain his spirits.

Prof. Kireet Joshiji is in the Chair and I request him to kindly conduct the proceedings of this Valedictory Session in which tributes will be paid to Prof. Hajime Nakamura in whose honour in particular, we have organized this Seminar and by now we are very well familiar with his Works and Thoughts, and with his contribution to Indian Culture in particular, and world culture at large.

KIREET JOSHI: It is a great honour to be together today at this Valedictory Session of this very important Seminar which we had for the last three days and in this particular session, we are going to pay tributes to Prof. Hajime Nakamura who was undoubtedly one of the greatest leaders of Asia who had influenced the world and even today we are happy that many of his students continue the legacy that he has left behind. It is a big and great legacy, a rich literature of philosophy for us to assimilate and to transmit. In the first place, I shall invite Mrs. Sumiko Miki to speak on this occasion.

SUMIKO MIKI: Good evening, Prof. Joshi, Prof. Bhatt, distinguished guests, ladies and gentlemen.

I wish to express my profound gratitude and thanks to all participants. This evening I feel very happy to be here because I have heard that this meeting is to commemorate my late father, Prof. Hajime Nakamura.

First of all, I would like to offer my sincere appreciation to Prof. Bhatt and his colleagues for organizing such a superior meeting and gave me this opportunity. My mother could not join me due to old age. She asked me to convey her best regards to everybody attending here. As a daughter of Late Prof. Hajime Nakamura I would like to relate to you a small story between this country and my father. In October 1999, my father passed away in Tokyo. During his life, he visited this country many times. The purpose of his visit was different from time to time; on many occasions to attend Conference or meetings or to take records and sometimes to visit historical places like Buddha's footsteps. Among them he liked to visit ancient marble image of Buddha located in the National Archaeological Museum at Sarnath.

Indeed my father loved this image of Buddha at Sarnath as well as this country very much. When my father was dead, our family conducted a funeral ceremony in accordance with the Buddhist customs in Japan. In the ceremony, we displayed the photograph of Buddha's image at Sarnath, together with photograph of my father. After the series of funeral ceremony had completed, our family wished to convey a small part of his ashes and spray them in this country because he loved India very much and regarded her as his second home country.

In December 2002, I visited this country for the first time together with my husband and my sister. We decided to visit such places as Varanasi and Sarnath. We saw the ancient marble image of Buddha at the Archaeological Museum at Sarnath. Then we conducted a small ceremony on the boat at the River of Ganga according to the instruction of a Hindu priest. After that we spread a small portion of my father's ashes in the River of Ganga. I had the kind of satisfaction and happiness because we believed my father would be able to sleep in this country forever. So, already four and half years have passed since my father passed away in 1999. However, huge amount of his books and literature in his room still remains unchanged, as if they are still waiting that my father might come back. I remember when I was an infant child, my father was always reading, discussing books or writing something on notebooks in his room. So, I could not play with my father like neighboring children.

In addition, my mother often complained that my father spent too much money to buy expensive books. So my family was always economically not so happy. Of course, I do not know whether it might be common fact or not, but I had an impression that those who studied Indian Philosophy were economically poor at that time. Especially whenever he returned from a trip to this country, India, a big cargo of books and literature used to follow him together with huge amount of invoices.

In the meantime, those studies of my father like a "History of Early Vedānta Philosophy" and "Ways of thinking of Eastern peoples" were fortunately appreciated in Japan and world wide and awarded from the Academy. Very frankly speaking, as a family member, I personally highly respected my father's continuous and tremendous effort, even though he was not economically happy and general environment was less favorable.

Among all, I remember the incident happened in connection with my father's Dictionary of Japanese Buddhist terms. After about twenty years' effort, the big volume draft of Dictionary was finally completed and passed to the publisher for publication. However, it happened that all of that draft was lost during the relocation of the warehouse of the publisher. Most likely by a series of mistakes, they were mixed up with waste material and finally incinerated at the fuses. Of course, my father was really disappointed and had fasted for several months to heal over this incident. However, shortly after this happening, he re-started the work to compile the Dictionary from the beginning. Several years later this Dictionary was successfully compiled and published.

At the time just before his retirement from the University of Tokyo, many students of the University of Tokyo were very radical and frequently they interrupted the lectures. My father really had deep apprehensions for these confusions. The reason why my father looked for the possibility to establish the Eastern Institute was that he really wished to keep and provide the places of study for those who really wished to study Indian Philosophy and Buddhism by eliminating the total confusions of the universities. Fortunately, many academic and business people understood his intention and the country supported him. Thus, the Eastern Institute was established in 1970. Up to today, many students, young and old are studying in this Institute. The Founder, my father, used to be the President of the Institute and later Prof. Mayeda succeeds this position.

In private life, he got two daughters including me and four grandchildren. He was a really gentle grandfather whenever any grandchildren visited his home. I still remember my Father's gentle and happy smile during the time he enjoyed a short nap, although my son and daughter were running around him.

As a family member I feel very happy to hear that my father's studies and books are still appreciated by many people and sincerely wish that his achievements could be succeeded and improved further by young generations.

I wish to say thank you very much again and sincerely wish everyone's health and prosperity. Thank you.

S.R.BHATT: Thank you very much Mrs. Miki for your very moving address. While you were reading out your paper and your tributes, we all felt ourselves pulsating with your emotions and we feel so proud that you are a worthy daughter of a worthy father and you are with us today to give us some of the personal intimate glimpses into the temperament and outlook of Prof. Nakamura. Thank you very much.

May I now request Prof. Sengaku Mayeda to speak to us.

SENGAKU MAYEDA: Prof. Kireet Joshi, Prof. Lokesh Chandra, Prof. Vyas, Prof. Bhatt and Dr. Helen. It is really a pleasure and honour for me to be given this opportunity to pay a tribute to my esteemed Guruji, Prof. Nakamura. It was in the fall of 1953, 51 years back when for the first time I attended his class of introduction to Indian Philosophy at the University of Tokyo. At that time, he was still young Associate Professor of Indian Philosophy who had just come back from the USA where he taught Indian and Buddhist philosophy at the Stanford University as a Visiting Professor. He was forty years old.

While lecturing, he laughed to himself merrily, looking at the ceiling of the Classroom. His lecture on History of Indian Philosophy was very illuminating and suggestive and very fresh. Ordinary books on the History of Indian Philosophy written in Japanese or foreign languages described only historical development of Indian Philosophy and nothing else. However, Prof. Nakamura approached Indian philosophy from a quite different point of view. He looked into the social and historical background in the formation of Indian thought. His understanding of Indian philosophy was very deep and inspiring, his lecture was so impressive that I made up my mind to study Indian philosophy under his guidance. Since then I have been one of his many, many students.

Nakamura was regarded among his students to be a great genius, who could be born only once in hundred years. As I said before, he was modest in his nature even to his students, but he was always pioneering and was in the forefront in the run. He opened and paved the new ways in many fields of study. One of them was the field of comparative thought or a comparative philosophy. In 1959, he published a Japanese book entitled "The Comparative Thought Beyond" and founded the Society for Comparative Thought on January 10, 1974 and he was elected its first President and Hon. President in 1983. The Society for Comparative Thought is still very active and has more than 1500 members.

In 1970, Dr. Nakamura established a non-profit organization, The Eastern Institute, the present President of which is Mrs. Hajime Nakamura, for the purpose of cultivating young scholars, promoting researches, mainly in the field of Indian and Buddhist Studies and disseminating Eastern Thought. Prof. Nakamura once told me his hidden intention to found such an Institute. The job market for researchers in the field of Indian and Buddhist studies had been and is still very small. So a young scholar although he was very able and promising man, he could not get any teaching job for a long time. Hence, he finally committed suicide. It was quite shocking to Prof. Nakamura, but he could not do anything for him. Therefore he founded such an Institute to save young and jobless young scholars. At present, we have more than thirty researchers in our Institute who have not yet got their full-time teaching positions. Among them, there are about ten post-Doctoral researchers. You will see how benevolent Dr. Nakamura was. He wrote a book entitled 'JISI' which means 'compassion' in Japanese. When he was writing this book, the second daughter was born to him. Then he gave her the name 'YASCO' which means a daughter of Compassion. Prof. Nakamura stresses that compassion is eternal truth. In this context, I would like to quote his sincerest wish again, which is inscribed on the grave stone placed side by side with the tomb of Nakamura family.

'May all creatures always abound in happiness and peace,

May all be always blessed with peace.

Rit Nankajole was despised as a fellow anywhere,

let none wish others harm,

Keep on this Compassion with all might.'

Dr. Nakamura himself translated these words from a Pali Buddhist text Metta Sutta of the Sutta nipāta and Mrs.

Nakamura wrote them down with a writing brush. This must be the last and sincerest wish for human kind that Nakamura had in common with Mrs. Nakamura.

I would believe that it is our duty, that is of the Eastern Institute's important duty, to make our best to realize his sincerest wish, as far as possible. As you know, as Mrs. Miki said, Prof. Nakamura is taking rest in India. Now he must be extremely pleased to see that this function is taking place in his honour as a grand success in India, a country which he loved very deeply and admired very highly. Thank you very much.

S.R.BHATT: Thank you very much, Prof. Mayeda. Through your words you have conveyed to us the great compassion of Professor Nakamura, compassion which is the real truth of Buddhism and you gave us a very moving account of some of the aspects of the inner personality of our Revered Prof. Nakamura. Thank you very much.

May I now request Prof. Lokesh Chandraji to speak to us about Prof. Nakamura.

LOKESH CHANDRA: I pay tribute to Prof. Nakamura who perhaps loved India more than his own country. When I first met him in Japan in 1970, he had established this Eastern Institute, took me there and said you have to bless this Institute. I said, how can I bless the Institute in your presence? You are my senior. He said, no, you come from India; so you have to bless it and then I asked him why have you established this Institute and as Miki pointed out the students were in turmoil and research and thought cannot flourish in all these turbulences. So, he had to create a place of silence. Buddhist thought developed in the remote forest and if you see the Zen paintings, you see the mountains, the streams where there is nothing of material life, they all transcend materiality.

He loved not only India, but also Buddhism in a very deep way. Perhaps, he was one of the last great scholars of that generation, who saw in Buddhism 'being' of their own country and he said, India is the mother of our culture and we are the daughter of India. So far as Indian culture is concerned all his life he strove to see that Indian Sanskrit studies are carried on. He wanted to speak Sanskrit, used to read Sanskrit journals. I used to send him a lot of these journals. Ultimately he wrote a book on contemporary Sanskrit vocabulary and Grammar, published by Motilal Banarsidass in Delhi. Besides his academic pursuits, he was keen that India and Japan should collaborate and try to extend each other's culture. He came here many times. I think he never expressed this idea, but from his face and general ambiance, I could feel that he felt that in India, we do not study Japanese culture, we do not study Japanese Buddhism and had we studied, perhaps we might have enriched the understanding of Japanese Buddhism, not only because we should study Japanese Buddhism, but we should enrich the understanding of Japanese Buddhism. For example, we read 'The Lotus Sūtra', the first chapter. I told him how as an Indian, I understand this Sūtra with of course my background in Buddhist studies. So, in a way, when we try to read a Buddhist text with all our background of Hinduism, it makes a difference.

Nakamura's interest was to study the relation between the Upaniṣads and Buddhist thought particularly in its original form, what he called Original Buddhism. He felt that Indians should have proper understanding of Buddhism and in particular of Japanese Buddhism. I think this Seminar anyway fulfils one of his wishes that on one level we understand the great contributions of Prof. Nakamura, on the second level we hope that a Nakamura Chair for Buddhist studies or whatever it is christened, will come into being and this may lead to a major fulfillment of our understanding of Japanese Buddhism. After all even to understand our own tradition, our Upaniṣadic tradition, some times it becomes important to look into what is Chinese, Japanese and the Korean scholarship as seen in the Buddhist thought for the last two thousand years or fifteen hundred years; and it is so revealing to see the whole exercise of thought, which originated in India and flourished in these countries; and I always had told Professor Hajime Nakamura that you know, we sent a bride to you and you have decorated her so beautifully. See the

Buddhist paintings. She was a tiny girl, but now she is a charming woman, and he was so pleased. I said, what you have done to Buddhism is beyond our comprehension and what you personally are contributing to the understanding of Buddhism is again of a colossal interest. This was because he was not only understanding Buddhism, but he was doing so in the total context of Upaniṣadic thought. After all Upaniṣadic thought is primarily a concern of the ksatriyas and they depart from the *karmakāṇḍa* and go into the *jñānakāṇḍa*. And Buddha was a *kṣatriya* and as Professor Hajime Nakamura has pointed out the role of the Upaniṣads in the formation of Early Buddhism, at least the ideas of Lord Śākya Muni himself, has been quite considerable and if not considerable, at least basic on certain very critical issues. So, this Seminar brings into the forefront India's understanding of the contribution of Japanese scholarship to their own tradition as well as to our tradition.

Somehow, we have looked too much to the West and too little to the East. Language is a barrier. I think there is a major communication gap, but we have to overcome it. So many Indians are studying Chinese, Japanese, Korean and many other languages of the world. Now it is time that we look more into the classical traditions of Japan. We celebrate Prof. Hajime Nakamura as a great Buddhist scholar. We also admire him as a great Japanese intellectual. He was very close to the Japanese Imperial family, Emperor and the Empress, and they sent special flowers at his funeral ceremonies. So he straddles across the whole Asian landscape or mindscape as a towering figure and just summons us, so that we should once again look to our neighbours. Whenever I met him, I was reminded of Syguyoa, a very eminent Japanese poet. He says, 'Had I not been told, never would I have known that hidden deep within the root lies a flower.'

So I always told Prof. Nakamura that you are the roots and you are the flower both. Buddhism originated in India, but somehow we have lost it. So today we have to seek the roots and their flowering in your country and with his incredible simplicity and spontaneity. I always called him the eyes of our culture and whenever we dişcussed I told him that ours is a culture of the mind, but yours is a culture of the eyes and the mind. Whatever you create is done with tremendous beauty. So you have given to Buddhism a new persona, a new life and a life which is so poetic, so artistic. Prof. Hajime Nakamura's memory is part of the great tradition. Bodhi Sena went to Japan, but very few Japanese have come to India. I think one or two Japanese must have come in ancient time. The way they describe India is very realistic. This cannot be done just on hearsay, but historically we cannot prove that, but Prof. Hajime Nakamura continued with the tradition of great Chinese pilgrims and brought luster to the inter-cultural context between India and East Asia.

We will always remember him for all the kindnesses that he showed us when we were in Japan. When we are in Japan, we have so many problems, linguistic problem, then the vast distances, you land at the Japanese airports and you do not know where to go. There are so many lanes and by-lanes in the international airport. So whenever I went to Japan, he was so nice, he would come and have a big flag or a big board with my name written. So I had no problem in finding him out and he treated me so affectionately. I think his affection lives so long as we live. And even beyond us he will be there in the Ganga with his ashes. Many Japanese have come to me. Only about a year ago a Japanese lady has passed away, her ashes were brought for being immersed into the Ganga and her sister had brought them and said, "I want to put these ashes into the Ganga', please bless them." So I did the Buddhist *Dhāraṇi* for placing them and used the *uṣṇiṣa* because that was the first *Dhāraṇi* that was used to consecrate the Constitution of Japan.

The role of Sarnath is very important in the life of the Japanese. One day Mrs. Indira Gandhi, the Prime Minister sent a Japanese to me. He had got a stone from Sarnath. He asked our Prime Minister, did Lord Buddha's feet touch this stone? Mrs. Gandhi was moved by this question. So she sent him to me to answer this question. He came to me and would not sit, would do nothing just asked me the question.

I said, yes, Lord Buddha's feet must have touched this stone because you have picked it up. There is a connection between you and the stone. Without waiting, he just ran away from my place. I did not get his card, which is unusual for a Japanese. He was so delighted. He was like a child and I think the same sentiments must have been in the mind of Prof. Nakamura when he saw this great image of Sarnath because it is here when the Dharma was declared, the *Dharma Cakra Pravartana*, the most sacred spot of the Buddhist world and of humanity. I think when we pay him tribute, we are paying tribute to the last fifteen hundred years of our contacts with Japan. Thank you friends.

S.R.BHATT: Thank you Prof. Lokesh Chandraji. You always throw a light unexpected, unimagined and we feel enriched and fulfilled. Your tribute to Prof. Nakamura and your reference to several anecdotes of your encounter with him, fill us with great happiness of reminiscence. Now I request Prof. Kireet Joshiji to say the final words.

KIREET JOSHI: Prof. Lokesh Chandraji, Prof. Mayedaji, Mrs. Miki, distinguished scholars and friends, this is one of the best Seminars that we have organised during the last several years and I must, first of all, congratulate Prof. Bhatt for the immense labour that he has poured into the making of this Seminar.

The significance of this Seminar, of course, is underlined by the fact that we have made a fresh study of Prof. Nakamura. Prof. Nakamura represents in the world thought a new trend, a trend which surpasses the national boundaries, a trend which surpasses narrow boundaries of philosophical systems, a trend which is wide and comprehensive and the fact that he established an Institute of Comparative Thought, is a testimony of his wide and soaring consciousness. The fact that he wrote on Vedānta and brought Vedānta into a kind of a focus in our own times, is once again a matter of great significance. Buddhism and Vedānta have great similarities, some do not see any difference at all between the two. In sharpness of language one can always make pronounced distinctions and trenchant distinctions, sharp distinctions and put one against the other. This is the sign of some kind of narrowness and lack of true comprehension. When we come to read Prof. Nakamura, these sharpnesses melt and we find ourselves flowing like the Ganges and feel that we are renewed by the new vigour that is drawn from the waters of Thought and Knowledge.

Often Buddhism has been misunderstood. Buddha's teachings have been often described in such a way as it was a petty ideal of escape from the world, but that it was a rigorous discipline of mastering the world and transcending the world and yet doing the works of verity and compassion on the earth. This message of Buddha requires to be recaptured in our own times.

I am sure that there is a new awareness about Buddhism all over the world today. The ultimate value of Buddhism is in the experience that Buddhism represents. The non-being of which the Buddha or Buddhism speaks may verbally be opposed to being, but when we come to experience, it may even be said that it is a being that surpasses being so that the limitations of being also are transcended. It may even be claimed that the *Brāhmic* experience is only the penultimate experience and that the ultimate experience transcends the Brahman, which can be described neither as being nor as non-being, ineffable 'X'.

I had a remarkable conversation once with Dalai Lama for about six hours, on the question of *śūnya* and it was a very revealing experience and his exposition of the concept of *śūnya* convinced me that it is futile to dabble in logic, which seems to be a kind of quibbling ultimately and that one must always transcend the barriers of words so that we can catch the real experience.

I was present at that time when he met the Mother in 1973, in the month of January and I was seated by his side. He was talking to the Mother and afterwards Mother made a remark after he left, that even his arms, that is, Dalai Lama's arms, are full of compassion. This is one of the great gifts of

Buddhism. To practice Buddhism is not only to love everybody, which is perhaps easier but to feel the compassion for the entire creation. Compassion transcends love and in that experience all distinctions and all quarrels melt and cease and we are overpowered by ineffable silence in which the whole creation seems to melt away and whether you call it *śūnya* or you call it Brahman or you call it by any other name, it is that 'That' which is *'Sat* and *Asat*' at the same time.

I think this is what came out also from this Seminar which we had during the last three days and although we had robust philosophical disputations and discussions, which we must always have, I think what came up as a cream of this Seminar was, as it were, that the doors were swung open before us and we felt the invasion of compassion.

For all this we should be very grateful to Professor Nakamura because whenever one encountered him, – in fact, I had a great privilege when in 1984 he paid a visit to my residence here in Delhi and we had a long conversation of two hours, ṭ and I could feel the same compassion. In fact, I feel that what world needs is not disputations or what they have through intellectual efforts at the determination of reality or unreality, but this experience of *Karuṇā*. It is because we live in ordinary narrowness, of I and thou, of inferior and superior, of my place and his place, '*asūyā*' a kind of jealousy. We escape the truth of the Upaniṣads that we should transcend these limitations. I think that ultimately, if philosophical studies lead us to this understanding, then all disputations can be forgiven. I believe that there are three great important lessons of Buddhism. First is the lesson that we derive from the life of Buddha himself. It is not for nothing that Buddha has been recognised in Hinduism as an *Avatāra*, even the Buddhist may not accept the theory of Avatārahood, even the Buddha himself might have rejected the idea that he was the *Avatāra*, but those in India who believe in Avatārahood and I am one of those who believe very firmly in the idea of Avatārahood, one can experience why Buddha is to be worshipped as an *Avatāra*. In the Fourth chapter of the Bhagavad Gītā, we have a brief, but very pregnant exposition and even a declaration that one who understands Avatārahood understands everything. Such is the great importance assigned to the idea of Avatārahood. God is not merely in heaven, looking on the world as a Judge rewarding boons and punishments, but he himself comes on the earth, he himself takes the cross on his shoulders and wears the crown of thorns so that the pain and suffering that is in the world is redeemed and he takes upon himself rightly and justifiably the burden of man's great labour.

The Buddha himself may be regarded as one who opened the path to the transcendental, beyond the transcendental and made it a gateway for humanity as a whole. In fact, every *avatāra* comes on the earth to open a gate. There are many gates of the Infinites and one of the gates is this experience of going beyond and to make it available and more easily to humanity, and that is a special significance according to me of the birth and life of the Buddha. For it is only in that consciousness of the transcendence that the suffering of the world can be endured. And it is only then that the real cure of sufferings of the world can be found.

This is according to me the teaching of the Buddha and for which I think humanity should prostrate at the feet of Buddha to receive eternal blessings so that with his compassion we can be delivered.

The second aspect that I learn from Buddhism and this was according to me a great lesson from Buddha himself, is that one should not to be tied up into philosophical disputations. When we examine the philosophers disputing with each other, we find that each one speaks as if he knows everything and yet we know that we hardly know anything and yet we take positions of disputations and we feel that the arguments that we have constructed are so sharp and so convincing, as though nobody can refute them and yet find refutations after refutations.

There is no argument in this world which cannot be countered by a counter argument. This is one of the great lessons of philosophical disputations. And that is why, I think, Buddha gave a very wise example when he refused to answer meta-physical questions. It is only because humanity has to pass through a period of intellectuality, that this intellectual exercise can be tolerated. And we can give a passport to it for some time, because human mind even if we do not give it philosophy, it will construct one. Therefore, it is best to recognize this need and to develop it so that we can come to some fixity in the mind whether that fixity takes you to Nyāya or to Vedānta or to Buddhism or to Jainism, from an ultimate point of view, it is the fixity which is important, not the particular doctrine in which the fixity has been achieved because it is only in the fixity of the mind that we can use it as a ladder to transcend the mind, and that is what we learn from the basic Buddhism. Although many Buddhists are highly disputative, very sharp, but if we go to the core of Buddhist Professors like Prof. Mayeda and Prof. Nakamura; in them we find that they have no disputations. Like the Buddha, they believe that if you answer one way, you will think other way and if you answer another way, you will think still in another way. Therefore, it is futile to discuss except insofar as it can take you to some kind of fixity of the mind, which is the basis of *'ekāgratā'* concentration and concentration is the key to the highest levels of consciousness.

The third lesson that I learn from Buddhism is its concern for the 'Earth'. This is why when people speak of Buddhism as an escape from the earth, I feel extremely unhappy. In fact, Buddha started his journey only because he felt concerned for the earth. He had a beautiful kingdom to rule, a great prospect of happiness of all kinds and yet he felt the pangs of the earth in his heart and he renounced the world in search. There is a beautiful conversation between the Mother and Buddha. The Mother was in Japan, when I speak of the Mother, I speak of Sri Aurobindo and the Mother. She is my teacher, the Mother herself; she was in Japan from 1916 to 1920 and she admired Japan tremendously. In fact, all her disciples are automatically great admirers of Japan. A huge number of people there during 1916 to 1920 were just dying and she was asked by somebody, what is the reason, can it be stopped? And she was a great spiritual master of the occult truths and she entered into the field. She received the disease herself in her body, almost herself came to a point of death and she discovered the cause, and she protected the whole of Japan. During her sojourn in Japan, she had meditations, and in one of her experiences, she experienced Buddha himself—this is to show that Buddha has not left the earth and Mother has recorded the following words about the Buddha. This was her conversation with Buddha on 20th December, 1916.

'Oh Lord, Thou hast spoken to me from the mouth of the one,

who has known Thee the best'

This is the tribute that Mother has paid to the Buddha, and then at that time the Mother herself had a question because she had reached herself that level of '*Nirvāṇa*' where Buddha had reached,—just when he gave this message in Sarnath—then she had the same problem and then Buddha manifested and told her—"I too had the same experience," Buddha said to her, "and I turned to the earth. So do I ask you to turn to the Earth". And that was the beginning of Mother's own mission of life, why she turned to the Earth.

This is the third message that I receive from the Buddhist philosophy 'Turn to the earth'. It is here that you have to work out this path. Sri Aurobindo has written a beautiful essay called 'The Way'. The way, he stated, is inexorable and none can abrogate it. Every one has to work it out, whether you start it now or tomorrow or later, but one day, you have to take staff in your hands and set out for the journey. This is the only meaning of life and the sooner we realise, the shorter will be our passage and greater will be the benefit that we can bring to ourselves and to the earth.

I think these are three messages I have learnt from Buddhism for which I am extremely grateful to this great philosophical tradition. This Seminar has given us a new occasion to pay our own tribute to Buddhism and particularly to our beloved Prof. Hajime Nakamura and the Lord, the Buddha himself.

S.R.BHATT: I now request Dr. Mercy Helen, Director of Indian Council of Philosophical research, to present a Vote of Thanks.

MERCY HELEN: Respected Chairman, Prof. Bhatt, Prof. Lokesh Chandra, Prof. Vyas, Prof. Mayeda and my dear friends.

It is my special privilege to perform this pleasant duty of presenting a Vote of Thanks. We have now come to the end of the three days of this enriching and enlightening Seminar on Buddhist philosophy with special reference to the Thoughts and Works of Prof. Hajime Nakamura. I feel extremely grateful to all who have participated in the Seminar to make this event a memorable and an unforgettable one. First of all, I would like to thank all the dignitaries who were with us during the Inaugural Session and initiated the Seminar with their most valuable thoughts.

The Chairman of the Inaugural Session, Prof. G.C. Pande and the Chief Guest, Dr. L.M. Singhvi deserve our special thanks.

Secondly, I express my deep gratefulness to all the Japanese scholars, scholars from Korea, China, Thailand and Viet-Nam who have not only participated in the deliberations, but also gave us a feeling towards better understanding on the philosophy of Nakamura. On this occasion I should thank Prof. Mayeda for having given an expository account of the rich bibliography of Nakamura. He had taken the trouble of bringing all the works of Nakamura for displaying them before us. I am also to thank all the Indian scholars from various parts of the country, who have contributed their ideas, their expertise on different aspects of the philosophy of Nakamura.

We are indeed thankful to all the Chairpersons of each and every session and the speakers too and all others who took part in the discussions.

My special thanks are for our esteemed and one of the leading thinkers of Indian Philosophy, Prof. R. Balasubramanian who was with us right from the beginning till now. He was with us and he gave us his very profound views. I also thank Prof. V.Kutumba Sastry, Vice-Chancellor of Rastriya Sanskrit Samsthan for chairing the Session on Vedānta and offering valuable thoughts.

I also take this privilege to extend our heartiest thanks to our Hon. Chairman, Prof. Kireet Joshi, who has not only sat through this Session, but also was with us all the three days in spite of his busy schedule and also for his scholarly contribution. He has helped us in all possible ways to organize this Seminar. We thank him for his significant address, which he delivered just now.

We express our deep felt gratitude to all the esteemed scholars who were in the Valedictory Session, who have paid their tributes to the great philosopher, Prof. Hajime Nakamura, namely, Mrs. Sumiko Miki for her sentimental remarks which she made, Prof. Mayeda for his personal, intimate, and scholarly account and our esteemed Prof. Lokesh Chandra for his respectful remarks for such a great scholar and intellectual.

On behalf of the ICPR and on behalf of all of us, I express our gratitude to the Japan Foundation for their generous financial support of a huge grant without which it would not have been possible for us to organize this Seminar.

We are also thankful to the Eastern Institute for their support. I cannot but remain without thanking Prof. S.R. Bhatt, the Director of this Seminar being the main figure behind not only in organizing the Seminar, but also in conceiving the theme, proposing, planning and implementing this mega event with meticulous care. His tireless efforts day in and day out, his preparations which he started months ago, have really enabled us to see the light of this day. His constant encouragement and help enabled the Council to go ahead with the Seminar. I am extremely thankful to him. I also thank all the Delhi local participants from Delhi University Buddhist Studies Department, from JNU and other institutions, who have been with us these days and participated in the deliberations.

I thank our Member Secretary, Prof. S.R. Vyas under whose guidance and advice this Seminar has been so successful.

I am also thankful to the Indian Council of Social Science Research and India Habitat Centre for having made us available the venue for holding the Seminar.

Finally, I would like to thank sincerely, the ICPR staff, especially, Mr. Chopra who was extremely cooperative, helpful and sincere in carrying out the task tirelessly day in and out and making this event a very successful and a grand one.

Lastly, I am deeply thankful to all the eminent scholars, who are present here right from the first day till today and for their tremendous patience in enjoying, participating and discussing the philosophical views of Nakamura in honour of him.

Once again, I thank you all. Thank you.

S.R.BHATT: We now close this Session and the Seminar. Thank you.

(At this stage the Seminar concluded)

List of Contributors

Acharya Kala, Professor
K.J. Somaiya Bharatiya Sanskrit Peetham
Somaiya Vidyavihar Campus
Ist Floor, Institute of Management Studies and Research,
Vidya Vihar
Mumbai - 400 077

Balasubramanian, R. Professor
5, Bhagirthi Street, Srinivas Avenue,
Chennai-600028

Bhatt, S.R., Professor
MP-23, Maurya Enclave
Pitampura,
Delhi-110088

Chandel Bhuvan, Professor
Director
Indian Institute of Advanced Study
Rashtrapati Nivas
Shimla - 171 005

Chandra Lokesh, Professor
J-22 Hauz Khas Enclave,
Sri Aurobindo Marg,
New Delhi - 110 016.

Chattopadhyaya D.P., Professor
25 Park Mansion
57-A Park Street
Kolkata- 700 016

Cho Yong-kil, Professor
Dean of Buddhist College and Professor,
Department of Buddhist Studies,
Dongguk University
Seoul
Korea

Chaudhuri Saroj Kumar, Professor
Guest Professor
Department of East Asian Studies
University of Delhi
Delhi
India.

Choudhuri Indra Nath, Professor
183 Tagore Park
Near Model Town
Delhi 110 009

Enoki Y., Mr.
H.E. The Ambassador of Japan
Japanese Embassy
New Delhi

Ghosh Raghunath, Professor
Department of Philosophy
North Bengal University
Rajarammohunpur
Dist. Darjeeling
West Bengal

Helen Mercy, Dr.
Director (P&R)
Indian Council of Philosophical Research
36 Tughlakabad Institutional Area
New Delhi - 110 062

Hino Shoun, Professor
Department of Liberal Arts
Gifu Pharmaceutical University
Gifu
Japan

Jindal Anu, Dr.
142 Sunder Nagar
2nd Floor
New Delhi-110 003

Joshi Kireet, Professor
Chairman
Indian Council of Philosophical Research
36 Tughlakabad Institutional Area
New Delhi - 110 062

Kar B., Professor
AM/26 VSS Nagar
Bhubaneswar - 751 007

Kim Sun-keun, Professor
President of Korea Society for Indian Philosophy
Professor, Department of Indian Philosophy,
Dongguk University
Seoul
Korea

Kumar Shashiprabha, Professor
Abhyudaya
H.No.295, Sector 15-A
NOIDA 201 301

Lee Geo-lyong, Professor
Research Professor
Brain Korea 21 Project of Buddhist Thought and Culture
Dongguk University
Seoul
Korea

Mayeda Sengaku, Professor
Executive Director of Eastern Institute
Professor Emeritus, University of Tokyo
Tokyo
Japan

Miki Sumiko, Mrs.
d/o Late Professor Hajime Nakamura
Director, Eastern Institute
Tokyo
Japan

Mishra Sabhajit, Professor
8 Professor's Colony
University Campus
Gorakhpur - 273 009

Motegi Shujun, Professor
Faculty of Education,
Shinshu University
Nagano
Japan

Mukherjee Asha, Professor
Dept. of Philosophy and Religion,
Visva-Bharati
Santiniketan-731235
India

Nara Yasuaki, Professor
Chancellor
Komazawa University
Tokyo
Japan

Narsimhan Sushila, Professor
Department of East Asian Studies,
University of Delhi
Delhi-110 007

Pande G.C., Professor
Chairman and President
Indian Institute of Advanced Studies,
Rashtrapati Niwas,
Shimla-171 005

Pillai Rajasekharan V.N., Professor
Vice-Chairman
University Grants Commission
Bahadurshah Zafar Marg
New Delhi - 110 002

Pradhan R.C., Professor
93, Doyens Township
Seri Lingampally
Hyderabad - 500 133

Samani Chaitany Pragya, Professor
Jaina Vishva Bharati,
Ladnun (Rajasthan) - 341 306

Seth Aftab, Shri
Ex-Indian Ambassador to Japan
Ministry of External Affairs
New Delhi

Shukla Karunesh, Professor
18 C-143/22 Andhirai Bagh
Gorakhpur - 273 001

Shikshu Satyapal, Professor
Head, Department of Buddhist Studies,
University of Delhi,
Delhi-110007

Singh Shyam Kishore, Professor
Professor of Philosophy
Manipur University
Palace Compound,
South of Shri Govindji Temple
Imphal - 795 001

Singhvi L.M., Dr.
Chairman
Indira Gandhi National Institute of Arts
Janpath
New Delhi - 110 001

Vyas S.R., Professor
Member-Secretary
Indian Council of Philosophical Research
36 Tughlakabad Institutional Area
New Delhi - 110 062

V. Kutumba Sastri, Professor
Vice-Chancellor,
Rashtriya Sanskrit Sansthan
New Delhi

Wada Toshihiro, Professor
Head, Department of Indian Studies
Graduate School of Letters
Nagoya University
Nagoya
Japan

Yajima Michihiko, Professor
Tsurumi Junior College
Yokohama
Japan